Perspectives of Management Accounting for Sustainable Business Practices

Ionica Oncioiu
Titu Maiorescu University, Romania

IGI Global
PUBLISHER of TIMELY KNOWLEDGE

A volume in the Advances
in Finance, Accounting, and
Economics (AFAE) Book Series

Published in the United States of America by
IGI Global
Business Science Reference (an imprint of IGI Global)
701 E. Chocolate Avenue
Hershey PA, USA 17033
Tel: 717-533-8845
Fax: 717-533-8661
E-mail: cust@igi-global.com
Web site: http://www.igi-global.com

Library of Congress Cataloging-in-Publication Data

Names: Oncioiu, Ionica, 1972- editor.
Title: Perspectives of management accounting for sustainable business practices / Ionica Oncioiu, editor.
Description: Hershey, PA : Business Science Reference, [2022] | Includes bibliographical references and index. | Summary: "This book examines the role of management accounting from other concepts point of view such as: green accounting, environmental indicators, e-accounting, KPI, lean accounting, controlling, auditing, reporting, etc. offering a number of new insights into management accounting"-- Provided by publisher.
Identifiers: LCCN 2022012063 (print) | LCCN 2022012064 (ebook) | ISBN 9781668445952 (hardcover) | ISBN 9781668445969 (paperback) | ISBN 9781668445976 (ebook)
Subjects: LCSH: Managerial accounting. | Business enterprises--Environmental aspects. | Sustainable development.
Classification: LCC HF5657.4 .P467 2022 (print) | LCC HF5657.4 (ebook) | DDC 352.4/3--dc23/eng/20220425
LC record available at https://lccn.loc.gov/2022012063
LC ebook record available at https://lccn.loc.gov/2022012064

This book is published in the IGI Global book series Advances in Finance, Accounting, and Economics (AFAE) (ISSN: 2327-5677; eISSN: 2327-5685)

British Cataloguing in Publication Data
A Cataloguing in Publication record for this book is available from the British Library.

All work contributed to this book is new, previously-unpublished material.
The views expressed in this book are those of the authors, but not necessarily of the publisher.

For electronic access to this publication, please contact: eresources@igi-global.com.

Advances in Finance, Accounting, and Economics (AFAE) Book Series

ISSN:2327-5677
EISSN:2327-5685

Editor-in-Chief: Ahmed Driouchi, Al Akhawayn University, Morocco

MISSION

In our changing economic and business environment, it is important to consider the financial changes occurring internationally as well as within individual organizations and business environments. Understanding these changes as well as the factors that influence them is crucial in preparing for our financial future and ensuring economic sustainability and growth.

The **Advances in Finance, Accounting, and Economics (AFAE)** book series aims to publish comprehensive and informative titles in all areas of economics and economic theory, finance, and accounting to assist in advancing the available knowledge and providing for further research development in these dynamic fields.

COVERAGE

- Investments and Derivatives
- Banking
- Behavioral Economics
- Economics of Risks, Uncertainty, Ambiguity, and Insurance
- Entrepreneurship in Accounting and Finance
- Economics Geography
- Bankruptcy
- Microeconomics
- Economics of Innovation and Knowledge
- Stock Market

The Advances in Finance, Accounting, and Economics (AFAE) Book Series (ISSN 2327-5677) is published by IGI Global, 701 E. Chocolate Avenue, Hershey, PA 17033-1240, USA, www.igi-global.com. This series is composed of titles available for purchase individually; each title is edited to be contextually exclusive from any other title within the series. For pricing and ordering information please visit http://www.igi-global.com/book-series/advances-finance-accounting-economics/73685. Postmaster: Send all address changes to above address.

Titles in this Series

For a list of additional titles in this series, please visit:
https://www.igi-global.com/book-series/advances-finance-accounting-economics/73685

Emerging Trends and Insights on Economic Inequality in the Wake of Global Crises
Shilpa Deo (MIT World Peace University, India) and A.V. Senthil Kumar (Hindusthan College of Arts and Science, India)
Information Science Reference • copyright 2023 • 300pp • H/C (ISBN: 9781668452899) • US $215.00 (our price)

Handbook of Research on Changing World Economic Order in the Post-Pandemic Period
Sushanta Kumar Mahapatra (IBS Hyderabad, The ICFAI Foundation for Higher Education, India) and Vishal Sarin (Lovely Professional University, India)
Business Science Reference • copyright 2022 • 470pp • H/C (ISBN: 9781799868965) • US $325.00 (our price)

Opportunities and Challenges for Multinational Enterprises and Foreign Direct Investment in the Belt and Road Initiative
Miraj Ahmed Bhuiyan (Guangdong University of Finance and Economics, China) and Isidora Beraha (Institute of Economic Sciences, Serbia)
Business Science Reference • copyright 2022 • 323pp • H/C (ISBN: 9781799880219) • US $250.00 (our price)

Advanced Machine Learning Algorithms for Complex Financial Applications
Mohammad Irfan (CMR Institute of Technology, India) Mohamed Elhoseny (American University in the Emirates, UAE) Salina Kassim (International Islamic University of Malaysia, Malaysia) and Noura Metawa (University of Sharjah, UAE)
Engineering Science Reference • copyright 2022 • 335pp • H/C (ISBN: 9781668444832) • US $270.00 (our price)

Finance for Sustainability in a Turbulent Economy
Abdul Rafay (University of Management and Technology, Pakistan)
Business Science Reference • copyright 2022 • 315pp • H/C (ISBN: 9781668455807) • US $250.00 (our price)

For an entire list of titles in this series, please visit:
https://www.igi-global.com/book-series/advances-finance-accounting-economics/73685

IGI Global
PUBLISHER of TIMELY KNOWLEDGE

701 East Chocolate Avenue, Hershey, PA 17033, USA
Tel: 717-533-8845 x100 • Fax: 717-533-8661
E-Mail: cust@igi-global.com • www.igi-global.com

Editorial Advisory Board

Table of Contents

Detailed Table of Contents

findings, the biggest problem created by the standards is the requirement for periodic reassessments and the option of selecting a method of assessing value, which offers grounds for the practice of creative accounting.

The results of scientific study and literature review indicate that new strategic transformations of entities are being examined for the adoption of a performance management system. This system has the responsibility of converting the strategic plan of long-term and medium-sized objectives into associated activities between the managerial plan and financial-accounting. An integrated system of performance indicators is implemented to properly estimate a company's worth in this chapter, which analyses the new research paths at the junction of accounting and management. The findings reveal that implementing performance management inside an entity satisfies a number of conditions that are directly connected to the level of achievement of the specified goals.

This chapter illustrates some aspects regarding the financial-accounting activity in the Romanian public system and obtaining a more realistic image of the financial reporting for the entities of the public system. The objectives of this chapter are to conduct an analysis on the implementation of financial reporting in the Romanian public sector in accordance with the requirements of International Public Sector Accounting Standards, which should include increased transparency and coherence, comparability of financial information, improved decision making, as well as the correct and real management of all approach arising therefrom. The issues presented by the author are based on the local and international specialized literature and university and specialized studies related to the treated topic. Thus, through the contribution brought, a new theoretical-empirical framework is created, which facilitates the identification of new ideas, themes, and debates of the aspects related to the financial-accounting reporting.

In a world where use of technology is not an option but a necessity, where new forms of work appear constantly, where change is everywhere and people must keep their distance from each other due to the pandemic, organizations must adapt and use new processes governed by using new technologies. In a sustainable environment, e-recruitment and non-financial compensations become the new tools to maintain performance and lower costs during a pandemic. Using bibliometric analysis, regression function, and correlation matrix, the authors obtained results for Romania and the top three countries, which indicated that e-recruitment is influenced by the use of the internet and availability of computers and productivity; the relations and the correlation between the analyzed variables are measured using simulation and mathematical modeling. The results indicate that there are benefits for individuals, for organizations, and also for environmental protection.

A company's conversion of financial statements is a well-known instrument in the development and management control domains, but its usage in the area of corporate disclosure reveals significant uses. In this chapter, the term "conversion" refers to the process that takes place whenever the currency in which the financial statements are created is different from the currency in which they are presented. Additionally, this chapter presents the significant managerial debates that arise throughout the process of converting financial statements. The findings reveal that financial statement conversion is only applicable if the firm whose financial statements are being converted has a functioning currency that is not in a hyperinflationary economy.

This chapter deals with developing a strategic map for improving the performance of medical services using the balanced scorecard (BSC). The main objectives of this chapter are to present the conceptual approaches of the balanced scorecard, the implementation and use of BSC in medical services, the advantages and limitations of BSC implementation in medical services. Based on the literature, the authors present the interpretations brought by specialists to the balanced scorecard concept and analyze the degree of implementation and use of BSC in medical services. A case study on the development of a strategic map for improving the performance of health services with the help of BSC is presented. Considering the factors that influence the size of medical organizations, the authors also present the advantages and limitations of adopting and using the balanced scorecard. The chapter ends with the general conclusions regarding improving medical services performance using BSC.

This chapter explores the notion of public relations accountability in the not-so-distant future with the integration of blockchain technology as championed and demanded by several brands, considering its impact on the dissemination of communication, coherency, and efficiency of the firm. Issues are around value delivery with reputation management, the new online ecosystem, and stakeholder relations. This text puts forward a radical proposition that would position the public relations profession and industry in a favourable position in relation to blockchain technology.

Because changes are quick in the digital age, the decision maker will actively seek the optimal solution for managerial accounting that he considers satisfactory and will put it into practice as soon as possible, given the conditions for materialising the decision. The use of digital programs and technologies to simulate the company's managerial accounting decisions can avoid these shortcomings, at least for a short period of time. This chapter illustrates that, in an increasingly digitalis environment, it is generally recognised that the use of IT technology in management accounting is critical for every company. Properly managing stakeholders' increasing expectations also contributes to the confidence required for a firm to survive and develop.

Preface

Management accounting takes on new elements in the 21st century, expanding the scope of its studies. Indicators of eco-performance offer information in a manner that is targeted and accurate to the environmental activity segment of the entity. Under these conditions, managerial choices must be changed and forcefully supported, taking into account the information needed by internal and external stakeholders, including financial reporting. As a result, the position of management in determining the company's success or failure has been increased to that of the most important factor in this process.

One of the challenges confronting today's corporate environment, and particularly management companies, is the management of sustainable performance. Profitability is the primary goal of every organization, but it must also consider the long-term viability of social, economic, and environmental factors. Under these conditions, managerial choices must be changed and forcefully supported, taking into account the information needed by internal and external stakeholders, including financial reporting. All of these discussions highlight the importance of users' role in creating accounting and finance models, and hence in modeling company information.

On the other hand, the merging of factors such as sustainability and corporate governance, as well as the rising demands of information users for access to information other than financial outcomes coming from the activity of organizations, have all led to the creation of non-traditional approaches that allow counterbalancing the advantages of finance. On top of that, management accounting shows the complete perspective of financial performance that experts in the area of accounting need to embrace in order to progress in an increasingly complicated corporate environment. This is because of the fact that management accounting is a reflection of management accounting. Companies recognize that such commitments are focused on improving their company image rather than core sustainability objectives. Organizations with a strong environmental orientation are more dedicated to adopting a green outlook. Green behaviors are described as the activities, acts, and practices that employees and stakeholders participate in that are related to, and contribute to, environmental sustainability.

Organizations implement trustworthy and green solutions with an ecological reputation and the ability to handle consumers' green demands and requirements through green practices, marketing management, and strategic transformation. Strategic green innovation combines and promotes management collaboration in production while taking into account environmental policies and regulations, green innovation practices and activities, environmental protection, and customer perception. Environmental customer wellbeing is the respect for customers' legal and moral rights through providing comprehensive information about products and services for customer satisfaction. The improvement of organizational sustainable development performance begins with lean and green practices and activities managed through a single unit, minimizing overlapping and separate implementation. The new models identify and explain how lean, green, and sustainable performance measures interact.

The book *Perspectives of Management Accounting for Sustainable Business Practices* is a comprehensive reference source that explores various theoretical and practical approaches to management accounting and its impact in the 21st century and investigates new accounting and financial approaches where economic and social aspects become mutually supportive to enhance their impact on community development. Covering topics such as CSR reporting, sustainability, and greenwashing, this book is an essential resource for academicians, specialty organizations, chief financial officers (CFOs), financial controllers, business analysts, financial planning and analysis (FP&A) analysts, budgeting managers, students, researchers, and business environment managers and specialists.

The authors Nabil Ahmed Mareai Senan, Ijaz Ali, Moin Uddin, Asma Khatoon, Asif Baig, and Imran Ahmad Khan of the first chapter, "Design Principles of Profitability Accounting and Accounting for Consistent Financial Management," suggested that the modern significance of profitability accounting from the perspective of the concept of accounting design that is consistent with financial management. In this sense, Beyer's concept of profitability accounting has not yet disappeared as a design concept for an accounting system that is consistent with financial management. They also describe how, as information technology advances, accounting information systems also undergo significant changes. But the question of what kind of information should be included in accounting and what kind of management philosophy should be used to create the necessary accounting system should be kept separate from the simple problem of the progress of information technology. The results showed that one of the reasons for maintaining consistent financial accounting is the influence of IFRS, which emphasizes the position of investors and considers it important to eliminate the information asymmetry between investors and management. Accounting treatment is necessary to harmonize the information that management uses to make management decisions with the financial-accounting information disclosed to investors. The part of the decision that is made by the company based on the current business situation must be made by management using a method of making management decisions and evaluating business performance. In addition, designing a unitary reporting framework could be the foundation to which businesses can relate in order to ensure a good correlation with users' requirements for accurate, reliable, and relevant information.

An interesting business perspective on the concept of non-financial reporting from a theoretical perspective is revealed by Teodora Breaz, Teodora Cucerzan, Cristina Didea (Castrase), and Rakos Ileana-Sorina, the authors of the second chapter, "A Holistic Picture of Non-Financial Reporting: The Stakeholders View." In comparison to conventional financial reporting, modern stakeholders want increasingly complex information and request supplemental disclosure. In addition to mandatory disclosure, corporations voluntarily provide additional data in the hope that this information will help the stock market better understand the driving constituents of company value. The authors present various aspects of non-financial reporting, such as the creation of value through non-financial reporting, its advantages and disadvantages, the trend toward standardization and the adoption of an integrated report, and the interpretation of the information provided to stakeholders through NFR. All aspects presented and analyzed are based on existing expert studies and university studies. The chapter ends with the authors' conclusions on the importance of integrated reporting. This input from the authors opens up new opportunities to exploit the information content specific to non-financial reporting, which is particularly relevant to all stakeholders.

The premises of strategic control that can drive an organization's digital transformation are illustrated by Alharbi Habbab Husam, the author of the third chapter, "Incorporating Corporate Social Responsibility Into Decision Making." The author demonstrates that there is a clear correlation between a company's business model and its financial decisions, such as investment and financial planning, in the case of successful companies with established CSR and sustainability initiatives. Increasing the knowledge of accounting managers about the strategic significance of environmental concerns is another key step once the concept of company-specific sustainability has been developed. One solution is to integrate decision-makers into interdisciplinary strategy teams. A company's leadership can also develop and promote a sustainability plan so that the company and society at large benefit from its implementation.

The priorities of the fight against the manipulation of accounting information are presented by Ionica Oncioiu, the author of the fourth chapter, "Creative Accounting Affects Corporate Performance: Theoretical Fundamentals and Specific Practices." Accounting creativity only addresses the same issue as management, but the solution resides at the border between the legal and recording of economic events, leaving accountants to cosmetic the entity's economic reality. From a variety of accounting treatments and rules, the entity's manager can select one that is most convenient and serves their own interests, which means that an outcome may be convenient but not necessarily accurate. On the other hand, the concept of creative accounting that is utilized by accountants within the context of attaining performance is very much a matter of innovation. This chapter shows the consequences and problems of creative accounting on performance. According to the findings, the biggest problem created by the standards is the requirement for periodic reassessments and the option of selecting a method of assessing value, which offers grounds for the practice of creative accounting.

In a descriptive manner, the interrelation of managerial accounting and the actions to increase the effect on performance is emphasized by Lavinia Essen Yildirim, the author of the fifth chapter, "Analysis of Performance From a Managerial Accounting Perspective." Accounting, the basic tool for knowledge, management, and control of patrimony and the results obtained by economic entities, is the only source capable of providing accounting information of informational value to the leadership of entities under pressure to adapt strategic decisions to economic uncertainty. This system has the responsibility of converting the strategic plan of long-term and medium-sized objectives into associated activities between the managerial plan and financial accounting. The findings reveal that implementing performance management inside an entity satisfies a number of conditions that are directly connected to the level of achievement of the specified goals. Credibility, opportunity, accessibility, dependability, relevance, consistency, simplicity, neutrality, and responsiveness are all quality standards. The identification and selection of relevant and meaningful KPIs that are incorporated in strategic planning processes must adhere to a set of rules that are supported by both theory and practice, rules that actively contribute to the imposition of quality criteria for these performance indicators.

In the sixth chapter, "Implementation of Financial Reporting in the Romanian Public System According to International Accounting Standards (IPSAS): Theoretical-Methodological approaches," Maria Ciurea and Rakos Ileana-Sorina present an analysis of the implementation of financial reporting in the Romanian public sector, in accordance with the requirements of International Public Sector Accounting Standards, which should include increased transparency and coherence, comparability of financial information, improved decision-making, as well as the correct and real management of all approach arising therefrom. Thus, through the contribution brought, a new theoretical-empirical framework is created, which facilitates the identification of new ideas, themes, and debates on the aspects related to financial-accounting reporting. The executive periodically requests information on the state of budgetary resources, in order to be able to ensure efficient implementation and evaluation of the comparative costs of the various programs. The solution to such a problem is to maintain the formats of the reporting documents in accordance with the requirements of the IPSAS standards, to present additional information when the situation requires it, and to continuously develop national rules in this area.

The importance of reducing HR Costs during pandemic time is presented by Nicoleta Valentina Florea, Constantin Aurelian Ionescu, Marinela Daniela Manea, Mariana Zamfir, Mihaela Denisa Coman, and Sorina Geanina Stanescu, the authors of the seventh chapter, “Sustainable Sources of Reducing HR Costs in Pandemic Time: E-Recruitment and Nonfinancial Compensation – A Mathematical and Accounting-Based Approach.” In a world where the use of technology is not an option but a necessity, where new forms of work appear constantly, where change is everywhere, and people must keep their distance from each other due to the pandemic, organizations must adapt and use new processes governed by using new technologies. In a sustainable environment, e-recruitment and non-financial compensations become the new tools to maintain performance and lower costs during a pandemic. Using bibliometric analysis, regression function, and correlation matrix, we obtained results for Romania and the top three countries, which indicated that e-recruitment is influenced by the use of the Internet, availability of computers, and productivity; the relations and the correlation between the analyzed variables are measured, using simulation and mathematical modeling. The results indicate that there are benefits for individuals, and organizations, but also for environmental protection. The research aims at academicians and practitioners who are concerned with the administration of a company through the budget system, with the purpose of satisfying the need for information in economic practice as the driving force.

A company’s conversion of financial statements is a well-known instrument in the development and management control domains, but its usage in the area of corporate disclosure reveals significant uses. Ionica Oncioiu and Alin Eliodor Tănase, the authors of the eighth chapter, “Different Approaches to Measure Conversion of Financial Statements and Disclosure Issues,” present the significant managerial debates that arise throughout the process of converting financial statements. Because several governments, market regulators, and operators have started enacting laws and regulations that compel corporations to report their environmental and social effects, there has been a recent rise in interest in understanding how actions linked to sustainability have an influence on a company’s business. Accounting and reporting are ways for organizations and their stakeholders to talk to each other and encourage social change. As a result, both stakeholder theory and legitimacy theory contribute to our understanding of sustainability disclosure since they both explain voluntary disclosure of sustainability challenges even in the absence of strong sustainability performance. The absence of trustworthy information is closely tied to the lack of available data. Compound measurements are based on information supplied by firms, which is not available to the general public. Thus, the validity of these measurements is dependent, at least in part, on company self-disclosure, which may have an incentive to present themselves in the best light possible. The findings reveal that financial statement conversion is only applicable if the firm whose financial statements are being converted has a functioning currency that is not in a hyperinflationary economy.

Performance measurement provides management of health care institutions with evidence of existing practices, beliefs, and assumptions, allowing management to create a strategic map for improving future health care services. In Chapter 9 dedicated to "Balanced Scorecard: Development of a Strategic Map to Improve the Performance of Medical Services," Adela Ioana Staras, Teodora Breaz, Melinda Timea Fulop, Dan Ioan Topor, and Sorinel Căpuşneanu present the conceptual approaches of the Balanced Scorecard, the implementation and use of BSC in medical services, and the advantages, and limitations of BSC implementation in medical services. It has launched new challenges related to the adoption and implementation of BSC within medical service institutions and beyond. Based on the literature, the authors present the interpretations brought by specialists to the Balanced Scorecard concept and analyze the degree of implementation and use of BSC in medical services. A case study on the development of a strategic map for improving the performance of health services with the help of BSC is presented. Considering the factors that influence the size of medical organizations, the authors also present the advantages and limitations of adopting and using the Balanced Scorecard. The chapter ends with the general conclusions regarding improving medical services performance using BSC.

The influence of blockchain technology on public relations and corporate communications is substantial, as firms that are proactive in recognizing and influencing future directions will have a stake in generating added value with seamless engagement. The author of the tenth chapter, "Public Relations Auditing and Accountability with Digitalised Decentralised Ecosystems: A Strategic Perspective," Ze Zook explores the notion of public relations accountability in the not-so-distant future with the integration of blockchain technology as championed and demanded by several brands, considering its impact on the dissemination of communication, coherency, and efficiency of the firm. Issues related to value setting, reputation management, the new online ecosystem, and stakeholder relations are addressed. This chapter puts forward a radical proposition that would position the public relations profession and industry in a favorable position in relation to blockchain technology. Increasing informational technological insights into blockchain technologies are inherently bound to influence the parameters as to how messages are received and given weight in terms of importance and relevance. PR, in line with its classical definition in contrast to marketing, is likely to lever an influence that can make a small yet incremental difference. In the opinion of the author, management should encourage PR professionals to get more involved with web developers so that they can share a common lingua franca.

The use of digital programs and technologies to simulate the company's managerial accounting decisions can avoid these shortcomings, at least for a short period of time. In the eleventh chapter, "The Impact of IT Technologies on Management Accounting," Alharbi Habbab Husam illustrates that, in an increasing digitalis environment, it is generally recognized that the use of IT technology in management accounting is critical for every company. Properly managing stakeholders' increasing expectations also contributes to the confidence required for a firm to survive and develop. From this perspective, the introduction of a new ERP system often affects everything at three levels, albeit to varying degrees. Processes are being redefined, which has a clear impact on a company's organizational chart and culture. It is clear that technological development has contributed to an expansion in the use of electronic accounting, and as a result, the use of new technologies has contributed to expanding the scope of the term "e-accounting." By integrating with IoT and changing from offline to online, experts discuss the e-accounting system using two concepts: accounting information system and computerized accounting system. The results highlight that the future is neither foreseeable nor predictable, and innovation has emerged as a critical component that may contribute value in any environment, whether individual, corporate, or societal. The development of information-technology-based systems for generating information for management purposes based on an integrated accounting information system has become a requirement in all businesses.

This overview of this book highlights the fact that each chapter contains interesting elements whose potential and degree of interest open new directions for future research. Authorized analyses indicate that accounting practices act as a mechanism to facilitate environmental management through compliance with environmental legislation, stakeholders' communication, employee and management engagement, and commitment to continuous improvement of environmental performance. Therefore, management accounting has a dual function in this respect: an environmental management facilitator and the benefit of environmental management based on accountability.

Ionica Oncioiu
Titu Maiorescu University, Romania

Acknowledgment

Looking back, we wish to thank all the persons who made the publishing of the present volume possible: Jan Travers, Melissa Wagner, Erin Wesser, Christina Henning, Nicole Elliott, Kristina Byrne, Lindsay Johnston, Joshua Witman, Nick Newcomer, Jaimie Watts, Josephine Dadeboe, Jordan Tepper, Sean Eckman, Elizabeth Barrantes, Katie McLoughlin and many other IGI Global team members, reviewers, collaborators, and all the contributing authors: without your efforts and dedication this editorial project would have never been possible.

Chapter 1
Design Principles of Profitability Accounting and Accounting for Consistent Financial Management

Ijaz Ali
https://orcid.org/0000-0001-5436-0624
Fahad Bin Sultan University, Saudi Arabia

Raj Bahadur Sharma
University of Bahrain, Bahrain

Asif Baig
https://orcid.org/0000-0002-5779-6164
Jubail University College, Saudi Arabia

Imran Ahmad Khan
https://orcid.org/0000-0003-2383-0608
Creative Heads Consultants, India

DOI: 10.4018/978-1-6684-4595-2.ch001

ABSTRACT

Design Principles of Profitability Accounting

One of the reasons for the advocacy of consistent financial accounting is the influence of IFRS, which emphasizes the position of investors and considers it important to eliminate the asymmetry of information between investors and management. The accounting treatment is required to harmonize the information that management uses to make management decisions with the financial accounting information disclosed to investors. The part of the decision that is made by the company based on the actual business situation, as referred to in IFRS, is required to be made by management using a method for making management decisions and evaluating business performance. This type of financial accounting (institutional accounting) is what is called the management approach. In the future, the demand from companies for an accounting system that is consistent with financial management is expected to increase. In this chapter, the authors examine the modern significance of profitability accounting from the perspective of the design concept of accounting that is consistent with financial management.

INTRODUCTION

Beyer published a book, *Profitability Accounting*, in 1963. This is a well-known book that shows the management accounting system of performance management accounting and decision-making accounting, which are widely supported in India. In 1972, the second edition was published with Trawicki as co-author.

What is Beyer's concept of profitability accounting? It is an integrated system that combines various elements such as profit planning, responsibility accounting, multidimensional classification of data, the contributory profit method, and reporting of exceptions, and can provide a variety of information that is useful for both financial and management accounting. In other words, Beyer's profitability accounting is oriented toward the accounting of unity of finances and management.

In the sections **Components of Profitability Accounting** and **Structure of Profitability Accounting**, the main points of profitability accounting are summarized based on the second edition of the book (1972). The reason for targeting the second edition is that the discussions are more organized than in the first edition and that there is a description based on the external reporting controversy of direct costing that took place in the 1960s. Then, in the section **Significance of Profitability Accounting from the Viewpoint of Financial Management Matching**, we examine in what sense profitability accounting has the design concept of the accounting system of financial management matching.

COMPONENTS OF PROFITABILITY ACCOUNTING

Financial Accounting and Management Accounting

Profitability accounting recognizes that accounting systems classify and represent information about an organization in financial terms. This form of financial terminology allows accounting to function as a language for communicating useful information in a standardized and easily understood format. Since almost everyone who interacts with a business organization has an interest in and need for quantitative financial information about the company, all of these information users make the accounting system the source of the financial information they need (Beyer & Trawicki, 1972, p. 4).

Depending on the interests and needs of these stakeholders, there are three purposes of an accounting system (Beyer & Trawicki, 1972, p. 4).

1. To provide shareholders, creditors, governments, and management with an accounting of the assets entrusted to the entity and an explanation of its financial condition and results over time.
2. To provide a mechanism to assist management in planning and controlling the entity's operations.
3. To provide quantitative information to support management decision-making.

Of these, accounting that contributes to objective (a) is called financial accounting. Since financial accounting is institutionally mandated, accounting systems should fundamentally contribute to this objective. Financial accounting "focuses on the management of assets, and the classification and recording of transactions that affect the enterprise. It is essentially a record of the past. Financial accounting is defined as "the computation and reporting of the financial condition and results of an enterprise as a whole over a period of time" (Beyer & Trawicki, 1972, p. 5). Financial accounting is characterized by the fact that the guiding rules and principles are prescribed by law or codified in GAAP. The purpose of these laws and regulations is explained as follows (Beyer & Trawicki, 1972, p. 5).

1. Ensure that important financial information is disclosed.
2. Ensure comparability of financial information among different organizations that issue securities.

On the other hand, accounting that serves the purpose of (b) and (c) is called management accounting. Management accounting is defined as "the provision of useful information to business managers in the operation of an enterprise" (Beyer

& Trawicki, 1972, p. 6). Such information is generally provided in the following two ways (Beyer & Trawicki, 1972, p. 5).

1. Control by ensuring quantitative agreement between schedule and actual performance.
2. Support planning and decision-making by providing information that helps evaluate alternatives.

The difference between management accounting and financial accounting is that management accounting must focus on the future, whereas financial accounting records the past. Another important feature of management accounting is that there are no laws regulating management accounting, and any system can be used as long as it is useful to business managers. Because business activities are so diverse, there is no single form of information that satisfies all management requirements, different objectives require different compilations, and many decisions require that the data elements contained in the accounting system be combined with external data elements such as market research and management decisions. (Beyer & Trawicki, 1972, p. 6).

Accounting System

As the life cycles of products and production equipment become shorter, situations will emerge in which managers will not have the experience or first-hand knowledge of all the information needed to effectively manage their companies, except in very small companies. In such a case, managers will have to place greater reliance on information produced by others inside and outside the company and communicated through efficient information systems. Managers will need specific information for each of the basic tasks of the management cycle. Providing the right information, at the right time, in the right format, and in the right place is necessary for business managers at different levels to perform their functions effectively (Beyer & Trawicki, 1972, pp. 7–8).

Increasing reliance on information systems does not diminish the need for sound judgment in decision-making. This is because there will always be situations where business managers make decisions based on incomplete or inappropriate information. In addition, the use of information systems is appropriate for such areas where the decisions of business managers are important. This is because the use of an appropriate information system can (1) reduce inappropriate information and (2) clarify the areas where information can be used. In particular, (2) has the merit of allowing business managers to invest more time in areas that require more subjective judgment. The use of such information systems enables managers to make decisions more objectively and efficiently, thus improving the quality of decision-making (Beyer & Trawicki, 1972, p. 8).

Here, the accounting system is expected to be a source of quantitative financial information. (Beyer & Trawicki, 1972, pp. 8–9).

1. To provide quantitative information on the effects of alternatives.
2. To provide quantitative information on the performance of business managers and various segments.

The method of using information is different between financial accounting and management accounting. However, since the input data required in financial accounting is also required in planning, decision making, and control in management accounting, the input data required in financial accounting is also required in management accounting (Beyer & Trawicki, 1972, p. 6). Therefore, a single integrated accounting system should simultaneously satisfy the objectives of financial accounting and management accounting (Beyer & Trawicki, 1972, p. 9). Profitability accounting is the one that integrates the two accounting.

Profit Concept

The calculation of corporate profits is regarded as an essential concept for the maintenance and development of the capitalist free economic system. The following are some examples of its uses:

1. As a basis for current and future creditors and investors to make predictions of companies.
2. Tax authorities use it as a basis for the taxation of companies.
3. As a basis for management performance evaluation and compensation decisions.

At the same time, however, the calculation and reporting of such profits is the subject of much controversy among corporate managers, professional accountants, investors, regulators, and tax authorities. On the other hand, business managers need a different profit measure than the one required for external reporting. The profit measures needed by such managers focus on how profit changes in response to specific changes in production, sales, or other factors. These profit measures are expressed in various forms depending on the purpose, such as ratio or absolute amount in units, or segment or whole company in terms of object. (Beyer & Trawicki, 1972, p. 40).

Profitability accounting was developed to provide this type of profit information. Under profitability accounting, a single system provides earnings information in different formats for different purposes, consistent within a company. Since the profit figures calculated by the accountant are used extensively to reconcile interests, the accountant must first of all emphasize objectivity. In terms of the role of accounting in the socio-economic system, the purpose of accounting is defined as the calculation of objective corporate profits for a certain period of time, which is relatively short in terms of the duration of the enterprise. On the other hand, from a purely conceptual point of view, profit is defined as follows: Profit = (enterprise value at the end of the period - enterprise value at the beginning of the period) + wealth distributed during the period. Such a profit is called an economic profit. This economic profit does not achieve the accounting objectives of a socio-economic system as described above. This is because there is no objective measure of the value of an ongoing enterprise at a particular point in time during the life of the enterprise. The value of an enterprise can be objectively calculated only when the enterprise is terminated. The replacement price or market price of an asset has a certain objectivity. However, since the value of a company depends on its ability to earn money in the future, which is inherently subjective and speculative, profit calculations based on such asset prices are inappropriate (Beyer & Trawicki, 1972, p. 41).

Because of these shortcomings, accountants have adopted an approach that calculates the difference between revenues and the cost of earning those revenues as periodic profit, rather than measuring and comparing the total value at a specific point in time (Beyer & Trawicki, 1972, pp. 42-43). Paton & Littleton (1940) describe cost as "effort" and revenue as "results", but this approach also has subjective evaluation problems on how to define revenue and when to recognize it To minimize the impact of this problem, accountants have adopted the realization principle, which states that "profits from sales arise when the realization of the sale is almost certain" In general, a sales transaction is an action that signals the conversion of goods into cash or cash equivalents Since sales transactions can be verified in the market, the revenue measure at the point of sale has objectivity. The cost is objectively measured by market transactions when goods and services are procured in the market before the sale. Therefore, the point of sales realization is the most rational time to measure net profit, because revenue and cost have the same objectivity when sales are realized One of the tasks of the accountant is to find a reasonable basis for allocating all costs to the period in which revenue, or income, is recognized. The search for such a criterion is conducted until all costs can be traced to a particular revenue or period, or until the costs of the task exceed its benefits (Beyer & Trawicki, 1972, p. 42).

Realization-based profit calculation has problems when there is a considerable interval between effort and achievement, and when the causal relationship is ambiguous. These problems occur mainly in the manufacturing industry, and total costing and direct costing are the approaches to profit calculation that address these problems (Beyer & Trawicki, 1972, pp. 43-46).

Total Costing and Direct Costing

In profit and loss accounting, products have long been used as a means of mapping revenue to manufacture costs. This is based on the idea that

...manufacturing costs arise only for the manufacture of a unit of product, and therefore the revenue generated from these costs should reflect the price received when the unit of product is sold (Beyer & Trawicki, 1972, p. 43).

Some manufacturing costs, such as material costs and direct labor costs, are directly related to a specific product unit and can therefore be easily associated with the product unit. However, most of the indirect manufacturing costs, which are also generated by manufacturing, cannot be directly traced to a product unit. Since these indirect costs do not vary in direct proportion to the manufacturing activities, the amount to be allocated per unit can be determined in advance by forecasting the manufacturing volume. As a result, the entire manufacturing cost is allocated to each product unit. For this reason, this type of costing is called total costing (Beyer & Trawicki, 1972, p. 43). The cost of inventories is deferred because it is actually a component of the production cost. Examples of manufacturing overheads that can be deferred on inventories in this way are plant, equipment, and rent (Beyer & Trawicki, 1972, p. 44). These costs are allocated to products through inventories and are eventually matched to the revenue earned from the sale of the products.

On the other hand, for the purpose of profit calculation, all other costs classified as selling, general, and administrative expenses also need to be associated with revenues in the period in which they contribute to revenues. However, most of these costs do not contribute to the manufacture of the product and are difficult to recognize in relation to the product unit. In general, with very few exceptions, there are no rational criteria that systematically relate selling, general, and administrative expenses to specific revenues. Some selling, general and administrative expenses are related to revenue that is recognized after the period in which they are incurred. However, because there is no objective criterion to determine the amount of cost to be deferred and the period in which it is deferred, selling, general and administrative expenses are associated with revenue in the period in which they are incurred. Such a procedure is convenient for-profit calculation because of its objectivity and conservativeness. Adopting such a procedure does not contradict the application of the principle of revenue-cost correspondence. Therefore, if there is a reasonable basis for deferring selling, general and administrative expenses, it is desirable to defer those costs for more appropriate profit calculation (Beyer & Trawicki, 1972, p. 44).

Along with total costing, direct costing is another approach to profit calculation. The difference between direct costing and full costing is that the direct costs of manufacturing and sales are subtracted from the revenue from the product to calculate the contribution margin. Contribution margin is such a margin that

...measures the net contribution of the period's earnings to realizing a profit by recovering the period's costs incurred in providing the manufacturing and selling capacity (Beyer & Trawicki, 1972, p. 45).

The usefulness of the decomposition of costs into variable and fixed costs in direct costing is as follows:

1. Estimate the break-even point and the contribution to fixed costs for profit planning.
2. Calculate the profitability of products and product lines.
3. To simplify budgeting
4. To support cost control

However, such usefulness for internal profit calculation and decision making is not a characteristic unique to direct costing, as it also exists in other techniques. The essential characteristic of direct costing is that this calculation method is performed within profit accounting for external reporting purposes (Beyer & Trawicki, 1972, p. 45).

Profit Calculations for External Reporting

Profit calculations used for external reporting have historically relied on full cost accounting, following the generally accepted interpretation of the principle of revenue/cost correspondence. The use of such profit measures provides information that is objective, consistent, and measures the economic progress realized by a company in a given period (Beyer & Trawicki, 1972, pp. 45—46).

At the same time, however, there are direct costing advocates who argue that the traditional profit calculation method used for many years is wrong and that direct costing is the only method that can calculate the correct period profit. The basic point of contention between the supporters of traditional cost accounting and the direct cost accounting advocates is the issue of whether or not to defer fixed manufacturing overhead costs in inventories (Beyer & Trawicki, 1972, p. 46).

The difference between direct costing and total costing in profit calculation is as follows. From the point of view of a company's entire existence, the amount of profit will be equal regardless of whether it is calculated by direct costing or total costing because the total cost of variable and fixed costs together corresponds to the total revenue. However, from a relatively short perspective, such as one year, manufacturing and sales are not necessarily balanced, so the reported profits calculated by the two techniques will be quite different. This is because, in full costing, some of the fixed manufacturing overhead is deferred to inventories, whereas in direct costing, all fixed manufacturing overhead is charged to the period In addition, in direct costing, fixed manufacturing overhead is the cost for production preparation and is not considered as the cost of products In other words, under direct costing, fixed manufacturing overhead is interpreted as a cost incurred to maintain production capacity, regardless of the manufacturing activity. Under direct costing, fixed manufacturing overhead is a cost associated with time because "the opportunity to use capacity comes at the expense of time, and the cost of providing this capacity is also associated with time" (Beyer & Trawicki, 1972, p. 46). This approach justifies that in direct costing, fixed costs are allocated directly to the period in which they are incurred, rather than being allocated to products and then being matched to the revenue from their sale. Proponents of direct costing further argue as follows:

Since gross profit can be realized only through sales transactions, net profit should vary with sales. Under total cost accounting, net income in a given period will either be reduced by a lower level of production activity or increased by a higher level of production activity, even if the volume of sales does not change (Beyer & Trawicki, 1972, p. 46).

Proponents of direct costing conclude that such a phenomenon is caused by the recognition of unrealized profits. On the other hand, there is a counterargument to such claims of the supporters of direct costing. Net income is a function of both revenue and cost and will increase either by an increase in revenue or by a reduction in cost. The concept of realization is related only to the timing of revenue recognition and is tied to sales transactions. Unrealized profit arises only when it is assumed that a sale has been made when no sale has been made. Since both direct costing and full costing use the same signal, the point of sale, for the timing of revenue recognition, the difference between the two methods has nothing to do with unrealized profits. The proponents of total costing state that the difference between direct costing and total costing is all in the timing of cost recognition. In direct costing, the difference between utilized and idle fixed capacity is ignored. All fixed costs are charged in the period in which they are incurred. In full costing, this difference is recognized. Fixed manufacturing overhead for unused capacity is treated as a loss for the period. This implies that the incurrence of these costs does not bring any benefit. The cost of the capacity utilized is deferred to correspond to the revenue when the product is sold. (Beyer & Trawicki, 1972, p. 47).

Table 1. Comparison of profitability accounting, direct costing, and total costing

Direct costing Profitability accounting Total costing **Sales $12,000,000 $12,000,000 $12,000,000** **variable cost 7,200,000 7,200,000** **Cost of sales 8,700,000**
Contribution profit $ 4,800,000 $ 4,800,000 Gross profit $ 3,300,000 Fixed and programmed costs 2,400,000 2,400,000 Inventory fixed cost adjustment 360,000 (subtraction) Selling, general and administrative 1,260,000 expenses
Profit before tax $ 2,400,000 $ 2,040,000 $ 2,040,000

(source: Beyer & Trawicki, 1972, p. 49)

Determining whether direct costing or total costing procedures are appropriate is a question of whether it is reasonable to use cost behavior as a basis for cost deferral. A cost is deferred if it has some comparable economic value that can reasonably be expected to contribute to earnings in future periods. If we deny this, as in direct costing, we deny the principle of revenue-cost correspondence, which links revenue to the cost of generating that revenue (Beyer & Trawicki, 1972, p. 47). As a practical matter, costs are not classified into direct costs or periodic costs because of their inherent characteristics. The concept of direct cost or period cost is not an inherent characteristic of cost, because the cost is assigned these characteristics, to a greater or lesser extent, as a result of decisions about organization, equipment, and cost control (Beyer & Trawicki, 1972, pp. 47-48).

Even though periodic profits vary greatly depending on how the concepts of direct costs and periodic costs are defined, these concepts are so confusing that different theorists have different definitions. The proportion of overhead costs allocated to

Table 2. Comparison of profitability accounting, direct costing, and total costing

Direct costing Profitability accounting Total costing **Sales $8,000,000 $8,000,000 $8,000,000** **variable cost 4,800,000 4,800,000** **Cost of sales 5,800,000**
Contribution profit $ 3,200,000 $ 3,200,000 Gross profit $ 2,200,000 Fixed and programmed costs 2,400,000 2,400,000 Inventory fixed cost adjustment (360,000) (subtraction) Selling, general and administrative 1,040,000 expenses
Profit before tax $ 800,000 $ 1,160,000 $ 1,160,000

(Source: Beyer & Trawicki, 1972, p. 50, partially modified)

inventories varies greatly from firm to firm, even within the same industry, because it depends on the concepts of direct cost and the period cost assumed by each business manager (Beyer & Trawicki, 1972, p. 48).

STRUCTURE OF PROFITABILITY ACCOUNTING

Income Statement in Profitability Accounting

The components of profitability accounting are profit planning, responsibility accounting, multidimensional data classification, contributed profit, exception reporting, comprehensiveness and elasticity. So, what kind of profit and loss is calculated in profitability accounting with such components? The income statement is shown in Table 1 and Table 2. The design principles are as follows.

Profitability accounting adopts the principle of revenue/cost matching. This is the basis for linking the problem of calculating the net income of the entire enterprise with the total costing method. Profitability accounting not only provides a measure of profit by full cost accounting but also allows full recognition of cost behavior by showing in the income statement, as in direct cost accounting, sales less variable costs for the period (Beyer & Trawicki, 1972, p. 49). Thus, in profitability accounting, the concept of contributory profit in direct costing is incorporated in the statement that reports profit consistent with the calculation by full costing. This allows the following benefits to be realized (Beyer & Trawicki, 1972, pp. 50–51).

1. The formal introduction of the concept of contributory profit facilitates planning and forecasting of decisions about increasing or decreasing production, or expanding or abandoning products or markets.
2. The concept of profit in total costing allows profit to be calculated and reported within a generally accepted framework.

Table 1 shows a case in which the sales volume exceeds the production volume and the inventories at the end of the period are lower than the inventories at the beginning of the period. By subtracting the difference of $360,000 between the beginning and the end of the period in fixed costs included in inventories from the contribution profit, the profit before tax of profitability accounting and full cost accounting is matched. On the other hand, Table 2 shows the case where production exceeds sales and inventories at the end of the period increase more than inventories at the beginning of the period. By adding the difference of $360,000 between the beginning and the end of the period in fixed costs included in inventories, the profit before tax of profitability accounting and full cost accounting will match.

Data Collection and Classification in Profitability Accounting

Responsibility Accounting and Data Classification

A major pillar of profitability accounting is the design of an accounting system based on responsibility accounting. For management information systems to function effectively, a clear allocation of responsibility is essential. This is because business activities are carried out by human beings, and data becomes useful information only when it is in a form that can be used by specific business managers in their actions (Beyer & Trawicki, 1972, pp. 19-20). In other words, a clear allocation of authority and responsibility identifies what kind of information is needed by business managers. Profitability accounting systems are built on this fact.

Therefore, in profitability accounting, the original data of revenues, costs, and profits are collected and classified according to the responsibility structure of the organization The planning and control system is constructed so that the necessary information can be communicated to management in the most useful form. Such a conformity process serves the dual purpose of providing managers with the information they need to perform their jobs and providing a basis for evaluating their performance

The information categorized by responsibility shows the results of each manager's past actions. Such information enables managers to identify important areas that need attention and consideration. Therefore, the information categorized by responsibility is extremely useful not only in evaluating the performance of managers but also in helping managers to perform their tasks. This is not only a control of the business manager but also control by the business manager. Therefore, the setting of responsibility in profitability accounting is not a restrictive concept, but a constructive concept (Beyer & Trawicki, 1972, p. 20).

In particular, it is difficult to establish cost responsibilities and allocate cost responsibilities in indirect departments that provide services to multiple product lines. This is a problem of clarifying who is responsible for which costs, and an organization chart should provide the necessary information to solve such problems. The process of setting responsibility for revenue and profit is similar to that of setting responsibility for the cost. This is done by the following procedure (Beyer & Trawicki, 1972, p. 20-22).

1. Allocate responsibilities to specific management personnel who have the authority to exercise control.
2. Set standards and targets for each area of responsibility.
3. Collect actual revenue and profit data for each area of responsibility and compare them to predetermined targets.

Multidimensional Data Classification

Multidimensional data classification is the classification of the inputs to the database that supports the accounting system in such a way that it has complete flexibility. By classifying input data in this way, an accounting system can process and provide the necessary information for almost any information request (Beyer & Trawicki, 1972, p. 15). The most essential property of a management information system is its ability to convey information in a meaningful and useful form for the management of a company. However, the realization of such a system is difficult because there is no single information format that is appropriate for all business management needs (Beyer & Trawicki, 1972, p. 22). Profitability accounting aims to satisfy all information needs of business control, profit planning, and various decision making, including financial accounting purposes, by a single system. Such a system is made possible by modularizing and classifying the data in a multidimensional manner. By combining and providing such modularized and multidimensionally classified data as needed, a system that can meet any information needs can be realized. The criteria for such multidimensional data classification are classification by information requirements of subunits and classification by data categories Responsibility for costs and revenues is the basis for one dimension of segmentation in all firms. This provides a mechanism for reporting costs, revenues, and profits according to the control and responsibility structure of the organization (Beyer & Trawicki, 1972, p. 23). However, in most cases, segmentation in a single dimension is not sufficient. Other examples of segmentation are product lines, sales regions, and distribution channels. Therefore, the data classification should be able to extract data for each of these identified subunits separately (Beyer & Trawicki, 1972, p. 24).

Setting up Accounts and Creating Account Charts

In profitability accounting, data is collected, classified, processed, and communicated using the following principles.

- Revenue, cost, and profit data are classified according to the organization's responsibility structure.
- Information is created for each responsibility of the business managers and communicated in such a way that it can be used for their actions.

The basic scheme for the collection and classification of all financial data is provided by the chart of accounts. The design of the chart of accounts is particularly important in profitability accounting, because the proper construction of the chart of accounts achieves the two principles of data processing in profitability accounting described above, as follows.

- Data classification by responsibility is performed.
- The data is edited and classified for reporting to business managers and external users.

At the same time, the classification system must recognize that the data can be sorted and edited to serve a variety of purposes. These principles of data classification are equally applicable to a wide variety of organizations, not only in manufacturing but also in services and distribution (Beyer & Trawicki, 1972, pp. 53—54). A chart of accounts reflects the organizational structure problems as they are, so creating a chart of accounts cannot solve the organizational structure problems.

Elements of the chart of accounts or the information and control system cannot correct the basic organizational weaknesses of the enterprise or the shortcomings of the organizational chart. If organizational problems exist, they must be solved before the management information system can function. (Beyer & Trawicki, 1972, p. 54). Acknowledging that the organizational structure of a company is influenced by many factors and that there is no one type of organizational structure that fits all companies, the following general principles of organization are essential to effective company operations.

- Each manager has a clear understanding of the responsibilities assigned to him/her.
- Each manager is given the authority necessary to carry out his or her responsibilities.

These principles allow the business manager to know what is expected of him and that the execution of his responsibilities is not constrained. This means that before constructing the chart of accounts, the following should be considered, and if necessary, management responsibilities should be reassigned, and the chart of accounts revised.

- Authority and responsibility in the organization should be clear, with no overlap or misunderstanding.
- The organization chart should reflect the actual situation in which the organization functions.

A company's accounting system is built and operated based on a set of procedures and schemes for organizing, classifying, recording, and summarizing the transactions that affect the company. As mentioned above, in profitability accounting, such a scheme is provided by an account chart. An account is a summary of transactions with certain common characteristics, and an account chart is a listing of all the accounts used to record financial information for a particular company (Beyer & Trawicki, 1972, pp. 54-55). The setting of accounts in an organization has the following characteristics:

- Subdivision of accounts is done to classify transactions that are related to the interests of the organization, or transactions for which the organization will benefit from the subdivision.
- Every transaction is recorded in some account.

The accounts include asset accounts, liability accounts, and equity accounts. These accounts are called balance sheet accounts, and the aggregate of all these accounts represents the financial position of a company at a given point in time (Beyer & Trawicki, 1972, p. 55).

Any transaction that occurs in an enterprise can be recorded directly in the above accounts. However, in reality, accountants choose to expand the accounts by setting up profit and loss accounts - revenue and expense accounts - to record and summarize transactions that affect the current year's profit and loss of the enterprise. These detailed accounts are used to classify data to help control and manage the operations of the firm. The profit and loss accounts are summarized and compiled at the end of a given period to show the net effect on profit and loss for that period. The asset, liability, and equity accounts may also be further subdivided to provide the information needed for control and reporting. However, unlike profit and loss accounts, these accounts do not need to be closed at the end of the period because they always represent the current state of affairs (Beyer & Trawicki, 1972, p. 56).

Whenever feasible, each account should be subdivided to reflect one type of activity, one person's responsibility, and one type of behavior, and each account should contain relatively homogeneous data. The advantages of such homogeneity in the accounts are as follows:

- It is essential for effective cost control.
- To reduce the need for special investigations of certain accounts.

To identify individual accounts, each account is given a code consisting of several digits. In the construction of the chart of accounts, each account is given a code consisting of several digits to identify the individual account. The basic principle of a coding system that assigns such a code is that the digits of each code have a definite meaning as well as their value. In the design of a coding system, the following contradictory principles should be satisfied simultaneously (Beyer & Trawicki, 1972, pp. 58—60).

Table 3. Coding of accounts

Account number	Account name (balance sheet account)
100	**cash**
110	101 Savings account 102 Deposits of salaries and dividends 103 Working capital for sales 104 Petty Cash **Marketable securities**
120	111 U.S. Treasury Bonds 112 Other marketable securities **Bills and accounts receivable**
	121 Bills receivable 123 Accounts receivable 125 Claims

(Source: Excerpted from Beyer & Trawicki, 1972, p. 74)

- Simplify the coding to the extent that it does not interfere with easy understanding and application.
- Coding should be detailed enough to be flexible enough to be modified and extended without recoding.

As mentioned earlier, in profitability accounting, the collection and recording of revenues and expenses are done by responsibility. The chart of accounts is designed to reflect the responsibilities embodied in the organization chart by using the above coding system and subdivided accounts. In this way, at any level of management, the actual and expected costs for which managers are responsible can be easily summarized and reported (Beyer & Trawicki, 1972, p. 60).

A selection of coding examples is shown in Table 3. In the main text, there are seven pages of coding examples.

THE SIGNIFICANCE OF PROFITABILITY ACCOUNTING FROM THE PERSPECTIVE OF FINANCIAL CONSISTENCY

The Concept of Consistency of Financial Management in Profitability Accounting

As mentioned in Section 2.2, Beyer & Trawicki (1972) does not develop a discussion based on a prior dichotomy between financial accounting and management accounting, but rather presents three roles of accounting and aims to construct an accounting system in which each is fulfilled in a single system. This is profitability accounting, and it can be said that Beyer & Trawicki originally aimed at an accounting system that is consistent with financial management. To be more precise, rather than integrating financial and managerial accounting into a single system, Beyer & Trawicki tried to construct an information system that could fulfill the roles of financial accounting and managerial accounting according to the objectives of the original one.

The structural essence of profitability accounting is direct costing designed from the perspective of responsibility accounting. Profitability accounting is designed so that it can be used not only for internal management (management accounting) but also for external reporting (financial accounting). In this regard, it can be said that it is close to the state of financial control agreement that Taipaleenmäki and Ikäheimo (2013) think. By the way they use the term "institutional accounting" instead of financial accounting and call it a control agreement. Taipaleenmäki and Ikäheimo show the relationship between management, institutional accounting, and management accounting, and the congruence of control and management (congruence of financial control) from the concept of management approach in IFRS, as shown in Figure 1 in the form of "Integration of Management and Accounting".

In profitability accounting, organizational segmentation and cost classification are conducted based on responsibility accounting. Segmentation and cost classification are not completely objective and there is no single "solution". The management philosophy of the manager enters into the process. Various management decisions are made using the numerical values of the accounting system designed in this way. The profits for management accounting are converted into profits for financial accounting and made public. This is exactly the relationship shown in Figure 1.

Figure 1. Integration of management and accounting

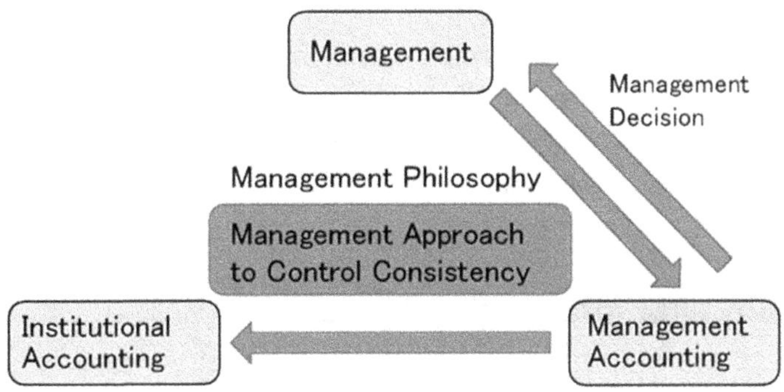

Fixed Cost Adjustment for Financial Consistency

As mentioned earlier, Beyer & Trawicki (1972) positions the essential characteristics of direct costing as including the function of external reporting. There are two reasons for them to make this point: first, the circumstances of the establishment of direct cost accounting. The first time direct costing had appeared in the literature was in Harris (1936), and the contributory profit method itself had been conducted as a special cost survey before. The reason why Harris is called one of the originators of direct costing is that he realized the calculation of contributory profit in the ordinary profit and loss account. The original aim of Harris was to create an income statement in which sales and profits are correlated, and it was more a modification of the profit calculation mechanism itself rather than an internal use of contributory profit. One reason is that there was a major controversy over external reporting between Horngren and Sorter (1961) and Ferrara (1963) between the first and second editions of Profitability Accounting. In this debate, Horngren and Sorter, a supporter of direct costing, argued that direct costing could be applied to external reporting from the perspective of accounting theory. The theory that became the pillar of this argument is the future cost avoidance theory, which states that the service potential of an asset is its ability to avoid incurring the same type of cost in the future. As this argument was developed, Beyer & Trawicki considered that the essential characteristic of direct costing is that it includes the function of external reporting.

However, Beyer & Trawicki argues that the profit concept used in external reporting is based on total cost accounting. In a series of arguments, Ferrara argued that the service potential of an asset lies in its ability to earn cash in the future and that there is no difference between variable costs and fixed costs in this ability. Therefore, he argued that the distinction between product cost and period cost should not be made based on cost behavior. As we saw in section 2 above, Beyer & Trawicki supports this view. For this reason, internal reporting accounting is based on direct costing, which is useful for responsibility accounting, and makes certain adjustments so that the reported profit matches that of full costing. The device is the so-called fixed cost adjustment. As can be seen in Table 1 and Table 2, the structure of profitability accounting itself is direct costing, which calculates the contribution profit. By applying fixed cost adjustment to it, the profit for external reporting is calculated. The systematic mechanism that facilitates this adjustment is the use of information systems as described below.

Relationship With Information Systems

Beyer & Trawicki (1972) state in Chapter 1 that profitability accounting systems should be designed to satisfy a wide range of information requirements of business managers, and that the system's database should contain all useful accounting input data for both financial and management accounting purposes. Then, in the final chapter describing the future outlook, "the direction of a new management information system," is shown, which is as follows (Beyer & Trawicki, 1972, p. 340).

1. Further use of business models
2. Inclusion of external information in company databases

In this paper, business models are simulation models that support planning, control, and decision-making. The authors point out that the development of computers will make it possible to use these models. Profitability accounting already assumed the use of EDP in the first edition (1963) and was intended to utilize computer systems. The second issue is the scope of the database. They point out that future information systems should include not only information within the enterprise, but also data about customers, competitors, markets, and the economic environment. This will make it possible to visualize comprehensive statements that explain the inputs and outputs of society and the environment (Beyer & Trawicki, 1972, p. 341). This is a point that foreshadows the use of big data in the modern era.

In addition, the multidimensional data classification and coding of accounts in profitability accounting are based on the assumption that information systems will be used. This concept is still applicable today. In many cases, ERP is assumed to be used when constructing an accounting system for a FILP. For example, Vaassen and Hunton (2009) present a case study of a credit company that built an accounting system based on ERP. In this case, SAP's ERP is used. In the constructed system, data flows in the same direction from the business system to financial accounting and management accounting via a data warehouse (DWH) that stores the data of the smallest unit of transactions. The concept of processing information from a single database into the necessary information according to the purpose, rather than using separate databases, is followed by Beyer & Trawicki (1972). The ERP and the next-generation information systems will enable smooth adjustment of fixed costs and calculation of profits consistent with those of the financial management.

CONCLUSION

As information technology advances, accounting information systems are also undergoing significant changes. However, the question of what kind of information should be provided as accounting, and what kind of management philosophy should be used to design the necessary accounting system, should be separated from the simple issue of the progress of information technology. Of course, there is no denying that new information needs arise as a result of the progress of information technology, but we should not forget that the needs for accounting information arise first of all from the business management needs (including the need to explain responsibility to the outside world) of business managers. In this sense, Beyer's concept of profitability accounting has not yet faded as a design concept for an accounting system that is consistent with financial management.

REFERENCES

Beyer, R. (1963). *Profitability accounting for planning and control*. Ronald Press Company.

Beyer, R., & Trawicki, D. J. (1972). *Profitability accounting for planning and control* (2nd ed.). Ronald Press Company.

Ferrara, W. L. (1963). Relevant costing—Two points of view. *The Accounting Review*, *38*(4), 719–722. https://www.jstor.org/stable/242395

Harris, J. N. (1936). What did we earn last month? NACA Bulletin, 501–527.

Horngren, C. T., & Sorter, G. H. (1961). Direct costing for external reporting. *The Accounting Review*, *36*(January), 84–93. https://www.jstor.org/stable/243122

Paton, W. A., & Littleton, A. C. (1940). *An introduction to corporate accounting standards*. American Accounting Association.

Taipaleenmäki, J., & Ikäheimo, S. (2013). On the convergence of management accounting and financial accounting—The role of information technology in accounting change. *International Journal of Accounting Information Systems*, *14*(4), 321–348. doi:10.1016/j.accinf.2013.09.003

Vaassen, E. H. J., & Hunton, J. E. (2009). An eclectic approach to accounting information systems. *International Journal of Accounting Information Systems*, *10*(4), 173–176. doi:10.1016/j.accinf.2009.10.004

Chapter 2
A Holistic Picture of Non-Financial Reporting:
The Stakeholder View

Teodora Breaz
1 Decembrie 1918 University, Romania

Teodora Cucerzan
1 Decembrie 1918 University, Romania

Cristina Didea (Castrase)
1 Decembrie 1918 University, Romania

Ileana-Sorina Rakos
University of Petrosani, Romania

ABSTRACT

This chapter addresses the concept of non-financial reporting from a theoretical perspective. The main objective of this chapter was to present the literature on the key issue of non-financial reporting. The authors present various aspects of non-financial reporting, such as the creation of value through non-financial reporting, its advantages and disadvantages, the trend toward standardization and the adoption of an integrated report, and the interpretation of the information provided to stakeholders through NFR. All aspects presented and analyzed are based on existing expert studies and university studies. The chapter ends with the authors' conclusions on the importance of integrated reporting. This input from the authors opens up new opportunities to exploit the information content specific to non-financial reporting, which is particularly relevant to all stakeholders.

DOI: 10.4018/978-1-6684-4595-2.ch002

INTRODUCTION

Despite advancements in sustainability reporting, rating agencies, investors, and benchmarking agencies continue to bombard firms with questions. As a result, several parties such as researchers, corporations, and interest groups are aiming for the adoption of a single standardized report that includes financial, social, and environmental performance reporting. All of these parties agree that there is a disconnect between the sustainability information that stakeholders want and the sustainability information that organizations give. Transparency is the force. Globalization, quick communication, structured civil society, and now a trust issue has all altered the game's rules. Firms are beholden to complicated and evolving sets of norms, ranging from unyielding webs of "stakeholders" who make judgements on business behavior to new and old legislation that control and frequently complicate ordinary activity. Every action and blunder are scrutinized in this transparent world of rapid communications. And any corporation with a brand to defend is at risk. Customers may now assess the quality of goods and services on previously unimaginable scales. Employees provide previously classified information regarding business strategy, management, and issues. Businesses and their partners must share personal information with one another in order to work efficiently. Today, powerful investors possess or manage the majority of money, and they are gaining X-ray vision. Finally, in an age of rapid communication, whistleblowers, investigative media, and Googling, people, NGOs, and communities constantly scrutinize corporations.

We require a complete, networked, real-time system that, via integrated reporting, gives a single version of the truth to all parties involved, both within and outside. When viewed in this light, redefining reporting is not a chore; it is at the core of a company's and even our economy's performance and survival. The objectives of this chapter are: *(1) presentation of non-financial reporting (NFR) as a tool for value creation to company's stakeholders; (2) establishing an overview of non-financial reporting's perspective; (3) achieving the transition from sustainability to integrated reporting; (4) presentation of non-financial reporting's skepticism and flaws; (5) presentation of key stakeholder in non-financial reporting.*

BACKGROUND

NFR as a Tool for Value Creation to Company's Stakeholders

In today's globalized corporate environment, providing high-quality services or products to clients has become increasingly difficult and demanding. Furthermore, corporations are under pressure to act in socially responsible ways to serve the interests of their internal stakeholders (e.g., shareholders, clients, creditors, suppliers, and employees) and external stakeholders (e.g., public authorities, community, non-governmental organizations, the environment) in terms of social and environmental (Korschun et al., 2016) and quality concerns (Frolova & Lapina, 2015).

In comparison to conventional financial reporting, modern stakeholders want increasingly complex information and request supplemental disclosure. In addition to mandatory disclosure, corporations voluntarily provide additional data in the hope that this information will help the stock market better understand the driving constituents of company value. Voluntary disclosure is critical for closing the knowledge gap between businesses and their stakeholders (Lim et al., 2007; Hassanein & Hussainey, 2015). The inclusion of non-financial information in corporate reports considerably adds to information transparency and is thus a major problem in economies across the world (Maroun, 2017). A rising number of organizations are disclosing information on the impact of their activities on the environment, corporate governance, society, and human rights. This greater availability of non-financial information has raised awareness of the value of these reports in reflecting organizational behaviors (Sierra-Garcia et al., 2018). The sharing of non-financial reports is a strategic measure that significantly enhances organizations' engagement with their stakeholders (Miska et al., 2013).

Creating value for stakeholders is a wide notion that balances the interests of several stakeholder groups at the same time. Because the firm is seen as a part of the environment, this notion serves as the cornerstone of long-term business. Corporate performance, according to that idea, is considered as a function of the balance between economic, social, and environmental components of business activity. There is no question that businesses operate in an environment with various interrelationships and interactions. As a result, a corporation should not be considered merely as a tool of the ownership, but as an organizational unity having control over multiple groups that should work in tandem (Kochalsky, 2016). Therefore, a company's performance must be judged on the basis of its economic performance, environmental quality, and social justice (Svendsen et al., 2001).

Business models have changed radically in recent decades, and non-financial reporting is considered justified, at least to some extent (Alcaraz & Rodenas, 2013). One of the claims that justifies running a business focused on the interests of stakeholders is that value creation is done through a process that involves all stakeholders (Asher et al., 2005). Risk is taken not only by shareholders but also by other stakeholders. When a company goes bankrupt, it affects not only shareholders but also workers. In this case, there is no reason to exclude the interests of these workers from their business strategy. This view changed the social nature of the company and the basic understanding of the relationships between its components (Retolaza et al., 2015).

The level and scope of stakeholder involvement in reporting mechanisms by companies and other organizations has increased (Bellucci & Manetti, 2018), in the recent years, which is not a coincidence. Crowther (2013) traces the archeology of corporate reports and, over time, the amount of information provided to shareholders first, then potential investors (Gilmore & Willmott, 1992), and other stakeholders shows an increase during the 20th century. Companies have recognized the benefits of broader disclosure. Similarly, disclosure of non-financial information has increased rapidly over the last decade as companies recognize the commercial benefits of increased transparency (Aras & Crowther, 2009). Bini et al. (2019) shows that, the rise of the information-based economy has made non-financial indicators more important to both business owners and stakeholders. Some studies argue that incorporating non-financial indicators into an organization's performance measurement system contributes to the strategic direction of the organization and has a significant impact on the effectiveness of the organization (Bini & Bellucci, 2020). Moreover, non-financial indicators are needed to understand past performance and future potential and to make informed investment decisions. These shed light on important aspects of the company that cannot be represented financial indicators (Bini et al., 2019). Non-financial reporting allows organizations to assess how they contribute (or are expected to contribute) to improving (or deteriorating) economic, environmental and social conditions at the regional and global level (GRI, 2016).

For decades, the debate over who a company should aim for is: short-term financial profits or long-term non-financial goals. Both terms are used to refer to conflicting goals of a company, emphasized by the shareholder theory (Friedman, 1970) proposed by Friedman and the stakeholder theory (Freeman, 1984) proposed by Freeman. There is an important part of the academic literature that states that taking into account the interests of stakeholders is not always in conflict with efforts to maximize profits. Therefore, the instrumental stakeholder theory described by Donaldson & Preston (1995) states that companies that consider all stakeholders also perform better in "traditional performance perspectives" such as profitability. The exercise of ethical principles aimed at meeting the company's social activities and stakeholder needs is a tool used to achieve financial performance (Jones, 1995). This is especially true when considering the long-term value that shareholders get from the company.

According to Hillman & Keim (2001), building better relationships with key stakeholders is an intangible value that gives companies a source of competitive advantage. Helping to develop an asset can lead to increased shareholder wealth (Verheyden et al., 2016). A study performed by Zumente & Bistrova (2021) suggests that qualitative and non-financial factors make the most significant contributions to value creation (Zumente & Bistrova, 2021). Categories such as stakeholder involvement, employees, reputation, customer value, and transparency show well-developed key stakeholder relationships. Stakeholder involvement and various aspects of relationship management are key drivers of shareholder value. These findings need to be considered by companies looking at potential means of increasing long-term shareholder value.

Companies with healthier ESG performance can benefit from a better reputation and image, facilitate employee recruitment and retention, and increase customer loyalty. These non-financial factors serve as a source of competitive advantage over other companies, leading, in the long run, to higher profits and lower costs associated with employee turnover, thus increasing shareholder value. Other variables that contribute to improved ESG performance, at the enterprise level, such as: higher quality operational skills, higher quality management. These factors demonstrate the ability of a company to make strategic, informed decisions, efficiently allocate capital, and operate the company efficiently and in a productive and value-added way. Reputation, management, and operational performance factors that have been shown to be actively associated with ESG disclosure do not directly lead to a higher corporate reputation, but investors can increase the efficiency and confidence of corporate governance (Zumente & Bistrova, 2021).

Long-term value creation is impossible if the organization does not consider the interests of key stakeholders. ESG policies and activities that consistently demonstrate strategic accountability and transparency develop trust that stakeholders will be rewarded through increased engagement and satisfaction. Trust is positive and focuses on adjusting profits. Non-financial reporting helps organizations set future directions and engage key stakeholders by proactively communicating key value opportunities and potential risks (Table 1).

Overview of Non-Financial Reporting's Perspective

The latter half of the 20th century and the beginning of the 21st century can be said to be a period of great change in the field of corporate reporting. The most important trends of recent years are the emergence and global expansion of corporate non-financial reporting practices. Concurrently, as the size of annual reports grows, so does the amount of non-financial data, and new types of corporate reports have become popular: social reports, reports on sustainable development, and integrated reports. It may also be positioned as an alternative to "traditional" financial reporting. Since 2000, corporate non-financial reporting practices have become increasingly standardized. Until recently, standardization was only concerned with how to create and audit new types of reports. These standards, issued by non-governmental professional organizations, are strictly for advisory reasons. But the most recent move in this direction is the implementation of EU Directive 2014/95/EU in 2017. This requires large companies to provide information on social responsibility (EU Commission, 2014).

Table 1. Company's stakeholders and possibilities for value creation through NFR

Type of Stakeholder	Possibilities for Value Creation
Investors	- By integrating financial and non-financial risks, opportunities, and performance, NFR can provide more transparent and meaningful disclosure. - Obtaining a lower cost of capital by offering an expanded overview of projected future risks and planned mitigation strategies - Exemplifying how upcoming investment based on various integrated resources might lead to financial capital growth.
Employees	- Assessing the experience of employees and how culture supports strategic priorities. - Identifying and prioritizing workforce engagement that are tied to organizational performance. - Supporting strategic staff planning, which includes identifying important skills for the organization's future direction, measuring competences, and developing suitable learning solutions throughout the organization.
Suppliers and vendors	- Improving visibility of supply chain risks, along with the financial consequences of poor performance management in terms of ESG. - Possibility of developing more sustainable vendor partnerships - Opportunities for collaborative learning to enhance the delivery of value-added goods and services based on defined financial and ESG objectives.
Regulators	- Explicitly illustrating how legal obligations are satisfied (and maybe surpassed) by releasing a broader collection of non-financial data and information - Trying to quantify the growing importance of ESG investments, as well as their impacts on public domain - Enhancing public trust and fortifying the organization's operating license by more transparency related to financial and ESG performance, outputs and results.
Society	- Improving societal openness and trustworthiness through more significant and complex reporting on major financial and environmental, social, and governance concerns and effects. - Exemplifying organizational "multi-capitalism" by linking traditional financial performance indicators and capital utilization with ESG-based capitals and their implications on social stakeholders. - Demonstrating financial and ESG value creation and risk reduction actions in the short, medium, and long term.

Source: BDO (2018)

There are about 30 worldwide frameworks for reporting on sustainability (Brown et al., 2009b). The Position Paper of the European Federation of Accountants (FEE) (2016) recognizes that nine international frameworks and guidelines are appropriate for compliance with the Directive. These frameworks have been provided by GRI, IIRC, SASB, AA, UNGC, OECD, EFFAS, and ISO. FEE also promoted another conceptual framework, Core and More, to integrate NFI into corporate reporting (FEE, 2015).

The framework in Table 2 creates a "new institutional global infrastructure" for NFR, which creates pressure to adopt NFR (Waddock, 2008). There are two main reasons for the following frameworks: Some provide compliant disclosure frameworks and standards through NFR's detailed instrumental methods (GRI,

SASB, EFFAS, ISO 26000), while the others, using principles-based methods, provide more flexible frameworks and structures for reporting (IIRC, AA, OECD, FEE). Some frameworks are in line with the perspectives of various stakeholders (GRI, AA, ISO, FEE). Others are primarily focused on financial stakeholders (IIRC, SASB, EFFAS etc.). Differences tend to focus on the principle of materiality and affect the type of information that should be included in non-financial statements. Current reporting frameworks address different stakeholders and cover a variety of characteristics and ideas in quest of a competitive advantage. FEE (2016) clearly states that "for clarity and comparability, businesses should properly disclose the frameworks used and why they are used." However, it can be difficult to adopt a framework that competes in a consistent manner across countries, and comparability is far from realistic in such a highly competitive institutional environment. These frameworks are also expected to help businesses create equivalent sustainability accounts. In practice, guidelines and frameworks contribute more to the common language than comparable information (Brown et al., 2009a). Therefore, as long as there is a contradiction between the reporting frameworks, the world is far from achieving harmonized and comparable information (Table 2).

From Sustainability to Integrated Reporting

Many separate reporting strategies have emerged throughout history in response to the needs of the business environment, including financial, corporate social responsibility, and sustainability reporting. Stakeholders now want more information in the simplest way possible, but many organizations continue to produce self-standing and truly long reports to illustrate their financial and non-financial results. However, independent analysis of reports to understand and decide on a company's actual performance is insufficient. In addition, the aspect of the value creation of these reports is still in dispute. As a result, corporate reporting needs to take a step forward to say more with less, a process known as "integrated reporting" (IR), which brings together all the pieces of the puzzle (Sarioglu et al., 2019).

In 1993, the Institute of Directors of South Africa invited Mervyn King, a former judge of the Supreme Court of South Africa, to head a corporate governance committee. The Committee's first report (King I) was published in 1994, followed by a revised edition (King II) in 2002. A third edition (King III) was launched in 2009. The Johannesburg Stock Exchange started to require listed companies to comply with King III criteria in March 2010. The annual reports in South Africa are expected to illustrate a company's leadership, sustainability, and good corporate responsibility, and are called "integrated" reports. Integrated reporting is seen as a "key challenge for leadership" in King III, with sustainability becoming "mainstream" (Downes, 2015).

Table 2. Frameworks, goals, and topic of reporting

Frameworks	Goal	Topic
GRI (since 1997)	Assist organizations in communicating their impact on social and environmental issues and provide shareholders with a tool for analyzing and comparing firms' CSR performance	Sustainability
AA (since 1999)	Provides a set of principles to shape and organize how they comprehend, manage, administrate, execute, assess, and communicate responsibility, as well as a high-level principles-based assurance standard emphasizing the significance of materiality, completeness, and responsiveness.	Materiality; stakeholder engagement
OECD (Since 1999)	Assist companies in making a good contribution to a healthier environmental, social, and economic environment. It aims to influence investment decisions by introducing a fresh perspective - by redefining the effect of corporations on society.	Disclosure
UNGC (Since 2000)	Aims to connect company operations and plans with ten globally acknowledged, guiding, and overarching principles in the areas of human rights, the environment, employment and anti-corruption.	Disclosure of company policies and activities that are ethical and sustainable
EFFAS (Since 2010)	Offer a foundation for incorporating CSR data into business performance reporting	KPIs, Capital market
ISO26000 (Since 2010)	Promote the dependability and openness of enterprises' CSR communication and transparency, and provide a consistent and universal framework for CSR concepts and processes	Social responsibility
IIRC (Since 2010)	By incorporating financial and NFI, the goal is to clarify how value-relevant information fits into the processes of the business and therefore assist integrate long-term decision making into the management of the undertaking.	Integrated thinking, Business model, Capitals, Key value drivers
SASB (Since 2011)	Support and implement accounting standards addressing social and environmental concerns	Financial regulation, KPIs, Materiality
FEE Core and More (Since 2015)	Intends to organize information in accordance with its significance to users. The Core report would convey what is deemed significant for a wide variety of stakeholders. Supplementary material, or information aimed at specific stakeholder groups, would be placed in the More reports.	Multi-stakeholder, Materiality, Relevance, Comparability Interactivity

Source: (FEE, 2016; La Torre et al., 2018)

King is the director of GRI, which advocates for the adoption of integrated reporting throughout the world. The Prince of Wales hosted a gathering of investors, corporations, accounting organisations, and UN representatives, including GRI experts, in 2009 to launch the International Integrated Reporting Committee (IIRC). The IIRC was renamed in 2012. portrays itself as a worldwide alliance of regulators, shareholders, corporations and NGOs leading the way in driving corporate entities throughout the world toward broader reporting on their operations. It is chaired by Mervyn King. PricewaterhouseCoopers developed a "value reporting" framework, in 1999, that highlighted information that was similar to all industries and businesses: market overview, strategy, value management and performance. It established an integrated sample reporting scheme including dozens of organizations from across the world in 2011. The paper is used to "speed up" the global adoption of integrated reporting.

Integrated reporting is a new standard for corporate communication that helps produce financial and other company reports. It is a process that results in concise communication on how an organization's strategy, governance, performance, and prospects contribute to the creation of value in the short, medium, and long term (IIRC, 2011). Instead of having a separate sustainability report, integrated reporting calls for merging the financial and sustainability reports into a single report. The idea of an integrated report is that by merging financial and non-financial reporting, companies will have a better chance of integrating sustainability into the whole business (Eccles & Krzus, 2010). The purpose of integrated reporting is to make the links between an organization's strategy, governance, and financial performance clearer, as well as the social, environmental, and economic context in which it operates (IIRC, 2011). Indeed, one of the distinctive features of integrated reporting is its objective to generate a concise report presenting the most important actions, outcomes, risks, and social, environmental, and economic opportunities of an organization in a way that reflects the interconnected nature of these factors (De Villiers et al., 2014).

Since its establishment in 2010, the International Integrated Reporting Council (IIRC) has gained much interest (Busco et al., 2014; Eccles & Krzus, 2010). IIRC is a global alliance of regulators, investors, businesses, standardization entities, the accountancy profession, and non-governmental organizations. This group agrees that the next step in the development of corporate reporting should include communication on value generation (IIRC, 2013b). IIRC recommends that companies provide a single report that includes both financial and non-financial data (Busco et al., 2014; de Villiers et al., 2014; Eccles & Serafeim, 2014). The aim of the IIRC is to move from a situation where financial and non-financial data are accounted for separately to a situation where integrated thinking is incorporated into the main management and accounting procedures, allowing integrated reporting to become the industry standard (de Villiers et al., 2014; IIRC 2013a, b).

An integrated report is defined as "a concise communication on how an organization's strategy, governance, performance, and prospects, in its external environment, deliver value in the short, medium, and long term" (IIRC, 2013b). The major aim of integrated reporting, according to the IIRC, is to present a bigger and more connected picture of organizational performance than traditional and/or sustainability-specific financial reporting (de Villiers et al., 2014). The purpose of an integrated report, in accordance with the principles of IIRC (2013b), is to provide a perspective on the resources and relationships of an organization, which are collectively referred to as "capital".

Non-Financial Reporting's Skepticism and Flaws

Companies are taking a significant step forward in non-financial reporting, but they face many challenges in designing, evolving, and sustaining reporting tools (Baret & Helfrich, 2016). Experienced companies are already facing problems with non-financial reporting tools. Therefore, it is clear that proper use of this tool is not easy for most businesses.

CSR-related issues and institutions form a complex social cognitive system. This is where the first difficulty emerges, as it is difficult for reporting tools to convey the nuances of such complex systems. This tool aims to codify components of this system with data and information and ensure that it is communicated to the participants of this system. This contributes to the principle of accountability and transparency to stakeholders according to logic that reduces information asymmetry.

Extensive literature arising from the information asymmetry problem and from the principal-agent problem was originally emphasized using convention theory (Lewis, 1969). The first one allows us to explain the situation in which the report is about to change. The second makes it possible to explain the circumstances under which this is standardized and legitimated. For non-financial reporting, the simplification to a purely quantitative approach is no longer possible because of the need to integrate qualitative factors (Baret & Helfrich, 2016). There are two sources for this: items that cannot be quantified and things that are too complicated to quantify. A qualitative part of the information is needed to ensure that non-financial reporting is not irreparably reduced to "technical concepts". In that case, non-financial reporting loses most of its meaning to its recipients (Baret & Helfrich, 2016).

Therefore, a company's NFR technique must always be readjusted. New applications, new constraints, and new measurement methods need to be integrated. This aspect directly contributes to the obligations associated with complexity. Another challenge a company may face is the expectations of its own management. Here we need to integrate three types of goals that can be inconsistent. The first one, NFR tools, must participate in CSR learning by all employees. The second one is that the tool must harmonize organizational details with legislators' expectations, both in its design and application. And the final one, reporting tools, addresses the dilemma between the need to stabilize indicators (to enable comparability) and the organizational routine of non-financial reporting.

A paradigm shift in our perception is reflected in the economy and business. Green economy and business are fresh viewpoints on the way to sustainable business that impose new requirements on corporations. "Green" is a style of conducting business and living, that respects and preserves environmental balance. Green and recycled products as well as the green process are examples of green initiatives that respond to rising customer interest. These initiatives definitely matter to eco-consumers, and industry statistics indicate that this segment is rapidly growing. A green economy is a low-carbon, resource-efficient, inclusive and sustainable approach to reducing environmental hazards and scarcity.

A growing number of organizations that choose to release non-financial reports allows research in this area. Because there are several standards and criteria for this kind of reporting, and organizations are allowed to set their own reporting standards, it is sometimes difficult to gather and process information and data, and furthermore, to compare different reports. There is a definite need to increase the comparability of the metrics provided in NFR, especially among businesses in the same industry (Roca & Searcy, 2012).

The next issue pertains to the type of data and information released, the way the data is acquired and processed, and the manner in which the data is provided in quantitative and qualitative form. IT support is essential in this process since gathering data for NFR is generally done manually, making document preparation more difficult and time-consuming. The NFR process is a challenge for every organization to rethink and reorganize business operations and report on their progress in this area (Bedenik & Barišić, 2019). The quantity of information is also a challenge: "the more information there is in a report about individual, social, environmental, and economic impacts, policies, and practices, the greater the likelihood of information overload for readers" (de Villiers et al., 2014).

Key Stakeholder in Non-Financial Reporting

Shareholders

Non-financial reports address the fewest issues directly connected to shareholders. The cause of this is the fragmentation of reporting. Characterization of a company's interaction with its own financial community is typically found in other materials devoted only to corporate governance problems. This fragmentation highlights the overall reporting standards' most serious flaw: the absence of a connection between non-financial themes and financial results in the reports. Companies are regarded as failing to communicate the consequences of the sustainability strategy for their economic prospects and to persuade shareholders of their ability to incorporate social and environmental concerns into daily operations (AccountAbility, 2003). In other words, managers should consider for future development of reporting practices, the opportunity to demonstrate the extent to which voluntary social and environmental activities are directly related to - not in contrast to - profit maximization and economic value creation.

Managers should evaluate the possibility of demonstrating the degree to which voluntary social and environmental actions are directly tied to - rather than in opposition to - profit maximization and economic value creation for future reporting procedures. Lai *et al.* (2018) discover, via interviews with integrated reporting preparers, that integrated reporting, in particular, allows reaching out to a larger audience through clearer communication. Despite the fact that shareholders are the primary users of the reports, integrated reporting helps enterprises be accountable to other stakeholders as well, which strengthens the conversation between the two sides. As a result, data on the implications of integrated reporting shows that there are advantages across ESG dimensions. Non-financial reporting reaches a wider audience than financial reporting. Non-financial information is increasingly important to investors and other shareholders who use financial reports for financial analysis (Dong, 2017; Kramer, 2020).

Prior research implies that when there is greater information asymmetry, corporations make more non-financial disclosures, which is especially true when there are more shareholders. In such cases, sustainability reporting may lower investors' expenses for information collection and analysis while also fostering cross-firm comparability, especially if investors' preferences are focused on certain CSR subjects.

CSR investments and the capacity to manage stakeholders have a direct influence on lenders' and potential investors' views of corporate risk. This can improve a company's access to market funding (Perrini et al., 2006). As a result, transparency can play a critical part in the process. The company's capacity to handle diverse stakeholder relationships reduces risk. Shareholders might utilize CSR efforts as a "sign of a firm's successful efforts at pleasing stakeholder groups" with the visibility acquired via transparency (Orlitzky & Benjamin, 2001).

Another potential is to provide more in-depth investor relations reporting to demonstrate a commitment to frequent engagement with shareholders. All of these actions, when presented in a methodical and cohesive "container," such as a non-financial report, can help to develop a new corporate image as a transparent and open organization based on reciprocal listening and broad participation (Hooghiemstra, 2000).

There is also a lack of information on shareholder and partner compensation, ratings, and stock price fluctuations. These topics should be covered more extensively in non-financial reports since they are critical for stakeholders attempting to fully comprehend a company's health status and potential to produce and distribute value and wealth (Perrini et al., 2006). Incorporating this information, particularly in the context of multi-year patterns, may provide additional opportunities to illustrate the link between CSR and financial success.

Europe is now ahead of the United States, where the issue of mandated sustainability reporting has just lately acquired traction. The existing voluntary framework is insufficient to satisfy the increasing information demand of investors on ESG, and a mandated structure is required (Hassan et. al, 2021). This may cause the topic of sustainability reporting to move more strongly (again) to shareholder orientation. As previously stated, the concept of giving ESG information stems from the need to supplement economic and financial information, the latter of which is obviously aimed solely at investors.

The double materiality criteria are required to guarantee that sustainability reporting is directed at a broader range of stakeholders and that social, environmental, and governance effects, as well as financial implications, are revealed. Only with such an all-inclusive strategy will a company's goods, services, and larger value chain be amenable to genuine change (Adams & Abhayawansa, 2021). This, in turn, may benefit shareholders, who increasingly seek non-financial information and favor investments with a good environmental effect. As a result, a broader materiality notion that is not limited to financial materiality alone may be required to meet the expectations of investors.

Employees

The notion of sustainability has permeated all management activities, including strategic management, organizational behavior, supply chains, and human resources (HR), and has piqued the interest of practitioners and academics alike (Randev & Jha, 2019). The HR function is crucial to the success of adopting sustainability inside firms. Sustainable management of personnel, which are critical organizational assets, makes use of HR resources and aids in the integration of sustainability strategies into enterprises (Cohen et al., 2012). HR management's purpose is to offer motivated, qualified, and loyal personnel and also to introduce sustainability into a company's operations. Among the topics that should be addressed by such information sharing is reporting on employee engagement and opportunities for workers.

HR discloses information like: employee recruitment; employee-management relationships; employee health and safety; employee training and education; inclusion and equal opportunities; Pay equity for women; Supplier evaluation in regards to work practices; Mechanisms for filing complaints about workplace processes (GRI, 2021).

Regarding worker matters, EU Directive 2014/95/EU proposes that the information given in the statement may concern actions made to ensure gender balance, implementation of fundamental norms, workplace conditions, and respect for workers' right to be consulted. In the context of employees, the UNCG framework establishes principles of human rights and working conditions. According to the OECD framework, in the context of employees, a firm should support human capital development by offering education and training opportunities, increasing awareness of the necessity of protecting workers and their rights, and refraining from all types of discrimination. The ISO 26000 HR component concentrates on corporate governance, labor relations, and human rights. Human rights are classified as follows: due diligence; circumstances in which human rights are threatened; avoidance of involvement; complaint processing; discrimination and disadvantaged groups; legal rights; and basic legal principles at work (Moratis & Cochius, 2011).

The number of corporations that report on workforce activities is increasing. Progress is obvious, and it can be stated that following the implementation of the Directive on nonfinancial reporting, the quantity of reported information about employment problems rose, particularly in the area of HRM practices.

Customers

Organizations know that revealing upgrades customers' impressions of corporate obligation and worry about their choices. It is significant for organizations to give trustworthy evidence that they mean to maintain all the objectives proclaimed. Portrayals of special approaches give additional evidence of an organization's capacity to tune in and to address key partner concerns.

Particularly with respect to client relations, non-monetary reports go about as "holders" in which to arrange and focus on every strong action. Managers should concentrate on covering market development patterns and how they can draw in new clients without revealing sensitive data that is being used to direct the advancement of new items and administrations. Investigates advancements can assist clients and partners with better understanding and surveying an organization's "tuning in and redoing" inclination. A few experimental examinations on shopper responses propose that "purchasers might shape surmising about missing item credits by drawing associations between an accessible snippet of data (e.g., organization notoriety for advancement and assembling capacity) and the missing trait (e.g., item refinement, innovativeness)." For instance, by liking the scope of new market drives advanced by organizations, new clients could be drawn in by organization dynamism, its restoration limit, and, surprisingly, its capacity to reevaluate itself to meet new market patterns.

Suppliers

In a global economy where corporations are rapidly relocating a portion of their manufacturing to low-cost suppliers, the accountability agenda and its associated reporting activities cannot conceivably reach the full supply chain. Reporting on the supply chain often takes a collaborative approach between a firm and its suppliers on topics such as human rights, overall workplace conditions, and environmental concerns. Companies frequently allude to particular management tools when defining supply-chain management in an attempt to provide proof of such collaborations, hence increasing trust. They hope to demonstrate to stakeholders the extent to which CSR in supply chain management has been integrated and has become a norm in this manner. Companies also prefer to share details regarding remedial steps taken to remove suppliers who do not comply with the company's CSR policy.

Non-financial reporting has the potential to pay much more attention to supplier relationships. They might, in particular, give more quantitative purchase data. Corporations, in fact, should wish to make it apparent that they have no unfair supplier rules. This would increase stakeholders' understanding of the importance they place on fair play. Again, a multi-year perspective might aid in the review process. It would illustrate the progress of both the corporation's supplier relationship and the supply chain's growing geographical dispersion.

Government

It is worth noting how data pertaining to compliance testing and inspections is now useful for a firm that wishes to declare its CSR interaction with government. The purpose is to draw attention to the lack of outstanding investigations or fines, as well as to confirm the conformity of proclaimed behavior with implemented behavior. Companies appear to be aware of the presence of a positive relationship among balanced disclosure of positive and negative information and the possibility of future regulatory costs The expense of adjusting operational practices and management systems to progressively rigorous safety, health, and environmental laws is one example. In this manner, non-financial report disclosures on present regulatory compliance minimize market reaction to subsequent leaks, perhaps lowering future regulatory costs.

Companies should pay greater attention to giving accurate information on duties and taxes on the one hand, and data regarding contributions, perks, and short-term financing obtained by the firm on the other, in order to enhance their report in this area. In reality, businesses may quantify their contribution to local development by stressing how much of their income they share with authorities, such as through fees and taxes. Adopting a multi-year perspective might supplement this reporting by outlining projects or initiatives undertaken in collaboration with local governments. These individuals display a proactive approach to community betterment.

Community and Environment Protection

According to studies, higher disclosures, and the use of non-financial KPIs are not motivated by shareholder demand. Rather, ecologists' pressure has been proven to enhance the quality of environment KPI disclosures (Zarzycka & Krasodomska, 2021). Furthermore, the usage of a company's social performance metrics looks to be increasing for economic purposes and with senior management's commitment (Lisi, 2018).

The fourth major CSR objective that clearly emerges from the examination of the content of non-financial reports is a company's socially responsible interaction with the community, notably in terms of active stakeholder involvement and corruption prevention. As stakeholders grow increasingly engaged and capable of contributing more to the formulation and assessment of corporate policy, their demands must be prioritized. One of the most essential is the prevention of corruption. A socially responsible firm is one that takes all necessary precautions to avoid unethical activity, beginning with strong, voluntary, self-regulatory standards and in-house norms. To that purpose, more emphasis may be placed in reports on a company's connection with the media. Media coverage of CSR-conscious businesses may educate stakeholders and a larger audience with new knowledge on the human factor of production and business methods. All of this, in turn, contributes to increased public knowledge of CSR-related issues, lowers information asymmetry, and significantly increases demand for CSR in all of its aspects.

Environmental protection is inextricably linked to community-based responsibilities. Companies are well aware that environmental conservation and respect are among their most essential duties. They are increasingly releasing a slew of management system to assess the environmental features of their operations and integrate them into day-to-day operations.

Environmental policy is frequently viewed on a global scale, influencing all firm operations and applied to all geographical circumstances in which they are engaged. Because of its extensive breadth, reporting on the company's interaction with the environment is one of the most difficult, in terms of both the resources required to gather and analyze data and comparability throughout the company's business divisions and geographically distributed departments. The lack of standard references expands the number of reporting techniques and measurement units as each organization provides its performance indicators, concentrating on its own interpretation of what "environmental impact" implies. As a result, it is becoming increasingly difficult for interested stakeholders to voice an impartial judgement on what firms have done in their efforts to respect and protect the environment.

SOLUTIONS AND RECOMMENDATIONS

In view of the problem addressed during this chapter, we propose the following solutions and recommendations:

- Investors place a high value on corporate reporting. Long-term investors are already well-known for looking beyond the financial numbers. Integrated reporting is a required next phase in reporting quality, as environmental, social, and governance data is already crucial for evaluating a company's performance and prospects.
- Companies cannot function without the support of the stakeholder community in which they operate.
- Integrated reporting may or may not lead to the refinement of an organization's strategy. Stakeholder responsiveness, however, should be mirrored in a company's business model, and this can often necessitate a strategy review.
- The core of integrated reporting is integrated management information that is consistent with an organization's long-term goal.

FUTURE RESEARCH DIRECTIONS AND LIMITATIONS

The topics studied in this article are of future interest for both the academic environment and the business environment. The information presented addresses the specialized literature in the field of non-financial reporting and its importance for stakeholders, as well as the importance of standardizing this type of reporting and migration to integrated reporting. There is a steady increase in interest in investigating this topic, yet accounting researchers have long been accused of making little contribution to practice. We suggest the following future research directions to all those interested in the topic of non-financial reporting:

- an analysis of value-creation through NFR, to see if companies generate money through non-financial reporting or whether they have greater costs and just report to comply with it (Maniora, 2017).
- a collaboration between academics and practitioners in the targeted field is necessary to discover the benefits and drawbacks of the NFR and so better assess its repercussions.
- an analysis of the reasons why entities report in accordance with a specific regulatory framework (Constantin et al., 2019; Constantin et al., 2020).

Several major topics for future study are mentioned, which address constraints inherent in the research reported in this chapter.

CONCLUSION

Companies have recognized the benefits of broader disclosure. Similarly, disclosure of non-financial information has increased rapidly over the last decade as companies recognize the commercial benefits of increased transparency. Studies show that, the rise of the information-based economy has made non-financial indicators more important to both business owners and stakeholders. Many separate non-financial reporting strategies have emerged throughout history in response to the needs of the business environment. Stakeholders now want more information in the simplest way possible, but many organizations continue to produce self-standing and truly long reports to illustrate their financial and non-financial results. However, independent analysis of reports to understand and decide on a company's actual performance is insufficient. In addition, the aspect of the value creation of these reports is still in dispute. As a result, corporate reporting needs to take a step forward to say more with less, a process known as "integrated reporting" (IR), which brings together all the pieces of the puzzle.

There are many benefits associated with integrated reporting – both within an organization and from an external perspective: Encouraging the organization to think in an integrated way, better articulation of strategy and business model, a single report that is easy to access, clear and concise, Creating value for stakeholders by identifying and measuring non-financial factors, more direct correlation of non-financial performance with the company, better identification of risks and opportunities, improved internal processes leading to a better understanding of the business and improved decision making (Deloitte, 2015).

The Integrated report serves as a tool for communicating with stakeholders on the progress and challenges facing companies in becoming more sustainable (Armbester et al., 2011). It paves the way for -internal benefits; benefits may include better resource allocation decisions, greater shareholder engagement and other stakeholders (Eccles & Krzus, 2010). It also benefits the external market, meeting investors' needs and ensuring that data providers report accurate non-financial information about the company. It manages risk, consisting in preparing a likely global wave of Regulation, responding to stock market demands; and prepared to cope with changes and developments in frameworks and standards (Eccles & Armbrester, 2011).

There is no doubt that integrated reporting is an important tool for business organization (Churet & Eccles, 2014; Havlová, 2015; Wadee, 2011). This tool integrates the characteristics of all types of reporting within it (Morros, 2016). Therefore, the IR is not just a business reporting, it is beyond reporting (Steyn, 2014). The benefits of IR adoption are so obvious that corporations can provide all the reports and benefit from it through internal business improvement (Busco et al., 2014; Steyn, 2014; Zhou et al., 2017). Integrated reporting is the most effective way to communicate with stakeholders, which will demonstrate the overall picture of a business as regards future objectives and the links between financial performance and reporting on corporate social and environmental responsibilities. IR also helps improve the business model and strategy by combining them with integrated thinking and decision-making support.

REFERENCES

AccountAbility. (2003). *Impacts of Reporting: The Role of Social and Sustainability Reporting in Organisational Transformation*. Retrieved February 10, 2022 from http://accountability.com

Adams, C. A., & Abhayawansa, S. (2021). Connecting the COVID-19 pandemic, environmental, social and governance (ESG) investing and calls for 'harmonization' of sustainability reporting. *Critical Perspectives on Accounting*.

Alcaraz, A. S., & Rodenas, S. P. (2013). The Spanish Banks in face of the Corporate Social Responsibility Standards: Previous analysis of the financial crisis. *Review of Business Management*, *15*(49), 562–581.

Aras, G., & Crowther, D. (2009). Corporate Sustainability Reporting: A Study in Disingenuity? *Journal of Business Ethics*, *87*(S1), 279–288. doi:10.100710551-008-9806-0

Armbester, K., Clay, T., & Roberts, L. (2011). Integrated Reporting: An Irreversible Tipping Point. Accountancy SA, 29-31.

Asher, C. C., Mahoney, J. M., & Mahoney, J. T. (2005). Towards a property rights foundation for a stakeholder theory of the firm. *The Journal of Management and Governance*, *9*(1), 5–32. doi:10.100710997-005-1570-2

Baret, P., & Helfrich, V. (2016). Cas 10. Rémy Cointreau. 10 cas de RSE, 219-232. doi:10.3917/dunod.baret.2016.01.0219

BDO. (2018). *Driving value creation through integrated thinking and reporting*. Retrieved February 10, 2022 from https://www.bdo.global/ getattachment/Insights/Audit-Assurance/BDO-integrated-thinking-and-reporting-journey-guid/IRSTF-IR-journey-guide-FINAL.pdf.aspx?lang=en-GB&ext=.pdf

Bedenik, N., & Barišić, P. (2019). Nonfinancial Reporting: Theoretical and Empirical Evidence. In M. Sarfraz, M. I. Adbullah, A. Rauf, & M. S. G. Shah (Eds.), *Business. Sustainable Management Practices*. IntechOpen. doi:10.5772/intechopen.87159

Bellucci, M., & Manetti, G. (2018). *Stakeholder Engagement and Sustainability Reporting*. Routledge. doi:10.4324/9781351243957

Bini, L., & Bellucci, M. (2020). *Integrated Sustainability Reporting: Linking Environmental and Social Information to Value Creation Processes*. Springer. doi:10.1007/978-3-030-24954-0

Bini, L., Dainelli, F., Giunta, F., & Simoni, L. (2019). Are non-financial KPIs in annual reports really "key"? An investigation of company disclosure and analyst reports in the UK. In *Business Integrated Sustainability Reporting*. ICAS.

Brown, H. S., De Jong, M., & Lessidrenska, T. (2009a). The rise of the Global Reporting Initiative: A case of institutional entrepreneurship. *Environmental Politics*, *18*(2), 182–200. doi:10.1080/09644010802682551

Brown, H. S., De Jong, M., & Levy, D. L. (2009b). Building institutions based on information disclosure: Lessons from GRI's sustainability reporting. *Journal of Cleaner Production*, *17*(6), 571–580. doi:10.1016/j.jclepro.2008.12.009

Busco, C., Frigo, M., Quattrone, P., & Riccaboni, A. (2014). Leading practices in Integrated Reporting. *Strategic Finance*, *9*, 23–32.

Churet, C., & Eccles, R. (2014). Integrated Reporting, Quality of Management, and Financial Performance. *Journal of Applied Corporate Finance*, *26*(1), 56–64.

Cohen, J., Holder-Webb, L., Kanellakou, L., & Wood, D. (2012). Corporate Reporting of Non-Financial Leading Indicators of Economic Performance and Sustainability. *Accounting Horizons*, *26*(1), 65–90. doi:10.2308/acch-50073

Crowther, D. (2013). *A Social Critique of Corporate Reporting; Semiotics and web-based integrated reporting*. Routledge.

de Villiers, C., Rinaldi, L., & Unerman, J. (2014). Integrated Reporting: Insights, gaps and an agenda for future research. *Accounting, Auditing & Accountability Journal*, *27*(7), 1042–1067. doi:10.1108/AAAJ-06-2014-1736

Deloitte. (2015). *Integrated Reporting as a driver for Integrated Thinking?* Retrieved February 8, 2022 from https://www2.deloitte.com/content/dam/Deloitte/nl/Documents/risk/deloitte-nl-risk-integrated-reporting-a-driver-for-integratedthinking.pdf

Donaldson, T., & Preston, L. E. (1995). The stakeholder theory of the corporation: Concepts, evidences, and implications. *Academy of Management Review*, *20*(1), 65–91. doi:10.2307/258887

Dong, L. (2017). Understanding investors' reliance on disclosures of nonfinancial information and mitigating mechanisms for underreliance. *Accounting and Business Research*, *47*(4), 431–454. doi:10.1080/00014788.2016.1277969

Downes, S. (2015). *Special GAAP Report 'Integrated Reporting*. GAAP Consulting.

Eccles, R. G., & Armbrester, K. (2011). Two Disruptive Ideas Combined: Integrated Reporting in the Cloud. *IESE Insight*, *8*, 13–20. doi:10.15581/002.ART-1890

Eccles, R. G., & Krzus, M. P. (2010). *One Report: Integrated Reporting for a Sustainable Strategy*. John Wiley & Sons.

EU Commission. (2014). *Directive 2014/95/EU of the European Parliament and the Council of 22 October 2014 Amending Directive 2013/34/EU as Regards Disclosure of Non-Financial and Diversity Information by Certain Large Undertakings and Groups*. Brussels: EU Commission.

FEE. (2015). *The Future of Corporate Reporting – creating the dynamics for change*. FEE.

FEE. (2016). *EU Directive on disclosure of nonfinancial and diversity information: Achieving good quality and consistent reporting*. FEE.

Freeman, R. E. (1984). *Strategic management: A stakeholder approach*. Pitman.

Friedman, M. (1970). The Social Responsibility of Business Is to Increase Its Profits. *New York Times Magazine*, 122-126.

Frolova, I., & Lapiņa, I. (2015). Integration of CSR principles in quality management. *International Journal of Quality and Service Sciences*, *7*(2/3), 260–273. doi:10.1108/IJQSS-03-2015-0033

Gilmore, C., & Willmott, H. (1992). Company Law and Financial Reporting: A Sociological History of the UK Experience. In M. Bromwich & A. G. Hopwood (Eds.), *Accounting and the Law* (pp. 159–190). Prentice-Hall/ICAEW.

Global Reporting Initiative (GRI) (2016). *Consolidated set of GRI sustainability reporting standards 2016: Global Reporting Initiative*. Academic Press.

GRI. (2021). Retrieved February 6, 2022 from https://www.globalreporting.org/standards/download-the-standards/

Hassan, A., Elamer, A. A., Lodh, S., Roberts, L., & Nandy, M. (2021). The future of non-financial businesses reporting: Learning from the Covid-19 pandemic. *Corporate Social Responsibility and Environmental Management*, *28*(4), 1231–1240. doi:10.1002/csr.2145 PMID:34220362

Hassanein, A., & Hussainey, K. (2015). Is Forward-Looking Financial Disclosure Really Informative? Evidence from UK Narrative Statements. *International Review of Financial Analysis*, *41*, 52–61. doi:10.1016/j.irfa.2015.05.025

Havlová, K. (2015). What Integrated Reporting Changed: The Case Study of Early Adopters. *Procedia Economics and Finance*, *34*, 231–237. doi:10.1016/S2212-5671(15)01624-X

Hillman, A. J., & Keim, G. D. (2001). Shareholder Value, Stakeholder Management, and Social Issues: What's the Bottom Line? *Strategic Management Journal*, *22*(2), 125–139. doi:10.1002/1097-0266(200101)22:2<125::AID-SMJ150>3.0.CO;2-H

Hooghiemstra, R. (2000). Corporate Communication and Impression Management – New Perspectives Why Companies Engage in Corporate Social Reporting. *Journal of Business Ethics*, *27*(1), 55–68. doi:10.1023/A:1006400707757

International Integrated Reporting Council (IIRC). (2011). *The International <IR> Framework*. Retrieved February 7, 2022 from http//:www.iirc.org

International Integrated Reporting Council (IIRC). (2013a). *Consultation draft of the international <IR> framework*. IIRC.

International Integrated Reporting Council (IIRC). (2013b). *Integrated reporting*. The IIRC.

International Integrated Reporting Council (IIRC). (2021). *The International <IR> Framework*. Available at: https://www.integratedreporting.org/resource/international-ir-framework/

Jones, T. M. (1995). Instrumental Stakeholder Theory: A Synthesis of Ethics and Economics. *Academy of Management Review*, *20*(2), 404–437. doi:10.5465/amr.1995.9507312924

Kochalski, C. (2016). *Green Controlling and Finance. Theoretical Framework*. Helion SA Publishing Group.

Korschun, D., Bhattacharya, C. B., & Swain, S. (2016). CSR and the Frontline Context: How Social Programs Improve Customer Service. *NIM Marketing Intelligence Review*, *8*(1), 24–29. doi:10.1515/gfkmir-2016-0004

Kramer, M. (2020). *Larry Fink Isn't Going to Read Your Sustainability Report*. Harvard Business Practices. Retrieved February 5, 2022 from https://hbr.org/2020/01/larry-fink-isnt-going-to-read-your-sustainability-report

La Torre, M., Sabelfeld, S., Blomkvist, M., Tarquinio, L., & Dumay, J. (2018). Harmonising non-ðnancial reporting regulation in Europe: Practical forces and projections for future research. *Meditari Accountancy Research*, *26*(4), 598–621. doi:10.1108/MEDAR-02-2018-0290

Lai, A., Melloni, G., & Stacchezzini, R. (2018). Integrated reporting and narrative accountability: The role of preparers. *Accounting, Auditing & Accountability Journal*, *31*(5), 1381–1405. doi:10.1108/AAAJ-08-2016-2674

Lewis, D. K. (1969). *Convention a philosophical study*. Harvard University Press.

Lim, S., Matolcsy, Z., & Chow, D. (2007). The association between board composition and different types of voluntary disclosure. *European Accounting Review*, *16*(3), 555–583. doi:10.1080/09638180701507155

Lisi, I. E. (2018). Determinants and Performance Effects of Social Performance Measurement Systems. *Journal of Business Ethics*, *152*(1), 225–251. doi:10.100710551-016-3287-3

Maroun, W. (2017). Assuring the integrated report: Insights and recommendations from auditors and preparers. *The British Accounting Review*, *49*(3), 329–346. doi:10.1016/j.bar.2017.03.003

Miska, C., Stahl, G., & Mendenhall, M. (2013). Intercultural competencies as antecedents of responsible global leadership. *European Journal of International Management*, *7*(5), 550–569. doi:10.1504/EJIM.2013.056477

Moratis, L., & Cochius, T. (2011). *ISO26000: the business guide to the new standard on social responsibility*. Greenleaf.

Morrós Ribera, J. (2016). The integrated reporting: A presentation of the current state of art and aspects of integrated reporting that need further development. *Intangible Capital*, *12*(1), 336–356.

Orlitzky, M., & Benjamin, J. (2001). Corporate Social Performance and Firm Risk: A Meta-Analytic Review. *Business & Society*, *40*(4), 369–396. doi:10.1177/000765030104000402

Perrini, F., Pogutz, S., & Tencati, A. (2006). *Developing Corporate Social Responsibility: A European Perspective*. Edward Elgar.

Randev, K., & Jha, J. (2019). Sustainable Human Resource Management: A Literature-based Introduction. *NHRD Network Journal*, *12*(3), 1–13. doi:10.1177/2631454119873495

Retolaza, J., Ruíz-Roqueñi, M., & San-Jose, L. (2015). An Innovative Approach to Stakeholder Theory: Application in spanish transnational corporations. *Review of Business Management, 17*(55), 1007–1020. doi:10.7819/rbgn.v17i55.2056

Roca, L. C., & Searcy, C. (2012). An analysis of indicators disclosed in corporate sustainability reports. *Journal of Cleaner Production, 20*(1), 103–118. doi:10.1016/j.jclepro.2011.08.002

Sarioglu, M., Dalkilic, A. F., & Durak, M. G. (2019). The Future of Corporate Reporting: Integrated Reporting. *International Journal of Contemporary Economics and Administrative Sciences, 9*(2), 327–347.

Sierra-Garcia, L., Garcia-Benau, M. A., & Bollas-Araya, H. M. (2018). Empirical Analysis of Non-Financial Reporting by Spanish Companies. *Administrative Sciences, 8*(3), 29. doi:10.3390/admsci8030029

Steyn, M. (2014). Organisational benefits and implementation challenges of mandatory integrated reporting. *Sustainability Accounting. Management and Policy Journal, 5*(4), 476–503.

Svendsen, A., Boutilier, R., Abbott, R. M., & Wheeler, D. (2001). *Measuring the business value of stakeholder relationships (part one)*. The Center for Innovation in Management (CIN).

Verheyden, T., Eccles, R., & Feiner, A. (2016). ESG for All? The Impact of ESG Screening on Return, Risk, and Diversification. *Journal of Applied Corporate Finance, 28*(2), 47–55.

Villiers, C., Rinaldi, L., & Unerman, J. (2014). Integrated Reporting: Insights, gaps and an agenda for future research. *Accounting, Auditing & Accountability Journal, 27*(7), 1042–1067. doi:10.1108/AAAJ-06-2014-1736

Wadee, N. (2011). Integrated reporting: An opportunity to reshape business. *Accountancy SA*, (December), 6–8.

Zarzycka, E., & Krasodomska, J. (2021). Non-financial key performance indicators: What determines the differences in the quality and quantity of the disclosures? *Journal of Applied Accounting Research, 23*(1), 139–162. doi:10.1108/JAAR-02-2021-0036

Zhou, S., Simnett, R., & Green, W. (2017). Does Integrated Reporting Matter to the Capital Market? *Abacus, 53*(1), 94–132. doi:10.1111/abac.12104

Zumente, I., & Bistrova, J. (2021). ESG Importance for Long-Term Shareholder Value Creation: Literature vs. Practice. *Journal of Open Innovation, 7*(2), 127. doi:10.3390/joitmc7020127

ADDITIONAL READING

Borin, N., Lindsey-Mullikin, J., & Krishnan, R. (2013). An analysis of consumer reactions to green strategies. *Journal of Product and Brand Management*, *22*(2), 118–128. doi:10.1108/10610421311320997

Constantin, D.-M., Topor, D. I., Căpuşneanu, S., & Manole, A. (2020). Sustainability Reporting: Stakeholders and Reporting of Sustainability Accounting Information. In I. Oncioiu, G. Cokins, S. Căpuşneanu, & D. I. Topor (Eds.), *Management Accounting Standards for Sustainable Business Practices* (pp. 92–117). IGI Global. doi:10.4018/978-1-7998-0178-8.ch005

Constantin, D. M., Topor, D. I., Căpuşneanu, S., Türkeş, M. C., & Anghel, M.-G. (2019). Green Reporting and Its Impact on Business Strategy: Computer Program for Evidence and Green Reporting. In I. Oncioiu (Ed.), *Network Security and Its Impact on Business Strategy* (pp. 91–109). IGI Global. doi:10.4018/978-1-5225-8455-1.ch006

Mahoney, J., Carleton, C., & Mahoney, J. (2004). Towards a Property Rights Foundation for a Stakeholder Theory of the Firm. *The Journal of Management and Governance*, *9*, 5–32.

Maniora, J. (2017). Is Integrated Reporting Really the Superior Mechanism for the Integration of Ethics into the Core Business Model? An Empirical Analysis. *Journal of Business Ethics*, *140*(4), 755–786. doi:10.100710551-015-2874-z

Sully, R. (2012). ISO 26000: The business guide to the new standard on social responsibility. *Impact Assessment and Project Appraisal*, *30*(3), 214–215. doi:10.1080/14615517.2012.681201

Chapter 3
Incorporating Corporate Social Responsibility Into Decision Making

Alharbi Habbab Husam
Mansoura University, Egypt

ABSTRACT

There is a clear correlation between a company's business model and its financial decisions, such as investment and financial planning, in the case of successful companies with established CSR and sustainability initiatives. Increasing the knowledge of accounting managers about the strategic significance of environmental concerns is another key step once the concept of company-specific sustainability has been developed. One solution is to integrate decision makers into interdisciplinary strategy teams. This chapter presents concrete tools with which accounting managers can promote and support sustainable, strategically planned corporate management.

INTRODUCTION

Since the financial crisis, the concept of corporate social responsibility (CSR) has become a distant memory (Alzola, 2017; Barth, Landsman, Young & Zhuang, 2014). When discussing CSR, the economic factor is given similar weight as environmental and social concerns. The many elements are frequently intertwined in such a manner that environmental and social factors have a direct influence on a company's financial success (Baker & Bettner, 1997; Caylor, 2010). Investors classify as riskier and accept less and less as sustainable investment businesses that pursue exclusively

DOI: 10.4018/978-1-6684-4595-2.ch003

financial objectives while neglecting the eco-social effects of their fundamental business and social interests (Allen & Ramanna, 2013).

The idea of corporate social responsibility (CSR) has long been argued in the corporate world, but more and more real-world instances illustrate that social responsibility is intimately tied to financial concerns and that the financial aspect of sustainability will be vital for the long-term viability of firms and whole sectors (Lukka, 2010). Ecological and social responsibility is impossible without economic and financial accountability - and vice versa (Li, Qi, Tian & Zhang, 2017).

Besides raising awareness, another crucial element in planning strategy work is the certification of accounting department staff (Hou, Jin, Yang, Yuan & Zhang, 2015). This first has an impact on personnel in command or strategic planning. If these concerns are to be addressed later in the strategy process, it is critical to teach the fundamentals of sustainability and environmental management.

The importance of the content of ecologically oriented particular issues or trends might be appraised differently by stakeholder groups than by the company's own management (Dennis, 2014). It is necessary to compile a list of the company's relevant stakeholders, such as shareholders, customers, suppliers, banks, and workers, and to methodically identify the environmental factors deemed particularly important for that group (Florou & Pope, 2012). Based on enhanced opportunities and risks as well as the profile of strengths/weaknesses, the first ecological areas of action can be defined as guidance for formulating the strategy (He, Pan & Tian, 2017).

The balancing of all ecological benefits and negatives may, of course, be applied to an individual product in addition to the ecological profit and loss account at the corporate level. Data is collected in the same manner as company-level data for this purpose. Because data gathering for individual items is far less complicated than data collection for a complete firm, the proportion of real data obtained may be raised here, and the use of extrapolated data can be eliminated.

As a consequence, sustainability initiatives may be focused in areas with the highest potential for savings at the lowest financial cost, or where control is required owing to the significant effect. Aside from the desirable objective of environmental protection, it may also be viewed as an essential contribution to the company's risk management.

Another element of the regulatory framework is the issue, ie the self-image of the company's mission or purpose (Damayant, 2013). Expect an issue of environmental orientation or sustainability here, especially in organizations whose primary business is built on sustainability (Ramanna, 2008). Stakeholders, at least in this case, normally anticipate a clear commitment to sustainability (Li, 2010).

Based on the regulatory framework and the strategic analysis conclusions, it is now required to identify the unique strategic value of those actions for the organization (Soltani, 2014). Internal views of managers or owners, as well as opinions of external interest groups, have an impact on this, resulting in very varied forms of strategy depending on the organization and the business climate (Richardson, 2011). Companies that place a high strategic value on all five levels of their business are thus pursuing a comprehensive green strategy.

As business partners, strategic controllers must support management in developing or planning, controlling, and adjusting strategies. Strategic Control 4.0 refers not only to the use of digital tools or offerings but also to their conscious design as part of a further digitally controlled development of the organization. It is of no use to a company to introduce a new (expensive) technology if it cannot be used properly. The digital business management model helps to identify areas where strategic control can drive an organization's digital transformation and how this change can be monitored and controlled.

A business model, in general, provides the logic of how a corporation produces value for its customers, benefits stakeholders, and consequently profits itself (Schleicher, Tahoun & Walker, 2010). The mechanisms of ecological success are predicted or sought with the integration of ecology-oriented content into an existing business model or with the new development of a green business model.

BACKGROUND

As a structural framework, a variety of business model techniques can be applied (Byard, Li & Yu, 2011). Customer value, customer segmentation, channels, customer connections, important processes, and critical resources/partnerships are among the main features of business models, as are financial components such as profit or cost structure and cash flows (Barth, Landsman & Lang, 2008; Chen, Qu & Sun, 2017).

This is an iterative process in many firms that can begin in departments depending on the scenario and the maturity of the strategy (Ahmed, Neel & Wang, 2013). Environmental strategic objectives, in addition to other strategic objectives, are an intrinsic aspect of those target systems (Andon, Baxter & Chua, 2007; Barth, 2013). If the content of the environmental strategy is subsequently consolidated in a sustainability map, the status of ecological sustainability implementation may be shown in real-time - with relevant criteria and metrics (Cahan & Sun, 2015).

Another important step in implementing ecologically oriented strategic objectives within the strategy process is integration into management systems and processes (Holthausen & Watts, 2001). A relationship with innovation management is an excellent notion for mobilizing the organization's innovative capacity in the direction of (green) sustainability (Ball, 2013). It promotes discussion of the topic within the organization, channels creative potential, and offers new impulses to sharpen the strategy if it incorporates aspects of ecological sustainability, for example, in the strategic orientation given for generating ideas or in the areas of strategic research (Chen, Tang, Jiang & Lin, 2010).

Ecological sustainability can only be successfully integrated into the strategy process if the managers participating in the process perceive it as a management task and incorporate it into the company's strategic management culture (Doukakis, 2014). In addition to analytical strategy work, fundamental management openness to environmental issues, entrepreneurial intuition and creativity in strategy development, organizational flexibility to incorporate the subject into company processes, and a strong will to implement the content of the environmental strategy all play important roles (Parker, 2012).

A company's environment continually changes, and it must adapt to these changes in order to remain viable (Ahrens, 2008). One of these shifts is our society's developing ecological challenges. On the one hand, businesses are the ones responsible for causing these issues, but on the other hand, they also have the potential to make a big contribution toward finding solutions (Arsenault & Faerman, 2014). More and more businesses view this as a strategic opportunity to set themselves apart from the competition.

Staff changes, no matter how essential, will result in changes to the organizational structure. Employees are required to work in addition to filling the vacancy. Rethinking several plans and maybe halting teamwork are feasible in situations when one of the partners is absent. If the individual was well-liked and liked by others in the organization, the shift might be due to a general drop in morale, which has a detrimental impact on motivation.

The choice that an employee makes regarding whether or not to continue working for a company is one that can be evaluated using the methods that are unique to the economics theory, just as we would anticipate the corporation to do when calculating it. The cost-benefit analysis may be used to justify the employee's decision to the organization; the determining factor is mostly the incentive structure that characterizes the organizational environment.

It's becoming more and more normal for top executives to get long-term remuneration, but leading organizations are also using specific sustainability criteria to ensure that they're making the right decisions for the future. the road to long-term corporate management The biggest impediment to widespread adoption of this promising method is the difficulty in creating workable sustainability metrics.

It is possible for unintended modifications to be made to the facts that are being researched; the components that are involved cannot be followed concurrently; the information that is gathered is frequently rather rich, but not all of it is of the same relevance. These are only some of the drawbacks that are associated with using this research approach.

THE ROLE OF CORPORATE SOCIAL RESPONSIBILITY IN MANAGERIAL PERFORMANCE

A company's success and all its CSR-related efforts (in regard to the social and environmental impacts of its main business) may at times appear to be different constructions during the intense public discussion (Ahmed, Neel & Wang, 2013). Management and control of sustainability were completely managed by specialized departments (such as an environment or sustainability department), whereas controllers had very little role in the process. One reason for this is that sustainability has always been regarded as secondary to the company's performance.

The relationship between sustainability and core business is a crucial aspect in finding such strategic areas of action with which organizations may achieve financial success beyond sheer image benefits (Ahrens, 2008). When it comes to serious execution of the company's sustainability plan, it is necessary to consider the ecological and social elements of the company's operations, as well as the three dimensions of sustainability. As a result, the entire business management must be linked with the economic, environmental, and social components of sustainability. The need for a sustainability strategy for an integrated sustainable corporate management that takes economic, ecological, and social factors into consideration is included in the company's management concept.

Corporate control activities include the merging of economic and environmental control information, as well as procedural accountability for modified control instruments (Alzola, 2017). However, due to the technical knowledge required in the field of environmental protection, ecological sustainability management necessitates collaboration with an environmental department, which is in charge of quality assurance of ecological data content and also serves as a coordination unit for operational implementation.

Additionally, one of the most significant tasks for Green Controlling is the incorporation of environmental information into corporate management procedures and tools (Ball, Li & Shivakumar, 2015). Due to the very specialized and frequently technical expertise required to assess sustainability measures, corporate control cannot handle some of these activities alone and must collaborate with other departments, such as environmental management.

Existing control procedures should be modified in order to take environmental sustainability into consideration and cooperate with other departments in processes after the organizational anchoring of environmental control has been understood (Jackson & Liu, 2010). It is possible to conduct surveys of the same nature about the creation of trash as well as the contamination of the air and water. The detrimental impact of acid rain, for example, might be utilized to assign a monetary value to soil and water acidification. It is also feasible to link the expenses of diseases caused by air pollutants to pollution emissions.

In terms of the consideration of environmental elements of sustainability in control instruments, it has been demonstrated that the more strategic the subject is for a corporation, the greater it is (Ozkan, Singer, & You, 2012). As a result, technological integration of Green Controlling into current IT systems is advised. On the one hand, because integration clearly stresses its relevance, the presentation of ecological sustainability as a distinct subject in corporate management may be avoided.

In order to be able to support even more efficient, effective, and fast management, strategic control should use the three forms of digitization. They have an impact on the fulfilment of strategic control tasks—or more precisely, on the perception of the activities within the control processes, on the control tools to be used, and, in general, on the design of the control systems. On the one hand, control should save the effort of the process and thus increase efficiency and speed. On the other hand, control should support strategic and more differentiated and therefore more efficient management through data and fact-based procedures, which are characterized by quantified driver models and success factors. In general, management will move away from reactive-analytical control and toward proactive, integrated corporate control between companies and cross-value added.

In essence, the strategic control reporting function refers to the addition of strategically relevant control information to a primarily operational reporting system. This contains internal information on the implementation of strategic plans (measures and initiatives) and, as a result, the progress of strategy implementation. Finally, the extent to which the company's strategic objectives have been attained, which is primarily decided by strategy execution, must be disclosed. However, this is insufficient for strategic information provision: external environmental information must also be supplied because certain predicted changes in the corporate environment are crucial premises for the strategic course of action - and this environment can alter at any time.

The mechanisms of strategic planning and control are intricate. A wide range of activities can be witnessed. Coordination, moderation, and time management are required in this situation. Strategic controllers take on the essential role of central manager of these processes as part of their coordination duty, especially when the impacted business units are included in the planning in accordance with the counter-current concept.

Changes in structural elements and core parameters are the main points of emphasis (measures). A basic scenario serves as the starting point. However, this is not generated from medium-term planning, but rather from a financial projection with a large horizon. If the financial projection horizon is created and extended automatically, the scenario analysis may be produced at any time using current data.

These digital technologies enable controllers to test the feasibility of strategy recommendations developed by specialized units and to develop their own impulses. Because, at the end of the strategic planning process, strategic control is judged by the output - specifically, feasible, well-founded, and easy-to-understand strategy initiatives that are presented to management for decision-making in an efficient manner that takes investment cycles into consideration.

If environmental information is automatically derived from existing data in the IT system, the human effort to gather the information and enter it into the reporting systems is reduced, and the continuing recording effort is reduced. Furthermore, this process guarantees a high degree of coherence between economic and environmental control information, increasing data trustworthiness and avoiding the effort of reconciling control information from diverse source systems. Because current systems are widely used, the installation effort for environmental management may be reduced to a minimum.

Corporate sustainability is more than just a passing fad; it is critically important to all of the company's constituents. In addition to the direct economic consequences (for example, cost reduction through environmental process optimization), there are an increasing number of indirect effects of social and environmental performance on the company's financial success (Soltani, 2014). Concerns about environmental and social sustainability have still not been taken into corporate governance, despite its strategic relevance and financial consequences.

For the financial sector and, in particular, control, the high strategic relevance implies that the duties involved in supporting the planning, measurement, management, and control of all corporate objectives should be performed to achieve sustainability objectives (Brown, 2010).

Corporate controlling's involvement in sustainability management has been shown to be a success factor in the development of sustainable corporate management since the subject's internal relevance might rise once again as a consequence (Ball, 2013). To successfully manage and regulate sustainability inside the organization, a variety of talents are required, therefore tight collaboration across different departments of the firm proves to be a significant aspect. Another success element in sustainability management is the use of current corporate management tools and procedures to collect data and report on the dimensions of ecological and social sustainability.

Approaches to sustainability control are merely a subset of feasible action possibilities. All existing control systems and instruments, in theory, may be expanded to include environmental and social elements of corporate management. The procedures and instruments that must be modified must be determined on a company-by-company basis and in accordance with the stated sustainability plan.

Companies determine the level to which they wish to accept responsibility for the environmental repercussions of their actions, and hence their corporate, through their day-to-day business choices (Lukka, 2010). The desire of management to consider environmental problems in business decisions is critical to regulating environmental performance. Consequently, environmental management systems and operational-level controls are needed to build the necessary competencies.

Control tools for monitoring environmental performance should also be built to identify the potential for value creation, help strategy formulation, and take human behavior knowledge into consideration. As environmental conservation is often viewed as a beneficial contribution to society, it remains a problem to align the company's incentive structures such that both objectives are satisfied. Control systems have a responsibility to guarantee that the company's resources are utilized in the most productive and efficient manner feasible in order to accomplish the company's goals. At the time, the focus was still on a more hierarchical top-down approach to accomplishing the goals.

The data that has previously been acquired can be extrapolated to similar or identical operations if the gathering of real data is too difficult or impossible owing to a lack of information in the supply chain. Where data extrapolation is not attainable, essential financial values in the purchasing region can be estimated utilizing eco-friendly input-output models and databases, as well as life cycle and material flow analyses.

The image of a company's situation (actual or supposed) sent by yearly financial statements attempts to affect the decision-making behavior of the receivers' balance sheet in the company's interest. The central purpose and checkpoints are therefore the appropriate annual financial statements (total assets and equity, particularly the outcome for the period), which are frequently used in the context of assessing important numbers to assess the company's trustworthiness.

Companies with a higher CSR score are more focused on their results and are less quick to communicate bad news. Furthermore, there is a link between corporate size and CSR excellence. The positive relationship between a company's performance in the CSR ranking and the level of profit management appears to be influenced by the company's size and its surroundings. This allows us to assume that organizations with a greater influence over their performance invest more in these areas since they are the focus of public attention - the marginal return on an improvement is thus larger.

Sustainable business management and its accompanying CSR initiatives have gained prominence over the past several years. The public's and investors' information needs and expectations have also grown. Social and environmental commitment is no longer evaluated benevolently without verification but is increasingly being rigorously questioned.

Companies that emphasize the client interface will be more successful. Appropriate (digital) procedures or technologies should be employed in this situation. On the other hand, it is critical for a corporation to build a digital strategy that can capitalize on the digital age's prospects. As a result, strategic control should assure the availability of relevant tools and procedures, as well as ensure or contribute to the modelling of digital strategy execution.

It is necessary to process the information that comes out of research on organizational performance and provide it in a manner that is understandable, synthesized, and pertinent. In practice, statistical and mathematical approaches, as well as graphical methods, such as prediction tests, group talks, in-depth dialogues, motivational studies, factorial, multidimensional analysis, and so on, are utilized.

SOLUTIONS AND RECOMMENDATIONS

The period's result (also known as profit or loss) of a firm is one of the most important measures of its success and is also used for other reasons, such as a measure of performance-related remuneration for management. The consequence of such increased attention to this result is reflected in a greater likelihood of being consciously controlled by a company's management - especially from an accounting point of view.

Accounting for environmental costs can be differentiated from accounting for other types of costs, such as accounting for cost types, cost centers, or cost units. This separation can help the organization better regulate its environmental performance. A rigorous review of all aspects of the balance sheet and profit and loss account is also advised in order to determine the components included therein in relation to the company's environmental performance.

It's important for businesses to keep account of environmental expenses that are not already factored into their bottom line but are instead absorbed (or outsourced) by them as a result of their everyday operations. To construct an ecological profit and loss account, the system's limitations must first be established, i.e., which sectors of a company's activity and which elements of the life cycle of the company's goods or services must be included in the ecological account. Profit and loss statement it is critical to strike a balance here between the desired thoroughness of the ecological profit and loss statement and the work necessary to calculate it.

The organization's most significant environmental factors (such as climate, water, and so on) are first characterized and then quantified using current data or data to be obtained via environmental management. Data gaps, particularly in the supply chain, can be filled by employing cost-effective input-output models or extrapolating data from product life cycle analysis.

There is no debate about the main instruments. Furthermore, only environmental performance components that conform with the currently relevant laws are reported. Amounts that can be quantified in money are therefore the only acceptable parameters for the investigation.

A company's total control administration could be greatly reduced if these circles of control were connected to the network through automated interfaces For example, if a firm intends to start a product development plan with changing production structures, a parallel automatic simulation of the consequences of these control rings would accelerate the preparation of a strategic control decision. Separate, cascade calculations unique to the control circuit are more difficult, take longer, and are prone to errors if performed manually.

Economic success remains a primary standard for judging corporations and their revenues, but it is increasingly evaluated in the context of a company's ties with the environment and society. However, this does not imply that the fundamental criteria for formal and accounting consistency are becoming less necessary. To be able to compare a company's equity, financial position, and earnings over time, it is important to methodically delimit them on a regular basis, as well as the similarity in the substance of the financial statements.

FUTURE RESEARCH DIRECTIONS

Companies may therefore better understand the environmental and monetary consequences of their energy and material use and develop improvement strategies. Quantity centres, like cost centres, are established in the first stage, and material flows and energy consumption that occur there are documented in physical units, i.e. all inputs and outputs.

The costs of an alternative in which the corporation actively accepts responsibility (action costs), some of which may be transmitted to other parties (acceptable costs), are compared to the costs of the alternatives. It contrasts the effects of a third-party reaction (costs of sanctions).

The planned production costs are typically raised as action costs due to the ecological focus. Customers, on the other hand, are frequently ready to pay for the additional advantage they obtain, particularly in the case of environmental performance.

The tools should ideally be utilized at all three levels of the organization. Other control methods may also have an impact on the obtained criteria. Firms need to develop what aims they want to achieve with the tools and hence why they want to take responsibility while installing their control systems.

An efficiency-enhancing potential that is not obvious through standard cost accounting can be recognized through differentiated control of environmental performance using techniques such as material flow cost accounting.

One of the most difficult obstacles in the future of expanding sustainability orientation will be your company's credible positioning and distinctiveness. In this perspective, CSR reporting is not an aim in itself, but rather an essential component of the entire business strategy. Sustainable financial reporting is critical to public image. CSR reporting should promote the impact of sound financial reporting rather than conceal its flaws (for example, in the form of accounting policy measures).

Obtaining a competitive advantage necessitates the ability to implement consumer expectations. This is especially true for the corporation application. This includes difficulties such as integrating into current strategies, budgets, and decision-making frameworks. Strategic control must guarantee that data adds value. Input sources (for example, competition analysis) and their integration, as well as storage and provisioning, are all part of the core data strategy.

CONCLUSION

A company's CSR profile is being viewed from an increasing variety of perspectives. This is also true for financial reporting. The recognition that a company's economic performance is an inherent aspect of CSR is decisive here.

The system limitation for the use of control tools must first be defined in order to assess the extent to which firms wish to accept responsibility for environmental performance in their choices. However, while ecological resources have value, they are seldom individually salable and exploitable, hence they are not fully integrated into standard accounting.

Competitive advantages can be determined using the net economic-ecological effect by thoroughly comparing the costs of doing something and passing them on vs the costs of doing nothing. It is essential for companies to utilize KPIs to determine if their firm is moving in the right way or whether it requires a shift in strategy. The correct collection of indicators will shed light on performance and reveal problem areas. Entrepreneurs/decision-makers are sailing blindly without the necessary KPIs. They comprehend the performance of all essential dimensions of their organization by condensing them down to vital KPIs that will provide them with the ability to comprehend, measure, and analyze the most critical parts of the business.

Furthermore, professional sustainability management, particularly at the quantitative level, is increasingly regarded as an indication of fundamentally sound business management. As a result of this finding, organizations with first-rate sustainability management will be considered as lower risk by analysts and investors. In order to convey the ideals and objectives of a business, many managers create and report on subordinates. Occasionally, video cassettes are sent to employees to highlight each employee's part in attaining the company's goals. Each manager is tasked with articulating the organization's ideals and incorporating these principles into their own activities.

It is apparent that the prospects for businesses originating from the social process of sustainable development cannot be used systematically and only partially by excluding the finance department from management. No corporation can afford this in the long term in a competitive market economy. Successive organizations are progressively displaying themselves as truly open systems, whose market position is dependent not only on their own internal resources, but also on their relationships with configuration and other entities that have complementing abilities as well. The company's external network is essentially an extension of the internal borders between the two types of networks, which are becoming increasingly difficult to distinguish.

Finally, research on the CSR-performance relationship give relatively little evidence on whether CSR improvements result in long-term changes inside the organization. This is where research that investigate the relationship between CSR services and the quality of financial reporting, particularly the quality of findings, come in. Furthermore, there is a considerable positive association between a company's share of discretionary accumulation and its CSR ranking performance. This indicates that the greater the scope of outcomes management, the greater the CSR score. A substantial negative association appears in terms of the degree of cautious accounting.

Given this inconsistent image, it is not easy for strategic controllers in particular to position themselves correctly in the digital age. In addition, during the digitalisation debate, tools - such as traditional regression analysis - are sometimes recommended that are known to be part of standard business education.

REFERENCES

Ahmed, A., Neel, M., & Wang, D. (2013). Does mandatory adoption of IFRS improve accounting quality? Preliminary evidence. *Contemporary Accounting Research*, *30*(4), 388–423. doi:10.1111/j.1911-3846.2012.01193.x

Ahrens, T. (2008). Overcoming the subjective–objective divide in interpretive management accounting research. *Accounting, Organizations and Society*, *33*(2), 292–297. doi:10.1016/j.aos.2007.03.002

Allen, A., & Ramanna, K. (2013). Towards an understanding of the role of standard setters in standard setting. *Journal of Accounting and Economics*, *55*(1), 1–66. doi:10.1016/j.jacceco.2012.05.003

Alzola, M. A. (2017). Beware of the watchdog: Rethinking the normative justification of gatekeeper liability. *Journal of Business Ethics*, *140*(4), 705–721. doi:10.100710551-017-3460-3

Andon, P., Baxter, J., & Chua, W. F. (2007). Accounting change as relational drifting: A field study of experiments with performance measurement. *Management Accounting Research*, *18*(2), 273–308. doi:10.1016/j.mar.2006.06.007

Arsenault, P., & Faerman, S. R. (2014). Embracing paradox in management: The value of the competing values framework. *Organizational Management Journal*, *11*(3), 147–158. doi:10.1080/15416518.2014.949614

Baker, C., & Bettner, M. (1997). Interpretive and Critical Research in Accounting: A Commentary on its Absence from Mainstream Research||. *Critical Perspectives on Accounting*, *8*(4), 293–310. doi:10.1006/cpac.1996.0116

Ball, R. (2013). Accounting informs investors and earnings management is rife: Two questionable beliefs. *Accounting Horizons*, *27*(4), 847–853. doi:10.2308/acch-10366

Ball, R., Li, X., & Shivakumar, L. (2015). Contractibility and transparency of financial statement information prepared under IFRS: Evidence from debt contracts around IFRS adoption. *Journal of Accounting Research*, *53*(5), 915–963. doi:10.1111/1475-679X.12095

Barth, M., Landsman, W., & Lang, M. (2008). International accounting standards and accounting quality. *Journal of Accounting Research*, *46*(3), 467–498. doi:10.1111/j.1475-679X.2008.00287.x

Barth, M. E. (2013). Global comparability in financial reporting: What, why, how, and when? *China Journal of Accounting Studies*, *1*(1), 2–12. doi:10.1080/21697221.2013.781765

Barth, M. E., Landsman, W. R., Young, D., & Zhuang, Z. (2014). Relevance of Differences between Net Income based on IFRS and Domestic Standards for European Firms. *Journal of Business Finance & Accounting*, *41*(3-4), 297–506. doi:10.1111/jbfa.12067

Brown, J. (2010). Accounting and visual cultural studies: Potentialities, challenges and prospects. *Accounting, Auditing & Accountability Journal*, *23*(4), 482–505. doi:10.1108/09513571011041598

Byard, D., Li, Y., & Yu, Y. (2011). The effect of mandatory IFRS adoption on financial analysts' information environment. *Journal of Accounting Research*, *49*(1), 69–96. doi:10.1111/j.1475-679X.2010.00390.x

Cahan, S. F., & Sun, J. (2015). The effect of audit experience on audit fees and audit quality. *Journal of Accounting, Auditing & Finance*, *30*(1), 78–100. doi:10.1177/0148558X14544503

Caylor, M. L. (2010). Strategic revenue recognition to achieve earnings benchmarks. *Journal of Accounting and Public Policy*, *29*(1), 82–95. doi:10.1016/j.jaccpubpol.2009.10.008

Chen, H., Tang, Q., Jiang, Y., & Lin, Z. (2010). The role of international financial reporting standards in accounting quality: Evidence from the European Union. *Journal of International Financial Management & Accounting*, *21*(3), 220–278. doi:10.1111/j.1467-646X.2010.01041.x

Chen, M., Qu, X., & Sun, X. (2017). Whose cost of equity capital reduces after IFRS convergence and why? Heterogeneity evidence from Chinese stock market. *China Journal of Accounting Studies*, *5*(1), 1–27. doi:10.1080/21697213.2017.1304539

Damayant, T. (2013). Who is afraid of Qualitative Research? A Compromise Accounting Research Failure in Improving Accounting Practices. *International Journal of Advances in Management and Economics*, *2*(2), 89-94.

Dennis, I. (2014). *The Nature of Accounting Regulation*. Routledge.

Doukakis, L. C. (2014). The effect of mandatory IFRS adoption on real and accrual-based earnings management activities. *Journal of Accounting and Public Policy*, *33*(6), 551–572. doi:10.1016/j.jaccpubpol.2014.08.006

Florou, A., & Pope, P. (2012). Mandatory IFRS adoption and institutional investment decisions. *The Accounting Review*, *87*(6), 1993–2025. doi:10.2308/accr-50225

He, K., Pan, X., & Tian, G. (2017). Legal liability, government intervention, and auditor behavior: Evidence from structural reform of audit firms in China. *European Accounting Review*, *26*(1), 61–95. doi:10.1080/09638180.2015.1100547

Holthausen, R. W., & Watts, R. L. (2001). The relevance of the value-relevance literature for financial accounting standard setting. *Journal of Accounting and Economics*, *31*(1-3), 3–75. doi:10.1016/S0165-4101(01)00029-5

Hou, Q., Jin, Q., Yang, R., Yuan, H., & Zhang, G. (2015). Performance commitments of controlling shareholders and earnings management. *Contemporary Accounting Research*, *32*(3), 1099–1127. doi:10.1111/1911-3846.12111

Jackson, S. B., & Liu, X. K. (2010). The allowance for uncollectible accounts, conservatism, and earnings management. *Journal of Accounting Research*, *48*(3), 565–601. doi:10.1111/j.1475-679X.2009.00364.x

Li, L., Qi, B., Tian, G., & Zhang, G. (2017). The contagion effect of low-quality audits at the level of individual auditors. *The Accounting Review*, *92*(1), 137–163. doi:10.2308/accr-51407

Li, S. (2010). Does mandatory adoption of international accounting standards in the European Union reduce the cost of equity capital? *The Accounting Review*, *85*(2), 607–636. doi:10.2308/accr.2010.85.2.607

Lukka, K. (2010). The roles and effects of paradigms in accounting research. *Management Accounting Research*, *21*(2), 110–115. doi:10.1016/j.mar.2010.02.002

Parker, L. (2012). Qualitative management accounting research: Assessing deliverables and relevance. *Critical Perspectives on Accounting*, *23*(1), 54–70. doi:10.1016/j.cpa.2011.06.002

Ramanna, K. (2008). The implications of unverifiable fair-value accounting: Evidence from the political economy of goodwill accounting. *Journal of Accounting and Economics*, *45*(2-3), 253–281. doi:10.1016/j.jacceco.2007.11.006

Richardson, A. (2011). Myth, Paradigms and Academic Accounting Research: A Comment on Reading and Understanding Academic Research in Accounting. *Global Perspectives on Accounting Education*, *8*, 67–77.

Schleicher, T., Tahoun, A., & Walker, M. (2010). IFRS adoption in Europe and investment-cash flow sensitivity: Outsider versus insider economies. *The International Journal of Accounting*, *45*(2), 143–168. doi:10.1016/j.intacc.2010.04.007

Soltani, B. (2014). The anatomy of corporate fraud: A comparative analysis of high profile American and European corporate scandals. *Journal of Business Ethics*, *120*(2), 251–274. doi:10.100710551-013-1660-z

ADDITIONAL READING

Ahmed, A., Neel, M., & Wang, D. (2013). Does mandatory adoption of IFRS improve accounting quality? Preliminary evidence. *Contemporary Accounting Research*, *30*(4), 388–423. doi:10.1111/j.1911-3846.2012.01193.x

Ball, R., Li, X., & Shivakumar, L. (2015). Contractibility and transparency of financial statement information prepared under IFRS: Evidence from debt contracts around IFRS adoption. *Journal of Accounting Research, 53*(5), 915–963. doi:10.1111/1475-679X.12095

Fan, J. P. H., Li, J., & Zheng, G. (2016). Revisiting the bright and dark sides of capital flows in business groups. *Journal of Business Ethics, 134*(4), 509–528. doi:10.100710551-014-2382-6

Ozkan, N., Singer, Z., & You, H. (2012). Mandatory IFRS adoption and the contractual usefulness of accounting information in executive compensation. *Journal of Accounting Research, 50*(4), 1077–1107. doi:10.1111/j.1475-679X.2012.00453.x

Chapter 4
Creative Accounting Affects Corporate Performance:
Theoretical Fundamentals and Specific Practices

Oncioiu Ionica
Titu Maiorescu University, Romania

ABSTRACT

Accounting creativity only addresses the same issue as management, but the solution resides at the border between the legal and recording of economic events. From a variety of accounting treatments and rules, the entity's manager can select the one that is most convenient and serves their own interests, which means that an outcome may be convenient but not necessarily accurate. The consequences and problems of creative accounting on performance are discussed in this chapter. According to the findings, the biggest problem created by the standards is the requirement for periodic reassessments and the option of selecting a method of assessing value, which offers grounds for the practice of creative accounting.

INTRODUCTION

Market valuation specialists and accountants are able to limit the potential impacts of creativity because of variables such as the severity of competition or the increased demand on enterprises to reveal substantial outcomes, especially from investors and analysts (Chen, Qu & Sun, 2017). Accounting alternatives have been around for a long time, and if the goal of creative accounting is to enhance a company's accounts (or

DOI: 10.4018/978-1-6684-4595-2.ch004

its image) by exploiting accounting regulations' vulnerabilities, the authors believe this notion is nothing new (Holthausen & Watts, 2001; Baker & Bettner, 1997).

The flexibility of international accounting rules promoted the creation of creative accounting (Damayant, 2013). In most circumstances, creative accounting is regarded negatively (negative creation), with the goal of creating value for intangible assets capable of responding to managers' demands regarding the company's financial status and performance (Doukakis, 2014). The concurrent consideration of creative accounting as a tool to fulfill accounting and accounting engineering goals is based on the accounting rules set by a patrimonial company to create and transmit information (Richardson, 2011; Ball, Li & Shivakumar, 2015).

Ethical challenges in creative accounting necessitate that accountants recognize that their decisions about accounting principles and transaction management might be abused (Byard, Li & Yu, 2011). Accountants in Anglo-Saxon economies have had more flexibility to practice such accounting, which has led to its rise (Chen et al., 2010; He, Pan & Tian, 2017). It was situated on the precipice between the legal form and the economic content of the many events and transactions (Barth et al., 2014). Creative accounting, as viewed from the perspective of accountants, has led to the development of both fundamental and alternative approaches for solving difficulties (Ahmed, Neel & Wang, 2013; Barth, Landsman & Lang, 2008; Fan, Li & Zheng, 2016). Of course, asset valuation concerns are examples of creative accounting practice including subjective reasoning in the professional accountant or expert assessor. Trying to estimate the true value of intangible assets is next to impossible due to the gray area supported by accounting regulations, which encourages the use of innovative accounting methods (Li, 2010; Ozkan et al., 2012, Barth, 2013).

Employees in the accounting departments of listed companies at lower hierarchical levels should be treated in particular as potential whistleblowers. They may report possible manipulations in financial reporting but are not legally obliged to do so. It may also be possible to include high-level employees and auditors (internal audit and auditors) as potential whistleblowers. However, their reporting situations are likely to differ significantly from the former, as they may have lower retaliation costs. They may even be asked to report by virtue of their role.

Measures to encourage denunciation, such as the introduction of rewards or guarantees, could lead to more reports of denunciation. On the other hand, it could also have negative effects because those who receive these messages have to assess their credibility.

As an alternative, credibility can also be interpreted as the informational content of a warning report. When an investigator is faced with a decision to initiate a special audit based on a report, the investigator will update his or her fraud expectations based on the informational content of the report. If the investigator considers that the reporting reports are not informative about the manipulation, then a report will not affect their expectations of fraud and they may decide not to investigate.

BACKGROUND

Several fields address the theme of innovative accounting techniques, including accounting, information technology, psychology, and management, but they have increased considerably in recent decades across the full spectrum of enterprises (Brown, 2010). Creative accounting operates in the shadows, where allegations of non-compliance with professional or legal standards might be filed, but where common sense reasoning indicates the presence of a certain amount of "pushing the note" (Bettner & Kate, 2013).

Identifying opportunities and incentives that alter the perception of control and rules is the goal of the Fraud Triangle. In turn, planned behavior theory gives further explanations of the aspects or elements that influence an individual's judgment, rationale, and purpose to behave (Parker, 2012).

The legal and institutional structure, in turn, has an impact on the channels through which people can denounce (Ball, 2013). When a person decides to report, he will recognize that he has the ability to control the situation. The aspects of the Fraud Triangle that impact the warning opportunities influence the perceived amount of control (Lukka, 2010).

Concerning the reporting of irregularities, the perceived potential of a successful correction has an effect on the perceived level of control. Company rules, processes, and perceived organizational impediments are other considerations (Dennis, 2014).

Extrinsic stimuli are rules because an individual does not want to be perceived as a rule-breaker by others. Individuals establish perceptions regarding norms at the same time (Singer & You, 2012). The social pressure is represented by perceived subjective norms, and the attitude is determined by the appraisal of the warning act.

The manner in which deviations are reported is determined by institutional systems. Reporting policies and processes may have an impact on warning possibilities. Internal justification of an activity is known as rationalization, and it helps to reconcile the disparity between the actual action and its ideal counterpart (Jackson & Liu, 2010). Moral problems, in particular, have a role in rationalization. There is no way for a potential whistleblower to judge whether or not an activity is improper or severe (moral sensitivity). Social incentives can impact his moral perception, and his personal morality and attitudes influence moral motivation (Caylor, 2010).

Extrinsic and intrinsic stimuli can both influence the intention to warn. Because of his moral commitment to do so and his expectation of compensation, an insider may denounce fraud if he feels compelled to do so. Furthermore, he generates ideas about those who act on his report. They also have their own goals, and one of their responsibilities is to evaluate the legitimacy of a whistleblower report or revelation.

On the other hand, there is a possibility that prospective warmers will be misled by misleading incentives or that their innate desire would wane. However, it should be noted that incentives might result in inaccurate reporting or the elimination of intrinsic drive. Furthermore, rewards may be ineffective because if individuals believe an act is a significant crime, they will be more ready to report it even without financial incentives.

Companies can better protect a whistleblower's identity by introducing anonymous reporting channels and setting or raising standards for reporting. A very high level of anonymity could be achieved, for example, by requesting external service providers to receive confidential and anonymous reports. A company could also save costs on setting up an internal system. From the employee's point of view, it could be an external channel, because it is reported to a part outside the company (although it was ordered by the company).

Creative accounting approaches for documenting intangibles may be divided into four groups (Schleicher, Tahoun, & Walker, 2010):

- Accounting standards may allow a corporation to select between multiple accounting procedures: accounting for development expenditures can either be treated as an expense when incurred or as a cost to be absorbed over the course of the project's life cycle, depending on how a company wants to portray itself.
- The estimates are often established within the organization or by an experienced assessor, and the creative accountant is able to set the estimate with both prudence and optimism.
- In order to manipulate intangible values on the balance sheet and shift profits across accounting periods (sale and lease-back), artificial transactions might be created.
- Real transactions involving intangibles might also be scheduled at different periods to provide the desired impression for accounting information users. Owners of real estate holding companies have complete discretion over when and how much they want to recoup on their intangible investment sales.

The procedures that disclose creative accounting for intangible assets may be categorized as:

- processes that model the outcome and management choices;

- processes and approaches intended to enhance the impact of balance sheet information;
- Processes that have an influence on how the findings are presented.

The approaches and procedures utilized for intangible assets that have an influence on the outcome are as follows:

- the capitalization of development expenses will occur if an optimistic attitude towards the prospects of success of a development project is maintained, which will have repercussions for the magnitude of the outcome, which will be the capitalization for the year. In future exercises, costs recorded with amortization will have a negative influence on the result. If the firm includes development expenditures in its profit and loss (expenditure), it will allege that at least one of the requirements specified in IAS 38 para. 43 is not satisfied.
- goodwill may be increased when a corporation acquires assets at a price that is below market value. Capitalization and amortization of goodwill during its useful life will have an impact on future performance (goodwill amortization costs lead to diminished results, with consequences on the course of action and competitiveness of competitive stock takeover bids). Due to the fact that goodwill amortization costs aren't included into future workouts, charging goodwill on equity has the unintended consequence of decreasing their lead (Hou et al., 2015).

In order to determine how anonymity affects the credibility of a report from the perspective of an investigator, it was analyzed how senior internal auditors (audit executive director and deputy audit executive director) respond to anonymous and non-anonymous reporting reports. Employees should assess the credibility of this report and allocate resources to review this report. On the other hand, the question arises as to the extent to which the detection of manipulation of accounting information is appropriate to represent a real allocation of resources.

CREATIVE ACCOUNTING AFFECTS CORPORATE PERFORMANCE: THEORETICAL FUNDAMENTALS AND SPECIFIC PRACTICES

Based on accounting regulations, accounting norms' inadequacies and shortcomings, and accounting mechanisms, financial engineering processes are used to manipulate financial outcomes. The determination accounting interpretation of a legally financial transaction or creation of a legally-financial mechanism to alter financial outcomes are examples of financial engineering (Florou & Pope, 2012; Allen & Ramanna, 2013).

Restricting the number of accounting techniques that may be used or defining the conditions under which each method must be utilized can both reduce the number of options available. It is worth noting that auditors should step up their efforts to discover any manipulations of financial statement information (Cahan & Sun, 2015). In order to avoid creative accounting or fraud, the audit function should evaluate the company's internal control system. Auditors must be prepared to confront their clients in order to obtain broader and more stringent monitoring. There is the potential for a significant shift in the interaction between auditors and management as a result of this. It should not be overlooked that principles such as honesty, objectivity, secrecy, competence, and, last but not least, credibility must be present in the conduct and documentation of any professional's work.

For the purpose of increasing the performance of an entity and attracting new customers, or even protecting one's reputation, accountants compile and present financial statements that encourage macro-manipulation and micro-manipulation, both of which the entity management even supports and encourages.

New accounting laws are being lobbied against by accountants, who believe they are impractical because they are aware of their existence. In this regard, they draw attention to an alternate depiction of economic reality that benefits them. This type of manipulation involves giving accounting information to a company's decision-makers that presents a different reality than the one that is meant to be given, rather than the actual reality.

The accounting outcome, however, also contributes significantly to a share's value (Andon, Baxter & Chua, 2007). There have been a few incidents of highly lucrative Romanian enterprises going bankrupt. That is why the stock exchange should educate investors on the importance of education and knowledge, but this is a long process.

According to this point of view, the concept of creative accounting that is utilized by accountants within the context of attaining performance is very much a matter of innovation. Entities must integrate their strategies, operations, performance, and actions with the Sustainable Development Goals, especially by 2030. (SDGs). Managerial culture is supposed to represent ideals, attitudes, and behaviors that are in conflict with the Yin field of creative accounting. To put it another way, the unfavorable effects of creative accounting can only be mitigated in an organization if there is a robust managerial culture in place, and this culture must have been cultivated by a leader who possesses the requisite abilities to understand the ramifications of making decisions based on accounting information.

Whether they are devices of corporations or individual actors, platforms that link assets throughout the industry in value-creating ways are emerging, and we are witnesses to their growth. These platforms are playing major roles in a variety of different industries, and they are built on Value-Based Indicators.

Another aspect to consider when evaluating studies is the influence of audit committees. Thus, the quality of audit committees could have a positive effect on the strength of the company's warning system (which includes identity protection measures) and could reduce the likelihood of retaliation. If the audit committee is of sufficient quality, this may result in improved circumstances for internal reporting, rendering unnecessary the process of external condemnation. But if the quality of the audit committee is inadequate, this might lead to a decrease in the quality of internal reporting and an increase in external reporting.

There is a correlation between audit committee quality and the chance of external reporting, as well as a link between audit committee quality and the risk of retaliation. The attributes of independence (proportion of independent members), competence (percentage of competent members), and diligence are used to assess quality (number of member meetings).

On the other hand, the usage of an external channel may imply that the previously utilized internal channels have been abandoned. Another opportunity for a possible whistle blower to exploit is a route that is external to the organization. The impact of adopting an external channel is complicated since the available reporting alternatives/ warning channels change based on the firm and the legal framework.

With regard to the reporting of data, many sectors of the economy make use of a variety of distinct modelling methodologies. Few theoretical models of leaking have been developed that can be applied directly to cases of accounting fraud and embezzlement in publicly traded firms without the whistle blower being implicated as a co-conspirator.

These models often contain two or three players: a possible perpetrator (for example, a manager), a potential whistle blower (for example, a corporate insider), and an investigator or judge. For example, a manager may be a potential perpetrator. The perpetrator can commit a crime, and the announcer can get information about a crime and determine whether or not to report it. The examiner may rule on his or her performance on the examination, and a court may rule on a conviction.

In the event that the internal auditor does not identify any instances of manipulation, an external denunciation will take place automatically. After this, he may be required to cover the expenses of litigation. You will not be charged if you do not receive a report. External reports can be used to promote internal denounce, but only if the internal denounce has already taken place. The author's compensation scheme for sequential reporting can therefore be implemented to advance internal reporting and support release regulators.

The significance of establishing trust in audits and financial reports from the perspectives of all stakeholders is universally acknowledged, but nations differ in their ability to achieve this critical aim or ensure the independence of auditors due to differences in their legal, regulatory, and political systems. To ensure audit quality, only French legislation utilizes joint auditing, which allows for cross-review and reciprocal monitoring. Additionally, having two auditors increases the auditor's level of independence from the organization being audited. Data on the market's supply and demand dynamics that are available or released differ by country as well.

Research on auditing partners' specific or individual characteristics, however, does not focus on the psychological aspects of audit processes or the ultimate decision-making process as a whole (Hou et al., 2015). Nonetheless, due to the fact that the audit process is entirely a decision-making process in which the talents, personalities, and competencies of auditing partners influence their professional judgment and, consequently, the audit opinion they finally provide, some researchers have proposed that auditing partner level characteristics be considered in audit quality research.

In order to define why and what should be done in terms of all business communications, researchers and regulatory authorities are greatly assisted by information asymmetry and agency theory. But the mental accounting paradigm and upper echelon perspective substantially aid in understanding these reporting procedures clearly and genuinely and give insights into why and what is going on in this great big world.

The specialists developed a new concept for a professional accountant dubbed a strategic management accountant, which takes into consideration the new attributes and qualities of the management accountant that were established by the strategic management accounting dimension. It is essential to collaborate with the strategic management accountant in the strategic management accounting practices, taking into consideration the changing nature of the company environment, the influence of cutting-edge technology that is now in use and will become more prevalent in the near future, as well as the complexity of the decision-making process.

SOLUTIONS AND RECOMMENDATIONS

According to what was mentioned before, creative accounting is considered to be a distinguishing characteristic of the Anglo-Saxon method of accounting. This method is distinguished from the European continental model, which is distinguished by precise traditions and prescriptions, by its flexibility, and reasonableness.

Either the discovery of lies (such as claims made knowingly or the spread of erroneous information) or the revelation of innovative accounting practices used to mask the true situation is the basis for financial scandals. As a result, professional accountants, who have long been mocked for their lack of imagination and strict conduct, have generated the surprise of producing creative accounting.

To maintain that level of anonymity as paper evaluation, companies can submit anonymous reports to a single national regulatory agency, which would then distribute these findings to randomly selected assurance providers. Because of this, the quality assurance process could be protected from managerial control or other problems. It is possible for assurance companies to determine if reporting business executives are biased toward overconfidence based on the most commonly used metrics in the literature. They should examine this business's reports more closely since the perceived risk of the reporting company increases when it has overconfident managers.

There has been an increase in the importance of all relevant information, including financial information since the economic crisis started in the United States and extended to practically all of the world's financial markets. This is attributable to the fact that businesses that are trying to remain viable in internationally competitive marketplaces are unable to achieve this objective by concentrating just on financial performance. Suggesting a method for companies to survive in this challenging environment, sustainability reporting has emerged as critical non-financial information that stakeholders want. There has been a lot of discussion on the legitimacy and accountability of this information as a result of the attempts to minimize information asymmetry, deal with agency difficulties, and improve stakeholder relations.

FUTURE RESEARCH DIRECTIONS

The entity's management then observes that the annual financial statements have a dual aim: on the one hand, to inform decision-makers about the entity's economic status, and on the other, to confuse them. The concerns given and evaluated are a synthesis of a great quantity of material developed by the writers to provide the foundation for understanding influencing corporate performance through creative accounting. As a result, there are new research directions for the future, such as:

- The number of accounting techniques that can be employed should be reduced, or the scenarios in which each method should be utilized should be specified. The imposition of consistent procedures is beneficial because a corporation that chooses a way that produces a positive image in one year must apply the same method in subsequent years when the results are less favorable.
- The exploitation of reasoning may be stopped in two different ways: first, by mapping rules to reduce the use of reasoning, and second, by establishing consistency in such a manner that if a corporation sets an accounting policy that advantages one of the years, they will be required to follow it throughout the subsequent years, even if it is no longer favoring them.

- According to the predominance of substance over form idea, economic substance rather than legal form dictates accounting substance in artificial transactions.
- There is no doubt that the moment of the transaction is an issue of leadership. However, the purpose of their usage can be decreased by requiring the frequent evaluation of the elements so that gains or losses of value change accounts are recognized in accounts for the years in which they occur. This will bring the purpose of their use closer to its original intent (and not entirely in the year are transferred).

It is imperative that any actions used to combat "fraudulent" accounting practices serve the dual objective of ensuring high-quality accounting information that accurately reflects reality and enabling informed decisions that promote equitable distribution of value creation amongst all participants.

The practice comes to light with two distinct but equally risky typologies. The first of these is made up of young individuals with no experience who actively use engineering without analyzing the dangers in order to just assert themselves. A mature individual who has expertise knows the entity for which he works and sees creative accounting as a way to enhance his own financial income falls into the second type.

A simple attempt to offer materials that may influence the choice, hide the reality of the company, or put it in a different shape than it is deemed deceit for a potential investor who has taken the decision to invest based on clear arguments in the financial statements.

CONCLUSION

The foundation of creative accounting is the same accepted accounting principles and procedures, to which other substrates are added or subtracted in order to show the company in a more persuading light from the standpoint of performance.

Accounting information can be manipulated both inside and outside of the law and accounting regulations (Li et al., 2017). In the latter situation, illegal conduct is taking place: accounting fraud. There is a distinct distinction between creative accounting and fraud, but there is always a distinct demarcation between the circumstances of creative accounting methods and the condition of accounting malpractice. Because the legislation is a two-edged sword - a control instrument as well as a basis for straying from the regulation - auditors should increase their efforts to discover potential manipulations of the information presented by financial statements. In this regard, the audit function should involve an evaluation of the company's internal control system in order to prevent creative accounting or fraud. Auditors need to be prepared to go to combat against their clients in order to secure a more comprehensive and rigorous level of transparency. This could inspire a major rethinking of the nature of the auditor-manager relationship. Integrity, objectivity, secrecy, competency, and, last but not least, credibility must all be present in the conduct and documentation of any professional's activity.

The underlying issue of accounting convergence is tied to the note of credibility provided to accounting. The assertion is based on user confidence in a circumstance in which the same public firm has various size images in equity and performance for the same period in different nations due to compliance with the regulations in these countries.

Consider that successful IFRS-US GAAP convergence in practical terms is dependent on the coordination of activity of the IASB and FASB interpretation, because even if the standards issued by the two bodies are identical, the financial statements (prepared in accordance with IFRS or US GAAP) will not be comparable (or will be only limited comparable), undermining convergence efforts (or comparable).

Europeans are more suspicious of the utility of fair value for other types of accounting information consumers, and the accounting model has numerous critics. Furthermore, the fair value is difficult to apply inside a Romanian accounting system, especially given the recent loss of confidence in capital markets, which has been exacerbated by the global economic crisis. This is due to the fact that fair value is a byproduct of the capital market (Ramanna, 2008). Even if the pros and cons of the fair value system are explored, it cannot be argued with certainty that it is preferable to the historical cost system. The latter has the undeniable benefit of being recognized and so mastered.

For these reasons, accounting information consumers prefer to work with a system that is uniform in its concepts, principles, and standards. As a criterion of credibility, the information in financial statements must be exhaustive with regard to two broad restrictions: cost-benefit analysis and materiality. Omissions can lead information to be inaccurate or misinterpreted, reducing credibility and significance.

As a consequence of this unfavorable trend, creative accounting has, for a considerable amount of time, been compartmentalized from various other disciplines and activities. When it comes to accounting, the one who saw it from a good viewpoint thinks that there may be a lot more freedom in accounting, which may provide a fair image of the accounts while also being utilized to serve financial statements and fraud, or to provide an inaccurate picture of the accounts.

REFERENCES

Ahmed, A., Neel, M., & Wang, D. (2013). Does mandatory adoption of IFRS improve accounting quality? Preliminary evidence. *Contemporary Accounting Research, 30*(4), 388–423. doi:10.1111/j.1911-3846.2012.01193.x

Allen, A., & Ramanna, K. (2013). Towards an understanding of the role of standard setters in standard setting. *Journal of Accounting and Economics, 55*(1), 1–66. doi:10.1016/j.jacceco.2012.05.003

Andon, P., Baxter, J., & Chua, W. F. (2007). Accounting change as relational drifting: A field study of experiments with performance measurement. *Management Accounting Research, 18*(2), 273–308. doi:10.1016/j.mar.2006.06.007

Baker, C., & Bettner, M. (1997). Interpretive and Critical Research in Accounting: A Commentary on its Absence from Mainstream Research||. *Critical Perspectives on Accounting, 8*(4), 293–310. doi:10.1006/cpac.1996.0116

Ball, R. (2013). Accounting informs investors and earnings management is rife: Two questionable beliefs. *Accounting Horizons, 27*(4), 847–853. doi:10.2308/acch-10366

Ball, R., Li, X., & Shivakumar, L. (2015). Contractibility and transparency of financial statement information prepared under IFRS: Evidence from debt contracts around IFRS adoption. *Journal of Accounting Research, 53*(5), 915–963. doi:10.1111/1475-679X.12095

Barth, M., Landsman, W., & Lang, M. (2008). International accounting standards and accounting quality. *Journal of Accounting Research, 46*(3), 467–498. doi:10.1111/j.1475-679X.2008.00287.x

Barth, M. E. (2013). Global comparability in financial reporting: What, why, how, and when? *China Journal of Accounting Studies, 1*(1), 2–12. doi:10.1080/21697221.2013.781765

Barth, M. E., Landsman, W. R., Young, D., & Zhuang, Z. (2014). Relevance of Differences between Net Income based on IFRS and Domestic Standards for European Firms. *Journal of Business Finance & Accounting, 41*(3-4), 297–506. doi:10.1111/jbfa.12067

Bettner, M., & Kate, K. (2013). Changes in annual reporting rituals of financial services firms in periods of market crisis. *International Journal of Critical Accounting, 5*(6), 577–593. doi:10.1504/IJCA.2013.059027

Brown, J. (2010). Accounting and visual cultural studies: Potentialities, challenges and prospects. *Accounting, Auditing & Accountability Journal*, *23*(4), 482–505. doi:10.1108/09513571011041598

Byard, D., Li, Y., & Yu, Y. (2011). The effect of mandatory IFRS adoption on financial analysts' information environment. *Journal of Accounting Research*, *49*(1), 69–96. doi:10.1111/j.1475-679X.2010.00390.x

Cahan, S. F., & Sun, J. (2015). The effect of audit experience on audit fees and audit quality. *Journal of Accounting, Auditing & Finance*, *30*(1), 78–100. doi:10.1177/0148558X14544503

Caylor, M. L. (2010). Strategic revenue recognition to achieve earnings benchmarks. *Journal of Accounting and Public Policy*, *29*(1), 82–95. doi:10.1016/j.jaccpubpol.2009.10.008

Chen, H., Tang, Q., Jiang, Y., & Lin, Z. (2010). The role of international financial reporting standards in accounting quality: Evidence from the European Union. *Journal of International Financial Management & Accounting*, *21*(3), 220–278. doi:10.1111/j.1467-646X.2010.01041.x

Chen, M., Qu, X., & Sun, X. (2017). Whose cost of equity capital reduces after IFRS convergence and why? Heterogeneity evidence from Chinese stock market. *China Journal of Accounting Studies*, *5*(1), 1–27. doi:10.1080/21697213.2017.1304539

Damayant, T. (2013). Who is afraid of Qualitative Research? A Compromise Accounting Research Failure in Improving Accounting Practices. *International Journal of Advances in Management and Economics*, *2*(2), 89-94.

Dennis, I. (2014). *The Nature of Accounting Regulation*. Routledge.

Doukakis, L. C. (2014). The effect of mandatory IFRS adoption on real and accrual-based earnings management activities. *Journal of Accounting and Public Policy*, *33*(6), 551–572. doi:10.1016/j.jaccpubpol.2014.08.006

Fan, J. P. H., Li, J., & Zheng, G. (2016). Revisiting the bright and dark sides of capital flows in business groups. *Journal of Business Ethics*, *134*(4), 509–528. doi:10.100710551-014-2382-6

Florou, A., & Pope, P. (2012). Mandatory IFRS adoption and institutional investment decisions. *The Accounting Review*, *87*(6), 1993–2025. doi:10.2308/accr-50225

He, K., Pan, X., & Tian, G. (2017). Legal liability, government intervention, and auditor behavior: Evidence from structural reform of audit firms in China. *European Accounting Review*, *26*(1), 61–95. doi:10.1080/09638180.2015.1100547

Holthausen, R. W., & Watts, R. L. (2001). The relevance of the value-relevance literature for financial accounting standard setting. *Journal of Accounting and Economics, 31*(1-3), 3–75. doi:10.1016/S0165-4101(01)00029-5

Hou, Q., Jin, Q., Yang, R., Yuan, H., & Zhang, G. (2015). Performance commitments of controlling shareholders and earnings management. *Contemporary Accounting Research, 32*(3), 1099–1127. doi:10.1111/1911-3846.12111

Jackson, S. B., & Liu, X. K. (2010). The allowance for uncollectible accounts, conservatism, and earnings management. *Journal of Accounting Research, 48*(3), 565–601. doi:10.1111/j.1475-679X.2009.00364.x

Li, L., Qi, B., Tian, G., & Zhang, G. (2017). The contagion effect of low-quality audits at the level of individual auditors. *The Accounting Review, 92*(1), 137–163. doi:10.2308/accr-51407

Li, S. (2010). Does mandatory adoption of international accounting standards in the European Union reduce the cost of equity capital? *The Accounting Review, 85*(2), 607–636. doi:10.2308/accr.2010.85.2.607

Lukka, K. (2010). The roles and effects of paradigms in accounting research. *Management Accounting Research, 21*(2), 110–115. doi:10.1016/j.mar.2010.02.002

Ozkan, N., Singer, Z., & You, H. (2012). Mandatory IFRS adoption and the contractual usefulness of accounting information in executive compensation. *Journal of Accounting Research, 50*(4), 1077–1107. doi:10.1111/j.1475-679X.2012.00453.x

Parker, L. (2012). Qualitative management accounting research: Assessing deliverables and relevance. *Critical Perspectives on Accounting, 23*(1), 54–70. doi:10.1016/j.cpa.2011.06.002

Ramanna, K. (2008). The implications of unverifiable fair-value accounting: Evidence from the political economy of goodwill accounting. *Journal of Accounting and Economics, 45*(2-3), 253–281. doi:10.1016/j.jacceco.2007.11.006

Richardson, A. (2011). Myth, Paradigms and Academic Accounting Research: A Comment on Reading and Understanding Academic Research in Accounting. *Global Perspectives on Accounting Education, 8*, 67–77.

Schleicher, T., Tahoun, A., & Walker, M. (2010). IFRS adoption in Europe and investment-cash flow sensitivity: Outsider versus insider economies. *The International Journal of Accounting, 45*(2), 143–168. doi:10.1016/j.intacc.2010.04.007

KEY TERMS AND DEFINITIONS

Accounting Engineering: The process whereby, given the existence of gaps in the rules to manipulate accounting numbers and taking advantage of flexibility, those practices are chosen for measurement and information that allow transforming synthesis documents from what they should be in what managers want.

Convergence of Accounting: The process by which accounting standards are developed in a manner that is able to lead to the same act or purpose, by showing the similarity of national, regional, international.

Corruptible Value: The amount for which an asset could be changed into a balanced transaction between informed and determined parties other than in a forced sale of liquidation.

Creative Accounting: A tool to create a distortion of the quality of financial information, creating uncertainty about the consistency and comparability of information for users, in which case we are dealing with an accounting of intent.

Chapter 5
Analysis of Performance From a Managerial Accounting Perspective

Lavinia Essen Yildirim
Ankara University, Turkey

ABSTRACT

The results of scientific study and literature review indicate that new strategic transformations of entities are being examined for the adoption of a performance management system. This system has the responsibility of converting the strategic plan of long-term and medium-sized objectives into associated activities between the managerial plan and financial-accounting. An integrated system of performance indicators is implemented to properly estimate a company's worth in this chapter, which analyses the new research paths at the junction of accounting and management. The findings reveal that implementing performance management inside an entity satisfies a number of conditions that are directly connected to the level of achievement of the specified goals.

INTRODUCTION

An organization's economic activity can be analyzed and diagnosed, and current approaches and techniques for assessing performance should be used, because accounting information is the primary source of support for the value creation indicators (Stettina & Hörz, 2015). The connection of an organization's ability to adapt to an environment is the major aim of the ongoing process of experimentation

DOI: 10.4018/978-1-6684-4595-2.ch005

and adaptation known as organizational change management (Chan, Shaffer & Snape, 2004).

One aspect of great importance to the existence, perpetuation and rise or fall of companies in the economy of any country is their contribution to creating new value, or, in other words, the value added in order to be more relevant, needs to be examined closely, along with the number of employees (Alhyari et al., 2013).

Entity risk management is to equip management with the tools necessary to recognize the element of uncertainty pertaining to the accomplishment of the goals set and the risk involved, as well as the chance to expand the capacity to add value, deliver more effective, economical, and efficient services, and uphold value accounts like equality and justice (Fisher, 2010). In a negative sense, the risk can be understood as uncertainty, threat, or obstacle; in a good sense, it can be understood as an opportunity.

Accounting, the basic tool for knowledge, management, and control of patrimony and the results obtained by economic entities, is the only source capable of providing accounting information of informational value to the leadership of entities under pressure to adapt strategic decisions to economic uncertainty (Arsenault & Faerman, 2014). Consequently, the attention of entity leadership is increasingly oriented towards the creation of an organizational culture orientated towards excellence and performance, and the crystallization of components that define and contribute to the formation of such an environment - Performance Indicators/ KPI's (Agha et al., 2012).

Around the middle of the nineteenth century, the word "performance" had its first appearance in written works (Becker & Huselid, 2006). Since then, it has been linked to the beginning of athletic competitions as a consequence of taking part in and ultimately winning such a competition. As the twentieth century progresses, the idea continues to expand, and new methods are ascribed to it by the theorists and practitioners of the era (Akgün et al., 2009). This is because, in the modern day, performance is recognized as the genuine measure of worth for any company leader or manager. Performance-related indicators that can be measured, compared to pre-established benchmarks, and used as a basis for future adjustments, added value, and competitive advantage are measurable (Amagoh, 2008).

Another approach for organizing and analyzing the values of individuals and corporate culture is value analysis (Taticchi, Tonelli & Cagnazzo, 2010). With respect to specific intents, expectations, and ideals, this technique reveals what individuals value more or less and what they consider desirable. In workplaces where employees are more preoccupied with addressing their most fundamental needs, their behavioral options are constrained, resulting in a decline in their contribution to enhancing the productivity of their job (Deutsch & Silcox, 2003; Ashkanasy, 2011). As a result of their increased expectations, employees are more likely to contribute to the success of the company (Olson et al., 2005; Andriole, 2010).

For the time being, the only options for growing enterprises are the capacity to generate new goods and services, the ability to enhance internal and external connections in order to favor the creation of competitive advantages that will assure market success. To be competitive in today's market, organizations must not only depend on their own internal resources, but also on their relationships with other configurations and external entities. The company's external network is essentially an extension of the internal borders between the two types of networks, which are becoming increasingly difficult to distinguish.

Performance management at the organizational level entails coordinating goal-achieving actions with the leadership vision, strategy, and culture. An organization's maturity and high use of human resources are indicators of alignment on both a group and an individual level. This can be shown in how well a team, department, or project accomplishes its goals through the use of operations management. As a result, individual performance evaluation is increasing, and the results have a direct impact on the performance management process, resulting in the emergence of the premise to develop new performance measurement tools and methods, which is reflected in the development of performance management systems.

Interdisciplinary approaches and extending the idea of performance have resulted from these interferences, which have allowed for a wider range of applicability. The interference of the organizational performance concept with other concepts such as management, leadership, profitability, predictability, and economic-financial indicators and metrics is revealed through specialized practice. The integrated performance indicators system would aid leadership in leading while also inspiring and motivating others, enabling them to have a holistic view of their clients and accomplish their goals by getting to the heart of the organization.

Performance management in an organization meets a number of needs that are closely connected to the success of the organization's goals. The first criterion is for leadership to analyze and manage poor performance compared to objectives, which has ramifications such as concentrating on the entity's strategic objectives, aligning resources with activities, feedback, and future growth orientations.

The problem is made even more difficult by the fact that the effect of the endogenous and exogenous elements of the entities is constant and difficult to control. Furthermore, the idea of performance brings together under one umbrella additional qualities beyond the economic and financial ones that contemporary entities need to include and develop in their own strategy. These characteristics include things like adaptability, flexibility, customer orientation, and the recruitment and retention of talent, as well as the capacity to innovate.

Theoreticians and practitioners who are interested in researching performance have come up with a variety of theories and approaches to the subject. The entity's leadership is forced to align managerial actions with financial-accounting conditions as well as industry-specific predictability reports due to performance.

According to field experience, performance management is a procedure whose goal is to position an entity among those with high levels of performance by gating the outcomes and enhancing individual skills and talents. One significant advantage of prize-based models is that they provide a balanced set of criteria and indicators against which entities may objectively analyze their performance management systems and compare their performance to global standards or that of other businesses.

BACKGROUND

Entities monitor their operations and outcomes in order to deal with competitive challenges, respond to these threats in real time via adaptation and flexibility, and achieve a competitive edge over direct competitors (Cocca & Alberti, 2010). Companies therefore are forced to often rearrange their structures in order to react to new trends brought on by the current scientific and technological progress, the increase of competition at the national and worldwide levels, the evolution of consumer tastes, and changes in demands as a result of the changing fever and quick succession rhythm.

The manifestations of economic efficiency may take the following forms: an increase in production per man-shift; a decrease in the consumption of raw materials, fuel, and consumables; a decrease in freight costs; an increase in firm profitability; and an improvement in product quality (Hurley, 2002; Ahearne et al., 2010). Consequently, the effectiveness of the case is reflected not only by its myriad forms and partial features, but also, and most importantly, via them reunite sequence.

Because of the limited nature of the resources, which must be carefully managed to ensure economic growth and the betterment of mankind's living standards, economic efficiency must be a fundamental component of all economic activity (Davila, 2012). A market economy framework necessitates an examination of economic efficiency from both a micro and macroeconomic perspective. In addition, this should also be considered from the perspective of the nations whose economies interact with one another, since the development of the activities carried out by the parties' leads to better products being acquired with less work being put in. Investment and fixed capital efficiency, in particular, have a forward-looking quality, which makes them particularly important when making economic decisions. Decisions will be made based on the presence of many project versions, allowing for the selection of the most efficient one. Due to the fact that it provides an absolute rise in results while requiring the same volume of work as input, economic efficiency is the primary qualitative aspect that contributes to the expansion of the economy (Cameron & Quinn, 2011).

It drives the leadership of the performing entities towards implementing customer-oriented management models such as CRM (Customer Relationship Management), Benchmarking, and Dash-Boards in order to align with the new requirements of the Global Market and meet the requirements of more and more sophisticated customers (Tallon & Pinsonneault, 2011).

To be considered efficient from a social perspective, an organization must be capable of effectively distributing and managing resources across a wide range of sectors in order to meet the needs of society at their greatest level. Social efforts shown in educational, cultural, hygienic, and societal assistance programs, and associated with social, individual, and collective consequences, define the idea of social efficiency (Behery et al., 2014). Outcomes such as the health of the people, the level of civilization, the degree of social security and protection, the welfare reflected by living standards, and the quality of socio-ecological life are all factors that may be used to justify the allocation of resources for the benefit of mankind.

Actual economic efficiency includes natural environment conservation and preservation through employing resources to research ecological balance, adopting sets of steps to minimize and eliminate negative impacts produced by disruptive causes, and preserving a life-supporting environment (Behery et al., 2014; Basten & Haamann, 2018). As a characteristic of environmental preservation, ecological efficiency represents the efforts required to achieve the normal evolution requirements imposed by ecological balance for natural environment characteristics.

Performance management is a determining factor in the process of achieving high performance and co-opting, retaining, and capitalizing on human resources with high potential, being the instrument of leadership to evaluate individual and team objectives in line with the company's strategic objectives, in order for the company to gain that competitive advantage in a constantly evolving market. An accurate evaluation of the effectiveness of any economic activity necessitates a systemic approach that considers economic, political, social, and ecological factors, as well as the multiplicity of impacts generated by the subject activity.

The Perspectives on Performance in Managerial Accounting

Entity leadership monitors the existing state, which is inseparably linked to the environment in which it evolves, to scan the internal environment and confirm by mandate the necessity to establish a Performance Management System in order to attain a State Desired Evolution. The identification of causes and resources for the consolidation of the enterprise's shared actions is a critical requirement for changing the existing situation (Tong & Arvey, 2015).

Alternatively, the special sensitivity of the organization, its distinctiveness, and the quick modification of consumer preferences supports the systemic and dynamic approach to efficiency, which takes into account the premises of a rational use of resources and their preservation in order to preserve the eco balance and the health of mankind (Hartnell et al., 2011).

There are still some issues with identifying KPI's in the field despite how clear the technique is conceptually, due to a wide range of activities. It is necessary that the entities clearly designate the field of activity for which KPI's unique bloodlines are to be produced in order to counteract the appearance of confusion. Whether we are speaking about the financial area, the human resources area, or the operations area, it is important that this field of activity be identified (Rowland & Hall, 2014). Each paradigm has several project versions at its inception point, each defined by a range of facts related efforts, impacts, the existing report between, duration of completion, and time until reaching the intended socio-economic consequences. The best alternative is then chosen objectively and qualitatively using a system of economic metrics. The use of an indicator system is necessitated by the complicated nature of economic efficiency since each component represents a different criterion of economic efficiency (Kaplan & Norton, 2006; Tapanainen, 2012).

One of the most useful classifications, when an analysis involves several activities, is one based on the nature of the analysis object, as in the cluster of general indicators for the overall economic activity; the cluster of efficiency indicators for the production elements; the cluster of structural indicators for the consumed resources and the produced outcomes; and the cluster of industry-specific indicators.

There are many different types of resources that may be used for a certain activity, and this particular indicator helps to show how much time and money is spent on those resources, no matter what kind they are. Achieving that certain profit was made easier thanks to the indicator, which was generated in this way and properly captures the effect of each component of the production process. It can be estimated for the full business unit or for each kind or product separately.

This indicator is important because certain economic analyses substitute the entire volume of the production capital allocated, which includes both fixed and working capital, for production expenses. To assess the value of a corporation while utilizing fixed capital, a set of indicators linked to the dynamical, structural, and functional status of the fixed capital; the extensiveness and efficiency of the equipment based on synthetically efficiency indicators are typically utilized.

The evaluation of efficiency in the industry must monitor the correctness of all investment efforts, notably the many economic consequences, direct or indirect, that they have on the industry's performance. Economic efficiency may be assessed by using a system of indicators that contains both static and dynamic elements as well as industry-specific indicators. This technique is known as the "complex system of indicators" approach (Anand & Kodali, 2010).

This approach assists managers in incorporating two fundamental ideas while making choices (Chen & Fu, 2008). A company's value is determined by two factors: first, the primary financial objective should be to enhance shareholder value; and second, the primary financial objective should be to increase shareholder value.

The European Management Journal defines EVA as "the difference between net sales and the amount of operating expenditures, taxes, and cost of capital (capital charges), where the cost of capital is determined as a weighted average cost of capital multiplied by total invested capital." When the return on net assets (return on average capital employed) is greater than the average cost of capital, EVA rises (Alstete & Beutell, 2018).

The EVA model was originally established as an internal measure of performance used by managers to assist them to make investment decisions, as seen in the graph. Tapanainen et al. (2008) found that an investment project that generates larger profits than the net cost of its financing does not inevitably raise the value of the firm. Only those investment initiatives that may provide a positive or even growing EVA should be considered by a corporation since this would boost shareholder value. Like a consequence of this, it is abundantly evident that businesses need to adjust their priorities in order to use the principles of this strategy.

To maximize the market value added, or the difference between the capital investors have invested in the original firm and the amount of money they can earn by selling shares they hold, it is necessary to maximize the market value difference between the company's market value and the nominal value of shares (the initial investment of shareholders) (Yadav & Sagar, 2013). Increased shareholder value can be achieved by widening the gap between the rich and the poor. The discrepancy between the firm's market value and its book value can be attributed to intangible assets, which are often ignored by the accounting papers of a company. This is evidenced by the fact that the disparity exists (Sarabi et al., 2016).

There was a new approach, VAIC (Value added intellectual coefficient), established to aid managers in estimating their firms' potential based on present performance because the value-added measure could not be fully completed either in this way (to establish whether the driveway destroys or creates value or measure intellectual potential) (Sementelli, 2016).

Many companies have realized the value of intellectual capital and are seeking for ways to evaluate this component and govern it (Jung et al., 2016). In order to accurately quantify intellectual capital's contribution to a company's bottom line, financial metrics are not enough. The creation of wealth in the knowledge economy is based on the combination of goods and services that provide value. Each business has its own collection of information, skills, ideals, and solutions, all of which are intangible resources. Value creation efficiency analysis may be used to keep track of and manage these resources, which managers should do in order to maximize production and minimize waste. VAIC indicates a firm's intellectual capacities by indicating the value creation efficiency of all resources. The more the usage of qualitative resources (human and intellectual capital), the greater the company's value generation efficiency (Lin et al., 2008).

Models of business excellence have been created by worldwide or national organizations and serve as the foundation for awarding important distinctions. The reasons why organizations utilize these models for self-evaluation include the capacity to see areas for improvement and their strengths, use the model as a foundation for future organizational development, and realize advantages that go beyond financial indicators. These benefits include increased creativity and idea generation, customer satisfaction, organizational growth (employees), employee satisfaction and participation, and product efficiency, effectiveness, and predictability.

Using the endogenous elements that impact the strategic values of an organization, Alstete and Beutell (2018) say that there are three ways to assess performance: first, by determining the actual performance of an entity; second, by utilizing a standard that measures the difference between the actual and standard performances; and third, by utilizing a combination of these methods. As a result of this rapid rate of change, economic entities are forced to adopt a true strategic aggressiveness attitude, expressed by the discontinuity of the companies' strategic movements and their rapidity.

The quality of the goods, which reflects the culmination of the manufacturing processes, is another factor that contributes to the value of a firm (Henczel, 2002). Additionally, it is summarizing the technological level, as well as the operational and economic performances, in contrast to the esthetic ones. In point of fact, the term "quality" refers to the degree to which the aggregate value of the characteristics of a certain product has been elevated to. Product quality measures how well a product meets the functional, aesthetic, and financial demands of the customer.

For a precise evaluation of the product's quality, we choose those characteristics that substantially influence the extent to which it meets consumer needs (Homburg & Pflesser, 2000). Technical, esthetical, hygienic-sanitary, comfort, use, operational, and economic characteristics make up the textile quality indicators. Each and every one of them has a designated place in the standards, task manuals, and specifications.

The amount of quality indicators that are present in completed textile goods is dependent not only on the quality of the design but also on the quality of the manufacturing process, as well as the quality of the raw materials.

SOLUTIONS AND RECOMMENDATIONS

There is a direct correlation between the growth of the system's component businesses and its overall efficiency. Following technological and revamping initiatives, increased company efficiency will have good consequences for the overall national economy, which will become increasingly competitive.

As well as reflecting the personality and conduct of stakeholders or powerful leaders, management culture also draws attention to the wants and goals of an entity's managers and influences managers at all levels of the hierarchy in terms of their decisions and actions. It is the managers' responsibility to be actively involved in the process of establishing norms, standards, and codes of behavior that are consistent with the values of the organization they work for. It is also why they accept to be assessed and motivated in reference to defined criteria, as do all of the people involved.

Using current methodologies and techniques to assess performance helps leadership to choose the optimum approach to deploy a tool that enables value generation for the entity, as well as the formulation of future-oriented policies and goals. In order to respond to the interruption, only a thorough understanding of the organization, its operations, the openness of management processes, the right use of accounting information, awareness of the external environment, in particular threats, and innovative thinking to boost performance, as well as the development and implementation of cutting-edge measurement techniques and ongoing improvement, can be considered.

Describe your goals in the most straightforward and compelling way possible. Accounting and management can only work together if they understand each other's resources in depth, including the whole management system as a whole, methodologies, and procedures used to produce KPI's performance indicators, and the function they play in the growth of the business.

FUTURE RESEARCH DIRECTIONS

In order to address the new difficulties posed by the phenomena of globalization, achieving the primary purpose of a company, which is to increase its economic efficiency, necessitates measures such as technologization and retooling procedures. For professionals operating in this delicate economic sphere, commissioning new manufacturing capacity as well as redesigning existing ones is a necessity.

It is through the use of Key Performance Indicators (KPIs) that a company's leadership can align its vision with its strategy in order to achieve its goals. As the market continues to change and new concepts like globalization and the circular economy develop, the number of Performance Indicators on which an organization's leadership focuses grows tremendously. A high degree of the inclusion of non-financial indicators and a link of the entity's strategy with the activities performed to attain the objectives are two important themes that have been relevant in recent practice.

At the entity level, performance indicators are the manifestation of leadership vision harmonization with strategy, and their values reflect correlation with defined goals, indicating whether they have been reached or not contributing value to the company. But, despite the fact that the concept is so well defined, current entities are performing at a far lower level than expected and pursued. Identifying, choosing, and implementing performance indicators suited to an entity's actions is more than essential in order to achieve this, with each of the strategy's objectives allocated a relevant performance indicator.

CONCLUSION

Companies now operate in an environment that is constantly changing, particularly from a technology standpoint and owing to market conditions (Basten & Haamann, 2018). In the context of large economic changes, the action of market current forces defines specific behavior of organizations, which become increasingly involved in resources, quality, consumers, and suppliers, with top quality management playing a key part.

The facts brought to light by the current age prompted major worries on the part of economic theorists and practitioners in order to boost the efficiency of businesses. They have also resulted in the emergence of specialized organizations primarily concerned with managing resources and controlling their use in relation to the necessities of human society. Their primary focus is on developing alternative, long-term solutions to ensure that future generations have at least equal possibilities for survival, knowledge, and advancement. The traditional approach of companies, without a detailed strategy for the long and medium term, cannot provide them any hope of extending their business, with the major concern today being a reality.

Due to global competition, technical advancements, and economic shifts, specialists must restructure the organization chart, alter corporate culture, and realign plans with external demands and possibilities. This may be done by aligning organizational development processes and methodologies with an organization's principles and culture. To successfully execute changes in organizational growth, specialists require structures, processes, tactics, and methodical and congruent organizational models.

Understanding the economic and managerial mechanics of operation underlies the making of meaningful, genuine, and especially timely decisions that play a role in counteracting turbulent environment dangers and expanding the entity's potential. This necessitates a continuous examination and re-evaluation of the entity's performance. In terms of sustainability and stewardship, performance in the current problematic, conflicting, vulnerable, and volatile setting is comparable to accomplishing the entity's economic and financial objectives while boosting customer happiness and respecting stakeholder interests.

Both ideas develop value over time, accounting information as a consequence of economic actions and KPIs as a result of a clear set of future directions for action, and They think that both concepts come into the core capabilities category. The foundation upon which a strong leadership may build their most critical decisions: whether it is about new markets, benchmarking, company scaling, market exit, globalization, or digitalization. There are really large-impact decisions at the entity level, decisions that can play a significant influence in market positioning, and economically justified actions that can offset external factors that apply pressure on the entity.

The present issues have made it necessary for entities to broaden their performance spectrum and take into consideration both economic and non-economic, economic, technological, managerial, and environmental mix, whereas up to now the indicators upon which the entities have concentrated were time and cost, along with their derivatives.

Credibility, opportunity, accessibility, dependability, relevance, consistency, simplicity, neutrality, and responsiveness are all quality standards. The identification and selection of relevant and meaningful KPIs that are incorporated in strategic planning processes must adhere to a set of rules that are supported by both theory and practice, rules that actively contribute to the imposition of quality criteria for these performance indicators. Finally, the findings that accounting practitioners present to leadership through financial statements and reports can permit access to the entity's current situation, as well as probable upward or downward trends that may affect its evolution favorably or adversely.

Corporate governance more explicitly refers to how the rights and duties are allocated among the several categories of participants in the company's activity, including the board of directors, management, shareholders, and other groups of interest. It also describes how decisions are made about the company's activity, how strategic objectives are created, what are the methods of fulfillment, and how the financial outcomes are monitored. It is the role of management to communicate and take responsibility for the non-fulfillment of their managerial tasks according to the sort of legal accountability that an organization's management owns.

REFERENCES

Agha, S., Alrubaiee, L., & Jamhour, M. (2012). Effect of core competence on competitive advantage and organizational performance. *International Journal of Business and Management*, *7*(1), 192–204.

Ahearne, M., Lam, S. K., Mathieu, J. E., & Bolander, W. (2010). Why are some sales people better at adapting to organizational change? *Journal of Marketing*, *74*(3), 65–79. doi:10.1509/jmkg.74.3.065

Akgün, A. E., Keskin, H., & Byrne, J. (2009). Organizational emotional capability, product and process innovation, and firm performance: An empirical analysis. *Journal of Engineering and Technology Management*, *26*(3), 103–130. doi:10.1016/j.jengtecman.2009.06.008

Alhyari, S., Alazab, M., Venkatraman, S., Alazab, M., & Alazab, A. (2013). Performance evaluation of e-government services using balanced scorecard. *Benchmarking*, *20*(4), 512–536. doi:10.1108/BIJ-08-2011-0063

Alstete, J. W., & Beutell, N. J. (2018). Designing learning spaces for management education: A mixed methods research approach. *Journal of Management Development*, *37*(2), 201–211. doi:10.1108/JMD-08-2017-0247

Amagoh, F. (2008). Perspectives on organizational change: Systems and complexity theories. *The Innovation Journal*, *13*(3), 1–14.

Anand, G., & Kodali, R. (2010). A mathematical model for the evaluation of roles and responsibilities of human resources in a lean manufacturing environment. *International Journal of Human Resources Development and Management*, *10*(1), 63–100. doi:10.1504/IJHRDM.2010.029447

Andriole, S. J. (2010). Business impact of Web 2.0 Technologies. *Communications of the ACM*, *53*(12), 67–79. doi:10.1145/1859204.1859225

Arsenault, P., & Faerman, S. R. (2014). Embracing paradox in management: The value of the competing values framework. *Organizational Management Journal*, *11*(3), 147–158. doi:10.1080/15416518.2014.949614

Ashkanasy, N. (2011). International happiness; a multilevel perspective. *The Academy of Management Perspectives*, (February), 23–29.

Becker, B. E., & Huselid, M. A. (2006). Strategic human resources management: Where do we go from here? *Journal of Management*, *32*(6), 898–925. doi:10.1177/0149206306293668

Behery, M., Jabeen, F., & Parakandi, M. (2014). Adopting a contemporary performance management system. *International Journal of Productivity and Performance Management, 63*(1), 22–43. doi:10.1108/IJPPM-07-2012-0076

Cameron, K. S., & Quinn, R. E. (2011). *Diagnosing and Changing Organizational Culture: Based on the Competing Values Framework*. Jossey-Bass.

Chan, L. L., Shaffer, M. A., & Snape, E. (2004). In search of sustained competitive advantage: The impact of organizational culture, competitive strategy and human resource management practices on firm performance. *International Journal of Human Resource Management, 15*(1), 17–35. doi:10.1080/0958519032000157320

Chen, H. M., & Fu, P. C. (2008). A systematic framework for performance appraisal and compensation strategy. *Human Systems Management, 27*(2), 161–175. doi:10.3233/HSM-2008-0674

Cocca, P., & Alberti, M. (2010). A framework to assess performance measurement in SMEs. *International Journal of Productivity and Performance Management, 59*(2), 186–200. doi:10.1108/17410401011014258

Davila, A. (2012). New trends in performance measurement and management control. *In Performance Measurement and Management Control. Global Issues (Washington, D.C.), 25*, 65–87.

Deutsch, P., & Silcox, B. (2003). Learning from other libraries: Benchmarking to assess library performance. *Information Outlook, 7*(7), 18–25.

Fisher, C. D. (2010). Happiness at Work. *International Journal of Management Reviews, 12*(4), 384–412. doi:10.1111/j.1468-2370.2009.00270.x

Hartnell, C. A., Ou, A. Y., & Kinicki, A. (2011). Organizational culture and organizational effectiveness: A meta-analytic investigation of the competing values framework's theoretical suppositions. *The Journal of Applied Psychology, 96*(4), 677–694. doi:10.1037/a0021987 PMID:21244127

Henczel, S. (2002). Benchmarking – measuring and comparing for continuous improvement. *Information Outlook, 6*(7), 12–20.

Homburg, C., & Pflesser, C. (2000). A Multiple Layer Model of Market-Oriented Organizational Culture: Measurement Issues and Performance Outcomes. *JMR, Journal of Marketing Research, 37*(4), 449–462. doi:10.1509/jmkr.37.4.449.18786

Hurley, R. F. (2002). Putting people back into organizational learning. *Journal of Business and Industrial Marketing, 17*(4), 270–281. doi:10.1108/08858620210431679

Kaplan, R. S., & Norton, D. P. (2006). How to implement a new strategy without disrupting your organization. *Harvard Business Review*, *84*(3), 100. doi:10.1108d.2006.05622had.002 PMID:16515159

Lin, C. H., Peng, C. H., & Kao, D. T. (2008). The innovativeness effect of market orientation and learning orientation on business performance. *International Journal of Manpower*, *29*(8), 752–772. doi:10.1108/01437720810919332

Olson, E. M., Slater, S. F., Tomas, G., & Hult, M. (2005). The performance implications of fit among business strategy, marketing organization structure, and strategic behavior. *Journal of Marketing*, *69*(3), 49–65. doi:10.1509/jmkg.69.3.49.66362

Rowland, C., & Hall, R. (2014). Management learning, performance and reward: Theory and practice revisited. *Journal of Management Development*, *33*(4), 342–356. doi:10.1108/JMD-08-2012-0110

Schneider, M., & Somers, M. (2006). Organizations as complex adaptive systems: Implications of complexity theory for leadership research. *The Leadership Quarterly*, *17*(4), 351–365. doi:10.1016/j.leaqua.2006.04.006

Stettina, C. J., & Hörz, J. (2015). Agile portfolio management: An empirical perspective on the practice in use. *International Journal of Project Management*, *33*(1), 140–152. doi:10.1016/j.ijproman.2014.03.008

Tallon, P. P., & Pinsonneault, A. (2011). Competing Perspectives on the Link Between Strategic Information Technology Alignment and Organizational Agility: Insights from a Mediation Model. *Management Information Systems Quarterly*, *35*(2), 463–486. doi:10.2307/23044052

Tapanainen, T. (2012). Information Technology (IT) managers' contribution to IT agility in organizations–views from the field. Publications of Turku School of Economics, serie A.

Tapanainen, T., Hallanoro, M., Päivärinta, J., & Salmela, H. (2008). Towards an Agile IT Organization: A Review of Prior Literature. In *Proceedings of the 2nd European Conference on Information Management and Evaluation* (pp. 425-432). London, UK: Academic Conferences Limited.

Taticchi, P., Tonelli, F., & Cagnazzo, L. (2010). Performance measurement and management: A literature review and a research agenda. *Measuring Business Excellence*, *14*(1), 4–18. doi:10.1108/13683041011027418

Tong, Y. K., & Arvey, R. D. (2015). Managing complexity via the Competing Values Framework. *Journal of Management Development, 34*(6), 653–673. doi:10.1108/JMD-04-2014-0029

Yadav, N., & Sagar, M. (2013). Performance measurement and management frameworks. *Business Process Management Journal, 19*(6), 947–971. doi:10.1108/BPMJ-01-2013-0003

ADDITIONAL READING

Basten, D., & Haamann, T. (2018). Approaches for Organizational Learning: A Literature Review. *SAGE Open, 8*(3), 1–20. doi:10.1177/2158244018794224 PMID:32983596

Jung, J., Nam, C., Lee, E., & Kim, S. (2016). Subculture by autonomy and group cohesion and its effect on job satisfaction of R&D professionals in an R&D organization. *Journal of Management & Organization, 22*(2), 154–172. doi:10.1017/jmo.2015.20

Sarabi, A., Naghizadeh, P., Liu, Y., & Liu, M. (2016). Risky business: Fine-grained data breach prediction using business profiles. *Journal of Cybersecurity, 2*(1), 15–28. doi:10.1093/cybsec/tyw004

Sementelli, J. (2016). OD, change management, and the a priori: Introducing parrhesia. *Journal of Organizational Change Management, 29*(7), 1083–1096. doi:10.1108/JOCM-12-2015-0234

Chapter 6
Implementation of Financial Reporting in the Romanian Public System According to International Accounting Standards (IPSAS):
Theoretical-Methodological Approaches

Maria Ciurea
University of Petrosani, Romania

Rakos Ileana-Sorina
University of Petrosani, Romania

ABSTRACT

This chapter illustrates some aspects regarding the financial-accounting activity in the Romanian public system and obtaining a more realistic image of the financial reporting for the entities of the public system. The objectives of this chapter are to conduct an analysis on the implementation of financial reporting in the Romanian public sector in accordance with the requirements of International Public Sector Accounting Standards, which should include increased transparency and coherence, comparability of financial information, improved decision making, as well as the correct and real management of all approach arising therefrom. The issues presented by the author are based on the local and international specialized literature and university and specialized studies related to the treated topic. Thus, through the contribution brought, a new theoretical-empirical framework is created, which facilitates the identification of new ideas, themes, and debates of the aspects related to the financial-accounting reporting.

DOI: 10.4018/978-1-6684-4595-2.ch006

INTRODUCTION

The financial accounting activity in the Romanian public system has registered remarkable progress, an aspect also identified by the tendency to prepare not only financial reports, useful for microeconomic analysis and decision making at the level of public institutions, but also various statistical reports, useful for macroeconomic analysis and decision making at the country and government level. The continuous improvement of national and international accounting references will lead to a much more realistic picture of financial reporting for public entities.

Therefore, the financial information of these entities gains more accuracy and more details, being available in real time and easier to verify by various actors, such as: the Ministry of Public Finance the chief authorizing officer or the Court of Accounts. The close monitoring of the financial-accounting situation in the public system strengthens the bases for the correct use of the resources of each institution, by strictly observing the budgeted provisions, so that the resulting information shows concrete proposals for the preparation of future budgets. Romania has been and still is actively involved in the effort to modernize public sector financial management, so that a commitment-based accounting system is currently applied in all sectors and at all levels of the public system, by taking over elements from International Accounting Standards for the Public Sector (IPSAS).

This new international approach to public management is a consequence of the increased diversification of accounting systems, the quality of government reporting and the interest of international financial institutions. In this sense, the institutions of the public system have gone through a long road of reforms that have considered the financial reporting system that must meet the needs of transparency and publicity of budgetary data related to the public system according to European or international regulations, trust of the data collected through cross-validations between the records of the system and the financial records of public institutions. Increasing efficiency in the activity of public institutions, transparency in their management using modern tools for communication and transmission of information are major objectives that are constantly found in the strategies of the public system. Therefore, one of the tools for implementing these objectives is the use of the ForExeBug system which allows the standardization of the reporting and transmission of various types of financial statements for each entity in the public system only in electronic format, standardized and secure which allows to increase confidence of data collected by cross-validation with system data.

The transmission option allows that in addition to the centralization of situations, simultaneously the data can be used for multicriteria analysis and time series by interconnecting with the IT system of the Ministry of Public Finance. Thus, the major advantage of using that system is obvious, if we consider the fact that the system allows electronic monitoring and control of legal and budgetary commitments, with a direct impact on improving financial discipline and preventing the formation of arrears of public institutions.

Therefore, through the implementation of this system, we also find a series of operational advantages that take into account: the aggregation, centralization and automatic consolidation of the data collected through the electronic reporting forms of the financial statements; automatic generation of summary reports based on the data collected and automatic validation of data on budget execution of revenues and expenditures; automatic validation of data on payments made by public institutions through treasury accounts with approved budgets; allows the control of the budgetary commitments of the reporting entities and provides the authorizing officers with information on the use of the approved budget at the level of all hierarchically subordinated public institutions; the reduction of the volume of data to be reported by each authorizing officer and, at the same time, the reduction of working time and related resources, as a result of the decrease of the data to be centralized and reported.

In this context, the purpose of our study is to perform an analysis on the implementation of financial reporting in the Romanian public sector in accordance with the requirements of International Public Sector Accounting Standards, which should include increased transparency and coherence, comparability of financial information, decision making as well as the correct and real management of all aspects arising therefrom.

The use of financial reporting standards provides a high-quality general reporting framework for the public sector that will allow for independent assurance, which requires the implementation of key institutional commitments to support their efficiency as a tool for improved public sector financial management. At the same time, it supports the ability to perform high quality audits on the financial statements of public system institutions, which is particularly important for public sector auditors and the Supreme Audit Institution (The Court of Auditors). Also, the adoption of IPSAS standards for financial reporting will facilitate the comparability of information at all levels and will help internal management in making decisions on the allocation of resources in the planning and budgeting process, monitoring and accountability will provide better information on the risks of the government's debt-related system. Finally, it will be an important step in achieving the country's financial transparency vis-à-vis other governments around the world. That is why, financial reporting in the Romanian public system guarantees budgetary discipline, clear rules applicable to the system of budgetary accounting and statistical reporting, aligned with the requirements of European Union directives and IPSAS standards. Through our study we hope to make our own assessment of the implementation process and the results obtained in the financial reporting of institutions in the public system.

BACKGROUND

International Public Sector Accounting Standards are the best international financial reporting practice used by public sector entities. They apply to general purpose financial statements prepared on an accrual basis or cash accounting, as appropriate. In most cases, the application of IPSAS requirements will lead to an increase in the confidence and transparency of financial reporting by governments and their subordinate structures. The approach of this issue in the national and international literature is extensively investigated as we will report in what will be presented.

The analysis specific to the financial reporting according to the IPSAS was performed by the respective author (Tiron-Tudor, 2010) to determine the extent to which the national accounting system implemented the IPSAS forecasts regarding the financial statements, an objective that was achieved through investigations carried out on the Romanian regulations in correspondence with the IPSASs, both from a theoretical point of view, and the empirical evidence resulting from the main similarities and differences of the respective regulatory documents. The results obtained in this study reported that there is a fairly high degree among the regulations analysed, but with the mention that further developments are still needed, according to which the most correct harmonization will be achieved. Other authors, Nistor & Deaconu (2016) approached this field by associating the adoption of accrual accounting in Romania with the need for international public managerial reform and internal factors.

A series of studies analysed the implementation process of IPSAS and to identify the factors that influenced their adoption. Such a study was undertaken by Antipova & Bourmistrov (2013) and Legenkova (2016) who analysed the accounting reform in Russia and found that the modernization of accounting practices at that time was in full evolution, this being attributed to the continued use of traditional local accounting practices that are cash-oriented and aimed at achieving them in accordance with the paths to be followed. Brusca & Martinez (2015) appreciated that the introduction of IPSAS in the public sector primarily demonstrates a shift from the traditional cash accounting system to the commitment-based accounting system that must be aligned with private sector practice.

The transition to the implementation of standards in international accounting was a complex process that involved important financial and human resources, an aspect also found in their implementation in Romanian public accounting, where Ristea et al. (2010) highlighted the many changes in the field of accounting regulations, aimed at harmonizing with European accounting directives and international accounting standards for the public sector and which have generated advantages and disadvantages in implementation. At the same time, the issue of convergence of public accounting in Romania with IPSAS standards is also found in the paper of other authors (Ilie & Alecu, 2011), whose analysis showed that, although convergence was achieved with the most important IPSAS by selecting some of them, however, there are significant omissions that have an impact on the quality of the information presented in the financial statements.

Among the significant reforms of the New Public Management (NPM), we also find the one that refers to the accounting of commitments that characterized the public sector of many countries. Due to the variety of public financial information systems, there is a need for harmonization with the International Public Sector Accounting Standards (IPSAS). In this regard, through his study Christiaens et al. (2015) examined the extent to which IPSAS accrual accounting has been adopted in central/local governments worldwide and revealed a degree of reluctance, especially at the level of central governments, in developing countries, a similar accrual accounting has been developed.

There are a multitude of studies that examine the performance of accounting reporting after the introduction of IPSAS in the public sector and have ignored investigations into the quality of financial reporting under IPSAS on a cash basis. This was despite the fact that cash-based IPSAS is a standard in the IPSAS provision and was adopted as a first step for countries that intended to make the transition to IPSAS based on commitments (IFAC, 2010). In this context, over time, numerous financial scandals have generated multiple concerns and comments regarding the effectiveness and quality of financial reports prepared by public system entities. Thus, in order to rectify this situation, the implementation of the International Accounting Standards for the Public Sector (IPSAS) has been implemented as the main solution, based on which Maruf et al. (2017) and Mnif & Gafsi (2020), considered it necessary to initiate a new conceptual framework to explains the main factors influencing the quality of financial reporting (FRQ) in a cash based IPSAS accounting system. Thus, their research showed that the possible organizational factors that would act on the practical activity of high-quality financial reporting in the public sector, as a result of the implementation of accounting standards are the quality of internal audit and the competence of accounting staff.

Convinced that the public and private sectors should not be managed differently, there has been widespread debate about the harmonization of public sector accounting systems and their convergence with private sector financial reporting standards, a situation that has created a strong need in the public sector for the implementation of high-quality standards that would substantially contribute to the development of financial reporting. In such a context, Roje et al. (2010) approached in their study an analysis of the state and perspective of public sector accounting and financial reporting in transition countries, in which they proposed an examination of the adequacy and the need for government accounting and financial reporting in the accounting regulations and financial reporting framework of countries such as

Croatia, Bosnia, Slovenia and Herzegovina. The results of this investigation referred to the degree and dynamics of the transformation for the accounting systems of these countries governments which are dependent on a number of specific factors that need to be taken into account when evaluating these systems and conducting various comparative analyses on system reforms of accounting policies implemented in the respective states.

The work of all governments to ensure compliance with IPSAS cash-based requirements is an improvement on transparent and conclusive financial reporting practices in these areas, so as to respond appropriately to the information needs of the various users concerned.

Accounting Harmonization, Implementation of IPSAS Standards and Financial Reporting

Accounting harmonization in the public system seemed out of the need to adopt a common language for financial reporting, which was achieved through the process of accounting standardization. Therefore, it was desired to improve and reduce the differences between national and international accounting regulations and their practices, which aimed at developing principles and rules, in general, to allow comparability of information provided by the content of financial statements of public sector entities (Man & Ciurea, 2016). Precisely in this regard, the harmonization of rules is considered an important means of improving clarity and comparability, leading to the improvement of the evolved decision-making process of the public system, from which stakeholders can make assessments of the performance achieved at the system different levels. Thus, the main benchmark of the accounting system at the level of the public system was the International Accounting Standards for the Public Sector (IPSAS).

With the integration of Romania as a full member of the European Union, a multitude of changes have appeared in the accounting of public institutions, which is why new accounting regulations have been developed in this field, approved by O.M.F.P. no. 2021/2013 and which were based on the international vision on public sector accounting and professional reasoning. From such a perspective, a number of elements of the IPSAS Standards have been included in this regulation. Therefore, by adopting and implementing IPSAS, both the quality and the comparability of financial information reported by public sector entities have been improved, and the management of public finances has been better strengthened, which will lead to a better assessment of resource allocation decisions, with a view to increasing the level of transparency and accountability (Nistor, 2017; Tudor and Crişan, 2017; Ristea et.al., 2010). At the same time, the need to use international practices in the public system aligned with the requirements of the IPSAS Standards appeared in the idea of standardizing the economic policies of various states in order to attract common economic and political interests.

According to some authors (Ciurea, 2018; Pitulice, 2013), the introduction of accrual accounting in the Romanian public sector was not perceived as a necessity and modernization, because it was an obligation imposed by the accession to the European Union. As at that time the political spectrum was involved in the adoption of accrual accounting only as a provider of government members, accrual accounting for public sector entities was introduced by order of finance ministers and not by laws to be approved by the legislature, respectively Parliament. For these reasons, the interest for the implementation of accrual accounting in the public sector was low, because the process was seen only as a necessary condition for harmonizing the Romanian regulations with the European ones, in order to receive the full membership of the European Union.

The reform of public accounting in Romania has had a number of implications at the macroeconomic level, among which we mention: increasing the responsibility of authorizing officers and civil servants; a new analytical development of public accounting; more efficient management of public money; harmonization of the Romanian systems with those of the European Union; transparency of public information, simultaneously with the increase of confidence in the status of civil servant (Nistor & Stefanescu, 2016); the adoption of new principles in public accounting, such as that of prudence aimed at predicting probable losses and the principle of the independence of the years, which implies the obligation in the case of accrual accounting. Therefore, the revolution of the Romanian public accounting system in order to achieve the objective of harmonization with IPSAS standards and compliance with European accounting directives was profound and with multiple implications on the part of all stakeholders.

At the same time, by adopting the IPSAS standards, multiple ***advantages*** have been identified, such as those aimed at:

- significant increase in the quality of financial reporting by public entities;
- more complete information that facilitates the management and administration of resources, the provision of efficient services and the achievement of results;
- increasing the credibility and transparency of the information presented;
- assessment of the responsibility at the level of all the resources that the public entity manages;
- better internal control and greater transparency of assets and liabilities;
- more detailed information on useful costs in facilitating results-based management;
- assessment of the financial situation, performance and cash flows of public entities;

- better consistency and comparability of financial statements due to the fact that each standard requires the presentation of uniform, detailed and specific information;
- making decisions regarding the provision of resources or the development of new activities.

Although those accounting rules were not mandatory, they were implemented by the Member States, but also by the accounting profession, which allowed their interpretation in accordance with the national law of each country. This has led us to believe that the IPSAS international standards are only partially implemented in each Member State, as it cannot be said that they have been fully adopted, as they are dependent on the available resources, the technologies developed, the economy of each state, the diversity of the fields in which they work and the specifics of the public system.

The high degree of transparency required in the application of IPSASs has led to the continuous improvement of the quality of financial reporting of public institutions in order to provide relevant, credible information and, at the same time, to ensure comparability between reporting periods. In their approach to investigating the implementation of IPSAS standards, some authors appreciated that, by even partially applying IPSAS standards in public entities in Romania, they led to increased credibility and transparency of reporting, while increasing the responsibility for costs and financial performance, improved reporting comparability were considered some of the additional benefits.

In this regard, there are several opportunities offered by the implementation of standards, such as avoiding the influence of the political factor on the content of accounting information and the opportunity to provide credibility for information provided to various bodies: European Commission, International Monetary Fund, World Bank. The many benefits of adopting the rules of these standards, which are able to ensure:

- increasing the quality of financial information will generate a number of opportunities in assessing the performance of the budget sector;
- improving the quality of strategic planning, developing budgetary and fiscal policies, managing public finances and increasing the efficiency of the allocation of budgetary resources;
- increasing the integrity of budget, financial accounting and statistical reporting;
- increasing the transparency of financial reporting;
- improving the management of state assets and providing accurate and more complete information;

- ensuring the possibility of comparison with the financial reports of other states;
- the ability to adapt more easily to various new changes.

Regarding the objectives of the financial statements prepared in accordance with IPSAS standards and those prepared in accordance with the statistical basis of financial reporting, they differ in certain respects in the sense that in the first case they provide useful information for decision making and for the resources entrusted to it and which it controls, in the latter case, the purpose is to provide adequate information for the analysis and assessment of fiscal policy. It is clear in this case that IPSAS standards are financial reporting standards developed specifically for governments and other public sector entities, with the primary objective of improving the quality and comparability of general purpose financial statements.

Therefore, accrual-based accounting in which IPSASs are used strengthens accountability by providing a comprehensive picture of government resources and how they have been used, contributing greatly to improving decision-making (Cohen & Karatzimas, 2017). Although IPSAS define the finished product, in this case the financial statements, there is no pre-established way to adopt and implement them, so the quality recommendations and principles allow them to be adapted according to various specific aspects and approach, but which requires that everything must be done in the context of consolidating public financial management.

The traditional financial reporting of public sector entities has focused on the budget as a core component of the financial statement set, the compliance with rules and regulations, and has been based on cash-based accounting principles. At that time, cash accounting corresponded to the information requirements of public sector entities in the context in which it was less involved in the production of goods, the financing of public institutions came largely from the state budget, and the compliance with applicable law was much more important than the effectiveness or quality of the results.

Thus, in the last decades, in order to cope with the constantly evolving economic environment, public entities have had to adapt to the new context. As a result, the shift to a commitment-based accounting system has led to a change in the mindset about the budget process, the transition from a rigid reporting of revenue and expenditure to a reporting that highlights achievements and forecasts for the future (Dabbicco & Mattei, 2020). More and more governments and intergovernmental organizations prepare financial statements based on accrual accounting in accordance with IPSAS or similar standards, considering that the information contained therein is useful for both accountability and decision-making.

The preparation of financial statements in accordance with these standards will allow users to assess the responsibility for all resources controlled by the entity and the use of those resources, assess the financial position, financial performance and cash flows of the entity and make decisions about the provision of resources or their realization. The current economic crisis and the major tax constraints facing some states have highlighted the need for them to report all their assets and liabilities in a transparent manner. Making such a decision in their reporting will improve internal control and provide more detailed cost information, with consequences for more accurate support for results-based management.

As a wide range of transactions are generally common in both the private and public sectors, there has been an attempt at some point to converge IPSAS with International Financial Reporting Standards (IFRS), a situation we find as a rule, in the regard that IPSAS standards maintain the accounting treatment and the original text of IFRSs, but with few exceptions when the situation specific to the public system requires it to deviate from them. The conclusion from the analysis of this aspect is that the current standards are either developed for financial reporting issues for which no adjustments have been made in accordance with an IFRS, or specific IFRS standards have not been developed for this purpose.

The International Public Sector Accounting Standards Board (IPSASB) through the conceptual framework of the International Accounting Standards Board (IASB) responds to the financial reporting needs of public sector entities in order to gain better credibility in this sector. As a result, the IPSASB has recognized that adopting commitment-based financial reporting is the ideal goal for all public financial reporting, but there is still the idea that the adoption of a cash-based IPSAS is a more realistic intermediate goal and has not failed to take into account, links to cash-based budgeting in some places and statistical reporting standards, such as International Monetary Fund government finance statistics (Nicula & Bragadireanu, 2017). In general, it was accepted that the information found in the reports on the basis of commitments is extremely useful, both for public accountability and for making relevant and timely decisions.

Consequently, the financial statements prepared on the basis of commitments will allow users to: assess the responsibilities for all the resources that the entity controls and the use of these resources; assessing the performance, financial position and cash flows of the entity and making decisions regarding the provision of resources or starting a business with that entity (Munteanu et. al., 2014). Also, at a much more detailed level, commitment reporting: shows how the government has financed its activities and met its liquidity needs; enables users to assess the government's continued ability to finance its activities and meet its obligations and commitments; shows the financial position of the government as well as the changes in the financial position; it also provides the government with the opportunity to demonstrate the proper management of its resources, and is also useful in assessing government performance in terms of service costs, efficiency and achievements.

The Specifics of Financial Reporting and Budget Execution in the Romanian Public System

The main purpose of any financial reporting system is to argue the ways in which the government manages its financial resources, revenues and expenditures, assets and liabilities, and is able to meet the following **objectives**: (Nistor, 2011)

- integrity of the budgetary process achieved through use of resources according to established and authorized legislation, obligations and responsibilities; the volume and share of unallocated budget allocations; the volume and structure of expenses engaged, but not incurred;
- functional performances represented by the obtained results; their way and/or their source of funding; the cost of various programs; the way of managing the patrimony by the Government; continuing to maintain obligations in order to maintain the results obtained;
- control systems are those that must ensure compliance with budgetary and financial regulations, the necessary performance, the correct and efficient management of assets.

Financial reporting is a very important tool for policy planning and formulation, which is why they need to provide information about ongoing programs and the main objectives of government ministries and agencies, as well as a source of information for parliament and the general public (Deaconu et. al 2011). Thus, this reporting will have to take into account the needs of various user groups, such as: the Government, ministries, agencies and their subordinate institutions, the leaders of the various programs; the legislature; citizens, the media, companies, universities, NGOs; interest groups, investors and creditors; financial investment institutions and financial markets. As it is known, the various user groups need complete and timely information about the budget.

The executive periodically requests information on the state of budgetary resources, in order to be able to ensure an efficient implementation and evaluation of the comparative costs of the various programs. The legislature and citizens need information about the costs and performance of programs that directly affect them. Financial markets, in turn, use information about the government's financial condition to assess the country's financial soundness and to judge the amount of debt and the appropriate level of interest rates and exchange rates.

Government reports, both for internal and external use, will need to be based on a number of **principles**, including: (Cîrstea et. al., 2017)

- complete, in the regard that the information, in consolidated form, will have to cover all aspects of the government's financial relations;

- legitimate for the form and content of financial reporting to be appropriate for target users and to meet accepted standards;
- easy to use to be understood by all well-informed and interested users to allow a quick search of the information and its easy communication. As not all citizens and legislators are familiar with budgetary concepts and methodological issues, it is necessary to contain additional explanations and interpretations;
- credible to make it easier to understand and verify the information presented;
- relevant in the regard that the information transmitted at the end of the year allows the legislature to control the budget execution. Not infrequently, financial reporting information is loaded with information that is extremely difficult for some users to interpret;
- constant, where established methodologies, purpose and coverage of financial reporting is required both over time and internally, and the established reporting or accounting method will need to be used for all transactions, unless there is a clear reason to change it. If this is necessary, it should be maintained in those reports;
- opportune, the usefulness of information decreases over time, but the value of timely information should not prevent the compilation of statistics and verification of data, even after the publication of preliminary reports;
- useful for all information on activities to be useful both inside and outside, contributing to the understanding of current and future activities, sources and use of funds, financial management of these funds, existing assets and liabilities.

Differentiating between reporting for a specific purpose, designed to meet specific needs, and general financial reporting for a wider audience can help define the presentation and dissemination of these reports (Man & Ciurea, 2017). For example, the reports required to monitor budget implementation are reporting for a specific purpose, and they are used primarily within the administration, while financial statements should be considered general reports. This differentiation is to some extent subjective and is dependent on various contexts and the need to respond to pressure from different interest groups.

With regard to reports on budget implementation, it is necessary to take into account:

- managing budget execution through daily, monthly and other reports;
- the dynamics of budget allocation accounts through an annual budget implementation report, which must be submitted to the Supreme Court of Auditors (Court of Accounts) and the legislature.

At the same time, the financial reporting must comply with certain reporting standards, namely:

- Minimum financial reporting requirements including reports, records and ancillary documents, including:
    - Consolidated general report where the Government will have to publish an analytical report on the consolidated financial operations in which to present the financial operations of the central, local and general administration, as well as those regarding the extra-budgetary funds;
    - The situation of arrears, in which a distinction will be made between arrears vis-à-vis the private sector, vis-à-vis regional entities and vis-à-vis the non-governmental public sector;
    - The summary report on the implementation of the government expenditure program shall cover, for a period of at least two financial years, budget expenditures and funds by functional areas and programs, a distinction between current and capital expenditures, situations from previous years for comparison and estimation to situations in the following years, for multiannual estimates;
    - Report on the medium-term external debt that will contain the remaining debt and the one repaid on account of the medium-term external debt, as well as projections of the debt service costs for the next 5 to 10 years;
    - Report on short-term loans;
    - Report on non-reimbursable external funds;
    - The situation of future commitments;
    - Cash flow statement;
    - The situation of fiscal facilities.
- Financial statements in the accrual-based accounting system will allow for undertakings that give a more complete picture of the financial statements than those presented in the reporting with minimum requirements;
- Administrative coverage of financial reporting refers to the fact that financial reporting must cover all public sector entities;
- Reports on capital investment expenditures on programs or projects;
- Special issues related to externally funded projects in which capital investment reporting will need to include the non-investment component of externally funded projects, so that this information can be used in the case of various funding received from various sponsors. Both the investment component and the current cost component must be separated on each project.

The core indicators of reporting and budget execution include financial operations that reflect *budget performance*, i.e. the analysis of initial budget forecasts compared to final figures and budget variations, *fiscal flexibility* as the extent to which an administrative entity can increase its revenues and reduce its expenditures, in the course of a crisis in order to maintain a balanced budget, without jeopardizing the timely repayment of obligations to creditors, as well as indicators covering aspects of other financial operations.

Considerations Regarding the Benefits of Implementing the Electronic Financial Reporting System "Forexebug"

Increasing the efficiency of public administration, administrative transparency, the use of modern tools for communication and transmission of information are major objectives that are constantly found in the strategies of Romanian public administration (Drăcea et. al., 2016). By implementing this reporting system, modern, standardized tools have been made available to public institutions for reporting financial statements and publishing detailed information on the use of public funds, in accordance with the budget classification and increase the reliability of the data collected by performing cross-validations with system data and providing conclusive information for the internal use of the Ministry of Public Finance (M.F.P.), public institutions, other competent institutions and the public, both at the level of detail as well as consolidated on various levels.

Thus, a new financial reporting methodology was developed, the documents of which are submitted by each reporting entity, in electronic, standardized and secure format, ensuring the electronic mechanisms for aggregating, centralizing, consolidating, reconciling these data on the hierarchies of reporting entities, sources of funding and other dimensions. Therefore, the data on the budget execution of revenues and expenditures are validated in the sense of their inclusion within the limits of the approved budgets and updated programs at the level of each public institution, realizing the automatic validation of payments made through the "Trezor" system, especially, regarding the preparation of budget execution statements and control of commitments by automatically verifying the allocation of the commitment reservation in the available budget.

The transmission of these documents allows that in addition to the centralization of situations, simultaneously the data can be used for multicriteria analysis and time series by interconnecting with the M.F.P. informatics system. Therefore, the major advantage of using the ForExeBug system is obvious, given that the system allows electronic monitoring and control of legal and budgetary commitments, with a direct impact on improving financial discipline and preventing the formation of arrears of public institutions.

The commissioning of this IT system was established by the Framework Loan Agreement with the International Monetary Fund, which would allow the introduction

Figure 1. The beneficiaries of the ForExeBug electronic system, respectively: main authorizing officers (from the central and local public administration), the County Directorates of Public Finance, secondary and tertiary authorizing officers (from the central and local public administration), other public institutions, economic operators with state capital, autonomous public institutions.
Source: Authors

of control elements for the fulfilment of Romania's obligations. As a Member State of the European Union, Romania is committed to applying the standards of economic classification of COFOG level 2 and 3 of the government activities for budget execution reporting, which involve the use of detailed information for approximately 15,000 public institutions and economic operators.

Therefore, financial reporting using the Forexebug system will help to automatically aggregate and consolidate them, accurate data, and reduce processing time. Taken as a whole, all of these will bring many benefits, including:

- improving budget management by reducing the tasks related to reporting activities and creating the possibility of reallocating time for activities in the area of analysis and decision;
- increasing administrative transparency by the fact that public institutions will use the same reporting system, resulting in a database to which any registered user of the ForExeBug system will have access;

- fast and easy centralization of data, as well as increasing the archiving capacity for the details of the financial reports of public institutions by using the electronic archive;
- decreasing the volume of data to be reported by each authorizing officer and at the same time the reduction of working time and related resources, as a result for the decrease of the data to be centralized and reported;
- automatic generation of summary reports based on the data collected and automatic validation of data on budget execution for revenues and expenditures;
- allows the control of the budgetary commitments of the reporting entities and provides the authorizing officers with information on the use of the approved budget at the level of all hierarchically subordinated public institutions;
- Romania's alignment with the accounting standards of the European public administrations, will allow the detailed reporting of the financial execution, to the standards imposed by the U.E. regarding the economic classification of COFOG level II and level III government activities.

Increasing the transparency and efficiency of public money is one of the priority objectives of the M.F.P. which launched an online platform, with the role to contribute to the transparency of expenditures made by public institutions in Romania. The platform is a national system for verifying, monitoring, reporting and controlling the financial statements, legal commitments and budgets of public entities in Romania. Its launching achieves both budgetary transparency and efficiency, by improving the management of budgetary resources and by introducing tools for full and automated budgetary verification and control, where stakeholders have access to various information, such as: number and structure public institutions, aggregate reports, budget, financial-accounting reports, as well as other aggregated information. It is hoped that the platform will be extended to state-owned companies and autonomous utilities.

At the same time, the use of the ForExeBug system has a substantial contribution to consolidated reporting through its benefits, such as: significantly reduced time and effort involved in reporting, automatic generation of consolidated reports, quick and easy access to information, and reconciliation and ensuring the quality of financial reporting data. In conclusion, the implementation of the ForExeBug system guarantees budgetary discipline, clear rules applicable to the system of budgetary accounting and statistical reporting, in line with the requirements of the European Union directives and the IPSAS Standards.

SOLUTIONS AND RECOMMENDATIONS

In the Romanian public system, the need for information and the need to provide comparable and transparent information have resulted in the development and implementation of IPSAS standards through which the quality of information presented in financial reporting is ensured. In order to provide relevant and credible information, it needs to be continuously improved to ensure comparability between reporting periods, between public entities in the country or in different countries, and between national accounts between states. The solution to such a problem is to maintain the formats of the reporting documents in accordance with the requirements of the IPSAS standards, to present additional information when the situation requires it and to continuously develop national rules in this area.

The reform of public accounting in Romania and the implementation of IPSAS standards has brought and continues to bring many benefits to public system entities. For this reason, we consider it justified that it is necessary to further develop this approach, for the realization of which we want to come up with a series of recommendations, such as:

- elaboration of budgetary - fiscal policies according to the results obtained by the public entities in the previous reporting periods;
- strengthening the decision-making process by developing strategies in the field of annual financial reporting;
- increasing the degree of involvement of decision makers in the process of achieving budget revenues and making expenditures;
- correlation of financial information with fiscal information, because not infrequently it has been proven that there are significant differences between them;
- more active involvement of M.F. P. and the Court of Auditors in implementing IPSAS standards to give a boost to the entity's management in terms of their role and importance in the sound management of public funds in accordance with the requirements of accrual accounting;
- the need to improve access to information on the M.F.P. concerning budgetary transparency, as at present it is not yet available to all interested parties;
- the elaboration by the accounting normalizer (M.F.P.) of some regulations, norms or methodologies, within which to be clearly specified the elements from the IPSAS standards that must be found in the financial reports;
- continuous improvement of modern tools for communication and transmission of information through the electronic financial reporting system;

- developing the skills of professional accountants in implementing standards and in the field of information technology for understanding and applying new technologies in recording and transmitting information, through active participation in professional development programs.

FUTURE RESEARCH DIRECTIONS

From the perspective of future research any scientific paper, no matter how profound, has been able to reach all aspects of the issue studied, so its added value is highlighted by the answers to a series of questions that were the basis for determining interest in studying the implementation of financial reporting in the Romanian public system according to the International Accounting Standards (IPSAS), as well as the ability to generate new questions in order to find answers to them as well. In our paper, the approached topic is a rich and complex one, through whose content, even if it is a theoretical-methodological one, we hope that through the approaches, ideas and opinions expressed to contribute to the consolidation of the investigated field, especially at this moment. according to IPSAS standards is evolving. Regarding the prospects of future research, we would like to extend this investigation as an empirical one, in which we will use various econometric models in which to analyze the degree of implementation of all IPSAS standards in the public sector regarding financial reporting, because in the literature national specialty, in the last 5 years no studies have been conducted on this topic. Further research could also focus on a study of the role of professional accountants in understanding and implementing financial reporting according to IPSAS standards, the quality and transparency of which is given by the professionalism of those who develop them.

CONCLUSION

In our opinion, Romania has been and is actively involved in the effort to modernize public sector financial management, so that a commitment-based accounting system is currently applied in all sectors and at all levels of the public system, by taking over and adapting some elements of the IPSAS Standards. The increasing resemblance of public accounting in Romania to that of private entities, from our point of view, has shaped even better the transition to indirect implementation of IPSAS standards, through which the Romanian public system has only gained in terms of maintaining a quality and competitive accounting standard, the existence of an internal control system at the level of each organizational structure, which was imposed by these standards and which will allow the correction of possible malfunctions, while requiring compliance by certifying the accurate picture of financial position, financial performance and the cash flows of public system entities, useful tools in the efficient management of funds and in providing relevant information in the decision-making process.

Therefore, the M.F.P. managed to put in place a high-performance IT service for the financial reporting of public institutions, through which it facilitated the application of the economic classification standards of COFOG level 2 and COFOG level 3 government activities for reporting budget execution, necessary for U.E. reporting. At the same time, the system facilitated the collection of the necessary information in relations with other international financial institutions, ensuring an efficient control of public resources. All these are elements of a pronounced technical character, but they present indispensable working tools, whose in-depth knowledge allows the achievement of new levels of performance in this field. Through this standardizer, the national regulations for accounting, auditing and control for the public sector are elaborated, aiming at achieving convergence on all three levels - national, European and global. Therefore, it becomes absolutely necessary for its work to be supported by other bodies such as the Body of Expert Accountants and Chartered Accountants (CECCAR) through its members, public sector professional accountants, whose activities contribute substantially to the improvement of the accounting and accounting system, financial reporting, and the translation of IPSAS and other standards or recommendations regarding the management of financial reporting in the Romanian public sector.

We can conclude that, by implementing the ForExeBug financial reporting system in the Romanian public system, an electronic mechanism was provided for aggregating, centralizing, consolidating, reconciling data and information on the hierarchies of reporting entities, funding sources and other dimensions has increased the degree of reliability for the data collected and the provision of reliable information for the internal use of the Ministry of Public Finance, public institutions, other competent institutions and the public, both in detail and consolidated at various levels, and has also increased the efficiency of the central public administration and local government and administrative transparency by providing public institutions with modern, standardized tools for financial reporting and the publication of detailed information on the use of public funds, in accordance with the budget classification. We believe that only by using IPSAS standards in high quality financial reporting for the public sector will it be possible to achieve independent assurance and important institutional commitments to support their efficiency as tools for developing public sector financial management in line with current requirements.

REFERENCES

Antipova, T., & Bourmistrov, A. (2013). Is Russian Public Sector Accounting in the Process of Modernization? An Analysis of Accounting Reforms in Russia. *Financial Accountability & Management, 29*(4), 442–478. Advance online publication. doi:10.1111/faam.12021

Brusca, I., & Martınez, J. C. (2015). Adopting international public sector accounting standards: A challenge for modernizing and harmonizing public sector accounting. *International Review of Administrative Sciences International, 0*(0), 1–21.

Christiaens, J., Vanhee, C., Manes-Rossi, F., Aversano, N., & van Cauwenberge, P. (2015). The effect of IPSAS on reforming governmental financial reporting: an international comparison. *International Review of Administrative Sciences (IRAS), 81*(1), 158-177. doi:10.1177/0020852314546580

Cîrstea, A., Nistor, C.S., & Tiron-Tudor, A. (2017). Consolidated financial statements – a new challenge for the public sector administration. *Journal of Economic and Administrative Sciences, 33*(1), 46-65. doi:10.1108/JEAS-04-2016-0012

Ciurea, M. (2018). Considerations on the Need to Implement International Accounting Standards for the Public Sector in Romania. *Annals of the University of Petrosani. Economics, 18*(1), 35–44.

Cohen, S., & Karatzimas, S. (2017). Accounting information quality and decision usefulness of governmental financial reporting. Moving from cash to modified cash. *Meditary Accounting Research, 25*(1), 95–113. doi:10.1108/MEDAR-10-2015-0070

Dabbicco, G., & Mattei, M. (2020). The reconciliation of budgeting with financial reporting: A comparative study of Italy and the UK. *Public Money & Management*, 1–11.

Deaconu, A., Nistor, S. C., & Filip, C. (2011). The Impact of Accrual Accounting on Public Sector Management: An Exploratory Study for Romania. *Transylvanian Review of Administrative Sciences, 32E*, 74–97.

Drăcea, M., Mitu, E. N., & Drăcea, R. (2016). *Elaboration and execution of the public budget* [Elaborarea şi execuţia bugetului public]. Editura Universitaria.

Gokten, S. (Ed.). (2017). Accounting and Corporate Reporting - Today and Tomorrow. IntechOpen. doi:10.5772/66609

Ilie, D., & Alecu, G. (2011). Convergence of public accounting with International Public Sector Accounting Standards (IPSAS) [Convergenţa contabilităţii publice cu Standardele Internaţionale de Contabilitate pentru Sectorul Public (IPSAS)]. *Revista Audit financiar, 10*, 36-43.

IPSASB. (2010). *Conceptual Framework for General Purpose Financial Reporting by Public Sector Entities: Elements and Recognition in Financial Statements*. IPSASB.

Legenkova, M. (2016). International Public Sector Accounting Standards Implementation in the Russian Federation. *International Journal of Economics and Financial Issues, 6*(4), 1304–1309.

Măcriş, M. (2015). *Accounting of public institutions, Edition II revised and added* [Contabilitatea instituţiilor publice, Ediţia a II- a revizuită şi adăugită]. Editura Universitas.

Man, M., & Ciurea, M. (2016). Elements of Corporate Governance Implementation in Romania, in the European Context. *Annals of the University of Petrosani. Economics, 16*(1), 151–166.

Man, M., & Ciurea, M. (2017). The current economic context to measuring performance in the Romanian public system. *Proceedings of the 29th IBIMA on Education Excellence and Innovation Management through Vision 2020: from Regional Development Sustainability to Global Economic Growth,* 370-379.

Maruf, M., Ku Nor Izah Ku, I., & Halimah Nasibah, A. (2017). Contingency for Financial Reporting Quality in the Public Sector under Cash-Basis IPSAS: a Conceptual Approach. *Proceedings of the Global Conference on Business and Economics Research.*

Mnif, Y., & Gafsi, Y. (2020). A contingency theory perspective on the analysis of central government accounting disclosure under International Public Sector Accounting Standards (IPSAS). *Meditari Accountancy Research, 28*(6), 1089-1117. doi/ doi:10.1108/MEDAR-04-2019-0480

Munteanu, V., Tilea, M. D., Bleotu, V., & Zaharia, L. D. (2014). *Accounting and financial reporting to public institutions* [Contabilitatea şi raportarea financiară la instituţiile publice.]. Editura Universitară.

Nicula, V. C., & Bragadireanu, C. (2017). International Accounting Standards for the Public Sector (IPSAS) in Romania [Standardele Internaţionale de Contabilitate pentru Sectorul Public (IPSAS) în Romania]. *Romanian Court of Accounts Journal, 9*, 11–18.

Nistor, C. S. (2011). A New Aproach of conceptual Framework for General Purpose Financial Reporting by Public Sector Entities. *Annals of Faculty of Economics*, *1*(2), 603–609.

Nistor, C. S., & Stefanescu, C. A. (2016). New approaches in public sector reporting at European Union level. *Studia Universitatis Babeş-Bolyai Oeconomica*, *61*(2), 49–66.

Nistor, S. C. (2017). European Union under the pressure of creating a competitive public accounting system. *International Journal of Competitiveness*, *1*(2), 136–154. doi:10.1504/IJC.2017.084726

Pitulice, C. (2013). Adoption of accrual accounting in the public sector in Romania [Adoptarea contabilităţii de angajamente în sectorul public din România]. *Revista Romana de Statistica*, *1*, 55–65.

Ristea, M., Jianu, I., & Jianu, I. (2010). Romania's experience in applying international financial reporting standards and international accounting standards for the public sector [Experienţa României în aplicarea standardelor internaţionale de raportare financiară şi a standardelor internaţionale de contabilitate pentru sectorul public]. *Revista Transilvană de Ştiinţe Administrative*, *12*(25), 169–192.

Roje, G., Vašiček, D., & Vašiček, V. (2010). Accounting regulation and IPSAS implementation: Efforts of transition countries toward IPSAS compliance. *Journal of Modern Accounting and Auditing*, *6*(12), 1–16.

Tiron-Tudor, A. (2010). Romanian Public Institutions Financial Statements on the way of Harmonization with IPSAS. *Accounting and Management Information Systems*, *9*(3), 422–447.

Tudor, A.T., & Crişan, A. (2017). IPSAS elements found in the Romanian accounting regulations for the public sector – Formal harmonization (I) and (II) [Elemente IPSAS regăsite în reglementările româneşti de contabilitate pentru sectorul public – Armonizarea formală (I) şi (II)]. *Expertiza şi auditul afacerilor, 36*, 37.

ADDITIONAL READING

Nistor, C. S., & Deaconu, A. (2016). Public accounting history in post-communist Romania. *Economic Research Journal*, *29*(1), 623–642.

Wise, V. (2010). Theory and Accountability: The Case of Government Consolidated Financial Reporting. *International Review of Business Research Papers*, *6*(5), 82–97.

KEY TERMS AND DEFINITIONS

C.E.C.C.A.R.: Body of Expert Accountants and Certified Accountants in Romania.

Court of Auditors: The Supreme Public Sector Audit Institution.

"ForExeBug": National financial reporting system.

IPSAS: International Public Sector Accounting Standards.

M.F.P.: Ministry of Public Finance, the Romanian accounting normalizer.

"Treasury": A system that automatically validates payments for budget execution in the ForExeBug system.

Chapter 7
Sustainable Sources of Reducing HR Costs in the Pandemic Time:
E-Recruitment and Nonfinancial Compensation – A Mathematical and Accounting-Based Approach

Nicoleta Valentina Florea
Valahia University of Targoviste, Romania

Constantin Aurelian Ionescu
https://orcid.org/0000-0001-6063-2921
Hyperion University of Bucharest, Romania & Valahia University of Targoviste, Romania

Marinela Daniela Manea
Valahia University of Targoviste, Romania

Mariana Zamfir
https://orcid.org/0000-0002-6906-0664
Valahia University of Targoviste, Romania

Mihaela Denisa Coman
https://orcid.org/0000-0002-5070-5303
Valahia University of Targoviste, Romania

Sorina Geanina Stanescu
Valahia University of Targoviste, Romania

DOI: 10.4018/978-1-6684-4595-2.ch007

ABSTRACT

In a world where use of technology is not an option but a necessity, where new forms of work appear constantly, where change is everywhere and people must keep their distance from each other due to the pandemic, organizations must adapt and use new processes governed by using new technologies. In a sustainable environment, e-recruitment and non-financial compensations become the new tools to maintain performance and lower costs during a pandemic. Using bibliometric analysis, regression function, and correlation matrix, the authors obtained results for Romania and the top three countries, which indicated that e-recruitment is influenced by the use of the internet and availability of computers and productivity; the relations and the correlation between the analyzed variables are measured using simulation and mathematical modeling. The results indicate that there are benefits for individuals, for organizations, and also for environmental protection.

INTRODUCTION

Using the Internet, the online recruitment process is getting real results for individuals and for organizations. Using the Internet for recruitment is a great and challenging opportunity, but its practical use is still up for debate. The official recruitment site of organizations may attract and retain the right candidates. At the same time, using recruitment agencies may be challenging even though it has real results during these times. Employees and candidates are the beneficiaries of using e-recruitment, according to the 24/7/365 principle. According to specialists in the HR field, during a pandemic, life, health, and business community are affected, and not just short term. A study made by CIPD in 2006, showed that 75% of employers used e-recruitment to reduce costs, so e-recruitment seems to be an efficient tool to manage this period affected by COVID-19. Researchers said that companies who used e-recruitment decreased their expenses by almost 88%, compared to the traditional method (Vatansever, 2017).

This paper analyzes the recruitment process under the influence of the Internet, the advantages, and disadvantages of e-recruitment from the two points of view: the individuals and the organization, and the factors which influence the e-recruitment efficiency. The study has other important objectives, such as identifying the many advantages of e-recruitment in pandemic time for candidates, for organizations, and for the environment, developing a plan based on e-recruitment as a source of reducing costs within the pandemic context, and developing a plan based on nonfinancial compensation during the pandemic for sustainable organizations and green candidates.

Interestingly, using a bibliometric analysis, and the mathematical modeling made on a group of analysis, yielded results that indicate there are benefits for individuals, for organizations, but also for environment protection. The implications of using sustainable HR processes based on reducing costs in pandemic times occur at individual level, at managerial level (by implementing the best HR practices along with green HR practices), and at environment level (by implementing green HR practices and green activities with long term effects).

The introduction described the recruitment process under the influence of the Internet. There are both benefits and disadvantages. The Methodology contains two points of view necessary to understand the importance of e-recruitment: on a theoretical level and on a practical level. The research was done using secondary data collected from: Web of Science and Scopus database, and data from EU level in order to make an analysis and to observe the relations between the analyzed variables and the correlation between e-recruitment and the factors which influence the adoption of this process. The analysis focused on four countries: Romania, and the top three European countries (France, Germany, and Spain) to observe the difference between them and make plans for improvement. A regression function and modeling were used in order to perceive a future performance. The findings of this research indicate that e-recruitment is influenced by the use of the Internet and some other activities mentioned and analyzed in this article; the relations and the correlation between the analyzed variables were measured using simulation and mathematical modeling. A plan for financial compensation as a good practice in pandemic time is developed, and some important conclusions were drawn.

BACKGROUND

Human capital is perceived as the most valuable asset of an organization. Attracting, retaining, and growing the human capital asset became a strategic objective for efficient organizations. Recruitment is a strategic process which helps firms attract and retain talented staff. In a world where technology's impact is expanding every day, new processes appeared which help employees and companies, including e-recruitment. If those interested in this process have a computer with an internet connection, they can communicate globally and recruit efficiently (Fielding, 2005). The Internet is becoming the most used communication tool in the world (Newsome, 2007) and especially in this time.

Recruitment is a strategic activity (Barraud et al., 2008), seen as the most visible outside the company (Cadin et al., 2009), and the entire performance of the company depends on its efficiency. By attracting talented candidates (van Esch et al., 2021;

Guillot-Soulez, 2009), learning how to retain them (Sims, 2002) and analyzing their knowledge objectively (Lakhdar et al., 2001), a company will obtain a competitive advantage in a changing environment (Cornet & Warlaud, 2008).

Mabuza (2019) added that the pandemic is having an impact on life, health, and business community. To overcome this, comapnies' leadership may implement an integrated response strategy. In our case, organizations can continue activity and may bring on new employees by using e-recruitment. Even if there is a health crisis, COVID_19, companies are still looking for a talented candidate, using e-recruitment (Meah & Sarwar, 2021). Implementation of technologies in the recruitment process is now a necessity for companies who want to obtain a competitive brand image and enter the niche market of searching for the adequate candidates (D'Silva, 2020). A study made by CIPD in 2006, showed that 75% of employers used e-recruitment to reduce costs (Bondarouk et al., 2011) and another research on 2,336 companies from 23 European countries revealed that two-thirds of all the analyzed organizations had already adopted e-HRM (Nguti & Mose, 2021).

Attracting talented candidates is an important issue and it depends on the most adequate recruitment sources (Armstrong, 2006). Recruitment is, in reality, a marketing job (Maurer & Liu, 2007), and this is the reason why e-recruiters must continue collaborating on "the creation of a virtual recruiting environment" in order to attract and retain talented staff and obtain long-term competitive advantage for the organization. Using the internet for recruitment is the most recent important technique in the field (Torrington et al., 2005), but its significance and use are topics for analysis.

Salehi (2009) wrote "The internet has made a new competitive environment for businesses to rethink and adapt technology to increase effectiveness and efficiency of the business processes". Nowadays, a life without internet is an isolated life. The internet plays a major role in changing everything around (Ghazzawil & Accoumeh, 2014).

Online recruitment helps organizations to meet the ever-changing HR needs to fill positions with dynamic and competent human resources. (Parry & Tyson, 2008a). There are many large organizations that are adopting online recruitment as a competitive strategy (Berry, 2005). The Internet is considered the latest tool in hiring (Kapse et al., 2015). This section on literature review touches on different theories relevant to our research.

A few articles tried to identify Internet recruitment techniques, methods and empirical models from relevant literature (Tyagi, 2012; Priyadarshini et al., 2017b); Singh, 2017; Fred & Kinange, 2018; Sherkar, 2012), to identify the changing trends for efficient hiring sources (Sinha & Thaly, 2013), their role and need for knowledge in organizations and for social networks in recruitment (Silva et al., 2017), the impact on the recruitment process (Sherkar, 2012; Sinha & Thaly, 2013), to describe their benefits (Sharma, 2014; Tyagi, 2012; Singh, 2017), if they are challenging for managers or influence the recruitment decision making and the development of the organization, or if they are attractive for potential and talented employees (Malik & Ullah, 2013), or to determine e-recruitment effects on organizational creativity and innovation (Cross, 2018).

In 2014 a research identified the influential factors that affect the success of using online recruitment instead of traditional recruitment and measured the effectiveness of each factor (Ghazzawi1 & Accoumeh, 2014). The main scope of Hada & Gairola (2015) was to discover the trends of e-recruitment and describe a few of the opportunities and challenges that candidates and recruitment specialists are facing in using e-recruitment methods. Mindia & Hoque K.'s (2018) study aimed to identify how e-recruitment and the internet are influencing the overall recruitment process, using a statistical analysis in order to analyze the relationship between these variables; the results of the study were to continue using e-recruitment to hire candidates by matching the strategy to the global environment.

Many other papers tried to identify the insights of e-recruitment: by showing the role of e-recruitment agencies (Galanaki, 2002); by exploring how accurate it is possible to assess candidate competency and personality traits based on their appearance (Zakrizevska & Litvina, 2016); by showing that the internet and a website are necessary to develop a strong new relationship between a brand and the candidates (Kapse et al., 2015); by investigating the effect of e-recruitment on the design of the recruitment process (Holm, 2012); through the prism of its advantages and disadvantages (Zin & Jaafar, 2016); by developing a scale to measure the benefits for companies (Badr & Aboul-Ela, 2014); by creating a job description for the online recruiter, suggesting new tasks, skills and qualifications for the traditional recruiter, with the purpose of transforming the traditional recruiter in an online recruiter (Boscai, 2017); by giving an overall assessment of the effectiveness of using the internet to recruit and select talented candidates (Gopalia, 2011); by determining what the most successful online recruitment platforms are, to find out what people need, which one is used most often and what they can provide for a better experience (Rosoiu & Popescu, 2016); by evaluating the intention to use e-recruitment which reveals: enjoyment, usefulness, and ease of use (Alsultanny & Alotaibi, 2015); job seekers' attitude which depends on the website's playfulness and usefulness (Priyadarshini et al., 2017b); efficiency and user-friendliness necessary to bring satisfaction (Sylva & Mol, 2009); informational characteristics of the website which influence the job seekers' pursuit intention (Priyadarshini et al., 2019); perceived usefulness and behavioral intention for using the Internet as a job search tool (Karim et al., 2015); subjective experience and perception of social media as a source of recruitment (Priyadarshini et al., 2017a; Ansari & Khan, 2020).

E-RECRUITMENT: CONCEPT, TOOLS, AND BENEFITS

The term online recruitment or e-recruitment implies using formal sourcing of job information online. E-recruitment can be defined as "the use of any technology to attract, select or manage the recruitment process" (Parry & Tyson, 2008b). E-recruiting is a method based on using web-based resources (Pande & Basak, 2015) and a part of electronic Human Resource Management (e-HRM). It is known as one of the most popular e-HRM applications used by organizations (Ghazzawi1 & Accoumeh, 2014). The term "E-recruitment" comprises an "e" from "electronic" and "recruitment" (Sills, 2014) and is involved in finding, attracting, assessing, interviewing, and procuring new talents (Singh, 2017). Muduli & Trivedi (2020) defined e-recruitment as recruiting candidates from job portals, career websites, and social networking sites that afford an alternative option.

E-recruitment tools: (i) websites - a study made on 820 people in 2017 indicated that the most used recruitment methods are: first and foremost websites (74%), followed by professional networks (LinkedIn with 60% and Facebook with 40%), Commercial job boards (58%), followed a great distance by the traditional recruitment method (Wilkinson & Dundon, 2021); (ii) The group of social networking sites (GSNS) is used for recruitment (Aqeel & Siddiqui, 2019) and keeps site users connected more than any other group. It's very used nowadays, since two out of three internet users visit it and it continues to expand (Mohammad et al., 2020). The most used and popular GSNS are Facebook and LinkedIn (Hosain & Liu, 2020; Kaur & Arianayagam, 2020). GSNS allows users to interact by building profiles with personal information, inviting contacts and peers to access those profiles, and exchanging texts with each other (Meah & Sarwar, 2021); (iii) job sites - these are processed and operated by specialized forms and can contain over 100,000 vacancies with 6-7 million CVs registered per month. Organizations pay to publish vacancies on these sites, which are usually not directly linked to agencies; (iv) agency sites - candidates register their CV online but will have detailed discussions in front of a commission, for the employer; (v) media sites - may contain a copy of an advertisement made in the press but may include an additional description of the station and the company (including its official website); (vi) interactive webpage or panel interviews - many organizations have implemented this type of recruitment and are aimed especially at students (eg Tesco) (Stredwick, 2000); (vii) E-college recruitment - managers now use email and website to transfer information needed by students to persuade them to apply for a position. Electronic programs identify the CVs that fit the job without too much financial effort. Online technical skills testing is now done before interviewing any candidate. Electronic profiles allow candidates to apply without an updated CV; (viii) CV-teque is a database that consists of existing CVs on the Internet (Guillot-Soulez, 2009); it's a bank of CVs which enables the search for candidates based on using multi-criterion (Berg & McCoy, 2012); (ix) employment blogs: some candidates choose to submit their CV on blogs, and some sites offer services for recruiting and managing these blogs; (x) SMS recruitment: the use of SMS in recruitment started in France; this method is used in particular for last minute recruitment for a vacancy, or for certain specialized jobs or for mass recruitment; it can replace e-mail recruitment, due to spam perception, is accorded more attention on mobile phone, it's cheaper than mail and phone contacts (Callegaro et al., 2015), it's instant, 1-to-1 message (Headworth, 2015), and it uses the world's biggest platforms such as WhatsApp or Facebook Messenger. Using both a SMS as a prenotification and an email for invitation will perform better; (xi) virtual professional networks refer to existing sites on the Internet that create professional recruitment networks (e.g. Viadeo, Xing); (xii) job dating - the method is often combined with other recruitment methods: several organizations gather on the same site and connect quickly with candidates in order to convince them to submit their resume as soon as possible (Benchemam & Galindo, 2009); (xiii) speed dating - allows the meeting between candidates and the recruitment team in the shortest time possible (Benchemam & Galindo, 2009), where the specialists may instantly like a candidate for the candidate's charm, attitude, or behavior (Billsberry, 2008).

Advantages of Using E-recruitment

E-recruitment offers many important benefits both for individuals and organizations, which are mentioned below by different specialists in the field: reduces searching time, improves speed (Sherkar, 2012), is cost efficient (Bournois et al., 2007; Galanaki, 2002; Florea, 2013; Armstrong, 2006), and offers a transparent method of information for candidates (Salmen, 2012); offers the opportunity to reach a larger set of potential employees and facilitate the selection process (Singh, 2017); offers geographical spread, gets to a larger audience (Bartram, 2006; Galanaki, 2002); finds the right candidate faster and with a greater effectiveness (Galanaki, 2002; Anand & Devi, 2016); is relatively cheap (Galanaki, 2002; Doran, 2001) and the most effective way for recruitment, reducing the costs by 85% (Bach, 2005); offers a higher quality for those making an application (Bartram, 2000), and also for smaller firms, to target a larger and more diverse pool of candidates; reduces the use of paper and printing (Doran, 2001); reduces the number of intermediaries (Hopkins, 2003); offers great productivity (Bournois et al., 2007), helps find many qualified employees (Bondarouk, 2009) and also has international access (Galanaki, 2002), new ideas and knowledge everywhere in the world; creates a preview for applications (Hopkins & Markham, 2003); is a new manner in receiving the resumes (Guillot-Soulez, 2009), based on using specific keywords (Hada & Gaiola, 2015; Armstrong, 2006); may offer a broad reach of job seekers (Posthumus, 2015); offers valuable and updated info for the candidates (Doran, 2001); is searching for new methods, such as using spontaneous resumes (Guillot-Soulez, 2009), even for passive candidates; helps reduce the number of unqualified candidates (Kapse et al., 2015); offers automatic processing of data, up to date, and modern image (Sharma, 2014).

Disadvantages of Using E-recruitment

Besides the many advantages presented above, there are also some disadvantages of e-recruitment, such as:

- **Disadvantages for organizations/employers:** fake profiles, high fees for access, lack of personal touch (Hada & Gaiola, 2015); poor segmentation of the market, net overwhelmed, discrimination towards nonusers, privacy issues (Sharma, 2014); vast pool of applicants, non-serious applicants, disclosure of information (Karim et al., 2015), which contributes to the dehumanization of the labor market; companies are invaded by an increased volume of CVs (Bondarouk et al., 2011), which implies higher costs (Torrington et al., 2005), and is time consuming (Kapse, 2015); corporate name recognition required and increased number of unqualified candidates (Galanaki, 2002);
- **Disadvantages for job seekers:** impersonal method, privacy issues (Bartram, 2000), outdated job posting, no response from companies, not suitable for all types of jobs (Hada & Gaiola, 2015); lack of human contact and transparency of data (Sharma, 2014); requires being computer savvy, legal consequences for using negative words or discrimination (Karim et al., 2015), lack of experience in using a recruitment website; the limited access of potential candidates due to some factors: age (this category is not prepared compared to the new "digital generation" (Bondarouk, 2009); many ads are not real (Torrington et al., 2005), outdated CVs; internet might not be the first option for applicants (Armstrong, 2006).

E-RECRUITMENT AND ITS FACTORS OF INFLUENCE

There are many factors that may have an influence on e-recruitment. According to Scarpello (2008), e-recruitment is influenced by reduced costs compared to the traditional method and by the access to personal computers, but also by age, education level and disabilities. Tsiakis (2015) adds that online recruitment adoption is influenced by technology development, content, interaction, learning, control, ethics, and privacy. Among many limiting factors in implementing e-recruitment we have: firstly, the cultural approach, secondly, the lack of knowledge and thirdly the internet usage (Tyagi, 2016). Banyiai (2019) said that using e-recruitment s depends on the socio-economic status of the candidates (sex, age, income, and computer skills) but also on the job market evolution. It also depends on IT infrastructure (internet access and evolution, use of internet, technology trend as website design, usefulness, ease of use and attraction, and number of personal computers) (Machado & Davim, 2019), on cultural values, personal relationships, and control (Gueutal & Stone, 2015). A study made in 2018 showed that from the perceived advantages of e-recruitment, the most important are the cost, the accessibility, large pool of candidates, time, and speed (the others obtained a much lower score). The most important three factors were analyzed below.

Internet Use

The main advantage of using the internet for communication is communication with anybody connected to the internet, anywhere in the world. As it can be observed, in the last years there has been an explosion of internet users (Table 1).

As we may observe, the number of internet users in 2021 compared to 2000 increased by 1322%; the biggest increase was in Europe by 570%, then in Australia by 273%, North America by 219%. Penetration rate is as follows: in North America - 93.9%, Europe -88.2%, Middle East - 74.9%, Latin America/Caribbean -75.6%, Oceania/Australia -69.9%, Asia -63.8%, and Africa -43.2%; thus, the world penetration rate in 2021 is 65.6% compared to 2020 -58.7%. This exponential growth is due to the constraints related to globalization. Physical persons and companies do not allow a technological fracture in this changing and global market. Internet penetration in Romania has seen an increase over the years as well (Table 2).

In Europe, Russia has the largest internet market at over 110 million users (in 2020), while Germany is the second with nearly 73 million users followed by Turkey and the United Kingdom. As for internet growth, Bulgaria, Cyprus and Latvia registered the biggest increase between 2017 and 2020. The best potential for internet growth is registered in southern Europe (Johnson, 2021).

Availability of Computers

Computers (PCs) are very important forworking, learning, studying, or recruiting. The total computing market is expected to grow annually by 0.6% in Europe, reaching 105.2 billion U.S. dollars in 2020, while the laptop and tablet market is expected to grow annually by 0.9% (Alsop, 2021). The computer market generated 59.2 bill US dollars in Europe in revenue in 2021, compared to 57.12 in 2020 or 57.67 in 2016, showing a continuous increase (Alsop, 2021).

Table 1. Internet users in the world

Year	Internet World Users	Growth (%)
2000	414,794,957	6.8
2001	502,292,245	8.1
2002	665,065,014	10.6
2003	781,435,983	12.3
2004	913,327,771	14.2
2005	1,030,101,289	15.8
2006	1,162,916,818	17.6
2007	1,373,226,988	20.6
2008	1,575,067,520	23.3
2009	1,766,403,814	25.8
2010	1,966,514,816	444.8
2012	2,405,518,376	566.4
2014	3,035,749,340	741.0
2015	3,366,261,156	832.5
2016	3,675,824,813	918.3
2017	4,145,932,140	1052.0
2018	4,208,571,287	1066.0
2019	4,574,150,134	1,167.0
2020	4,929,926,187	1,266.0
2021	5,168,780,607	1,331.9

Source: (Internet world stats, 2021)

Table 2. Internet penetration in Romania/EU-28 countries (2000-2021)

Year	in RO	in EU-28 Countries
2000	3.6%	30%
2004	18.7%	57%
2007	23.9%	60%
2010	35.5%	70%
2012	44.1%	76%
2015	56.8%	83%
2021	73.8%	88%

Source:(Internet Live Stats, 2016; Internet world stats, 2021; Statista, 2020)

Switzerland leads the world with 65 personal computers per 100 residents. Luxembourg has 46 personal computers per capita. Norway has 49 personal computers per capita, one of the highest rates in Europe, 51 in Denmark and Sweden own a personal computer (Sawe, 2017).

Labor Productivity

By only attracting talented candidates, the company will obtain sustainable competitive advantage. The costs of recruitment and selection grow at the same time with the level of experience and the job specialization (Billsberry, 2007). The efforts made for the recruitment process is very expensive (Sims, 2002). The cost of recruitment is considered to be directly proportional to the productivity of the organization (Bovenberg & Zaidi, 2010). Analyzing the trend between 2005 and 2020 at EU level there is a stagnation, even a slow decrease of labor productivity per person employed and hour worked (101.6 in 2005 and 100 in 2020). In Romania, this labor productivity has almost doubled (from 36.7 in 2005 to 74.7 in 2020). Compared to the evolution of e-recruitment at EU27 level there has been an evolution from a value of 11 in 2006 to 17 in 2020 and in Romania from 3 in 2006 to 6 in 2020. We will observe the correlation between these variables in the research study below.

RESEARCH METHODOLOGY

Theoretical Interest in E-recruitment

To observe the interests of researchers in the topic of e-recruitment, the content of published articles in the database available in Web of Science and Scopus was analyzed. In Web of Science data base 265 articles were published between 1992 and 2021 and in the Scopus database 347 articles were published between 1970 and 2021.

Analyzing the 265 articles on e-recruitment published on Web of Science, and using VOS viewer it represents the map of the countries who published in this field (Figure 1); it is noted the interest for this field of three European countries from the top ten countries (France with 22 articles, Spain 15 articles, and Germany with 11 articles), besides USA (71 articles), Canada (19 articles), England (18), Australia (17), India (14), Malaysia (13), and China (10).

From the Scopus database, USA has published 69 articles, India 29, France 26, UK 24, Canada 20, Australia 15, Germany 15, China 14, Malaysia 14, and Spain 13.

Analyzing the two graphical representations (Figure 2), the common keywords for the two databases are: for Scopus (e-recruitment, human, manpower, feasibility, motivation) and for Web of Science (e-recruitment, growth, performance, impact, strategy).

Figure 1. Published articles in Web of Science on countries

Figure 2. representation of keywords used in the published articles in Web of Science and in Scopus

Figure 3. Graphical representation of the first authors on e-recruitment

Figure 4. Published articles in Scopus on e-recruitment in the four analyzed countries (<2007-2021)

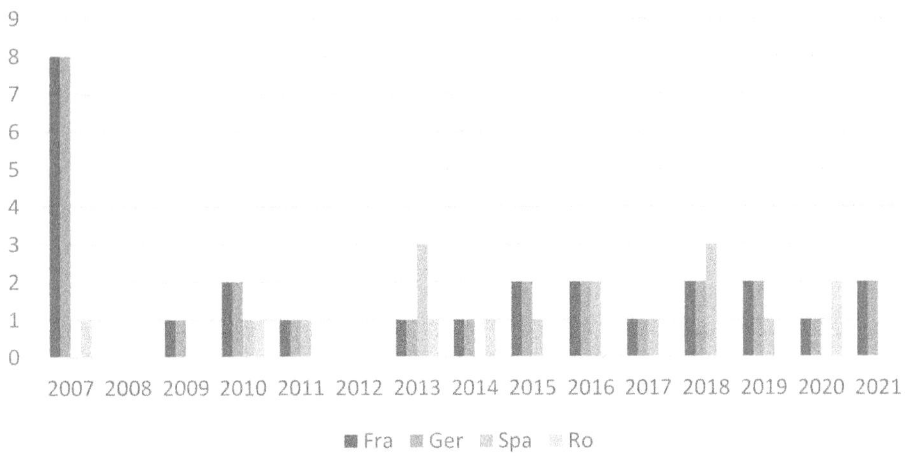

From this graphical representation (Figure 3) and the Scopus database we see that Fagliagka E. is on the first place with 8 articles, followed by Martinez Gil J. (6), Rigou M. (5), Trichet F. (5), Tzakalidis A. (5), Tzimas G. (5), Fallery B., Girard A., Holm A.B., and Malherbe E., each with 4 articles.

Table 3. Articles published on e-recruitment in the four analyzed countries in Scopus and Web of Science

Scopus	**<2007**	**2008**	**2009**	**2010**	**2011**	**2012**	**2013**	**2014**	**2015**	**2016**	**2017**	**2018**	**2019**	**2020**	**2021**	**Total**
RO	1			1			1	1						2		6
FRA	8		1	2	1		1	1	2	2	1	2	2	1	2	26
GER	8				1		2				1			1	2	15
SPA				1	1		3		1	2	1	3	1			13
T																60
Web of Science	**<2007**	**2008**	**2009**	**2010**	**2011**	2012	**2013**	**2014**	**2015**	**2016**	**2017**	2018	**2019**	**2020**	**2021**	**Total**
RO					1		1	2		1	1			2		8
FRA	6		1		1			1	2	2	3	1	2	1	2	22
GER	4				1		1			1	1			1	2	11
SPA				1	1		3		1	2	1	3	2		1	15
T																56

The first three European countries were, in both analyzed data bases, France, Germany, and Spain. Thus, the comparison method between these three top countries and Romania in articles published in e-recruitment topics was used (Table 3).

Below are the two situations for the four countries for Web of Science and Scopus on e-recruitment topics (Figure 4 and Figure 5).

As can be seen, Romania registered the lowest level in publishing articles in the field of e-recruitment out of all four countries, the maximum number of articles - only two were published in 2020 (registered in Scopus/Web of Science data base).

The first year when an article on e-recruitment was published in Romania in these two databases was 2007 by Chis G. et al and for Web of Science and 2011 by Ionescu B. et al for Scopus; the second being published by one of the authors of this chapter, formed by the team Florea N.V. and Badea M. in 2013.

There is a decreased interest in publishing in this field, due to the different factors which influence this field (such as factors which are taken in analysis for practical interest - as in our case internet use, availability of computers).

Figure 5. Published articles in Web of Science e-recruitment in the four analyzed countries (<2007-2021)

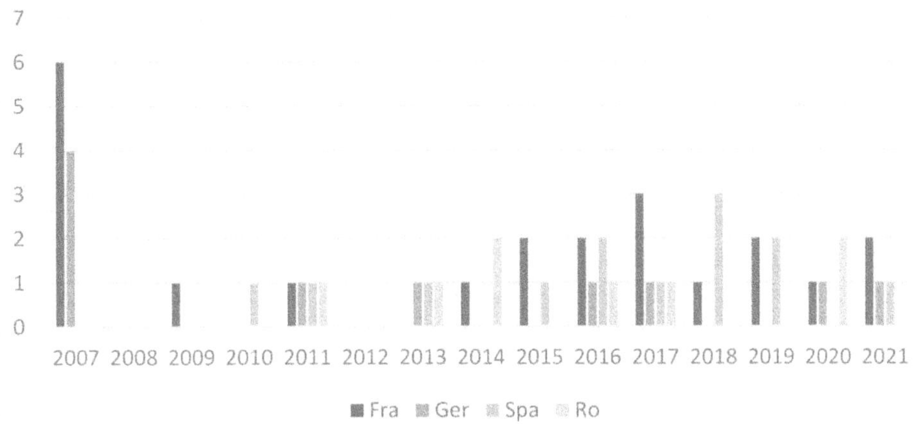

Practical Interest in E-recruitment

- **Goal:** to examine the impact some factors could have on e-recruitment and to determine the correlation between e-recruitment and its influential factors.
- **Data collection**: data was collected from EU level, from four analyzed countries - Romania and three countries considered the best in class for e-recruitment, due to the above points of view, in order to make a comparison and to observe the gap and implement some plans to improve the existing recruitment practices.
- **Tools**: the tools used in this research were statistical methods such as the Pearson coefficient and correlation test in order to observe the relations between the analyzed variables and compare the values for Romania with the other three top countries; the modeling - regression function and Excel-Data Analysis were used.

Research hypotheses:

- **Hypothesis One:** There is a relationship between e-recruitment and the analyzed variables.
- **Hypothesis Two:** There is a correlation between e-recruitment and these factors of influence which impact the overall performance.
- **Hypothesis Three:** E-recruitment is directly proportional with labor productivity.

Analysis of Relationship Between E-recruitment and Internet Use, Availability of PCs, and Labor Productivity per Person

Sampling: data about e-recruitment, internet use, availability of computers and labor productivity per person was used from the four analyzed EU countries between 2010 and 2020, in order to make a comparison and to observe the difference between Romania and the three top EU analyzed countries.

A graphical representation was used to observe the differences between the compared countries and then a regression function for modeling the analyzed variables was applied (Table 4).

As can be seen from the graphic above (Figure 6), analyzing the e-recruitment process at the analyzed group level, the three countries considered the top increased their values over time, only Romania reduced its values, especially during the pandemic, when e-recruitment was a necessity for individuals and organizations. This indicates that organizations reduced the number of recruited persons in this period

Figure 6. E-recruitment 2010-2020 in France, Germany, Spain, and Romania

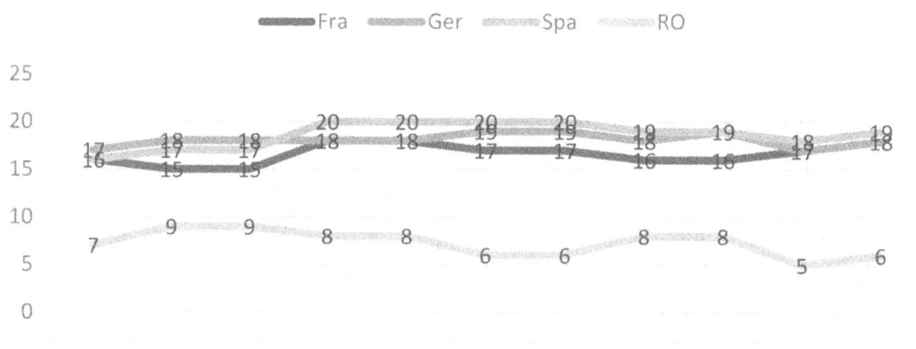

Figure 7. Internet usage 2010-2020 in France, Germany, Spain and Romania

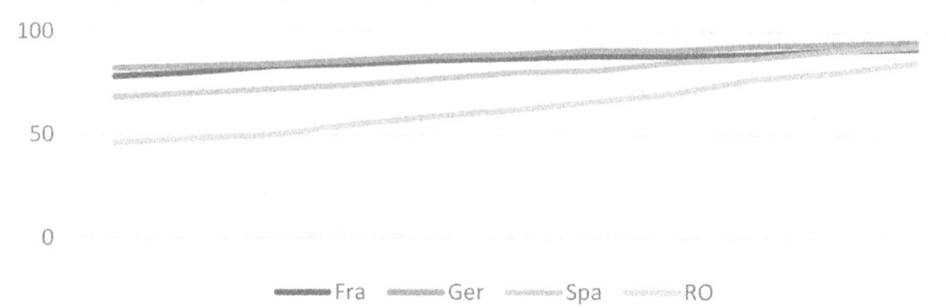

Table 4. Data about the analyzed variables on the four countries

Year	Y (e-recr)				X1- I use				X2- avail of PC				X3- lab prod/pers			
	Fra	Ger	Spa	RO	Fra	Ger	Spa	RO	Fra	Ger	Spa	RO	Fra	Ger	Spa	RO
2010	16	17	16	7	78	82	68	46	76	86	67	48	117.4	104.8	102.1	53.2
2011	15	18	17	9	80	83	70	48	78	87	70	51	116.7	106.0	101.1	54.6
2012	15	18	17	9	83	84	72	50	81	89	73	57	115.6	105.2	103.1	55.5
2013	18	18	20	8	84	86	74	55	82	89	73	61	117.0	104.5	103.6	56.3
2014	18	18	20	8	86	88	77	59	82	91	76	69	116.4	106.5	103.5	56.9
2015	17	19	20	6	87	89	80	62	84	93	78	73	115.8	105.3	102.3	58.6
2016	17	19	20	6	88	91	81	66	85	95	80	77	115.5	106.0	102.0	63.0
2017	16	18	19	8	88	91	85	70	86	96	82	81	114.7	106.3	101.9	66.0
2018	16	19	19	8	89	93	87	77	88	97	84	83	115.3	105.8	99.8	68.4
2019	17	17	18	5	91	94	91	80	90	98	86	85	117.5	103.7	97.9	72.6
2020	18	18	19	6	92	95	93	85	92	99	88	87	114.8	103.6	95.7	74.7

Source: (Eurostat, 2020; Eurostat, 2021a; Eurostat, 2021b; Eurostat, 2021c)
Note: missing data from the official statistics, was added as an yearly average.

Table 5. Summary output for the four analyzed countries

Regression Statistics	France	Germany	Spain	Romania
Multiple R	0.678	0.628	0.792	0.589
R Square	0.459	0.395	0.627	0.347
Adjusted R Square	0.228	0.136	0.467	0.068
Standard Error	0.984	0.651	1.045	1.301
Observations	11	11	11	11

and continued to use traditional recruitment methods instead of all the advantages brought by e-recruitment.

Even if internet usage increased for Romania (Figure 7), almost reaching the values of the other three countries, organizations and individuals maintained low values for the e-recruitment process.

As seen from this graphical representation (Figure 8), in 2010 the difference between the analyzed countries was double, and just in 10 years, Romania almost reached the same values obtained by France, Germany, and Spain for computer availability.

Figure 8. Households- availability of PCs 2010-2020 in France, Germany, Spain and Romania

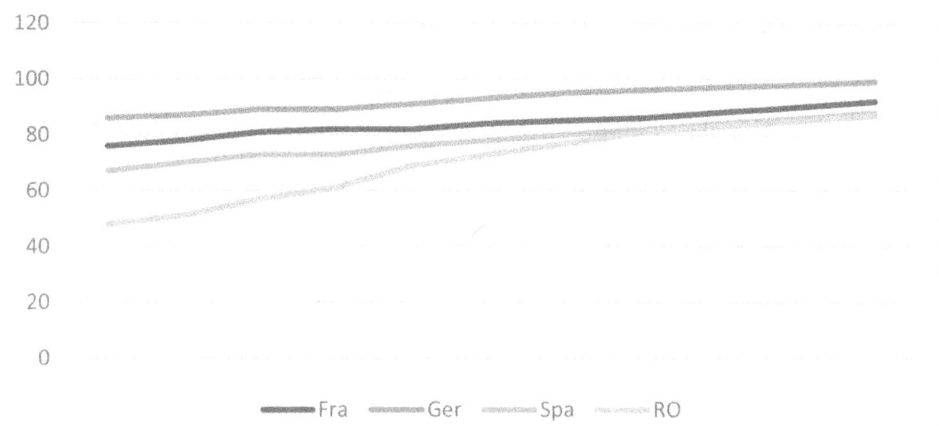

Regression Analysis

R squared means that a percentage in variation of the dependent variable (e-recruitment) is explained on account of independent variables (Florea, 2017). Excel - Data Analysis (Table 5) was used to calculate R squared.

Analyzing the values obtained for R squared, for France R squared is 45.96%, for Germany (39.54%) and Romania (34.79%) is an influence under the average, however positive and strong, hypothesis 1 is partially fulfilled (the lowest percent, but positive are obtained for Germany and Romania, with France near the average). For Spain (62.75%) R squared is above average, positive, and stronger than in the other cases, and hypothesis 1 is totally fulfilled. Thus, Hypothesis One - a relationship between e-recruitment and the analyzed variables is partially fulfilled, because three values are positive but under the average.

The conclusion of this study is that if the organizations would adapt new technologies in the process of recruitment (use of the internet and the availability of PCs) and if the costs of recruitment would depend on productivity, then all these factors would facilitate a recruitment online service more performant for all the employees, and also for organizations and implicitly for analyzed countries and the online recruitment process would be more effective. Penetration of the internet in France is 92.3%, 96% in Germany, 92.5% in Spain, and 73.8% in Romania. This information (https://www.internetworldstats.com/stats4.htm) also reflects the low influence of internet usage and availability of Pcs on e-recruitment - the fact that the population that has access to the internet in Romania is lower than in the other analyzed three countries.

To observe how each factor influences e-recruitment the regression function and Excel-Data Analysis were used (Table 6).

In the table above the coefficients necessary for regression function and the lower and the upper values for each variable are determined.

Resulting:

$$Y_{France}=-54.75+0.52\times X_1-0.31\times X_2+0.45\times X_3$$

To increase with a monetary unit e-recruitment will get an increase of 0.52 monetary units of X_1, a decrease of 0.31 m.u. of X_2, and an increase with 0.45 m.u. of X_3. We note that the value of free term (- 54.75) reveals that the variables which were included in the econometric model have a negative effect on the evolution of e-recruitment. The coefficients for Germany (Table 7) are also determined.

The regression function for Germany is:

$$Y_{Germany}=-31.37+0.13\times X_1-0.06\times X_2+0.41\times X_3$$

To increase with a monetary unit e-recruitment will get an increase of 0.13 monetary units of X_1, a decrease of 0.06 m.u. of X_2, and an increase with 0.41 m.u. of X_3. We note that the value of free term (- 31.37) reveals that the variables which

Table 6. Regression function for France

France	Coefficients	Standard Error	t Stat	P-value	Lower 95%	Upper 95%
Intercept	-54.75	46.078	-1.188	0.273	-163.714	54.204
X Variable 1	0.525	0.341	1.538	0.167	-0.282	1.334
X Variable 2	-0.316	0.303	-1.040	0.332	-1.034	0.402
X Variable 3	0.454	0.361	1.256	0.249	-0.400	1.309

Table 7. Regression function for Germany

Germany	Coefficients	Standard Error	t Stat	P-value	Lower 95%	Upper 95%
Intercept	-31.376	23.965	-1.309	0.231	-88.045	25.293
X Variable 1	0.133	0.333	0.401	0.699	-0.654	0.921
X Variable 2	-0.068	0.327	-0.209	0.840	-0.842	0.705
X Variable 3	0.417	0.214	1.945	0.092	-0.089	0.924

Table 8. Regression function for Spain

Spain	Coefficients	Standard Error	t Stat	P-value	Lower 95%	Upper 95%
Intercept	-56.786	25.744	-2.205	0.063	-117.664	4.090
X Variable 1	0.125	0.401	0.312	0.763	-0.824	1.075
X Variable 2	0.094	0.468	0.201	0.846	-1.013	1.202
X Variable 3	0.573	0.236	2.427	0.045	0.014	1.132

Table 9. Regression function for Romania

Romania	Coefficients	Standard Error	t Stat	P-value	Lower 95%	Upper 95%
Intercept	10.798	10.290	1.049	0.328	-13.535	35.132
X Variable 1	-0.066	0.316	-0.211	0.838	-0.815	0.682
X Variable 2	0.002	0.147	0.016	0.987	-0.345	0.350
X Variable 3	0.008	0.359	0.024	0.981	-0.841	0.859

were included in the econometric model have a negative effect on the evolution of e-recruitment. The coefficients are also determined for Spain (Table 8).

The regression function for Spain is:

$$Y_{Spain}=-56.78+0.12\times X_1+0.09\times X_2+0.57\times X_3$$

To increase with a monetary unit e-recruitment will get an increase of 0.12 monetary units of X_1, an increase with 0.08 m.u. of X_2, and an increase with 0.57 m.u. of X_3. We note that the value of free term (-56.78) reveals that the variables which were included in the econometric model have a negative effect on the evolution of e-recruitment. The specific coefficients for regression function for Romania are presented below (Table 9).

Applying the regression function for Romania, we get:

$$Y_{Romania}=10.79-0.06\times X_1+0.002\times X_2+0.008\times X_3$$

To increase with a monetary unit e-recruitment will get a decrease of 0.06 monetary units of X_1, an increase with 0.002 m.u. of X_2, and an increase with 0.008 m.u. of X_3. We note that the positive value of the free term (10.79) allows us to conclude that the influence factors considered in the model have an important impact on the evolution of e-recruitment.

Analysis of the Correlation Matrix Between the Three Factors and E-recruitment for the Four Analyzed Countries

Using the Pearson method, correlation coefficient may have values between (-1; +1); when it's 0 there is no correlation, when they are + or – 1 they are perfectly correlated, when it's between + or – (0; 0.3) the correlation is weak, between + and – (0.3; 0.5) it's reduced, between + and – (0.5; 0.7) it's moderate, between + and – (0.7; 0.9) it's high (Wilson, 2017; Webber, Wallace, 2011; Watson & Reissner, 2014; Florea & Duica, 2019). This method was applied to our analysis group using Excel-Data Analysis (Table 10).

For France, all the analyzed variables positively influence e-recruitment, internet usage is above average (correlation is moderate) and availability of computers is a little below average (correlation is reduced, but positive). Thus, for France, the Hypothesis Two - There is a correlation between e-recruitment and these factors of influence is partially fulfilled. For Germany and Spain, all the analyzed variables positively influence e-recruitment, but they are all a little below the average, so, the correlation is reduced and Hypothesis Two is partially fulfilled.

For Romania, it may be observed the negative correlation between the influencing factors and e-recruitment. Thus, e-recruitment and Internet usage are not related, showing the existence of a negative and moderate relationship between them (the value obtained is -0.58). The same thing for availability of computers (-0.57), and productivity (-0.577). The calculations may be explained as follows: even if individuals are using the internet frequently, e-recruitment remains at a low level of use; even if the availability of computers increases, e-recruitment does not register increased values. Romanian organizations still prefer to use old traditional recruitment methods, face-to-face, not online, even if the pandemic conditions such measures. As for productivity, it confirms the fact that if it, recruitment costs are directly proportional with productivity.

Productivity does not influence e-recruitment in France (0.04) or Spain (0.099). Only in Germany there is a real influence, almost close to the average value (0.479).

Table 10. Correlation matrix for the four analyzed countries

Variable/ Country	France			Germany			Spain			Romania		
	Y	X_1	X_2	Y	X_1	X_2	Y	X_1	X_2	Y	X_1	X_2
X1	0.509			0.261			0.430			-0.580		
X2	0.439	0.977		0.257	0.990		0.469	0.992		-0.570	0.966	
X3	0.040	-0.500	-0.484	0.479	-0.264	-0.250	0.099	-0.763	-0.721	-0.577	0.981	0.917

In Romania, labor productivity registered increased values for the entire analyzed period (except for other three countries which decreased in the last two years), and even so, e-recruitment is not positively or strongly related to productivity (there is a negative and moderate correlation of - 0.577).

Thus, making the correlation matrix between e-recruitment and labor productivity, there is a very weak correlation: for France (4.08%) and for Spain (9.97%), a strong correlation for Germany (47.91%), and a negative correlation and above average for Romania (-57.76%). So, the Third Hypothesis: E-recruitment is directly proportional with labor productivity- is not fulfilled (only one of the four analyzed countries has a better correlation, but below average).

Internet usage positively and strongly influences the availability of computers (0.977), but productivity influence is negative and strong between productivity and internet usage (-0.5) and availability of computers (-0.484). The same thing is valid for Germany and Spain (the first influence over 0.9 and the following influences of productivity negative values).

For Romania: there is a strong relation between internet usage and availability of computers (0.966), but also between productivity and internet usage (0.981) and availability of computers (0.917). This could mean that, the more individuals use the Internet, the greater the computer availability, and productivity positively influences the two analyzed variables.

Reducing Costs in the Pandemic Context Using E-recruitment

There are a few points that employers and candidates should consider: (i) The threat of this pandemic does not mean no one is hiring or no one is actively looking for a job; (ii) The state, the official organizations and the companies have the means to prepare and protect people in the workplace; (iii) Employees can easily work from home using e-skills or companies to use e-recruitment to attract candidates; (iv) Using recruitment plans based on knowledge, skills, and attitudes, in order to improve performance (recruiting the right persons, the costs will be reduced); (v) Increase employees' retention, because a retention plan is five times cheaper than a recruitment plan ; (vi) Create a strong and positive company culture based on strong values, attitudes, trusts, habits, which can retain talented staff and recruit only according to a growing plan; (vii) Develop employees constantly and consistently with training programs, and in this time with e-training, e-coaching, -mentoring programs (viii) Offer flexibility to employees - the pandemic era has forced companies to use hybrid program or totally work from home for long periods of time, so, offering a flexible program to employees will retain talented staff long-term; (ix) Using e-recruitment means developing attractive websites for recruitment, lowering recruitment costs, improving e-skills for HR recruitment specialists, improve personalized communication with the candidate (a 1-to-1 relationship), keeping the distance during the pandemic and solving recruitment objectives. No one knows how much the Covid-19 pandemic will last, but we do know that the recruitment process does not have to stop, even if the pandemic crisis will continue for a while; (x) Involve all the adequate persons: management, specialists in the field, IT specialists, HR specialists in order to ensure a good and efficient e-recruitment plan; (xi) Establishing the right objectives in order to find the right candidate, with the right skills and knowledge necessary for a job; (xii) Use effective recruitment marketing based on an integrated communication plan (virtual channels with real results, getting the lowest costs to the right candidate).

Reducing HR Costs Using Accountability of Nonfinancial Compensation in Pandemic Time

Financial compensation satisfies the employees' needs short term, and nonfinancial compensation satisfies them on medium and long term, trying to win their trust, loyalty, and attachment (Bradutanu, 2015). During this period of crisis, many companies resorted to pandemic staff reductions, until the total closure of the company. But these are not long-term or performance-enhancing solutions. Therefore, necessary measures are required to maintain talented employees and to find innovative and inexpensive solutions. It is said that after increasing the salary of an employee, the employee shortly forgets this financial measure, considering the increase worth it, while nonfinancial measures are not forgotten so easily. Thus, it is necessary to develop a non-financial compensation plan, given that studies indicate that these measures, which are not so easily forgotten, lead to performance and attachment to the company: (i) good communication between managers and employees - based on transparency, trust, speed, accuracy, implication in intercommunication, a very clear set of rules, positive collegial atmosphere between employees, or employees and managers, respect between employees (managers treat employees correctly, clearly assign tasks, set realistic goals, clear determination of rights and obligations, conclusion of formal employment contracts, apply incentives, give employees confidence, a transparent promotion system which any employee can access, a clear knowledge of the tasks to be performed, a satisfactory level of authority, a transparent salary system, employees' opinions to be heard; (ii) working in teams - the sum of team knowledge and experience is bigger than individuals, so working in different teams will offer both parts new knowledge and the principle of knowledge sharing, promoting work in interdisciplinary teams, offering training programs, learning-development (gaining new knowledge through transitions to other positions, team building, special events, counseling and support programs especially in moments of resistance to new methods of work or in moments when the level of self-esteem, anxiety and homework are high; (iii) delegating the power to talented staff or implicating them in taking decisions or finding solutions for different problems, offering opportunities for group membership, achievement, autonomy; (iv) motivating the best employees with diplomas, plaques, distinctions, mentions on the notice board or in meetings, going out for lunch, having parties, or participating to team building programs, a flexible schedule built around the employee and tailored to their needs, job security, job simplification, job rotation, recognition of merits in front of others, career development opportunities, skills development, involvement, commitment, motivational speeches and e-mails of thanks, stimulation and encouragement of the collective mind by organizing team building programs, etc.; (v) encouraging to continue to achieve performance and objectives by using nonverbal communication - looking someone straight in the eye, using a smile, using a touch on the arm, on the shoulder, shaking hands as tools specific for phaptic from nonverbal communication; (vi) establishing a fair work environment - working according to not-discrimination principles, sustainable development, ethics, empathy, equity, decorating employees with very good results, establishing anti-corruption measures.

CONCLUSION

The scope of this study is to show that e-recruitment (a cost-effective virtual method, which brings real results for future employees but also for organizations) and nonfinancial compensation are two efficient HR methods which will bring performance in the long run for companies, especially in pandemic times. Specific purposes of the study are: to identify the many advantages of e-recruitment but also a few disadvantages, to analyze the factors which have a real influence on e-recruitment implementation, to observe the influence of productivity on e-recruitment, linked by costs, to develop a plan based on e-recruitment as a source of reducing costs in the pandemic context, to develop a plan based on nonfinancial compensation during the pandemic for sustainable organizations and green candidates.

The novelty of this study is the double analysis of e-recruitment process: one based on e-recruitment from the theoretical point of view (where a bibliometric analysis is made from 1970 till 2021 using Web of Science and Scopus database), and from a practical point of view (where a mathematical analysis is made using regression function and correlation matrix). The peak of articles written in the analyzed database was reached in 2013 for Scopus (five articles) and for Web of Science in 2016 and 2017 (with six articles). Therefore, the interest is currently low for the theoretical, scientific part, even if there are real benefits for individuals and companies.

In the practical part the regression function, the correlation matrix, and Excel-Data Analysis are used but also the development of two important plans for e-recruitment and nonfinancial compensation. The analysis is made at Romanian level, and other three countries were chosen, according to the data registered in bibliometric analysis: France, Germany, and Spain. A comparison was made using modeling and simulation. R squared calculated for each country means that a percentage in variation of the dependent variable (e-recruitment) is explained on account of independent variables. For all the four analyzed countries, the percentage of R squared is reduced or above the average (between 34% for Romania and 62% for Germany), indicating that the variation of e-recruitment is explained by individual's internet usage, availability of computers, and productivity by low percent or average, as mentioned above.

The correlation between e-recruitment and its factors of influence is also low or average (between 0.040 and 0.509) for the top three countries and for Romania, all the correlations are negative (between -0.57 and -0.58), showing that the three factors taken into account are not important as is considered. Productivity, as we may observe, does not influence the recruitment process so much (values between 0.099 and 0.479 and negative for Romania (-0.577- even if it is a growing trend for the registered period) as it is said in the studies and practice.

Results indicate that even if this process brings benefits for all stakeholders and the environment it is still not used at maximum power. Lack of trust, experience, interest in innovation, lack of face-to-face communication, are preventing e-recruitment from becoming a powerful tool, as it is considered.

Recruitment is changing, an e-labor market has appeared, so using e-recruitment is not trying to exclude traditional recruitment methods, but to improve this process, by reducing its costs, getting to new candidates, with new knowledge and skills. E-recruitment offers the right candidates the right opportunity for growth, growth of individuals and of the company. E-recruitment is getting anywhere, to anybody interested in a specific job, and anytime. The pandemic showed us that we can continue to work, to recruit and develop without considering the distance. The virtual process is getting real results: for individuals (24/7/365, reduced cost and time, gaining new knowledge, and improve e-skills), for companies (reduced costs and time, speed, efficiency), and also for the environment.

The article will offer a broader view for specialists, for candidates, for future employees and also for employers regarding the real benefits from a virtual world, that of e-recruitment, such as reduced costs, accessibility, ease of use, anytime, anywhere, according to the 24/7/365 principle. It will also provide a clear plan based on e-recruitment as a real source of reducing costs and increasing relationships and collaboration, and more importantly increasing ethics, reducing discrimination, increasing equity, social responsibility, and sustainable development, as the author called the ENERD principle.

REFERENCES

Alsop, T. (2021). *PC market in Europe - Statistics & facts.* https://www.statista.com/topics/3889/pc-market-in-europe/

Alsultanny, Y. A., & Alotaibi, M. F. (2015). Evaluating the Factors Affecting on Intension to Use of E-Recruitment. *American Journal of Information Science and Computer Engineering, 1*(5), 324–331.

Anand, J., & Devi, C. S. (2016). The Impact of e-recruitment and challenges faced by HR professionals. *International Journal of Applied Research, 2*(3), 410–413. https:// www.allresearchjournal.com/archives/2016/vol2issue3/PartG/2-2-84.pdf

Ansari, J. A. N., & Khan, N. A. (2020). Exploring the role of social media in collaborative learning the new domain of learning. *Smart Learning Environments, 7*(1), 9. Advance online publication. doi:10.118640561-020-00118-7

Aqeel, S., & Siddiqui, D. (2019). The effect of social media following on recruitment in service industries of Pakistan. *Business Management and Strategy, 10*(1), 41–77. doi:10.5296/bms.v10i1.14633

Armstrong, M. (2006). *A handbook of human resources management practice.* Kogan Page.

Bach, S. (2005). *Managing human resources: personnel management in transition.* Blackwell Pub.

Badr, G., & Aboul-Ela, E. (2014). Development of a scale to measure the perceived benefits of e-recruitment from the viewpoint of the recruiter. *The Journal of Business and Retail Management Research, 9*(1), 40–51.

Banyai, T. (2019). *Sustainable Human Resource Management.* MDPI.

Barraud, J., Guillemin, M., & Kittel, F. (2008). The Human Resources function-3rd ed.: Trades, skills and training [La fonction Ressources Humaines-3e éd.: Métiers, compétences et formation]. Hachette.

Benchemam, F., & Galindo, G. (2009). Human Resources Management [Gestion des resources humaines] (2nd ed.). Gualino ed..

Berg, R. J., & McCoy, H. (2012). *Let's Talk Business!: Introduction to economic and commercial French* [Parlons affaires!: Initiation au français economique et commercial]. Cengage Learning.

Berry, M. (2005). *Top companies lead online recruitment revolution.* www.personneltoday.com

Billsberry, J. (2008). *Experiencing recruitment and selection*. John Wiley & Sons.

Bondarouk, T., Ruël, H., & Looise, J. K. (2011). *Electronic HRM in theory and practice*. Emerald Group Publishing. doi:10.1108/S1877-6361(2011)8

Boşcai, B. G. (2017). The evolution of e-recruitment: The introduction of online recruiter. In *Management and Organization: Concepts, Tools and Applications* (pp. 161-170). Pearson. http://real.mtak.hu/54549/1/162_Management_and_Organization-Pearson-2017j%C3%BAn08-DOI_CrossRef-2017j%C3%BAn13f.pdf

Bournois, F., Point, S., Rojot, J., & Scaringella, J. L. (2007). *RH: Les meilleures pratiques du CAC 40/SBF 120*. Editions Eyrolles.

Bovenberg, L., & Zaidi, A. (2010). *Ageing, Health and Pensions in Europe*. Springer. doi:10.1057/9780230307346

Bradutanu, D. (2015). *Resistance to change: a new perspective*. Lulu Press.

Cadin, L., Guerin, F., & Pigeyre, F. (2009). *Human resources management* [Gestion des ressources humaines]. Dunod.

Callegaro, M., Manfreda, K. L., & Vehovar, V. (2015). Web survey methodology. *Sage*.

Cornet, A., & Warlaud, Ph. (2008). *Human resources management and diversity management* [Gestion de ressources humaines et gestion de la diversité]. Dunod.

Cross, O. D. (2018). E-Recruitment and its Effects on Organizational Creativity and Innovation in Nigerian Manufacturing Firms. *Nile Journal of Business and Economics*, *8*, 3–12.

D'Silva, C. (2020). A study on increase in e-recruitment and selection process. *International Journal of Research in Engineering, Science and Management, 3*(8), 205-213. https:// www.journals.resaim.com/ijresm/article/view/162

Doran, A. (2001). *E-work arhitect-how HR leads the way using the Internet*. IHRIM Press Book.

Eurostat. (2020). *Labour productivity per person employed and hour worked (EU27_2020=100).* https://ec.europa.eu/eurostat/databrowser/view/tesem160/default/table?lang=en

Eurostat. (2021a). *Individuals using the internet for looking for a job or sending a job application.* https://ec.europa.eu/eurostat/databrowser/view/tin00102/default/table?lang=en

Eurostat. (2021b). *Internet use by individuals.* https://ec.europa.eu/eurostat/databrowser/view/tin00028/default/table?lang=en

Eurostat. (2021c). *Households - Availability of computers.* https://appsso.eurostat.ec.europa.eu/nui/show.do?dataset=isoc_ci_cm_h&lang=en

Fielding, M. (2005). Effective communication in organizations (3rd ed.). Juta & Co. Ltd.

Florea, N. V. (2013). Human resources audit [Auditul resurselor umane]. C.H. Beck.

Florea, N. V. (2017). *Simulation and modeling in business* [Simulare si modelare in afaceri]. Mustang.

Florea, N. V., & Duica, A. (2019). *Customer relationship management* [Managementul relatiei cu clientii]. Mustang.

Fred, M. O., & Kinange, U. M. (2018). Effectiveness of E-Recruitment in Organization Development. *Management and Economic Journal*, *2*(4), 294–301.

Galanaki, E. (2002). The Decision to recruit Online: A Descriptive Study. *Career International Development*, *7*(4), 243–251. doi:10.1108/13620430210431325

Ghazzawi, K., & Accoumeh, A. (2014). Critical Success Factors of the E-Recruitment System. *Journal of Human Resources Management and Labor Studies*, *2*(2), 159–170.

Gopalia, A. (2011). *Effectiveness of Online Recruitment and Selection Process: A Case of Tesco.* http://www.pbr.co.in/2011/2011_month/Jan_March/0002.pdf

Gueutal, H., & Stone, D. L. (2015). *The Brave New World of eHR: Human Resources in the Digital Age.* John Wiley & Sons.

Guillot-Soulez, C. (2009). *Human resources management* [La gestion des ressources humaines] (2nd ed.). Gualiano.

Hada, B. S., & Gairola, S. (2015). Opportunities & Challenges of E- Recruitment. *Journal of Management Engineering and Information Technology*, *2*(2), 1–4.

Headworth, A. (2015). *Social media recruitment.* Kogan Page Publishers.

Holm, A. B. (2012). E-recruitment: Towards an Ubiquitous Recruitment Process and Candidate Relationship Management. *German Journal of Human Resource Management*, 241-259.

Hopkins, B., & Markham, J. (2003). *E-HR: using intranets to improve the effectiveness of your people.* Gower Pub.Ltd.

Hosain, M., & Liu, P. (2020). LinkedIn for searching better job opportunity: Passive jobseekers' perceived experience. *Qualitative Report*, *25*(10), 3719–3732. doi:10.46743/2160-3715/2020.4449

Internet Live Stats. (2016). *Romania Internet Users.* https://www.internetlivestats.com/internet-users/romania/

Internet World Stats. (2021). *Internet users in the world.* https://www.internetworldstats.com/stats.htm

Johnson, J. (2021). *Internet usage in Europe - Statistics & Facts.* https://www.statista.com/topics/3853/internet-usage-in-europe/#dossierKeyfigures

Kapse, A. S., Patil, V. S., & Patil, N. V. (2012). E-recruitment. *International Journal of Engineering and Advanced Technology*, *1*(4), 82–86.

Karim, M. R., Miah, S., & Asma, K. (2015). E-Recruitment in Practice: A Study on Jobseekers' Perception in Bangladesh. *Munich Personal RePEc Archive*, 33-42.

Kaur, J., Arianayagam, S., & Singh, P. (2020). The usage of social media networks as a tool by employers to screen job candidates. *The European Journal of Social & Behavioural Sciences*, *3*(3), 191–207. doi:10.15405/ejsbs.282

Lakhdar, S. (2001). *Human Resources Management* [Gestion de ressources humaines]. Universite de Boeck.

Mabuza, M. P. (2019). *Evaluating international public health issues.* Springer Nature.

Machado, C. F., & Davim, J. P. (2019). *Higher Education and the Evolution of Management. Applied Sciences, and Engineering Curricula.* IGI Global. doi:10.4018/978-1-5225-7259-6

Malik, Z., & Ullah, R. (2013). The Role of E-recruitment Towards Attraction of Workforce: A Case of Telecom Sector Organization. *Abasyn Journal of Social Sciences*, *6*(1), 104–115.

Maurer, D. S., & Liu, Y. (2007). Developing effective e-recruiting websites: Insights for managers from marketers. *Business Horizons*, *50*(4), 305–314. doi:10.1016/j.bushor.2007.01.002

Meah, M. M., & Sarwar, A. (2021). Social Networking Sites for e-Recruitment: A Perspective of Malaysian Employers. *Journal of Asian Finance, Economics and Business*, *8*(8), 613–624. doi:10.13106/jafeb.2021

Mindia, P. M., & Hoque, K. (2018). Effects of E-recruitment and internet on recruitment process: An Empirical study on Multinational companies of Bangladesh. *International Journal of Scientific Research and Management*, *6*(1), 2321–3418. doi:10.18535/ijsrm/v6i1.em01

Mohammad, J., Quoquab, F., Sulaiman, A., & Salam, Z. (2020). I voice out because I care: The effect of online social networking on employees' likelihood to voice and retention. *Asia-Pacific Journal of Business Administration*, *13*(1), 117–137. doi:10.1108/APJBA-05-2020-0142

Muduli, A., & Trivedi, J. (2020). Social media recruitment: The role of credibility and satisfaction. Evidence-based HRM: A global forum for empirical scholarship. *Evidence-based HRM*, *8*(2), 237–251. doi:10.1108/EBHRM-08-2019-0069

Newsome, D. A. (2007). *Bridging the gaps in global communication*. Blackwell Pub.

Nguti, V. N., & Mose, T. (2021). The Role Of E-Recruitment And Selection Functions on the Organizational Outcomes in Helb, Kenya. International Academic Journal of Human Resource and Business Administration, 3(9), 554-565.

Pande, S., & Basak, S. (2015). *Human resource management: text and cases*. Vikas Publishing House.

Parry, E., & Tyson, S. (2008a). Can technology transform HR processes? The case of UK recruitment. *The Second European Academic Workshop on Electronic Human Resource Management*.

Parry, E., & Tyson, S. (2008b). An analysis of the use and success of online recruitment methods in the UK. *Human Resource Management Journal*, *18*(3), 257–174. doi:10.1111/j.1748-8583.2008.00070.x

Posthumus, J. (2015). *Use of Market Data in the Recruitment of High Potentials*. Springer. doi:10.1007/978-3-658-10376-7

Priyadarshini, C., Kumar, Y., & Jha, R. R. (2017a). Employer Attractiveness Through Social Media: A Phenomenological Study. *Qualitative Report*, *22*(4), 969–983. doi:10.46743/2160-3715/2017.2663

Priyadarshini, C., Sreejesh, S., & Anusree, M. R. (2017b). Effect of information quality of employment website on attitude toward the website A moderated mediation study. *International Journal of Manpower*, *38*(5), 729–745. doi:10.1108/IJM-12-2015-0235

Priyadarshini, C., Sreejesh, S., & Jha, R. R. (2019). Impact of Informational Characteristics of the Recruitment Website on Graduating Students' Job Pursuit Intention: A Moderated Mediation Study. *International Journal of Human Capital and Information Technology Professionals*, *10*(2), 1–19. doi:10.4018/IJHCITP.2019040101

Rosoiu, O., & Popescu, C. (2016). E-recruiting Platforms: Features that Influence the Efficiency of Online Recruitment Systems. *Informações Econômicas, 20*(2), 46–55. doi:10.12948/issn14531305/20.2.2016.05

Salehi, M. (2009). *Investigating Website Success in the Context of e-Recruitment: An Analytic Network Process (ANP) Approach* [Master's thesis]. Lulea University of Technology.

Salmen, S. (2012). What's Next -Die nächsten Trends. In *Recruiting im Social Web*. BusinessVillage GmbH.

Sawe, B. E. (2017). *Countries With The Most Personal Computers Per Capita.* https://www.worldatlas.com/articles/countries-with-the-most-personal-computers-per-capita

Scarpello, V. G. (2008). *The Handbook of Human Resource Management Education.* SAGE.

Sharma, N. (2014). Recruitment Strategies: A power of E-Recruiting and Social Media. *International Journal of Core Engineering & Management, 1*(5), 15–35.

Sherkar, A. (2011). A Study on Use of E- Resources in Recruitment and Selection Process in 5 Star Hotels. *Atythia: A Journal of Hospitality*, 14-19. http://www.publishingindia.com

Sills, M. (2014). *E-recruitment: A comparison with traditional recruitment and the influences of social media. A qualitative and quantitative review.* https://www.theseus.fi/bitstream/handle/10024/80428/Sills_Maureen.pdf

Silva, S., Silva, C., & Martins, D. (2017). Online Recruitment for Organizational Knowledge Management: A Quantitative Study. *Proceedings of the 18th European Conference on Knowledge Management, 1*(2), 890-896.

Sims, R. R. (2002). *Organizational success through effective human resources management.* Greenwood Pub. Inc.Group.

Singh, S. (2017). Recruitment: A New Dimension of Human Resource Management in India. *International Journal of Advance Research in Computer Science and Management Studies, 5*(3), 99–105.

Sinha, V., & Thaly, P. (2013). A Review on Changing Trend of Recruitment Practice to Enhance the Quality of Hiring in Global Organizations. *Management, 18*(2), 141–156.

Statista. (2020). *Share of households with internet access in the European Union (EU) from 2007 to 2020.* https://www.statista.com/statistics/377585/household-internet-access-in-eu28/

Stredwick, J. (2000). *An introduction to HRM, Butter-Heinemann.* Reed Edu & Prof. Pub. Ltd.

Sylva, H., & Mol, S. T. (2009). E-Recruitment: A study into applicant perceptions of an online application system. *International Journal of Selection and Assessment, 17*(3), 311–323. doi:10.1111/j.1468-2389.2009.00473.x

Torrington, D., Hall, L., & Taylor, S. (2008). *Human resources management.* Pearson Edu. Ltd.

Tsiakis, T. (2015). *Trends and Innovations in Marketing Information Systems.* IGI Global. doi:10.4018/978-1-4666-8459-1

Tyagi, A. (2012). Effective Talent Acquisition Through E-Recruitment:A Study. *International Journal of Multidisciplinary Research, 2*(3), 302–312.

Tyagi, A. (2016). *Impact of e-recruitment on human resource.* Horizon Books.

van Esch, P., Black, J. S., & Arli, D. (2021). Job candidates' reactions to AI-enabled job application processes. *AI Ethics, 1*(2), 119–130. doi:10.100743681-020-00025-0

Vatansever, K. (2017). Using multi criteria decision making approaches for evaluating and selecting website: A literature review. *International Journal of Current Advanced Research, 6*(4), 3388–3399. doi:10.24327/ijcar.2017.3399.0281

Watson, G., & Reissner, S. (2014). *Developing skills for business leadership.* Kogan Page Pub.

Webber, L., & Wallace, M. (2011). *Quality control for dummies.* JohnWiley&Sons.

Wilkinson, A., & Dundon, T. (2021). Contemporary HRM. *Sage (Atlanta, Ga.).*

Wilson, E. (2017). School-based researcg: A guide for education students. *Sage (Atlanta, Ga.).*

Zakrizevska, M., & Litvina, A. (2016). First Impresion And Belief Importance In Candidate Recruitment Decisions. *SGEM, Psychology And Psychiatry, Sociology And Healthcare, Education Conference Proceedings*, 1, 177-184.

Zin, S. M., & Jaafar, N. N. (2016). *E-Recruitment Technology: The Effective Source of Recruitment.* https://www.semanticscholar.org/paper/E-Recruitment-Technology%3A-The-Effective-Source-of-Zin-Jaafar/490e8d7069007b8ee4105d714c0ad725dddbed4b

Chapter 8
Different Approaches to Measure Conversion of Financial Statements and Disclosure Issues

Oncioiu Ionica
Titu Maiorescu University, Romania

Alin Eliodor Tănase
Titu Maiorescu University, Romania

ABSTRACT

A company's conversion of financial statements is a well-known instrument in the development and management control domains, but its usage in the area of corporate disclosure reveals significant uses. In this chapter, the term "conversion" refers to the process that takes place whenever the currency in which the financial statements are created is different from the currency in which they are presented. Additionally, this chapter presents the significant managerial debates that arise throughout the process of converting financial statements. The findings reveal that financial statement conversion is only applicable if the firm whose financial statements are being converted has a functioning currency that is not in a hyperinflationary economy.

INTRODUCTION

The currency of an entity's primary economic environment has been defined as the functional currency. A functional currency does not exist in a group, but the functional currency is determined at the level of each group entity (Ball, Li &

DOI: 10.4018/978-1-6684-4595-2.ch008

Shivakumar, 2015). Determining each functional currency at each component of a group is made by looking at several factors. Stakeholder theory, institutional theory, signaling theory, legitimacy theory, and socioeconomic theory are all capable of explaining why commercial, public, and third-sector entities choose to engage in sustainability reporting.

In recent years, there has also been an increase in interest in understanding how sustainability-related activities affect a company's profitability, as numerous governments, market regulators, and operators have started to establish regulations and laws requiring corporations to report their environmental and social effects (Al Lawati & Hussainey, 2022).

When accounting for transactions denominated in foreign currency or translating financial statements into the presentation currency, the International Accounting Standard (IAS) should be applied (Iatridis, 2010; Guthrie & Parker, 2016). When the currency in which the financial statements are created differs from the presentation currency, the conversion occurs (Zéghal et al., 2011; Lobo & Zhou, 2001). Concerning financial statement conversion, it should be highlighted that this standard only applies if the entity whose financial statements are converted has a functional currency that is not a hyperinflationary economy (Jones & Smith, 2012; Watts & Zimmerman, 1978; Ball et al., 2015).

The presence and impact of possible voting rights that are now exercisable or convertible, including potential voting rights owned by other companies, will be taken into consideration when determining whether there is considerable influence (Choi et al., 2013; Barth et al., 2008; Cairns et al., 2011). An entity may own warrants on shares, options to acquire stocks, debt or equity securities that are convertible into common shares or other financial instruments, which, if exercised or converted, can either give an entity that possesses greater voting rights or diminish the voting rights of another party's financial and operating policies. Potential voting rights that are now exercisable or convertible must be taken into consideration (i.e. potential voting rights).

Because they are not currently usable or convertible, any potential voting rights that cannot be exercised or converted until a future date or until an event occurs are regarded to be inactive. If the investor loses the ability to participate in decision-making about the investee entity's financial and operating policies, we may argue that it has lost considerable influence (Allen & Ramanna, 2013; Bozec, 2008; Tendeloo & Vanstrelen, 2005).

A sort of shared commitment is known as a joint venture in which the partners share control over the enterprise and the rights to its net assets (Daske & Gebhardt, 2006; Marra et al., 2011). For joint commitments, each party has rights to the assets and responsibility for liabilities associated with the agreement (Ghosh & Olsen, 2008; Landsman, Maydew, & Thornock, 2012). This is referred to as a joint venture business, and it is not discussed in this literature, nor do we use the equity technique (Pieper, Trevor, Weller & Duchon, 2017).

When a foreign operation is a subsidiary, branch, associate, or joint undertaking of the reporting company, the foreign operation's functional currency is the same as that of the reporting entity (Schleicher et al., 2010). According to the Standard, an entity's functional currency should represent the relevant transactions, events, and underlying conditions (Xiong, 2006; Leuz et al., 2003). Therefore, once defined, the functional currency only changes if the underlying transactions, events, and conditions change (Chen, Tang, Jiang & Lin, 2010).

Transactions in foreign currency are those that are denominated in a foreign currency or that allow for settlement in a foreign currency (Zeghal et al., 2012; Dechow et al., 1996). A company's foreign currency-denominated purchases and sales, borrowings and lendings, as well as other asset acquisitions and debt support and repot transactions are all included under IAS 21, according to which these transactions are reported (Pope & McLeay, 2011).

Following the two moments of first recognition and subsequent recognition, a foreign currency transaction may be recorded in the functional currency once the functional currency has been created as follows: Initial recognition - the functional currency and foreign currency exchange rates at the time of the transaction; subsequent recognition (at the end of each reporting period) - the items will be converted according to their type, monetary or non-monetary items (Ahmed et al., 2013; Thong et al., 2008; DeFond, 2010).

It is the carrying amount of the equity method investment in an associate or a joint venture, and any long-term interests that are part of the net investment in the associate or joint venture created under that method (Barth, 2013; Kothari et al., 2005). After the holding company's value has been brought down to zero, any subsequent losses should be accounted for, and a liability must be recognized only to the extent that the entity has either been legally or constructively obligated to do something or has made payments on behalf of the associate or joint venture (Richardson, 2011). Only once its share of profits equals the share of losses not recognized does the entity begin to recognize its portion of the earnings reported by the associate or joint venture.

BACKGROUND

Today, there are prominent exceptions of nonfinancial and CSR disclosure regulation systems (Carnini et al., 2022). The consolidated financial statements are thought to be more beneficial for management, owners, and lenders of the firm acquirer (Barth et al., 2008). A company, an investor in an associate, or a venture in a jointly managed corporation may produce separate financial statements in which investments are accounted for more on the basis of direct equity than on the reported results and net assets of the investee (Alzola, 2017; Jeanjean & Stolowy, 2008). All of the following are included in the entire set of financial statements: consolidated statement of financial position, consolidated statement of comprehensive income in the period, consolidated statement of changes in equity over time, and consolidated cash flow period notes (Lang et al., 2006; Fu et al., 2012).

International Financial Reporting Standards (IFRS) 10 is used to generate the consolidated financial statements. Individual financial statements for the main and its subsidiaries will be produced on the same reporting date as the consolidated financial statements (Messier et al., 2008). In the event that the end of the reporting period for a subsidiary differs from that of the main company, the subsidiary is required, for the purposes of consolidation, to prepare extra financial statements on the same date as the main company's financial statements, unless doing so would be impossible. In certain cases, the subsidiary will make some adjustments to account for the consequences of important transactions or events that occur between that date and the day the main company's financial statements are issued (Klein, 2002). The interval between the end of the reporting period of the subsidiary and the end of the reporting period of the parent business, however, should not be less than three months (Fan et al., 2016). The reporting periods themselves, as well as any differences in the ends of the reporting periods, are required to be consistent from one period to the next (Rittenberg & Schwieger, 2005).

Changes in the capital shares of the parent company in a subsidiary that do not result in a loss of control are accounted for as transactions with own capital, just like operations (meaning transactions with the stockholders). Additionally, the carrying amounts of controlling interests (ICI) and non-controlling interests (INC) should be updated to reflect changes relating to ownership in the subsidiary. These adjustments should be made in accordance with generally accepted accounting principles. Adjusted non-controlling interests (INC) are immediately recorded in equity as a difference between the fair value of consideration paid or received and the adjusted non-controlling interests (INC). This difference is ascribed to the owners of the primary business (Louwers et al., 2007).

The amount of packages of shares held by the parent business and its subsidiaries in an associate or joint venture, or "group share," is determined by IAS 28. (Whittington & Pany 2008; Lin et al., 2012). It is not taken into consideration that the group has stakes in other partners or joint ventures for the purposes of this calculation The profit or loss, other comprehensive income, and net assets that are considered when adopting the equity method when an associate or joint venture has subsidiaries, associates, or joint ventures are those that are recorded in the associate's or joint venture's financial statements (including share of associate or joint venture of profit or loss and other comprehensive income and net assets of its associates and joint ventures).

In contrast, the financial asset is the investment made by the parent firm in the subsidiary's net assets (Iatridis, 2012). The subsidiary's net assets are equal to its equity. Because the subsidiary's assets and debt are added to those of the parent company in the consolidated balance sheet, it is customary to remove the asset representing the parent company's investment in a subsidiary in exchange for the subsidiary's equity to avoid counting double of these assets net (Beasley et al., 2009). There will be no equity in the consolidated financial statements that is not owned by the parent firm. Non-controlling interests (ICN) will be disclosed separately from the equity of the primary company's owners.

CORPORATE DISCLOSURE AND PRESENTATION CURRENCY

There is a correlation between determining the functional currency and the mechanism used to translate foreign firms' financial statements. In spite of this, there are institutional and legal measures that push businesses and other organizations to actively engage in non-financial disclosure (Barth et al., 2014). These initiatives are in addition to the voluntary reasons for social reporting. Because several governments, market regulators, and operators have started enacting laws and regulations that compel corporations to report their environmental and social effects, there has been a recent rise in interest in understanding how actions linked to sustainability have an influence on a company's business. This interest has also risen over the past few years. (Balachandran & Faff, 2015).

Business model disclosure should have two primary components in order to be relevant to stakeholders: a narrative description that demonstrates the most essential pillars of a company's business model and a set of quantitative metrics that strengthen the trustworthiness of narratives (Brüggemann et al., 2013).

It is possible to reach the conclusion that massive corporations produce sustainability reports for the sole purpose of complying with the ever-increasing number of requirements that pertain to the reporting of social and environmental factors (Houque et al., 2012). Nevertheless, compliance with the law is not the sole reason that businesses, particularly large ones, publish sustainability reports. Publish material in unregulated areas is a common commercial practice, which backs this up. Corporate sustainability reporting has been and remains mostly a voluntary activity aimed at presenting an account of the social and environmental impacts of doing business to both internal and external stakeholders, despite the fact that many governments and organizations have fostered this type of disclosure directly or indirectly.

Although these concepts are not used expressly in IAS 21, their range of applicability suggests that such is the case (Barth & Konchitchki, 2013). There will be consideration given to the rules in Section 3 pertaining to how foreign currency transactions in a functional currency should be registered at the level of each individual company, whether or not it is a part of a group, as well as how financial statements denominated in foreign currency should be translated into a functional currency.

Temporal balance is handled according to the item's nature: Monetary items (e.g., cash, receivables, or trade payables) are translated using the closing rate, and the resulting differences in differences are recognized in profit or loss; non-monetary items (e.g., tangible, intangible, etc.) are converted: using the exchange rate at the transaction date if they are valued on the historical cost basis, or using the exchange rate from the date they were measured at fair value (Chebaane & Othman, 2014).

On non-controlling interests (ICN), the standard makes the following statement regarding the fair value at the acquisition date: acquirer may measure a non-controlling interest held in the acquire at fair value at the acquisition date; if available prices in an active market for shares - the acquirer can measure the fair value at the acquisition date of INC given these prices; if not available prices in an active market for shares - the acquirer must measure the fair It is probable that the fundamental difference is the inclusion of a first control in the fair value per share of the acquirer's interest or, conversely, the inclusion of a discount for lack of control (also known as a shrinking minority) in the fair value per share of controlling interest.

The sum of the first three components (VJ of the transferred consideration, INC, and VJ of purchase of previously held ownership interest) is the transaction's default (VI) (Doukakis, 2010).

It should also be noted that prior years' financial statements should be translated using the currency rates that were in effect at the time of conversion. In other words, they will not update at the closing rate or the current average rate used in previous period financial statements. In the event that this upgrade is implemented, the values of these chairs will be different from what they would be if they did not record motions.

When dealing with matters pertaining to income and spending, it can be quite challenging to produce accurate results when using transaction dates and currency rates (Horton et al., 2013). As a consequence of this, one may use a conversion rate to convert exchange rates based on the transaction dates, for example by taking the average of the rates for that time period. This can be deduced from practical reasoning.

The variety of reporting requirements is certainly the biggest challenge for companies right now and requires a variety of discussions within the company and the appropriate resources. However, when applied correctly, reporting can add significant value and support the integration of disclosure issues across the organization. Companies should decide for their specific situation which cadres they use and what they want to communicate externally and to whom. Progress in these areas should then be reported regularly, using clear indicators and targets. Many unanswered questions in reporting will be clarified as data, processes, systems, and reporting mature. There is still a long way to go to the proper maturity of non-financial indicators compared to financial indicators. In the medium and long term, the stated goal should be to report in a standardized, focused, and comparable manner with high and significant quality.

SOLUTIONS AND RECOMMENDATIONS

Accounting and reporting are ways for organizations and their stakeholders to talk to each other and encourage social change. As a result, both stakeholder theory and legitimacy theory contribute to our understanding of sustainability disclosure since they both explain voluntary disclosure of sustainability challenges even in the absence of strong sustainability performance. The absence of trustworthy information is closely tied to the lack of available data. Compound measurements are based on information supplied by firms, which is not available to the public. Thus, the validity of these measurements is dependent, at least in part, on company self-disclosure, which may have an incentive to present themselves in the best light possible.

Exchange rate discrepancies are included in the company's equity as a distinct component until the overseas operation is sold. In the event that these differences are associated with a foreign business that is not entirely owned (that is, there are non-controlling interests) and that is strengthened, then the portion of these differences that pertain to non-controlling interests will be recognized as part of the non-controlling interest of the consolidated statement of financial position.

As of the date of the acquisition, the difference in value between the involved in the transaction value and the accounting values will be assigned in the acquired assets and assumed liabilities in order to achieve the fair value of such assets and liabilities. The commercial background receives the extra. It is critical to remember that this allocation table will be created just once, at the time of purchase, and will stay unmodified. The revenue and costs of a subsidiary are included beginning with the date of purchase and ending when the mother society no longer has control. It is critical to understand that the value of the assets and liabilities as of the acquisition date will have an impact on the consolidated result.

The values disclosed by the subsidiary do not take into consideration the fair values as of the purchase date when referring to fixed assets that are not depreciable (land). The difference between accounting values and fair values as of the date of the business combination will be represented solely in the mother society and the worksheet required to acquire the consolidated financial conditions. However, because the land is not depreciable, this disparity does not affect any of the purposes of an adjustment. In any case, if the land is not sold or there is a temporary depreciation, we must make modifications in the spreadsheet as well.

None of the entities will register the commercial backdrop that results from the business merger in their own individual financial positions. For an indefinite amount of time, the commercial background will only exist in the mother society's consolidated financial problems.

A depreciation test will only affect its worth if we discover any depreciation. This depreciation will be recorded as a cost, and the consolidated result will be discounted. In contrast to the subsequent years, where depreciation is visible, the first year shows no evidence of it.

Information regarding the value of the exchange discrepancies should be disclosed in an organization's financial accounts, and this information can either be included in the net profit or net loss for the period, or it can be categorized as equity. It should also reconcile the opening and closing balances to the total exchange difference recorded as equity. There should be additional information included in financial statements on the functional currency, such as: if the functional currency is different from the country's currency, the cause for using a different currency should be specified; the reason that was considered when making the choice to change the presentation or functional currency; if financial statements are presented in other than functional currency, the reason for currency change should be indicated.

FUTURE RESEARCH DIRECTIONS

Business model disclosure, as a framework for non-financial information, could also be a useful tool for sustainability reporting. The sustainable business model literature has come up with a variety of ways for managers to incorporate environmental and social concerns into their day-to-day activities. Furthermore, it is acknowledged in the literature on sustainability management that effective internal and external communications are essential components of any effort to integrate sustainability inside a business.

Regarding the statement of equity and the status of other items included in the comprehensive income, we would like to elaborate once again on the following points: The total amount of exchange rate differences are shown as a distinct component of equity to the disposal of the foreign operation; the position of other parts of the overall result includes correcting the conversion as an increase or reduction.

Determining and establishing pertinent indicators is crucial, as is grouping them into distinct categories (e.g., quantitative or qualitative components of a company's operations, such as its workers, or macro concerns), rather than merely lumping them all together. Each category should also be given a specific weight when determining the final conclusion.

Another difficulty would be to generalize the link between business combination and firm success to other nations and sectors, rather than going on forever with instances and studies. Disclosure of a firm's business model could be beneficial for stakeholders in this regard since it offers information that must be kept succinct and focuses solely on pertinent details that are associated with the process of value generation at a company.

CONCLUSION

It is important for social groups to remember that their efforts to implement IFRS adjustments will be disclosed to investors because: many managers view confidential management and discovery as going too far; (Mechelli & Cimini, 2014). They also favor the IFRSs' high level of openness and comparability.

It may be a priority for a group's management team to retain such secrecy - such as progress achieved in applying IFRS, on the day-to-day activities of societies, or more specific initiatives. Overwhelmingly, managers interviewed acknowledge that they are well-versed in IFRS and its implications. More than three-quarters are aware of the impact of IFRS on firms in their nation and, similarly, are extremely or adequately confidential in terms of comprehending the consequences on the companies in which they invest.

An overview of the above conversion rules on the financial statements of a foreign firm would be as follows: all assets and liabilities are converted to the closing rate; social capital accounts are converted to the historical exchange rate from the date of purchase; accounts that constitute cumulative profits.

Some social and environmental disclosures have recently been consolidated with financial disclosures in single reports, probably in reaction to the rising complexity and length of stand-alone reports. In contrast to previous social and environmental disclosures made inside annual reports, which did not connect social and environmental information with financial information, these new developments have attempted to integrate social, environmental, financial, and governance information.

As a standard for corporate communication, Integrated Reporting supports in the preparation of financial as well as other reports and is a process that results in effective communication about how a company's long-term strategy, governance, performance, and prospects lead to value creation.

REFERENCES

Ahmed, A., Neel, M., & Wang, D. (2013). Does mandatory adoption of IFRS improve accounting quality? Preliminary evidence. *Contemporary Accounting Research, 30*(4), 388–423. doi:10.1111/j.1911-3846.2012.01193.x

Al Lawati, H., & Hussainey, K. (2022). Does Sustainable Development Goals Disclosure Affect Corporate Financial Performance? *Sustainability, 14*(13), 7815. doi:10.3390u14137815

Allen, A., & Ramanna, K. (2013). Towards an understanding of the role of standard setters in standard setting. *Journal of Accounting and Economics, 55*(1), 1–66. doi:10.1016/j.jacceco.2012.05.003

Alzola, M. A. (2017). Beware of the watchdog: Rethinking the normative justification of gatekeeper liability. *Journal of Business Ethics, 140*(4), 705–721. doi:10.100710551-017-3460-3

Balachandran, B., & Faff, R. (2015). Corporate governance, firm value and risk: Past, present, and future. *Pacific-Basin Finance Journal, 35*(A), 1-12.

Ball, R., Li, X., & Shivakumar, L. (2015). Contractibility and transparency of financial statement information prepared under IFRS: Evidence from debt contracts around IFRS adoption. *Journal of Accounting Research, 53*(5), 915–963. doi:10.1111/1475-679X.12095

Barth, M., Landsman, W., & Lang, M. (2008). International accounting standards and accounting quality. *Journal of Accounting Research, 46*(3), 467–498. doi:10.1111/j.1475-679X.2008.00287.x

Barth, M. E. (2013). Global comparability in financial reporting: What, why, how, and when? *China Journal of Accounting Studies, 1*(1), 2–12. doi:10.1080/21697221.2013.781765

Barth, M. E., Konchitchki, Y. L., & Landsman, W. R. (2013). Cost of capital and earnings transparency. *Journal of Accounting and Economics, 55*(2–3), 206–224. doi:10.1016/j.jacceco.2013.01.004

Barth, M. E., Landsman, W. R., & Lang, M. H. (2008). International accounting standards and accounting quality. *Journal of Accounting Research, 43*(3), 467–498. doi:10.1111/j.1475-679X.2008.00287.x

Barth, M. E., Landsman, W. R., Young, D., & Zhuang, Z. (2014). Relevance of Differences between Net Income based on IFRS and Domestic Standards for European Firms. *Journal of Business Finance & Accounting*, *41*(3-4), 297–506. doi:10.1111/jbfa.12067

Beasley, M. S., Buckless, F. A., Glover, S. M., & Prawitt, D. F. (2009). *Auditing Cases. An Interactive Learning Approach* (4th ed.). Prentice Hall.

Bozec, Y. (2008). Ownership Concentration, Separation of Voting Rights from Cash Flow Rights, and Earnings Management: An Empirical Study in Canada. *Canadian Journal of Administrative Sciences*, *25*(1), 1–15. doi:10.1002/cjas.52

Brüggemann, U., Hitz, J.-M., & Sellhorn, T. (2013). Intended and unintended consequences of mandatory IFRS adoption: A review of extant evidence and suggestions for future research. *European Accounting Review*, *22*(1), 1–37. doi:10.1080/09638180.2012.718487

Cairns, D., Massoudi, D., Taplin, R., & Tarca, A. (2011). IFRS fair value measurement and accounting policy choice in the United Kingdom and Australia. *The British Accounting Review*, *43*(1), 1–21. doi:10.1016/j.bar.2010.10.003

Carnini Pulino, S., Ciaburri, M., Magnanelli, B. S., & Nasta, L. (2022). Does ESG Disclosure Influence Firm Performance? *Sustainability*, *14*(13), 7595. doi:10.3390u14137595

Chebaane, S., & Othman, H. B. (2014). The Impact of IFRS Adoption on Value Relevance of Earnings and Book Value of Equity: The Case of Emerging Markets in African and Asian Regions. *Procedia: Social and Behavioral Sciences*, *145*, 70–80. doi:10.1016/j.sbspro.2014.06.012

Chen, H., Tang, Q., Jiang, Y., & Lin, Z. (2010). The role of international financial reporting standards in accounting quality: Evidence from the European Union. *Journal of International Financial Management & Accounting*, *21*(3), 220–278. doi:10.1111/j.1467-646X.2010.01041.x

Choi, Y.-S., Peasnell, K., & Toniato, J. (2013). Has the IASB been successful in making accounting earnings more useful for prediction and valuation? UK evidence. *Journal of Business Finance & Accounting*, *40*(7–8), 741–768. doi:10.1111/jbfa.12025

Daske, H., & Gebhardt, G. (2006). International financial reporting standards and experts' perceptions of disclosure quality. *Abacus*, *42*(3/4), 461–498. doi:10.1111/j.1467-6281.2006.00211.x

Dechow, P., Sloan, R., & Sweeney, A. (1996). Causes and consequences of earnings manipulation: An analysis of firms subject to enforcement actions by the SEC. *Contemporary Accounting Research*, *13*(1), 1–36. doi:10.1111/j.1911-3846.1996.tb00489.x

DeFond, M. L. (2010). Earnings quality research: Advances, challenges and future research. *Journal of Accounting and Economics*, *50*(2-3), 402–409. doi:10.1016/j.jacceco.2010.10.004

Doukakis, L. C. (2010). The persistence of earnings and earnings components after the adoption of IFRS. *Managerial Finance*, *36*(11), 969–980. doi:10.1108/03074351011081286

Fu, R., Kraft, A., & Zhang, H. (2012). Financial reporting frequency, information asymmetry, and the cost of equity. *Journal of Accounting and Economics*, *54*(2–3), 132–149. doi:10.1016/j.jacceco.2012.07.003

Ghosh, A., & Olsen, L. (2008). Environmental uncertainty and managers' use of discretionary accruals. *Accounting, Organizations and Society*, *34*(2), 188–205. doi:10.1016/j.aos.2008.07.001

Horton, J., Serafeim, G., & Serafeim, I. (2013). Does mandatory IFRS adoption improve the information environment? *Contemporary Accounting Research*, *30*(1), 388–423. doi:10.1111/j.1911-3846.2012.01159.x

Houque, M. N. (2012). The effect of IFRS adoption and investor protection on earnings quality around the world. *The International Journal of Accounting*, *47*(3), 333–355. doi:10.1016/j.intacc.2012.07.003

Iatridis, G. (2010). International Financial Reporting Standards and the quality of financial statement information. *International Review of Financial Analysis*, *19*(3), 193–204. doi:10.1016/j.irfa.2010.02.004

Iatridis, G. (2012). Hedging and earnings management in the light of IFRS implementation: Evidence from the UK stock market. *The British Accounting Review*, *44*(1), 21–35. doi:10.1016/j.bar.2011.12.002

Jeanjean, T., & Stolowy, H. (2008). Do accounting standards matter? An exploratory analysis of earnings management before and after IFRS adoption. *Journal of Accounting and Public Policy*, *27*(6), 480–490. doi:10.1016/j.jaccpubpol.2008.09.008

Jones, D. A., & Smith, K. J. (2012). Comparing the value relevance, predictive value, and persistence of other comprehensive income and special items. *The Accounting Review*, *86*(6), 2047–2073. doi:10.2308/accr-10133

Klein, A. (2002). Audit committee, board of director characteristics and earnings management. *Journal of Accounting and Economics*, *33*(3), 375–400. doi:10.1016/S0165-4101(02)00059-9

Kothari, S. P., Leone, A. J., & Wasley, C. E. (2005). Performance matched discretionary accrual measures. *Journal of Accounting and Economics*, *39*(1), 163–197. doi:10.1016/j.jacceco.2004.11.002

Landsman, W. R., Maydew, E. L., & Thornock, J. R. (2012). The information content of annual earnings announcements and mandatory adoption of IFRS. *Journal of Accounting and Economics*, *53*(1-2), 34–54. doi:10.1016/j.jacceco.2011.04.002

Lang, M., Raedy, J. S., & Wilson, W. (2006). Earnings management and cross listing: Are reconciled earnings comparable to US earnings? *Journal of Accounting and Economics*, *42*(1-2), 255–283. doi:10.1016/j.jacceco.2006.04.005

Leuz, C., Nanda, D., & Wysocki, P. D. (2003). Earnings management and investor protection: An international comparison. *Journal of Financial Economics*, *69*(3), 505–527. doi:10.1016/S0304-405X(03)00121-1

Lin, S., Riccardi, W., & Wang, C. (2012). Does accounting quality change following a switch from U.S.GAAP to IFRS? Evidence from Germany. *Journal of Accounting and Public Policy*, *31*(6), 641–657. doi:10.1016/j.jaccpubpol.2012.10.006

Lobo, G. L., & Zhou, J. (2001). Disclosure quality and earning management. *Asia-Pacific Journal of Accounting & Economics*, *8*(1), 1–20. doi:10.1080/16081625.2001.10510584

Louwers, T. J., Ramsay, R. J., Sinason, D. H., & Strawser, J. R. (2007). *Auditing and Assurance Services* (2nd ed.). McGraw-Hill Irwin.

Marra, A., Mazzola, P., & Prencipe, A. (2011). Board Monitoring and Earnings Management Pre- and Post-IFRS. *The International Journal of Accounting*, *46*(2), 205–230. doi:10.1016/j.intacc.2011.04.007

Mechelli, A., & Cimini, R. (2014). Is comprehensive income value relevant and does location matter? A European study. *Accounting in Europe*, *16*(25), 1–35. doi:10.1080/17449480.2014.890777

Messier, W. F., Glover, S. M., & Prawitt, D. F. (2008). *Auditing and Assurance Services. A Systematic Approach* (5th ed.). McGraw-Hill Irwin.

Pope, P., & McLeay, S. (2011). The European IFRS experiment: Objectives, research challenges and some early evidence. *Accounting and Business Research*, *41*(3), 233–266. doi:10.1080/00014788.2011.575002

Richardson, A. (2011). Myth, Paradigms and Academic Accounting Research: A Comment on Reading and Understanding Academic Research in Accounting. *Global Perspectives on Accounting Education*, *8*, 67–77.

Rittenberg, L. E., & Schwieger, B. J. (2005). *Auditing. Concepts for a Changing Environment* (5th ed.). Thomson South-Western.

Schleicher, T., Tahoun, A., & Walker, M. (2010). IFRS adoption in Europe and investment-cash flow sensitivity: Outsider versus insider economies. *The International Journal of Accounting*, *45*(2), 143–168. doi:10.1016/j.intacc.2010.04.007

Tendeloo, B., & Vanstrelen, A. (2005). Earnings management under German GAAP versus IFRS. *European Accounting Review*, *14*(1), 155–180. doi:10.1080/0963818042000338988

Thong, T. Y., Ding, D. K., & Lim, C. Y. (2008). Firm diversification and earning management: Evidence from seasoned equity offerings. *Review of Quantitative Finance and Accounting*, *30*(1), 69–92. doi:10.100711156-007-0043-x

Watts, R., & Zimmerman, J. (1978). Towards a Positive Theory of the Determination of Accounting Standards. *The Accounting Review*, *53*(1), 112–134.

Whittington, O. R., & Pany, K. (2008). *Principles of Auditing & Other Assurance Services* (16th ed.). McGraw-Hill Irwin.

Xiong, Y. (2006). Earning management and its measurement; a theoretical perspective. *The Journal of American Academy of Business, Cambridge*, *9*(1), 214–219.

Zeghal, D., Chtourou, S., & Fourati, M. Y. (2012). The effect of mandatory adoption of IFRS on earning quality: Evidence from the European Union. *Journal of International Accounting Research*, *11*(2), 1–25. doi:10.2308/jiar-10221

Zéghal, D., Chtourou, S., & Mnif, S. Y. (2011). An analysis of the effect of mandatory adoption of IAS/IFRS on earnings Management. *Journal of International Accounting, Auditing & Taxation*, *20*(2), 61–72. doi:10.1016/j.intaccaudtax.2011.06.001

ADDITIONAL READING

Ball, R., Li, X., & Shivakumar, L. (2015). Contractibility and transparency of financial statement information prepared under IFRS: Evidence from debt contracts around IFRS adoption. *Journal of Accounting Research*, *53*(5), 915–963. doi:10.1111/1475-679X.12095

Cui, R., Ma, Z., & Wang, L. (2022). Allocation of Decision Rights and CSR Disclosure: Evidence from Listed Business Groups in China. *Sustainability*, *14*(7), 3840. doi:10.3390u14073840

Fan, J. P. H., Li, J., & Zheng, G. (2016). Revisiting the bright and dark sides of capital flows in business groups. *Journal of Business Ethics*, *134*(4), 509–528. doi:10.100710551-014-2382-6

Guthrie, J., & Parker, L. D. (2016). Whither the accounting profession, accountants and accounting researchers? Commentary and projections. *Accounting, Auditing & Accountability Journal*, *29*(1), 2–10. doi:10.1108/AAAJ-10-2015-2263

Pieper, J. R., Trevor, C. O., Weller, I., & Duchon, D. (2017). Referral Hire Presence Implications for Referrer Turnover and Job Performance. *Journal of Management*, *19*, 14–20.

Chapter 9
Balanced Scorecard:
Development of a Strategic Map to Improve the Performance of Medical Services

Adela Ioana Staras
National Institute for Chemical Pharmaceutical Research and Development (INCD-ICCF), Romania

Teodora Breaz
1 Decembrie 1918 University, Romania

Melinda Timea Fulop
Babeş-Bolyai University, Romania

Dan Ioan Topor
1 Decembrie 1918 University, Romania

Sorinel Căpuşneanu
https://orcid.org/0000-0003-3799-3993
Titu Maiorescu University, Romania

ABSTRACT

This chapter deals with developing a strategic map for improving the performance of medical services using the balanced scorecard (BSC). The main objectives of this chapter are to present the conceptual approaches of the balanced scorecard, the implementation and use of BSC in medical services, the advantages and limitations of BSC implementation in medical services. Based on the literature, the authors present the interpretations brought by specialists to the balanced scorecard concept and analyze the degree of implementation and use of BSC in medical services. A

DOI: 10.4018/978-1-6684-4595-2.ch009

case study on the development of a strategic map for improving the performance of health services with the help of BSC is presented. Considering the factors that influence the size of medical organizations, the authors also present the advantages and limitations of adopting and using the balanced scorecard. The chapter ends with the general conclusions regarding improving medical services performance using BSC.

INTRODUCTION

The health care system is one of the most critical sectors of society and the economy, especially in countries with a developed economy, growing significantly in recent years. However, despite all the investments made by governments, this system is complex and has difficulties measuring performance, is characterized by long waiting times, low productivity, stressed medical staff, or patients dissatisfied with the medical services provided.

Performance measurement provides management of health care institutions with evidence of existing practices, beliefs, and assumptions, allowing management to create a strategic map for improving future health care services (Cokins & Căpușneanu, 2020). The development of the strategic map is closely linked to the Balanced Scorecard (BSC) and the perspectives of approaching the performance of an organization: the financial perspective, the internal perspective, the client perspective and the learning and growth perspective. Being composed of a complex set of entities, processes and activities, the health care system is subject to dramatic changes due to its functioning, the increase of the competitive level, the alternatives of services offered to the clients, the increase of the quality of the medical services offered.

To cope with these changes, the management of a healthcare institution must have reliable and timely information to make appropriate decisions with an impact on future business and increase performance, especially given that healthcare services are based on the most accurate information possible. of the customer. The improvement of the performance measurement system in the field of medical services must be rethought and adapted to the pressures of reducing costs, the quality of the level of care of patients/clients, ETC. Therefore, IT is very important to select specific indicators with an impact on highlighting those issues pursued by the objectives set by the management of health care institutions (Holban et al., 2021). In this regard, the purpose of this chapter is to highlight the following aspects: (1) *the presentation of the Balanced Scorecard (BSC) concept and its development*; (2) *the use of BSC in medical services*; (3) *presentation of the critical factors that influence the medical services industry*; (4) *presentation of the advantages and limitations of BSC implementation*; (5) *conducting a case study on developing a strategic map for improving performance with the help of the BSC at a healthcare institution.*

BACKGROUND

Balanced Scorecard: Concept and Development

At the end of the 20th century, Kaplan and Norton (1996) first introduced a Balanced Scorecard (BSC) as a tool for implementing its strategy. Since its inception and implementation, many profitable organizations have successfully analyzed and applied BSC in various industries and at different organizational levels (Lueg & Carvalho e Silva, 2013; Hoque, 2014) but also in non-profit organizations (Rodrigues Quesado et al., 2017), each of them depending on the objectives pursued, personalizes the model chosen by BSC.

Specialists analyzed the impact of using the Balanced Scorecard in terms of effectiveness (Amado et el., 2012) on the organization, and their findings were reflected in the following aspects: the BSC model through the four business perspectives focuses on both the past and the future through the indicators it calculates (Kaplan & Norton, 1996; Wade & Recardo, 2001; Kumbakara, 2008; Celma et al., 2017). Other experts have focused their research on analyzing the concept of BSC and its links to key perspectives, establishing many causal relationships, both within and between perspectives, resulting in the achievement of financial goals (Nørreklit, 2000; Bryant et al., 2004; Čizmić & Crnkić, 2010).

Experts have captured the impact of companies' strategy on the BSC's outlook by including financial or non-financial indicators specific to the outlook or strategic indicators for their interconnection (Bryant et al., 2004; Huang et al., 2009; Parmenter, 2010; Janeš, 2014) and the performance measurement system is thus aligned with the company's strategy (Bourne et al., 2000; Radnor & Lovell, 2003; Atkinson, 2006). In order to strike a balance between the internal and external performance prospects of the BSC, it is necessary to combine several indicators in a single framework between short-term and long-term objectives (Daft, 2010). Comprising all stakeholders in the company, BSC provides a complete reflection on implementation and strategy becoming a holistic system (Ittner et al., 2003; de Geuser et al., 2009; Cheffi et al., 2010). Starting from the concept of Balanced Index for Balanced Scorecard BSC (BSC BI), some experts believe that it offers a balance between multiple perspectives that will allow the organization to develop all its organizational capabilities equally (Olsson et al., 2000; Osama, 2006; Funck, 2007; Stefanovska & Soklevski, 2014; Shin et al., 2015). Specialist research has focused on deepening how organizations handle measurements and use the information collected to provide management and support management (Zelman et al., 2003; Kollberg, 2007; Aidemark & Funck, 2009).

Balanced Scorecard: Use in Medical Services

The use of BSC in healthcare has resulted in correcting errors in performance standards, the monitoring of organizational results to achieve the objectives and level of organizational strategy. The current purpose of BSC is to define, communicate, and strengthen core values, the purpose, and the direction of the organization to encourage opportunity-seeking behavior (Kollberg & Elg, 2011). Funck (2009) suggests the following functions of BSC: (1) management control; (2) strategic management tool; (3) information and communication tool; (4) quality management tool; (5) benchmarking tool; and (6) the complementary budgeting instrument.

According to specialists, BSC is used in health services for several reasons: (1) as a system for improving the quality of health care (Funck, 2009); (2) support in the long-term survival of companies (Zelman et al., 2003); (3) system for reducing the uncertainty of objectives within the organization (Aidemark, 2001); (4) creating a common language for improving health care services (Hallin & Kastberg, 2002); (5) improving customer orientation (Rahm et al., 2002); (6) implementation of the support strategy (Atkinson, 2006).

BSC promotes multidimensional thinking (Andersson et al., 2000), including a series of performance measures necessary to represent all dimensions of the organization, considering in the case of healthcare: patients, health care processes, professional staff learning (Aidermark, 2001). Thus, in health care, it is necessary to measure and monitor medical activities such as time of care and physical condition of the patient, operations and treatments, number of diagnoses, etc. but also administrative activities such as: waiting and care times, compliance, productivity, efficiency, rationality, economic measures (Kollberg & Elg, 2011). Therefore, several experts believe that BSC is a relevant framework. However, the concept needs to be developed in local departments (Rahm et al., 2002) and modified and adapted to an organization's specific requirements (Zelman et al., 2003), which will guarantee successful implementation of the BSC.

To successfully implement BSC in medical services, it is necessary to analyze the factors that determine BSC use. According to specialists, these factors are mainly related to (1) the approach that requires changes in organizational culture (Chavan, 2009); (2) understanding, commitment and support from both senior management and all employees (Kollberg & Elg, 2011); (3) developing and communicating a causal model of the strategy used by organizations that have implemented BSC (Othman, 2006); (4) decentralization of measures in terms of process, management interest, BSC demand and support, the flexibility of BSC design and use (Aidemark

& Funck, 2009). BSC is the dominant performance measurement system in the industry, but its implementation is complex due to the difficulties translating into concrete actions (Bhagyaschree et al., 2006).

Critical Factors Influencing the Healthcare Industry

According to the specialists, a series of critical factors have been identified as contributing to the implementation and development of the medical services industry, such as:

1. *Performance and improvement of performance indicators*. The BSC approach provides management with the necessary framework to transform the goals set by an organization's strategy into a set of performance measures (Baker & Pink, 1995; Atkinson, 2012). As a result, operational and strategic approaches are transformed into actions that measure performance (Cifalino & Baraldi, 2009; Yuen & Ng, 2012) and measuring performance helps reduce costs, improve the quality of care, and adhere to strict guidelines (Peng et al., 2007). Some of the indicators used in the BSC perspectives are based on:
    a. *Productivity and profitability.* The productivity indicator indicates the capacity of the staff employed in the health system (Kershaw & Kershaw, 2001), while the profitability indicator shows the efficiency of the management of the health system (Zelman et al., 2003).
    b. *Waiting time* refers to the length of time from the time of requesting a patient's consultation to its actual consultation (Chen et al., 2006).
    c. *Outpatient waiting time* is the difference between total operating income and total operating expenses divided by total operating income. In addition, customer satisfaction or the superior quality of medical services can help to improve the profit margin obtained. (Bamford & Chaziaislan, 2009).
    d. *The occupancy rate* is related to productivity, and if it is higher, it means the profit obtained by the health institution is the result of dividing the outputs at the inputs. (Chen et al., 2006).
2. *Satisfaction of customers, staff and quality assurance of medical services.* Customer satisfaction is a critical component of profitability for any product-oriented (health and wellness) quality of life business that helps the organization gain a competitive advantage over its competitors (Bakar et al., 2008). Clients' perception is determined by the success or failure of medical services. The quality control of healthcare provided by competing private contractors led to BSC measurement (Aidemark, 2010). Employee satisfaction contributes to improving customer service by showing a positive attitude towards the quality of future services (Zelman et al., 2003). Ensuring the quality of medical services means controlling the various

care processes within the health system (Urrutia & Eriksen, 2005). On the one hand, providing high-quality medical services would help to improve outcomes, customer and healthcare satisfaction, and on the other hand, reducing costs would create long-term competitive advantages. (Chen et al., 2006).

3. *Commitment of senior management*. Without the support of senior management, all changes related to the implementation of BSC in the medical services cannot be achieved (Zelman et al., 2003), which plays a significant role in forming an equal relationship between organizational interests. (Funck, 2007).
4. *Strategic planning and employee training*. Strategic planning is crucial given that the implementation of BSC requires a certain level of commitment from the hospital's senior management, volunteers and board members through their education, recognition, and support (Purbey et al., 2007). In addition, employee training is an essential factor in ensuring the quality of services; it is the training of employees and the administrative team, department directors, medical staff (Cifalino & Baraldi, 2009).
5. *Culture, courtesy, and respect*. Culture and faith influence patients' health care experiences, significantly contributing to increasing their satisfaction and improving health care (Zelman et al., 2003). A global survey on the use of BSC and best practices in health care (Gurd & Gao, 2007) or the use of the strategic map of BSC in health care organizations and health systems (Chan, 2009) would create a clearer vision in the field of health.
6. *Communication and adaptation to new technologies*. Communication is relevant in the field of health as it contributes, on the one hand, to the prevention of boils and health promotion, and on the other hand to the improvement of personal and public health through studies and the use of communication strategies for information and influence (Zelman et al., 2003). Healthcare institutions should include an additional perspective in the BSC that provides information on the socio-demographic and environmental factors in which they operate (Urrutia & Eriksen, 2005) and identify opportunities for improvement on existing issues (Chen et al., 2006). Adaptation to new technologies ensures the continuous improvement of medical services for clients (Kershaw & Kershaw, 2001).

Advantages and Limitations of BSC Implementation

In the opinion of specialists, the essential advantages that BSC brings in the field of medical services are the following: (1) it contributes to the evaluation of the application of the vision and strategy of the institution on these issues (Assiri et al., 2006; Juhmani, 2007); (2) contributes to the control and improvement of operations related to effective benchmarking (McAdam & Walker, 2003; Phillips, 2007) but also to the identification of opportunities to reduce costs (Anand et al., 2005);

(3) contributes to the encouragement and involvement of staff at all levels of the institution (McAdam & Walker, 2003).

Considering the stage of BSC implementation (design, processing, or use), the specialists identified the following disadvantages or difficulties:

- *in the design stage*: difficulties related to data collection (Kocakülâh & Austill, 2007), indicators to be chosen (Assiri et al., 2006; Kaufmann & Becker, 2005) and identification of cause-effect relationships between them (Anand et al., 2005; Malina & Selto, 2001); the existence of started and unfinished BSC implementation projects (Kaufmann & Becker, 2005).
- *in the processing stage*: difficulties in translating the strategy and communicating with the design team (Malina & Selto, 2001; Beer & Eisenstadt, 2004) are generally based on subjectivity and a certain tension in terms of performance measures (Malina & Selto, 2001), namely the effects of time on organizational results (Nørreklit, 2003); difficulties in holding senior management accountable for the implementation of the BSC (Galas & Forte, 2005; Atkinson, 2006; Prieto et al., 2006); difficulties in how employees perceive their contribution to improving performance through the BSC (Decoene & Bruggeman, 2006).
- *in the use stage*: difficulties related to the continued use of BSCs (environmental uncertainty, lack of assessment and reporting, insufficient communication, lack of up-to-date market and performance data etc.) (Kaufmann & Becker, 2005); difficulties in making investments and creating future value, the need to provide advice, the rigidity of existing hierarchical structures and the lack of a common culture (Prieto & de Carvalho, 2006, 2009).

Case Study on Developing a Strategic Map for Improving Medical Services With Balanced Scorecard

1. The long-term strategic performance objectives of a private medical clinic (medical services) (Table 1, figure 1).
2. Preparation of the strategic map for the improvement of medical services using BSC (Figure 2).
3. Defining each strategic performance objective and establishing the measurement indicator (Table 2).
4. Defining the performance target for 2 years (Table 3).
5. Possible courses of action for each strategic performance target (Table 4).
6. Balanced Scorecard Synthesis (Table 5).

Table 1. The long-term strategic performance objectives of a private medical clinic

Perspectives	Strategic Performance Goal	Number of Objectives to Be Formulated in the Project
1. Customers' perspective	Providing patients with unparalleled clinical care	3
2. Financial perspective	Turnover increase	4
3. Internal processes perspective	Conducting state-of-the-art research to eradicate the disorder	3
4. Learning and growth perspective	Developing advanced skills in future specialists	3

Figure 1. The long-term strategic performance objectives of a private medical clinic

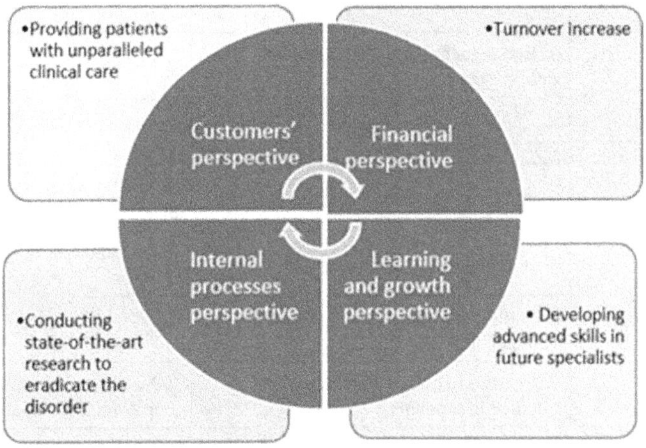

Figure 2. Strategic map for the improvement of medical services using BSC

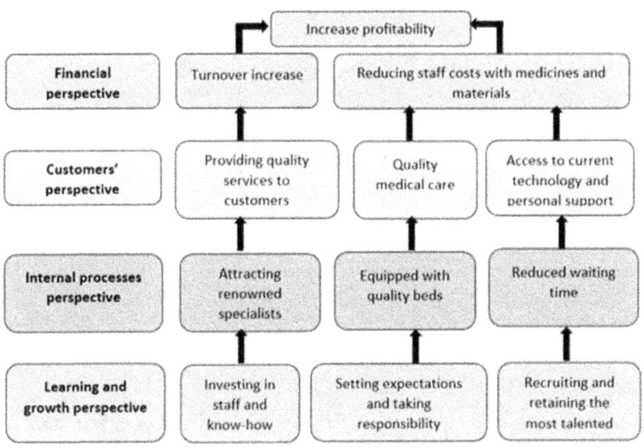

Table 2. Defining each strategic performance objective and establishing the measurement indicator

	Strategic Performance Goal	Measuring Indicator
1. The Customers' perspective	1. Providing patients with unparalleled clinical care	% Satisfied patients / Total patients
	2. Quality care with access to the latest tools and support staff	% No. patient complaints / No. total patients
	3. Quality care, comfort, and compassion	% No. appointments confirmations / No. Appointments
2. The financial perspective	1. Increase in revenue relative to costs	% Total revenues / total costs
	2. Personnel cost management	% Staff costs / total costs
	3. Management of daily costs on the clinic bed	Average bed expenses per day
	4. Management of drug and material costs	% Drugs and material costs / Total costs
3. The perspective of internal processes	1. Endowment with beds in the best quality conditions	% No. beds available / No. total beds
	2. Improving (reducing) waiting times and quick access for patients	Customer waiting time / Maximum waiting time
	3. Attracting renowned specialists	% No. renowned specialists / No. Specialist
4. The perspective of learning and growth	1. Investing in staff and know-how	% Personnel training expenses in total expenses
	2. Setting expectations and taking responsibility	% No. absents / No. total staff
	3. Recruiting and retaining the most talented individuals	% No. recruited individuals / No. employed individuals

Table 3. Defining the performance target for 2 years

Strategic Performance Goal	Measuring Indicator	Strategic Performance Target	Year 1	Year 2
Providing patients with unparalleled clinical care	% Satisfied patients / Total patients	90%	85%	90%
Quality care with access to the latest tools and support staff	% No. patient complaints / No. total patients	8%	10%	8%
Quality care, comfort and compassion	% No. appointments confirmations / No. appointments	90%	80%	90%
Increase in revenue related to costs	% Total revenues / total costs	80%	75%	80%
Personnel cost management	% Staff costs / total costs	60%	50%	60%
Management of daily costs on the clinic bed	Average bed expenses per day	1,500 lei	1,600 lei	1,500 lei
Management of drug and material costs	% Drug and material costs / Total costs	45%	48%	46%
Endowment with beds in the best quality conditions	% No. beds available / No. total beds	90%	80%	90%
Improving (reducing) waiting times and quick access for patients	Customer waiting time / Maximum waiting time	7 minutes	10 minutes	7 minutes
Attracting renowned specialists	% No. renowned specialists / No. specialists	50%	40%	50%
Investing in staff and know-how	% Personnel training expenses in total expenses	40%	30%	40%
Setting expectations and taking responsibility	% No. absents / No. total staff	10%	12%	10%
Recruiting and retaining the most talented individuals	% No. recruited individuals / No. envious employees	22%	12%	22%

Table 4. Choices for each strategic performance target

Strategic Performance Goal	Measuring Indicator	Strategic Performance Target	Courses of Action
Providing patients with unparalleled clinical care	% Satisfied patients / Total patients	90%	Improving medical services and attracting new patients
Quality care with access to the latest tools and support staff	% No. patient complaints / No. total patients	6%	Improving the quality of medical services, purchasing state-of-the-art tools and hiring experienced staff
Quality care, comfort, and compassion	% No. appointments confirmations / No. appointments	90%	Hiring specialised, experienced staff and ensuring a comfortable climate for patients
Increase in revenue related to costs	% Total revenues / total costs	80%	Attracting projects, new business partners
Personnel cost management	% Staff costs / total costs	60%	Improving staff pay levels
Management of daily costs on the clinic bed	Average bed expenses per day	1,300 lei	Elimination of certain facilities provided by unnecessary providers for patients
Management of drug and material costs	% Drug and material costs / Total costs	45%	Provision of an additional amount for medicines and materials in the budget
Endowment with beds in the best quality conditions	% No. beds available / No. total beds	90%	Attracting projects from non-reimbursable funds
Improving (reducing) waiting times and quick access for patients	Customer waiting time / Maximum waiting time	7 minutes	Hiring specialised and efficient staff in receiving patients
Attracting renowned specialists	% No. renowned specialists / No. Specialists	50%	Hiring specialised and well-paid staff
Investing in staff and know-how	% Personnel training expenses in total expenses	40%	Attracting projects from non-reimbursable funds
Setting expectations and taking responsibility	% No. absents / No. total staff	10%	Hiring serious and efficient staff
Recruiting and retaining the most talented individuals	% No. recruited individuals / No. envious employees	20%	Hiring specialised, talented staff with good prospects for the future

Table 5. Synthesis of Balanced Scorecard for medical services

Perspectives	Strategic Performance Goal	Measuring Indicator	Strategic Performance Target	Courses of Action
1. The customers' perspective	Providing patients with unparalleled clinical care	% Satisfied patients / Total patients	90%	Improving medical services and attracting new patients
	Quality care with access to the latest tools and support staff	% No. patient complaints / No. total patients	8%	Improving the quality of medical services, purchasing state-of-the-art tools and hiring experienced staff
	Quality care, comfort and compassion	% No. appointments confirmations / No. appointments	90%	Hiring specialised, experienced staff and ensuring a comfortable climate for patients
2. Financial perspective	Increase in revenue related to costs	% Total revenues / total costs	80%	Attracting projects, new business partners
	Personnel cost management	% Staff costs / total costs	60%	Improving staff pay levels
	Management of daily costs on the clinic bed	Average bed expenses per day	1,200 lei	Elimination of certain facilities provided by unnecessary providers for patients
	Management of drug and material costs	% Drug and material costs / Total costs	45%	Provision of an additional amount for medicines and materials in the budget
3. The perspective of internal processes	Endowment with beds in the best quality conditions	% No. beds available / No. total beds	90%	Attracting projects from non-reimbursable funds
	Improving (reducing) waiting times and quick access for patients	Customer waiting time / Maximum waiting time	7 minutes	Hiring specialised and efficient staff in receiving patients
	Attracting renowned specialists	% No. renowned specialists / No. Specialists	50%	Hiring specialised and well-paid staff
4. The perspective of learning and growth	Investing in staff and know-how	% Personnel training expenses in total expenses	40%	Attracting projects from non-reimbursable funds
	Setting expectations and taking responsibility	% No. absents / No. total staff	10%	Hiring serious and efficient staff
	Recruiting and retaining the most talented individuals	% No. recruited individuals / No. envious employees	20%	Hiring specialised, talented staff with good prospects for the future

SOLUTIONS AND RECOMMENDATIONS

Given the issues addressed during this chapter, we propose to specialists and all those interested the following improvement solutions:

- Identifying better performance indicators to highlight their calculation and analysis for more extended periods, but also constantly updating information.
- Full involvement of senior management and all staff categories in a health care institution in deepening the knowledge of BSC, its role and importance, but also in its successful implementation benefiting from its advantages in the future.
- Preparing a BSC implementation team or hiring specialists to contribute to the successful implementation of the BSC, long-term monitoring of the indicators used to assess the prospects of the BSC agreed with the objectives set by the senior management of the health care institution.
- Extending the BSC by including an environmental perspective would also help measure environmental performance under current integrated reporting or the direct use of the Sustainability Balanced Scorecard. (SBSC) (Cokins & Căpuşneanu, 2020).
- Based on the concepts discussed above, we recommend specialists and all those interested in deepening the BSC and the impact it has on the performance of a health care institution the following aspects:
- research of the specialized literature regarding the adoption and implementation of SBC, its advantages, and limitations.
- research at a national and global level of the impact produced by the implementation of BSC on strategic managerial accounting at the level of the medical service institutions that implemented them.
- adapting and expanding the company's culture among employees in terms of the advantages offered by adoption and implementation internally but also externally.
- publicizing the adoption and implementation of BSCs among health care institutions as a tool for measuring and monitoring their future performance.

FUTURE RESEARCH DIRECTIONS

Through the objectives launched in this chapter, we consider that we have reached our proposed goal within the business or academic environment. The chosen topic is current and of future interest for all specialists. The amount of information presented in this chapter covers a wide area of the international literature dedicated to adopting and implementing the BSC within the health care system, more precisely, the medical services. This amount of information has been carefully selected and synthesized to present only those significant aspects in adopting and implementing BSCs within healthcare institutions with accurate future research directions. We suggest the following research directions to specialists and all those interested:

- analysis of the possibilities to adapt and implement BSC to the specifics of the organizations, entities in the sanitary-medical field.
- analysis of the position of companies, entities, organizations regarding the BSC concept, medical legislation and the points of view of the management, the BSC implementation team, the employees.
- analysis of the impact of strategic managerial decisions resulting from the BSC implementation within the medical service institutions, of the performances obtained and on the extension of the BSC perspectives by including the environmental perspective or SBSC.

This paper aimed to present a review, analysis, classification, and coding of the Balanced Scorecard (BSC) literature to identify BSC implementation issues. Several issues were identified and classified as related to the BSC project, the BSC process, and difficulties in using the BSC. The results are not conclusive and could not be generalized. The methodology used in this study and the initial results can be replicated using a more extensive database, perhaps including, and properly analyzing consulting documents.

CONCLUSION

Through its structure, this chapter summarizes some aspects dedicated to the description of BSC and its conceptual evolution within health care institutions, the critical factors underlying the successful adoption and implementation of BSC within these institutions and the advantages and disadvantages offered. The following can be mentioned as strengths of this chapter:

- brings some clarifications regarding the adoption and implementation of BSCs within healthcare institutions.
- analyzes the critical factors that influence the implementation of BSC within medical service institutions.
- presents the advantages and disadvantages of implementing BSC within healthcare institutions
- analyzes health care institutions and their environment in terms of perspectives by presenting a case study on developing a strategic map for measuring performance with the help of BSCs within a health care institution.

- the BSC model used in the case study can be adapted to different types of organizations and new strategies. In particular, the model can be applied to public organizations and the service sector.
- BSC model promotes the commitment and participation of all employees due to the relationship between strategy and the process of continuous improvement.

This chapter has launched new challenges related to the adoption and implementation of BSC within medical service institutions and beyond. We are confident that the implications of BSC on the performance of a healthcare institution will not go unnoticed. However, efforts to identify new opportunities for the design, deepening, and diversification of BSC perspectives at the level of healthcare institutions need to be stepped up.

REFERENCES

Aidemark, G. (2010). Cooperation and competition: Balanced scorecard and hospital privatization. *International Journal of Health Care Quality Assurance*, *23*(8), 730–748. doi:10.1108/09526861011081868 PMID:21125968

Aidemark, L. G. (2001). The meaning of Balanced Scorecards in the health care organization. *Financial Accountability & Management*, *17*(1), 23–40. doi:10.1111/1468-0408.00119

Aidemark, L. G., & Funck, E. K. (2009). Measurement and health care management. *Financial Accountability & Management*, *25*(2), 253–276. doi:10.1111/j.1468-0408.2009.00476.x

Amado, C. A., Santos, S. P., & Marques, P. M. (2012). Integrating the Data Envelopment Analysis and the Balanced Scorecard approaches for enhanced performance assessment. *Omega*, *40*(3), 390–403. doi:10.1016/j.omega.2011.06.006

Anand, M., Sahay, B. S., & Saha, S. (2005). Balanced Scorecard in Indian Companies. *Vikalpa*, *30*(2), 11–25. doi:10.1177/0256090920050202

Andersson, P. M., Persson, J. E., & Ramberg, U. (2000). Balanced Scorecard i landsting: erfarenheter från tolv projekt i region Skäne. Institutet fo¨r ekonomisk forskning vid Lunds universitet, Lund.

Assiri, A., Zairi, M., & Eid, R. (2006). How to profit from the balanced scorecard: An implementation roadmap. *Industrial Management & Data Systems*, *106*(7), 937–952. doi:10.1108/02635570610688869

Atkinson, H. (2006). Strategy Implementation: A Role for the Balanced Scorecard? *Management Decision*, *44*(10), 1441–1460. doi:10.1108/00251740610715740

Atkinson, M. (2012). Developing and using a performance management framework – a case study. *Measuring Business Excellence*, *16*(3), 102–132. doi:10.1108/13683041211257402

Bakar, C., Akgün, H. S., & Assaf, A. F. (2008). The role of expectations in patients' hospital assessments: A Turkish university hospital example. *International Journal of Health Care Quality Assurance*, *21*(5), 503–516. doi:10.1108/09526860810890477 PMID:18785349

Baker, G. R., & Pink, G. H. (1995). A balanced scorecard for Canadian hospitals. *Healthcare Management Forum*, *8*(2), 7–21. doi:10.1016/S0840-4704(10)60926-X PMID:10156487

Bamford, D., & Chaziaislan, E. (2009). Healthcare capacity measurement. *International Journal of Productivity and Performance Management*, *58*(8), 748–766. doi:10.1108/17410400911000390

Beer, M., & Eisenstat, R. A. (2004). How to have an honest conversation about your business strategy. *Harvard Business Review*, *82*(2), 82–89. PMID:14971272

Bhagyashree, P., Margaret, R., & Victor, P. (2006). Performance measurement systems: Successes, failures and future? A review. *Measuring Business Excellence*, *10*(3), 4–14. doi:10.1108/13683040610685748

Bourne, M., Mills, J., Wilcox, M., Neely, A., & Platts, K. (2000). Designing, implementing and updating performance measurement systems. *International Journal of Operations & Production Management*, *20*(7), 754–771. doi:10.1108/01443570010330739

Bryant, L., Jones, D. A., & Widener, S. K. (2004). Managing Value Creation within the Firm: An Examination of Multiple Performance Measures. *Journal of Management Accounting Research*, *16*(1), 107–131. doi:10.2308/jmar.2004.16.1.107

Celma, D., Buil, M., & Patau, J. (2017). Management control in startups with high growth success in the Technology sector: The case of Netrivals. *European Accounting and Management Review*, *3*(2), 17–44. doi:10.26595/eamr.2014.3.2.2

Chan, Y. L. (2009). How strategy map works for Ontario's health system. *International Journal of Public Sector Management*, *22*(4), 349–363. doi:10.1108/09513550910961628

Chavan, M. (2009). The Balanced Scorecard: A new challenge. *Journal of Management Development*, *28*(5), 393–406. doi:10.1108/02621710910955930

Cheffi, W., Rao, A., & Beldi, A. (2010). Designing a Performance Measurement System: Accountants and Managers Diverge. *Management Accounting Quarterly*, *11*(3), 8–21.

Chen, X. Y., Yamauchi, K., Kato, K., Nishimura, A., & Ito, K. (2006). Using the balanced scorecard to measure Chinese and Japanese hospital performance. *International Journal of Health Care Quality Assurance*, *19*(5), 339–350. doi:10.1108/09526860610671391 PMID:16961099

Cifalino, A., & Baraldi, S. (2009). Training programs and performance measurement: Evidence from healthcare organizations. *Journal of Human Resource Costing and Accounting*, *13*(4), 294–315. doi:10.1108/14013381011010141

Čizmić, E., & Crnkić, K. (2010). Enhancing Organizational Effectiveness and Efficiency through Balanced Scorecard Application. *Problems and Perspectives in Management*, *8*(4), 14–26.

Daft, R. L. (2010). *Organization Theory and Design* (10th ed.). South-Western Cengage Learning.

De Geuser, F., Mooraj, S., & Oyon, D. (2009). Does the Balanced Scorecard Add Value? Empirical Evidence on its Effect on Performance. *European Accounting Review*, *18*(1), 93–122. doi:10.1080/09638180802481698

Decoene, V., & Bruggeman, W. (2006). Strategic alignment and middle-level managers' motivation in a balanced scorecard setting. *International Journal of Operations & Production Management*, *26*(4), 429–448. doi:10.1108/01443570610650576

Funck, E. (2007). The Balanced Scorecard Equates Interests in Healthcare Organizations. *Journal of Accounting & Organizational Change*, *3*(2), 88–103. doi:10.1108/18325910710756122

Funck, E. K. (2009). Ordination Balanced Scorecard – översättning av ett styrinstrument inom hälso- och sjukvården [Prescription Balanced Scorecard – Translation of a Management Control Instrument in Health Care]. Ekonomihögskolan, Växjö universitet.

Galas, E. S., & Forte, S. H. A. C. (2005). Fatores que interferem na implantação de um modelo de gestão estratégica baseado no balanced scorecard: estudo de caso em uma instituição pública. *Revista de Administração do Mackenzie*, *6*(2), 88-111.

Gurd, B., & Gao, T. (2007). Lives in the balance: An analysis of the balanced scorecard (BSC) in healthcare organizations. *International Journal of Productivity and Performance Management*, *57*(1), 6–21. doi:10.1108/17410400810841209

Hallin, B., & Kastberg, G. (2002). Balanced Scorecard i teori och praktik. En flerdimensionell styrmodell i hälso- och sjukvå rden. Göteborgs universitet.

Hoque, Z. (2014). 20 years of studies on the balanced scorecard: Trends, accomplishments, gaps and opportunities for future research. *The British Accounting Review, 46*(1), 33–59. doi:10.1016/j.bar.2013.10.003

Huang, H.-C., Chu, W., Lai, M.-C., & Lin, L.-H. (2009). Strategic Linkage Process and Value-Driven System: A Dynamic Analysis of High-Tech Firms in a Newly-Industrialized Country. *Expert Systems with Applications, 36*(2), 3965–3974. doi:10.1016/j.eswa.2008.02.038

Ittner, C. D., Larcker, D. F., & Randall, T. (2003). Performance Implications of Strategic Performance Measurement in Financial Services Firms. *Accounting, Organizations and Society, 28*(7-8), 715–741. doi:10.1016/S0361-3682(03)00033-3

Janeš, A. (2014). Empirical Verification of the Balanced Scorecard. *Industrial Management & Data Systems, 114*(2), 203–219. doi:10.1108/IMDS-04-2013-0195

Juhmani, O. I. H. (2007). Usage, motives and usefulness of the Balanced Scorecard (BSC): Evidence from Bahrain. *International Journal of Business Research, 7*(5), 106–117.

Kaplan, R. S., & Norton, D. P. (1996). *The Balanced Scorecard: Translating Strategy into Action*. Harvard Business School Press.

Kaufmann, L., & Becker, A. (2005). Overcoming the barriers during Implementation and use of the balanced scorecard by multinational companies in Brazil. *Latin American Business Review, 6*(3), 39–62. doi:10.1300/J140v06n03_02

Kershaw, R., & Kershaw, S. (2001). Developing a balanced scorecard to implement strategy at St. Elsewhere hospital. *Management Accounting Quarterly, 2*(2), 28–35.

Kocakülâh, M., & Austill, A. D. (2007). Balanced scorecard application in the Health Care Industry: a case study. *Journal of Health Care Finance, 34*(1), 72-99.

Kollberg, B. (2007). *Performance Measurement Systems in Swedish Health Care Services, Division of Quality Technology and Management*. Linköping University.

Kollberg, B., & Elg, M. (2011). The practice of the Balanced Scorecard in health care services. *International Journal of Productivity and Performance Management, 60*(5), 427–445. doi:10.1108/17410401111140374

Kumbakara, N. (2008). Managed IT Services: The Role of IT Standards. *Information Management & Computer Security, 16*(4), 336–359. doi:10.1108/09685220810908778

Lueg, R., & Carvalho e Silva, A. L. (2013). When One Size does not Fit All: A Literature Review on the Modifications of the Balanced Scorecard. *Problems and Perspectives in Management*, *11*(3), 86–94.

Malina, M. A., & Selto, F. H. (2001). Communicating and controlling strategy: An empirical study of the effectiveness of the balanced scorecard. *Journal of Management Accounting Research*, *13*(1), 47–90. doi:10.2308/jmar.2001.13.1.47

McAdam, R., & Walker, T. (2003). An Inquiry into Balanced Scorecards within Best Value Implementation in UK Local Government. *Public Administration*, *81*(4), 873–892. doi:10.1111/j.0033-3298.2003.00375.x

Nørreklit, H. (2000). The Balance on the Balanced Scorecard a Critical Analysis of Some of Its Assumptions. *Management Accounting Research*, *11*(1), 65–88. doi:10.1006/mare.1999.0121

Nørreklit, H. (2003). The balanced scorecard: What is the score? a rhetorical analysis of the balanced scorecard. *Accounting, Organizations and Society*, *28*(6), 591–619. doi:10.1016/S0361-3682(02)00097-1

Olsson, B., Karlsson, M., & Sharma, E. (2000). Towards a Theory of Implementing the Balance Scorecard: A Study in Association with the Swedish Telecommunication Firm Ericsson. *Journal of Human Resource Costing & Accounting*, *5*(1), 59–84. doi:10.1108/eb029064

Osama, A. (2006). *Multi-Attribute Strategy and Performance Architectures in R&D: The Case of The Balanced Scorecard*. PhD Thesis.

Othman, R. (2006). Balanced Scorecard and causal model development: Preliminary findings. *Management Decision*, *44*(5), 690–702. doi:10.1108/00251740610668923

Parmenter, D. (2010). *Key Performance Indicators: Developing, Implementing, and Using Winning KPIs* (2nd ed.). John Wiley & Sons.

Peng, T. A., Pike, S., & Roos, G. (2007). Intellectual capital and performance indicators: Taiwansese healthcare sector. *Journal of Intellectual Capital*, *8*(3), 535–556. doi:10.1108/14691930710774902

Phillips, P. A. (2007). The balanced scorecard and strategic control: a hotel case study analysis. *Service Industries Journal*, *27*(6), 731-746.

Prieto, V. C., & de Carvalho, M. M. (2009). *Literature review on Balanced Scorecard – Types of research, difficulties and benefits.*, Annual Conference on Production and Operations Management Society, Orlando, FL.

Prieto, V. C., Pereira, F. L. A., de Carvalho, M. M., & Laurindo, F. J. B. (2006). Critical Factors in Balanced Scorecard Implementation. *Gestão & Produção*, *13*(1), 81–92. doi:10.1590/S0104-530X2006000100008

Purbey, S., Mukherjee, K., & Bhar, C. (2007). Performance measurement system for healthcare processes. *International Journal of Productivity and Performance Management*, *56*(3), 241–251. doi:10.1108/17410400710731446

Radnor, Z., & Lovell, B. (2003). Success factors for implementation of the balanced scorecard in a NHS multi-agency setting. *International Journal of Health Care Quality Assurance*, *16*(2), 99–108. doi:10.1108/09536860310465618 PMID:12870249

Rahm, C., Henriks, G., & Skreding, M. (2002). *Insiktsboken – en skrift om ett nätverk som arbetar med Balanced Scorecard*. Landstingsförbundet.

Rodrigues Quesado, P., Frenandes Branco, J. C., & Rodrigues, F. J. (2017). Proposal to Implement the Balanced Scorecard in a Non-profit Organization. *European Accounting and Management Review*, *4*(1), 49–74. doi:10.26595/eamr.2014.4.1.3

Shin, J., Choi, J., & Kim, I. (2015). Development of BIM Performance Measurement System for Architectural Design Firms. In G. Celani, D. M. Sperling, & J. M. S. Franco (Eds.), *Computer-Aided Architectural Design Futures. The Next City - New Technologies and the Future of the Built Environment* (pp. 348–365). Springer Berlin Heidelberg. doi:10.1007/978-3-662-47386-3_19

Stefanovska, L., & Soklevski, T. (2014). Benefits of Using Balanced Scorecard in Strategic and Operational Planning, *Universal. Journal of Management*, *2*(4), 165–171.

Urrutia, I., & Eriksen, S. D. (2005). Application of the balanced scorecard in Spanish private health-care management. *Measuring Business Excellence*, *9*(4), 16–26. doi:10.1108/13683040510634808

Wade, D., & Recardo, R. (2001). *Corporate Performance Management: How to Build a Better Organization Through Measurement-Driven Strategic Alignment*. Butterworth-Heinemann. doi:10.1016/B978-0-87719-386-9.50005-7

Yuen, P. P., & Ng, A. W. (2012). Towards a balanced performance measurement system in public health care organization. *International Journal of Health Care Quality Assurance*, *25*(5), 421–430. doi:10.1108/09526861211235919 PMID:22946241

Zelman, W. N., Pink, G. H., & Matthias, C. B. (2003). Use of the balanced scorecard in health care. *Journal of Health Care Finance*, *29*(4), 1–16. PMID:12908650

KEY TERMS AND DEFINITIONS

Balanced Scorecard: A performance measure used to identify, improve, and control the various functions and the results.

Strategic Map: A form of graphical representation that indicates the cause-and-effect connection between an organization's strategic objectives.

Sustainability Balanced Scorecard: The fifth pillar of the SBC is a tool used to measure performance (for the four perspectives: financial, processes, customers, learning and development) and environmental performance to identify, improve and control certain functions of a business and the results obtained.

Chapter 10
Public Relations Auditing and Accountability With Digitalised Decentralised Ecosystems:
A Strategic Perspective

Ze Zook
University of Portsmouth, UK

ABSTRACT

This chapter explores the notion of public relations accountability in the not-so-distant future with the integration of blockchain technology as championed and demanded by several brands, considering its impact on the dissemination of communication, coherency and efficiency of the firm. Issues around value delivery with reputation management, the new online ecosystem and stakeholder relations are raised and explored.

INTRODUCTION

This chapter addresses the nature of public relations (PR) today. It assumes there is no schism between online and offline PR, and the definition of PR connotes both and is explored in relation to contemporary society. The subject is then addressed conceptually within a marketing framework and as a business function from the 1970s before discussing how and why it relates to blockchain technology, with specific insights into what blockchain technology is, how it works and how communication models are influenced to change.

DOI: 10.4018/978-1-6684-4595-2.ch010

The topic of marketing and PR security is discussed from a vantage point of B2B and B2C brands, with key themes such as General Data Protection Regulation (GDPR, 2018) and privacy. The chapter then addresses the issue of trustlessness, intelligent agents and Web 3.0.

The concept of social equity brands is analysed along the theme of 'trust', whilst the debate around artificial intelligence (AI) and machine learning (ML) is discussed hypothetically using the Hunt and Vitell ethics model (2021).

Aligning trust and trustlessness into building social capital, the focus–adjust–cast model is adapted from Bourgoin et al. (2018) and integrated into an optional dialogue strategy before concluding by stating the implications for management.

THE LEGACY OF PR

Traditionally, after 1945, the birth of PR since the 1920s has been amplified in its consistency of championing a top–down centralised approach. Indeed, this falls in line with the Grunigian orthodoxy that PR is a management function itself (Thompson, 2020) that is particularly focused on the task of managing communication with the public.

The legacy of this direction that PR has emerged from is what Thompson (2020) has defined as the classical approach – dating approximately between 1923 and 2010, epitomised by Ivy Lee and Edward Bernays, who depicted PR as being largely organisational and corporatist, and blending characteristics with a mixture of practice and theoretical orthodoxies. However, it is the societal role that PR plays in a neoliberal economy that is the focus of this research, understanding its contribution to a marketplace of ideas (Coombs & Holladay, 2007).

The importance of laying out the adequate groundwork for critically appraising opportunities within the environmental sphere raises the necessity of an understanding of classical and postclassical PR phrases, implying (a) classical PR conformance, operating through relational advantage, sensitivity to others, rationality and civility, and (b) postclassical PR nonconformance, characterised by a solitary and distinct positioning focus on self and incivility (Thompson, 2020). Building from this, some insight into what PR entails needs to be put forward. Sriramesh and Verci (2012) have framed PR as 'a specific form of management of communication and relationships. It is strategic in its intent and focused on the production of envisioned changes among groups of people, organizations or the society at large'.

The rationale behind grappling with PR in the Fourth Industrial Age, where changes in society are fast and rampant, is to disseminate and capture some entanglements and contradictions that unfold in power-orientated relationships through social exchange (Blau, 1964) in a client relationship concerning stakeholders and other agents where PR amalgamates in its operations (Thompson, 2020) with the legal remedies of injunctions, defamation and other court actions, with the risk and investigative work of private security specialists.

Considering the nature of PR and that PR operates as an adjunct activity, never done for the sake of itself but on behalf of organisations or individuals who seek promotional or persuasive advantage (Thompson, 2020), from a postclassical perspective, the societal role of PR includes being 'promotional intermediaries' (Davis, 2005) since it plays a key role in the production, consumption and promotion of commodities and culture to inform or persuade their public. Their ability to do this is fostered by access to specific networks (owned media), which are protected and layered with high levels of trust and reliability, so that media messages achieve the desired effect (Thompson, 2020). With this in mind, the organisational PR role is to permeate not only the organisation but also those who facilitate stakeholder engagement, facilitating trust. In this capacity, PR functions as a 'cultural intermediary', managing social relations that closely align and manifest through values and behaviours in the form of reputation management, which can be thought of as the Holy Grail in PR, as it contributes to business value and success. It involves cultivating goodwill among stakeholders and managing perceptions, relationships and the media (Meintjes & Grobler, 2014). In the 21st century (partly with the assistance of various media tools such as Social Mention, Twitter, etc.), enduring relationships are built by stakeholders by listening to their needs and expectations (Falconi, 2009), thus improving both organisational reputation and organisational decision-making (Niemann-Struweg, Meintjes & Grobler, 2007).

This element of PR, building relationships, is the crux of this analysis to benchmark best practice success in realms concerning blockchain technology and, specifically, digital agents that facilitate new power governance paradigms in these emerging ecosystems (Zwitter & Hazenberg, 2020).

PR'S RELATIONSHIP WITH MARKETING

Before examining the nature of blockchain technology and relating this to PR, it would be beneficial if a contextual understanding of PR in relation to marketing is relayed and perceived through the lens of digital marketing.

At the least, the relationship between marketing and PR has been tenuous and has been altered over the ages because of trends, technology movements and other external factors. In 1978, the renowned marketing author Philip Kotler and William Mindak highlighted this in their paper titled 'Marketing and Public Relations: Should They Be Partners or Rivals?' They predicted that a pattern of interrelation and operations would help combine distinctions between them and that their function, as a component of the business unit, would merge and become singular.

Before this exposition, marketing was considered as the professional business unit that dealt with markets in the sense of identifying a population from which a product or service could fuel demand, whilst PR used the term 'publics', which was aligned with groups or organisations that organised and mobilised whenever companies needed to make concessions that affect a group adversely (Grunig et al., 1980). They were also seen as being concerned with more general views of a company as opposed to being product-specific.

During the 1970s and 1980s, the economic ethos was heavily influenced by the Chicago school mantra of Nobel Prize–winning economist Milton Friedman that the core purpose of a business was to increase profits (Friedman, 1970). Marketers Kotler and Mindak later stated that '[m]arketing exists to sense, serve and satisfy customer needs for a profit', whilst PR exists to produce goodwill with the company's various publics.

However, turning to the other side of the Atlantic, throughout the 1980s and into the early 1990s, the UK financial industry went through a period of deregulation (Elliott, 2015), which was precipitated in the USA with supply-side economic policies on stimulating consumer spending (Corporate Finance Institute, n.d.). Its knock-on effect across industries raised media costs (Wood, 2020). Organisations such as the Body Shop in the UK epitomised this, as it was a company with a social conscience that championed ethics first and foremost as its axis of interaction with its body and skincare products, which included ethically sourced, natural, cruelty-free lotions and perfumes. The company understood the need to leverage marketing budgets and followed a corporate policy of ensuring credibility in their products and services before raising credibility (Smith 2003) through a dynamic application of a communication mix on issues such as store décor and exceptional customer service, which all contributed to the Body Shop making use of PR as their central communications tool as well as fulfilling and executing its marketing business function. Other consumer brands, such as Starbucks, followed the Body Shop model by making publicity their central communication point, which lent weight to the argument of both marketing and PR being given even weight: marketing PR (Kotler & Mindak, 1978).

However, between the mid-1990s and 2005, the relationship between marketing and PR oscillated in varying degrees with emphasis at times being placed more on PR than on marketing and vice versa; nevertheless, layers of complexity and contradictory practices enmesh between the two functions, influenced by both micro and macro factors (Moore, 2017).

Conceptually, what emerged in this fluctuating relationship between PR and marketing was the concept of integrated marketing communications (IMC), within which marketing was the dominant, distinct discipline, as it subsumed and integrated the other communication channels including PR. From this, however, hybrids and nuances of PR began to appear within the communications paradigm, such as cause-related marketing and sponsorship. In relation to the former, Tesco, in 2005, executed a cause-related marketing campaign by donating computers to schools through the process of offering customers one voucher for every £10 they spend over 10 weeks (Pratley, 2005). Although it was considered controversial in relation to the actual value of its vouchers, it was deemed a success. Meanwhile, concerning sponsorship in the motor industry, the Mercedes-AMG Petronas F1 Team sponsored engineering teams and drivers, which assisted in raising the brand profile and leveraged partnerships, allowing the brand to compete with competitors that had large advertising budgets.

The rise of social media as a critical component of the marketing arsenal was a significant factor in changing the relationship between various marketing communication tools. Initially, it was dwarfed off as relatively insignificant in relation to budget allocation (Netimperative, 2022); however, the fact that the media, both owned and earned, could be leveraged to the potential value of paid media, gradually took hold, and video, blogs, images, audio and text soon became staples in the PR media toolkit. Ultimately, from this, brands endorsing 'content' were later merged with marketing, becoming content marketing, from which branded content later unravelled and companies such as Red Bull and GoPro became leaders in this field. This product-driven approach, distinct from content marketing, in some ways can be considered the absolute synthesis between marketing and PR, as it facilitated direct conversations with the consumer. A classic example was Coca-Cola's Share-a-Coke campaign, where first names in localised regions were publicly emblazoned on the side of a Coke bottle and then featured in media, on buses, in billboards, in train stations and others. The wow factor of people seeing their name publicly was a catalyst for the media content/message to go viral (Coca-Cola, 2022).

In many ways, this campaign, from a theoretical standpoint, can be put forward as the ultimate balance between the marketing and public relations models (Kotler and Mindak, 1978).

Digital marketing, which at one point was labelled as cyber marketing (Bickerton, 2000), has accentuated this debate somewhat concerning the blurring of the line between the marketing and PR role or function.

With so many new and different definitions and terminologies appearing across the marketing lexicon, it can be difficult to keep up with new terms applied and their meanings in a fast-changing technological space.

When we decode the term 'digital marketing', it refers to the electrification of the marketing function and states that the binary nature of digitalisation allows for speed, agility and accuracy to be leveraged and aligned with other business functions (Bickerton, 2000). Renowned marketing author Dave Chaffey defines digital marketing as 'achieving marketing objectives through applying digital media, data, and technology' (Chaffey, 2022).

The roles and functions of different entities within a business are critical and it can be argued even more so in the current postindustrial age where different business entities such as decentralised autonomous organizations (DAOs) operate within a business ecosystem, distribute assets and execute business operations through smart contracts, which have been preprogrammed into the DNA of the organisation. Examples of such companies are Friends with Benefits (FWB) DAO, which is a social club DAO (Hackl, 2021), and the cryptocurrency derivative exchange BitDAO (Shuttleworth, 2021).

The backdrop to this new ecosystem that this chapter addresses is blockchain technology, in which there is a native web of embedded protocols and nascent appendages that aligns itself with the digital marketing and online PR world, through which stakeholders such as employees and investors will be expected to respond to communication professionals, who will then be expected to influence attitude and behaviour (Cornelissen, 2020).

PR'S RELATIONSHIP TO BLOCKCHAIN IN A POSTMODERN WORLD: WHAT IS BLOCKCHAIN?

This fast-paced industry is driven by the principles of Satoshi Nakamoto (2008) and his white paper titled 'Bitcoin: A Peer-to-Peer Electronic Cash System', which, like other cryptocurrencies, is driven by blockchain technology. Before discussing PR in this realm, a denominating understanding of blockchain technology must be established before examining certain key concepts and relating them to marketing PR.

At its core, blockchains are types of databases that take a certain amount of records and place them in a block, which in turn is 'chained' to the next block using a cryptographic signature, storing the transaction history, which is then replicated on every node, which is a cluster of computers or ancillary devices that can receive or send information (Lehdonvirta & Ali, 2016; Balva, 2017). Part of its uniqueness is that it is interconnected with other computers, enabling it to be used like a ledger that can be shared and corroborated by those with appropriate permissions. They can also be constructed or modified for specific purposes. For example, generally, there are shared ledgers – which refer to any database that is shared by industry or private consortiums or that is open to the public (DLT: Beyond BlockChain, 2016).

Ledgers have different nuances that may be best suited for certain purposes and functions. For example, distributed ledgers are databases that are commonly accessible to the public (permissionless). Records are commonly stored one after the other in a continuous ledger rather than sorted into blocks, and as an added protection, additional records can only be added when the participants reach a quorum. Ripple is an example of such a ledger in the fintech industry. It has its own list of validators (known as unique node lists or UNLs) from up to 150 known, unknown or partially known validators who are trusted not to collude (XRPL, n.d.).

The issue of governance is of high importance when it comes to blockchains, as it provides a framework and guideline as to how the technology works. Governance, in its most basic terms as a working item, is referred to as '[t]he system by which entities are directed and controlled' (Governance Today, n.d.).

Public blockchains such as Bitcoin and Ethereum are unpermissioned, which means they are open to the public, whilst private blockchains such as the Icertis blockchain framework in the Daimler supply chain system are not (Icertis, n.d.). Since the blocks on the blockchains are interconnected, they are considered as networks, where it is possible for transactions to occur. The approval of a transaction on a network can be validated in several ways. One is proof of work, for example, Bitcoin, and another is proof of stake, where certain nodes have specifically been selected to assist in confirming whether a transaction on the chain will go through and achieve consensus (DLT: Beyond Blockchain, 2016) among those computers participating in such a task. This process is undertaken through a concept known as 'hashing', which addresses how much computational power is used by the network to calculate transactions (Robinhood.com, n.d.), followed by the authentication of the transaction on the blockchain via computer, and the fastest computer to solve the cryptographic mathematical puzzle receives an incentive or reward.

Two key characteristics of blockchain technology are that they are immutable, as Zwitter and Boisse-Despiaux (2018) implied that it is it impossible for any entity to alter the transaction (Kavanagh, 2022), and that they inherently have trustlessness features, in this sense implying not the removal of trust but rather a shift in where an individual's trust is placed. In decentralised systems, the very notion is the removal of a central (Parry & Collomosse, 2021) authority in controlling and consenting to specific actions through smart contracts: pieces of computer code that sit above the application layer of software computer stacks, removing intermediaries, binding and confirming agreements (DLT: Beyond Blockchain, 2016). Smart contracts are based on property laws, which are rights related, and are at the epicentre of postindustrial capitalism, codifying business logic in a dynamic and efficient way (Mack, 2018).

From smart contracts, tokens can be issued, for example, Ethereum Improvement Proposals (EIP-20), which can be considered as digital assets to which value can be ascribed. The difference between tokens and cryptocurrencies is that the former is built on an existing blockchain whereas cryptocurrencies are the native asset of a particular blockchain, for example, BTC (Bitcoin) and RBTC (Smart Bitcoin) (RSK, n.d.), and this limits the use of cryptocurrencies. This is important when we want to address how blockchain protocols fulfil their mandate of transparency (immutability) and trustlessness with the integration of AI, to facilitate mobility across different platforms and incentivise models of human behaviour through what is termed 'token economics' (Kampakis, 2018).

WHAT IS DECENTRALISATION AND WHY IS IT RELEVANT TO BLOCKCHAIN PUBLIC RELATIONS?

Decentralisation sits at the heart of blockchain technologies, its prime characteristic being that no one entity or organisation controls the network (Bhalla, n.d.), just like the first iteration of the Internet, Web 1.0, which was the ability to interconnect to another webpage or server through hyperlinks. We are now moving beyond Web 2.0, the sharing of rich media through social media networks, to Web 3.0, blockchain, which is about P2P networks executing transactions at fractions of milliseconds with the potential to radically alter behaviour and business communication (Nield, 2021).

A point of caution needs to be adopted in line with definitions that have been put forward. The only true decentralised blockchain network operating in line with the characteristics in Satoshi's 2008 paper has been Bitcoin. Ethereum, which offers various other amenities aside from cryptocurrencies, is not technically decentralised since hardware systems used to fulfil its obligations are predominately centralised (Anthroplous, 2018); this means servers that run the chain can be disrupted if the key source hosting the servers are disrupted.

A further division exists between distributive and decentralised networks. A network can be centralised and distributive as well as decentralised and distributive. The two are not mutually exclusive, and in this respect, the power of blockchain security is based on its distributed and decentralised storage of data (Yanik & Kiliç, 2018).

The relevance of blockchain technology's impact on PR as well as corporate communications is significant, as companies who are proactive in understanding and shaping future directions will be the ones who will have a stake in leveraging added value with engagement in a seamless manner. Professor Greyser (2012) stated that the real challenge in business is that communications need to be supported by behaviour. This raises issues around group dynamics and governance, concerning how people operate in relation to organisational duties, internal PR and stakeholder relations. Stakeholder governance takes on different dimensions in different blockchain networks, depending on whether the blockchain network has an on-chain or off-chain system. Both systems have their pros and cons, and it depends on the utility of the blockchain network as to which system may be preferred.

Teszos and Difinity blockchains both have on-chain mechanisms. This implies that when decisions arise that can cause ambiguity or uncertainty, the resolutions are resolved within the network. Although technocrats may see this as positive, the process can be cumbersome and time-consuming. Off-chain governance refers to the traditional governance system of crypto miners, i.e., those seeking to solve the cryptographic computation puzzle; core developers and token holders will follow the preexisting guidelines as to how the dispute or disagreement should be resolved. For example, in the Bitcoin community, if some stakeholders want to put forward changes to the network, the Bitcoin improvement protocol (BIP) would be the formal structure to follow (RSK, n.d.). Voting would need to take place, and a consensus of having to reach a quorum would need to be achieved (Bitcoin Magazine, 2020).

Stakeholder communication takes place through the network, which is the rock bed of the community and social interaction; it also tends to be influenced by norms within any social sphere. Within and in relation to the blockchain, communication takes place on various levels between different entities and stakeholder groups.

TRADITIONAL COMMUNICATION MODELS

PR traditionally aligns with B2B asymmetric communications where the message is sent and facts can be used to persuade and win over sceptic audiences for any brand-worthy cause (Cialdini, 2007). Quality, speed and time are all key variables that will influence the resonance of messages (Target, 2022).

On the other hand, symmetric communications can both exist within the same paradigms. It has been understood within the PR fraternity as communications that are fuelled with the intention of reaching mutual agreement. Likewise, symmetric communications can be used strategically to engender trust amongst team members in an organisation, for example, where a company deploys work to an external agency (Target, 2022).

AI and ML drive key elements of blockchain technology that are interwoven with token economics (Kampakis, 2018) all playing pivotal roles in shaping Web 3.0 for both B2B and B2C behaviours, with the frequency of communication altering the intention of the message itself (Jenkins et al., 2013). Companies need to decide what type of code of conduct they want their employees to adopt and accept, such as whether digital distribution platforms including Discord may be used privately by an individual in an organisation or as an employee on behalf of an organisation to facilitate or broker business deals.

Power hierarchies are influenced by these technological drivers and play a significant role in influencing groups and individuals, receiving and sending messages across channels. Depending on the nature of the brands, consumer or industrial, a stable and professional marketing approach ensures a brand is clear, consistent, competitive and concise (Pulford et al., 1999) and should be the legacy and modus operandi fostering multidimensional nodes of communication when considering the advanced web communication model as put forward by Smith and Taylor (2004).

Figure 1. An advanced web communications model (Smith & Taylor, 2004)

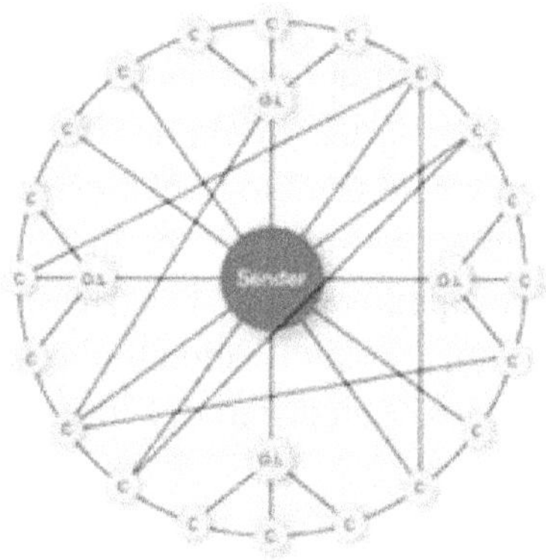

Blockchain digital assets, such as nonfungible tokens (NFTs) and gaming, are likely to become more prominent through culture and industry influencing groups and social trends through the interaction of tech, such as VR and AR (Ray, 2021) in service sector economies, providing an opportunity for brands that adopt a proactive approach, fuelling multiple conversations across channels and being strategically placed to take opportunities for PR to influence power hierarchies from monologues and dialogues on P2P networks with the capability of messages going exponential.

DIGITAL MARKETING AND PUBLIC RELATIONS SECURITY ISSUES

Marketing security habitually orchestrates itself in various forms since various blockchain security identification processes and procedures exist, which, as a whole, is a specific subject area beyond the remit of this chapter. However, our central concern in this context is its impact and relation to the marketing/PR function from both a B2B and B2C perspective since both permutations influence the behavioural traits of the end-user.

Within the complex web of inter- and intracommunicative messages sent under the umbrella of digital marketing and online PR. Organisations today commonly blend cloud and blockchain platforms seamlessly.

Since May 2018, when the GDPR came into effect within the European Union (EU), personal identity information (PII), has had to be taken much more seriously by all organisations in both big and small business spheres. A similar law was enacted in the United States through the California Consumer Privacy Act (CCPA) 2018, which, like its counterpart, has been the de facto guardian of privacy and security for consumers and individuals (Myers & Ulloa, 2018).

An example of how B2C companies ensure they are in tune with consumer concerns and sentiment is when the car company manufacturer Daimler made use of the B2C blockchain. The Daimler Mobility Service focused on finance, insurance and other service-oriented demands. The brand is a steward of consumers' PII information security, which is increasingly a must-have feature (Madhavaram et al., 2005) for consumer relations. Daimler has also integrated blockchain technology for greater efficiency, transparency and privacy within their systems (Williams, 2019).

Blockchain identification can get more complex depending on whether a user is on-chain or off-chain with the outcome instigating different identification procedures as required. The Ethereum Attestation Service, which leverages on-chain transactions that default to public and immutable, has attempted to remedy this issue (Bailey, 2021) by allowing one to prove their identity when browsing Web 3.0 through a personal identifier, such as an e-mail address (Alphawallet, n.d.). In this sense, this service is similar to two-factor authentication (2FA) and verifies identification by integrating another personal device such as a mobile phone in real time with knowledge authentication (Griffith, 2022).

The quest for a chain-agnostic solution for managing contextual data from any blockchain's public address has fuelled the race for developers to develop Web 3.0 architecture. Decentralised identity is also known as personal identity, self-sovereign identity, distributed identity and, collectively, decentralised identifiers (DIDs). Their purpose is to give users more control, as the model allows individuals to store identity-related data in a digital wallet on their mobile device. Three central parties are essential for the process to work: ***issuers,*** who may be the official sources of data, such as universities, credit bureaus, etc.; ***users,*** who may be individuals, employees, customers, etc., who store, for example, a driver's license, on the digital wallet; and ***verifiers,*** who may be businesses, individuals or entities that need to confirm something about someone (Griffith, 2021).

In line with this development is the overt marketing–oriented, transactional-based ID verification blockchain method called zero-knowledge protocols, which are techniques and methods, based on maths, used to verify things without sharing or revealing underlying datasets (Hay, 2019).

Increasing informational technological insights into blockchain technologies are inherently bound to influence the parameters as to how messages are received and given weight in terms of importance and relevance. PR, in line with its classical definition in contrast to marketing, is likely to lever an influence that can make a small yet incremental difference.

GDPR VS BLOCKCHAIN PRIVACY AND INTERNET ACCESS

Although GDPR quashed consumer concerns of businesses improperly obtaining and misusing as well as divulging their PII, privacy issues have been an ongoing saga when it comes down to website browsers capturing cookie personal information and storing them in information systems (McParland & Connolly, 2007).

Nevertheless, paradoxically, blockchain is the antithesis of GDPR in the sense that PII data on the chain cannot be removed if requested, and this would be a severe breach of the GDPR and other privacy regulations (Griffith, 2022).

In this sense, PII does not belong on the blockchain, whilst laws like GDPR and CCPA are vehemently at odds with being public and immutable and the documentation of personal data on behalf of users since privacy cannot be flexible, consensual and continuously evolving if it is public and immutable (Serto, 2021).

With the utility of browsers remaining the same, to retrieve information from servers, different types are likely to carve out niches more tailored towards blockchain, for example, Tor, Brave and Osrisis, integrating security as an advantage benefiting PR and marketing.

Blockchain digital marketing and PR security have an advantage of a protective layer mechanism built into the technology as native within the platform; asymmetric encryption, digital signatures and access control allow brands to make the most of decentralisation so that they can create and communicate as synchronised networks within their ecosphere. From a marketing consumer-driven perspective, this could take the form of increased personalisation of an offering at a particular price and certain venues in the form of discounts, promotional benefits, or other incentives that can be real time and empowering to customers.

From a stakeholder perspective, PR can play a particular role in clarifying the intention of an organisation when collecting customer data and company policy as well as when companies are hit by denial of services (DoS) attacks (Helebrandt et al., 2018). The fact that particular types of communication may be required at specific times can be of benefit to PR as a communications channel bridging the gap between business and private with the additional reassurance of security due to end-to-end encryption. New networks such as the Wire private messaging service and Signal, the private messenger, can be assets in the PR artillery.

The very nature, orientation speed, capacity and variation of messages and formats that take place on blockchain platforms are vast and multifaceted. For instance, in messaging and digital distribution platforms such as Discord and NFT platforms such as Opeansea, one-to-one and one-to-many messaging are facilitated by the integration of crypto wallets, which is being incorporated by more browsers through natural design and seamlessly intersects with smart contracts and the execution of specific instructions. These actions take place in a fraction of a second and through nonhuman intervention. The verification of digital identities and crypto wallets enables particular software embedded in the architecture platform called 'agents' to run on behalf of validators or other aligned entities to control and manage decentralised identities (Terbu, 2020).

Figure 2. The relationship between the agent, trust and behavioural layers (Hawlitschek et al., 2018)

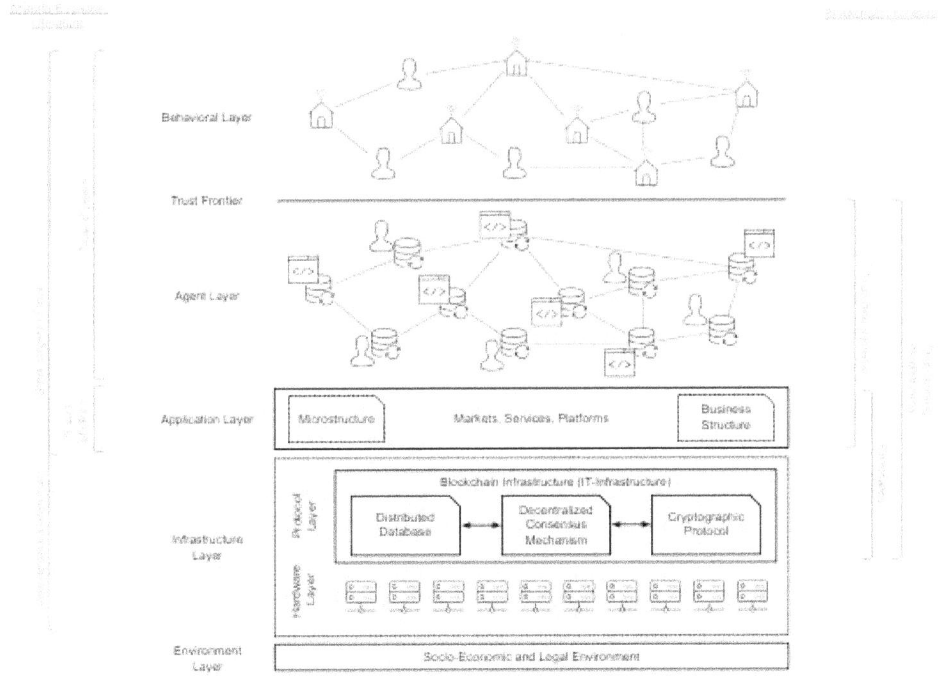

This process is known as disintermediation in traditional digital marketing. It accelerates exponentially, and it is facilitated by smart contracts and Native currencies, which provide targeted incentives that will influence consumer and corporate behaviour. Through this silent digital process, the use of consented data becomes the cornerstone for engagement and the development of brand equity, impacting both marketing and PR (Hayes, 2021).

An example of this is the Daimler Group, of which Mercedes Benz is a central part, which joined the MobiCoin consortium, a virtual currency that rewards drivers for adopting ecodriving reflexes, to accentuate the brand.

The way the project worked was that data from the vehicles were transmitted to Daimler and converted into MobiCoins, which are stored in a mobile app, and participants with the most MobiCoins were reportedly to receive VIP tickets to events such as the Deutsche Tourenwagen Masters (DTM, German Touring Car Masters) Races, the Mercedes Cup Final or Fashion Week in Berlin. (Coin Insider, 2018; MOBI, n.d.).

Blockchain has been described as the 'trust machine'; however, the thought may also lead to degrees of blindness and possibly a 'lack of questioning of the data' (Rogerson & Parry, 2020). The technology makes use of AI and its derivative of ML, which attempts to mimic human intelligence (Brown, 2021).

To date, no unified definition of AI exists. The importance of a consistent definition is not just for legal purposes but also for a conceptual understanding of its capability. The consulting firm Accenture (2021) described it as 'a constellation of many different technologies working together to enable machines to sense, comprehend, act, and learn with human-like levels of intelligence'. The United Nations also stepped in with the aim of clarifying its remit. Aside from producing an ethical AI framework, late in 2021, they put forward a definition very close to the iteration in the Oxford Dictionary, stating that

it is the theory and development of computer systems that can perform tasks normally requiring human intelligence, such as visual perception, speech recognition, decision-making, and translation and interpretation, whilst academics, Ostrom et al, define it as States it as define AI as 'non-biological intelligence'. Whatever definition we prefer AI is closely linked to ML, which concerns us more in this chapter, as it is based on the Deep Learning Principle, in that the machine can be fed and immersed in data with the outcome of being able to perform specific relative tasks requested from it by analysing mathematical outcomes, assisting Blockchains to solve complex problems by use of pattern recognition, speech recognition and other technologies Kai-fu-lee. (n.d.)

In his book *The Four Waves of A.I.*, Ku Fu Lee maps AI out into four phases: 'Internet AI' is the first, powered by vast amounts of data flowing through the web. The second wave is about 'business AI', where algorithms can be trained on proprietary datasets and complex business processes can be undertaken. The third wave is 'perception AI', and the last wave is 'autonomous AI', which integrates all previous waves.

It remains to be seen how organisations will deploy the PR business function in addressing some of the 'why' questions around the need for integrated data into blockchain networks, both on- and off-chain, since ML allows for the introduction of code-based rules (Hassan & De Filippi, 2017).

ML bleeds into the trustlessness schema, as it is distributed in a type of economy that incentivises certain behaviours (academy.binance.com). In lay terms, it means the participants involved do not need to know or trust each other or a third party for the system to function. Through ML organisational trust, the service provider can extend their ecosystem of unseen partners and system-level trust (Sekhon et al., 2013). In this sense, senior practitioners and decision-makers in organisations using blockchain systems cede authority to algorithms to provide information that is considered true and to direct action (Lustig & Nardi, 2015).

The question as to whether trust can be fully replaced by an algorithm (Lustig & Nardi, 2015) raises the issue of the reliance of AI by organisations at both system organisational and individual levels. This raises the issue of not just Web 3.0 but also how both marketing and PR operations will have to make strategic decisions regarding how they want to engage and optimise these layers and how different browsers with distinct privacy settings will be interoperable with organisational web presence and in the distribution of their goods and services (Buhalis & Licata, 2002).

WHAT IS WEB 3.0 AND WHY IS IT IMPORTANT?

It has been stated that we are at the tail end of Web 2.0, which has been characterised by FAANG companies, which all dominate the Internet in the sense that they all use centralised servers, and therefore, activity and traffic on these platforms are influenced by whatever policies and procedures are put in place by them (Burgess, 2021).

Tuten and Solomon (2014) divided social media activities over the Internet into the following categories: (1) social entertainment, (2) social commerce-ecommerce, (3) collaboration/community and (4) social publishing. Even though our definition of the Internet should be understood as encompassing more than the above, FAANG companies operate as platform companies (Cusumano et al., 2019), with business models that generate revenue from a combination of spheres within their ecosystems: advertising, hardware, licencing and so on.

Web 2.0, a legacy from 1.0, operates through various groups of multistakeholders – most notably the Internet Corporation for Assigned Names and Numbers (ICANN), which pays attention to Internet protocol standards and domain name registration. So what is Web 3.0? To date, no unified definition of it exists, but it is considered as a decentralised version of the web based on the blockchain (Wall Street Journal, 2022) that harkens back to Berners-Lee's original idea of the semantic web, where no permission is needed from a central authority, and there is no central controlling node (Brahambhatt, 2021).

While Web 3.0 technologies are difficult to define precisely, the outline of emerging applications has become clear over the past year. The academic Jim Hendler (2009) refers to it as 'intelligent agents that can automatically manipulate Web services (read-write-execute) and help firms react to changes quickly'.

Fuchs et al. (2010) referred to it as 'developed networked digital technologies that support human cooperation'. Conceptually, the Internet will be run by a protocol that links private data centres as opposed to private networks (Dominic Williams, 2019) which have the tendency to become monopolistic.

The advent and development of Web 3.0 are set to change and influence how business and relationships are conducted over the years to come as communication between devices accelerates. The potential of this amorphous Internet is for relationships and transactions over the Internet to be conducted through private servers, from which individuals will have the capability to own, control, and broker their personal data (PII) (Diehl, n.d.), through Dapps, which are decentralised applications that store the data on a blockchain where it gets distributed among several nodes, which eliminates the presence, and power, of a central authority and thus providing a more democratic web experience (Genesis, 2018).

These essential characteristics of Web 3.0 will be accentuated through privacy and trust for brands to foster competitive advantage and a new role for PR due to blockchain and Web 3.0 partly because of the desire, need and trends for brands, most especially consumer brands, to be much more vocal on social issues, for example, Nike, Coca-Cola etc. It remains to be seen how companies will adjust their business models to take advantage of direct consumer interaction that can be facilitated through blockchain technologies. For example, Tesla cars can only be purchased directly from their website, giving leverage to PR as a medium to play a pivotal role in harnessing and championing brand values, building brand equity through an integrated communications approach, amalgamating both online and offline interaction with the demarcation between private and public being blurred.

FOSTERING A SOCIAL EQUITY BRAND SOCIAL, ON THE BLOCKCHAIN

New Web 3.0 social spaces are emerging. LBRY, the social file-sharing site; OpenChat, the decentralised alternative to WhatsApp; Steem, another social media platform and others are championing blockchain technologies holding both corporate and consumer brands accountable and transparent, which has the potential to change communication strategies of brands. For example, Daimler ensures all the cobalt used in their car batteries are Initiative for Responsible Mining Assurance (IRMA) compliant. Gucci have also used technology to ratify the traceability of their products and services against counterfeits and fraud (Consensys, n.d.), enabling the brand to be amenable to conversations relating to corporate social responsibility and accumulating brand equity through various communication channels from which, pending the weight, degree and intensity reciprocity of such engagements, the brand can enjoy a network effect because of Metcalfe's law (Cornerstone, n.d.).

Practitioners/academics Champniss and Vila (2011) labelled such brands that are constituted that way as social equity brands, a term which they state distinguishes brands investing in society for the long term and are acknowledged as having an authentic brand voice – an example is when Google staff told their board they no longer wanted to work on a national defence contract. Trust is the key work that binds the DNA of the brand together, and dialogue is one of the social equity traits that Champniss and Vila (2011) developed as a dynamic ingredient of social brand equity development.

Internal communication channels in organisations influence behaviour. In the Google example, 3,100 signatures were gathered when staff stated their discontent (Shane & Wakabayashi, 2018) at having to work on the defence contract. Internal PR should be strategically developed as extensions of private communications, reiterating and overlapping personal and business values (Simonite, 2021).

This Google scenario, according to Champniss and Vila (2011), is a classic example of how the staff has bonded and formed kinship-like affinities which have led to reflective thinking, in a dyadic manner, into what the authors term the cognitive thought process, whereby codes and symbols are expressed through Google's corporate work culture. The process as to how this occurs, through discussions and committees, via dialogue, cements relational trust between the respective parties, and on the back of this emerges the outcome, otherwise known as the 'linking phase' in their theory, which is a distinct characteristic of the social capital process. The decisions were made by the staff and agreed upon and confirmed by management. The meso 'linking' element of this when this decision was communicated to the U.S. government (Daniel, McCalla & Schwier, 2002; Champniss & Vila, 2011).

The progression of AI sits at the very heart of trustlessness and the execution of commands at fractions of seconds. The consequences for brands, which may find their organisations in unforeseen scenarios, when operations and smart contracts do not go to plan, raises the issue of ethics, or what is sometimes called situational ethics, which occurs where moral judgments must be made within the context of the entirety of a particular situation. It is both vital and imperative that the brands are understood through traditional accepted norms as well as holistically (Waller, 2005).

Figure 3. The Revised Hunt–Vitell (H–V) model guide to implementing AI ethics (Ferrell & Ferrell, 2021)

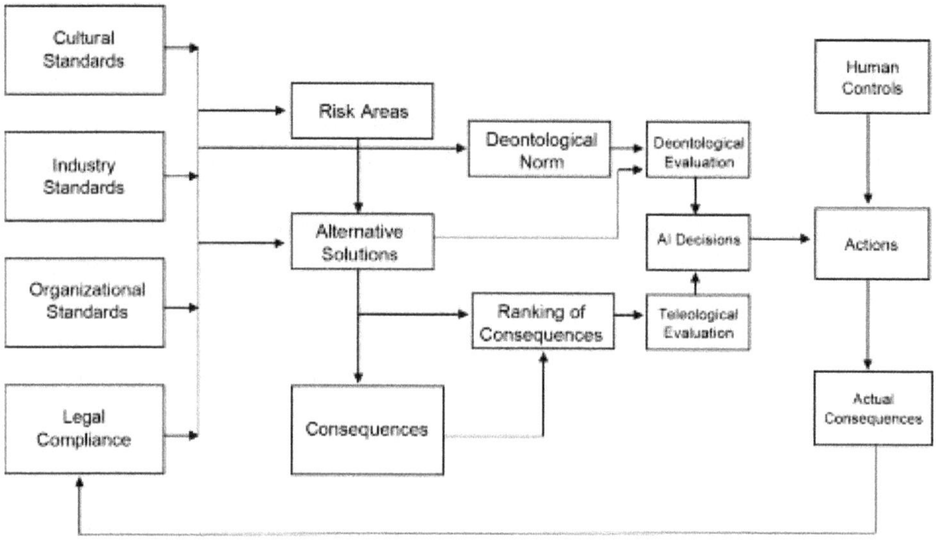

This can happen for example, when an organisation suffers from an unusual bio-cyberattack event; it needs to be communicated, bringing the role of PR to the fore.

The renowned academic and PR theorist Prof James E Grundig understood that different stakeholders needed to be communicated to in different ways that were consistent with their particular situations. He developed a theory of communication behaviours, from which he understood that stakeholders could be best understood by measuring how members perceived situations, in other words, focusing on the impact and consequences to the organisation. The 2010 BP oil spill off the Gulf of Mexico would be an incident where an appropriate communication form to deal with the scenario should have been advocated (Lustgarten, 2012).

Unforeseen consequences and scenarios always occur in business operations, and this raises the issue of trustlessness on blockchain platforms of which PR would be required to win corporate and external stakeholders with special emphasis on staff communications.

Let us explore a hypothetical scenario. Company A exists and works with several stakeholder companies, but one particular company, T1, is an OEM, as it makes and supplies interior fabrics for parent company A, the final product being a motor car. It is significant to note that company T1 has a deal with Company A that they are allowed to leave their insignia, as a sub-brand logo, discretely on the end product: the motor car.

Company A has evolved into making use of blockchain technology for greater efficiencies, and this is put to use in supply chain verification, where raw materials being used are sourced responsibly and ethically.

In this manner, the use of smart contracts is put to full use, and company A has insisted on the use of public permissionless blockchains for interoperable reasons, and complex deployment of ML with AI robotic integration is implemented. Operations across the board seem on track and according to the schedule.

However, what occurs next during production is unexpected. On one particular Monday morning in the summertime, T1 company received an announcement that possible power fluctuations were imminent. Later that same day, a 7-minute power interruption takes place at 11:05 a.m. and later at 3:20 p.m. Nothing nefarious is thought to have occurred, and business continues as usual. It is only a week later that it is found out that a new patch on the supply chain traceability system had been compromised. It is later found that counterfeit car interior products were produced as the smart contract was compromised. The items produced were later found to have been sold on the black market.

Whilst it is evident that serious ethical implications beyond the remit of this paper have been raised, it can be argued from a chief executive officer (CEO) perspective that mitigating risk concerning cyber security should be addressed. However, from an organisational and corporate communications perspective, what kind of crisis management procedure changes should an organisation ensure are in place in contrast to Web 2.0 ecosystems?

Furthermore, this raises denotative questions. How will this case be assessed internally by the organisation? What kind of risk management and insurance procedures were in place? What will happen to the protection of the brand? Will the case be judged following dutiful assumed norms that it was business as usual and the software can take no fault for being tricked or ostensibly fooled into following through the transaction without suspecting any flaw, focusing on individual rights and intentions? On the other hand, will a more prevalent societal teleological stance of focusing on the business as a whole with its communal lineages be considered when deciding what decisive steps need to be taken to weigh the consequences of such organisational conduct recurring?

One possible option for resolving the above ethical scenario is to listen, engage and take onboard recommendations and suggestions from internal capital sources and staff.

SOCIAL CAPITAL, STAKEHOLDERS AND DIALOGUE STRATEGIES

The process of dialogue can be the mechanism to bring the alignment of the business vision and practice, taking onboard that employees in an organisation are the first line of trust, combined with trustlessness in any organisation, and equate to brand social capital, an asset that PR can strategically leverage when the art of balancing the two mutually inclusive variables has been perfected.

The principle of dialogue is to have intentional outcomes through conversations used to improve mutual understanding, appreciation and respect amongst people and groups. Such a level of engagement acknowledges the amount of equity each party brings to the table and the process that facilitates collaboration during decision-making (Tsoukas, 2009).

Borrowing from human resource management, the renowned Harvard organisational behaviour specialist Jack Gabarro developed four stages of trust (see Appendix 1) required for trust to be cemented in an organisation PR, as a communication tool, about blockchain and Web 3.0 and that can broaden its native role by making use of employees by listening to them. This is where the art of dialogue comes into play.

One element of dialogue is the process of self-distanciation (Tsoukas, 2009), which occurs when practitioners come together in a specific enclosed environment to achieve balance by distancing themselves from their customary and unreflective ways of acting. Relational connections in this type of connection fuels entities to actively take responsibility and become involved in issues that might have effects on others (Champniss & Vila, 2011).

Dialogue, in the context of social equity brands, includes the rich, varied and dynamic dialogue that takes place amongst a far broader cross-section of stakeholders. Internal PR that innately can be deemed as credible (Smith & Zook, 2019) can be used to identify with such entities, in this sense fostering a broader, almost 'antitargeting' approach to brand-led communications.

Brands are able to foresee a Web 3.0 world where the battle for brand salience to stay above the clutter of noise, positioning the brand strategically, may see equity brands reinforcing their positions proactively through a brand dialogue approach.

In 2018, a group of Canadian consultants and researchers (Bourgoin et al., 2018) developed a framework that can help business executives get the best out of dialogue situations. It is called **the focus–adjust–cast model**, which has been modified and centred towards organisations to bridge the chasm between brand trust and trustlessness.

Table 1. Adaptation of the focus–adjust–cast model (Bourgoin et al., 2018)

Pillars of Dialogue	Purpose/Intent	Symmetrical Tactics ³ Strategy
Decision-Making	Partnerships Human/AI	Viral Capabilities Time Liquid vs Nonliquid Assets
Communication Style	Minimal/Query Exploratory	Personable/Functional and Adaptable
Leadership	Governance	Consultant/Amenable

Power is always a centrifugal force when assisting the level of quality and interaction during the dialogue process within organisations depending on their structure. PR should access the nature of power play by analysis and understand social networks in relation to the organisation as well as the in- and outflow of informational channels.

An essential role corporate communications play in any organisation is in guiding staff and consumers with clear policies in relation to its values and code of conduct, which reflects the organisation's attitude, what is acceptable and what is not; ostensibly, some organisations have adopted central positions and/or frameworks on the topic of AI.

Although the UN has set up an AI framework, companies have not been complacent, as few industry leaders have forged ahead and taken it upon themselves to set up their frameworks to endear trust from the public. Bosch, Cisco and Daimler Group AG are three such companies.

Bosch have established an ethical code guideline for the use of AI, which will govern, amongst other things, the use of their Internet of Things (IoT), intelligent products. The company's AI code of ethics is based on the following maxim: Humans should be the ultimate arbiter of any AI-based decisions, as the company aims that future products either contain AI or have been developed or manufactured with its help. The essence of the code is based on Bosch's 'Invented for life' ethos, which combines a quest for innovation with a sense of social responsibility.

The company believes in observing all legal requirements and orienting them to ethical principles, with the underlying premise that AI should be a tool for humans, and any decision that will affect people should not be made without a human arbiter.

Cisco, the American networking communications company, also has an AI responsible framework based on the six principles of transparency, fairness, accountability, privacy, security and reliability, which focus on inclusion.

With their products generally split into two components, hardware and software, according to the International Data Corporation (IDC), they account for approximately 33% of the global market.

Cisco as a whole company conducted extensive research into how businesses perceiving the impact of AI can transform their businesses (Columbus, 2017), and their focus is to form a bedrock from which AI will assist in this new ecosystem, with their products and solutions providing advanced intelligence across the value chain.

The last company is Daimler Group AG. The organisation has set up a framework of four principles around AI (see Appendix 2).

From a customer-focusing end, the company realises that integration of this technology can assist in it being a major technological advantage, as the motor industry enters a new age of autonomous vehicles with interlinked navigation systems, smart voice assistants and integrated mobility systems.

The company pushes the use of AI through all aspects of its business initially through research by harnessing the use of its data compliance centre, which leverages targeted analysis of vast quantities of data. Its production procedures integrate real-time augmented manufacturing practices in its Factory 56 plant in Sindelfingen, southwestern Germany, and align this with blockchain solutions through the Daimler Financial Services Mobility unit (Mobility as a service (MaaS)).

IMPLICATIONS FOR MANAGEMENT

Because of the nature of blockchain platforms and how they are likely to develop, with the onslaught of Web 3.0, PR and marketing should present themselves as distinct appendages of the business function, as there is likely to be a clear need for brands to accentuate credibility and authenticity consistently. However, despite their differences, both should also join together where necessary firms engage and implement digital transformations and upgrades. Although particularly focused on marketing, a recent 2018 study of 1,500 U.S. companies from Standard and Poor's firms highlighted that only 2.6% of corporate board members have any significant marketing experience (Dimov, 2021). In an age of digital marketing analytics, this implies the discipline still has an uphill battle.

In line with the proposition that has been put forward in this chapter, brands need to realise that their first and greatest asset is human resources, which needs to develop healthy relationships facilitated through listening and dialogue. Not only is it extremely likely that consumer brands who leverage this to great effect will witness higher brand salience and social capital. In this sense, PR can accommodate more stakeholder relationships within the ecosystem of the firm.

PR is highly likely to play a pivotal role concerning both corporate and blockchain governance. This is because the latter is an evolving medium in which new ground rules are being established. For example, Teszos, with its on-chain protocol, needs to ensure that what is communicated to stakeholders is received and understood as expected and that the automated processes of governance have the necessary notifications to provide alerts in the case of malfunction.

On the issue of ethics, as shown from the previous examples, firms need to be bold and take and command strong positions around AI and ML by developing their own frameworks and leading when it comes to regulation. Corporate communications and PR are ever more central in ensuring the appropriate message reaches its desired and expected destination as well as providing contingencies by mitigating the necessary channels and taking advantage of strategic insights.

Ultimately, PR could play the role of the arbiter by making use of appropriate engagement data to keep informed, for example, TweetDeck and Social Mention, and assess stakeholder relations to influence decision-making as to whether the organisation will manage communications channels through intelligent agents or have a threshold or ceiling from which human intervention will be a policy requirement on matters of a pressing nature or of high significance.

Lastly, management should encourage PR professionals to get more involved with web developers so that they can share a common lingua franca. This is important, as this not only intertwines issues related to trust and trustlessness but also fosters professional mutual respect amongst different entities and understanding that again links the bridging dimension of social capital. Such relationships could be developed to foster digital Web 3.0 insights so that PR, as a communications channel, can embed itself within the protocol of blockchain software.

CONCLUSION

The nature of PR is changing and will change much further because of the advancement of blockchain technologies. This chapter has earmarked some of the critical issues likely to be involved and provided some progressive strategies companies can adopt to position themselves in comparative advantage.

REFERENCES

Accenture. (2021). *Artificial intelligence.* Retrieved from https://www.accenture.com/gb-en/insights/artificial-intelligence-summary-index

Anthroplous, A. (2018). *Mastering Ethereum: Building smart contracts and dApps.* O'Reilly Publication.

Attestation. (n.d.). Retrieved from https://alphawallet.com/for-user/attestation/

Bailey, A. (2021). *Roadblocks and concerns on the way to a decentralized ecosystem.* Retrieved from https://www.kuppingercole.com/insights/decentralized-identity#Chapter4

Balva, C. (2017). *The blockchain: Reinventing relationships of trust* [La Blockchain: réinventer les rapports de confiance]. Retrieved from https://www.youtube.com/watch?v=JID9c-MABis

Bellini, E., Iraqi, Y., & Damiani, E. (2020). Blockchain-based distributed trust and reputation management systems. *IEEE Access: Practical Innovations, Open Solutions*, *8*, 8. doi:10.1109/ACCESS.2020.2969820

Bernays, E. (1928). *Propaganda*. Horace Liveright.

Bhalla, A. (n.d.). *What is decentralization in blockchain?* Retrieved from https://www.blockchain-council.org/blockchain/what-is-decentralization-in-blockchain/

Bickerton, P., Bickerton, M., & Pardesi, U. (2000). *Cybermarketing*. Routledge.

Bitcoin Magazine. (2020). *What is a Bitcoin Improvement Proposal (BIP)*. Retrieved from https://bitcoinmagazine.com/guides/what-is-a-bitcoin-improvement-proposal-bip

Blau, P. (1964). *Blau, exchange and power in social life*. John Wiley and Sons.

Blockchain Framework. (n.d.). Retrieved from https://www.icertis.com/contract-management/blockchain

Blockchain-governance. (n.d.). Retrieved from https://101blockchains.com/blockchain-governance/

Bock, E. D., Wolter, S. J., & Ferrell, C. O. (2020). Artificial intelligence: Disrupting what we know about services. *Journal of Services Marketing*, *34*(3), 317–334. doi:10.1108/JSM-01-2019-0047

Bosch. (n.d.). *AI code of ethics*. Retrieved from https://www.bosch.com/stories/ethical-guidelines-for-artificial-intelligence/#:~:text=Bosch's%20AI%20code%20of%20ethics,based%20products%20that%20are%20trustworthy

Boukis, A. (2020). Exploring the implications of blockchain technology for brand–consumer relationships: A future research agenda. *Journal of Product and Brand Management*, *29*(3), 307–320. doi:10.1108/JPBM-03-2018-1780

Bourgoin, A., Marchessaux, F., & Bencherki, N. (2018). We need to talk about strategy: How to conduct effective strategic. *Business Horizons*, *61*(4), 587–597. doi:10.1016/j.bushor.2018.03.008

Brahambhatt, R. (2021). *What is Web 3.0? A new horizon for your online life.* Retrieved from https://interestingengineering.com/web-3-the-new-internet-is-about-to-arrive#:~:text=Web%203.0%3A%20The%20internet%20of%20tomorrow&text=Web%203.0%20is%20in%20many,is%20no%20central%20controlling%20node

Brown, S. (2021). *Machine learning, explained.* Retrieved from https://mitsloan.mit.edu/ideas-made-to-matter/machine-learning-explained

Buhalis, D., & Licata, M. C. (2002). The future etourism intermediaries. *Tourism Management*, *23*(3), 207–220. Advance online publication. doi:10.1016/S0261-5177(01)00085-1

Burgess, M. (2021). How France tamed Google. *Wired Magazine.* Retrieved from https://www.wired.co.uk/article/google-france-fines

Campbell-Verduyn, M. (Ed.). (2019). *Bitcoin and beyond cryptocurrencies, blockchains, and global governance*. Routledge.

Chaffey, D. (2022). *What is digital marketing?* Retrieved from https://www.smartinsights.com/digital-marketing-strategy/what-is-digital-marketing/

Champniss, G., & Vila, R. (2011). *Brand valued: How socially valued brands hold the key to a sustainable future and business success*. Wiley and Sons.

Chavez-Dreyfuss, G. (2019). Harvard, Levi Strauss, U.S. think tank in blockchain tie-up on worker welfare. *Reuters.* Retrieved from https://reut.rs/3alm7g

Chitkara, H. (2019). *Daimler will use a blockchain platform to track the value of used cars in real time.* Retrieved from https://www.businessinsider.com/daimler-to-use-blockchain-platform-for-valuing-used-cars-2019-9?r=US&IR=T

Cialdini, R. (2007). *Influence: The psychology of persuasion*. HarperBus.

Cisco. (n.d.). *The Cisco Responsible AI Framework.* Retrieved from https://www.cisco.com/c/dam/en_us/about/doing_business/trust-center/docs/cisco-responsible-artificial-intelligence-framework.pdf?CCID=cc000742&DTID=odicdc000016

Coca-Cola. (2022). *Coca-Cola's Coke's Share A Coke Campaign*. Retrieved from https://www.coca-colacompany.com/au/faqs/what-was-the-share-a-coke-campaign

Coin Insider. (2018). Daimler AG launches MobiCoin; a cryptocurrency that rewards eco-friendly driving. *Coin Insider.* Retrieved from https://www.coininsider.com/daimler-ag-mercedes-benz-mobicoin/

Columbus, L. (2017). How artificial intelligence is revolutionizing business in 2017. *Forbes Magazine*. Retrieved from https://www.forbes.com/sites/louiscolumbus/2017/09/10/how-artificial-intelligence-is-revolutionizing-business-in-2017/

Compeau, R. D., & Higgins, A. C. (1995). Application of social cognitive theory to training for computer skills. *Information Systems Research*, *6*(2), 118–143. Advance online publication. doi:10.1287/isre.6.2.118

Consensys. (n.d.). *Blockchain in retail fashion & luxury*. Retrieved from https://consensys.net/blockchain-use-cases/retail-fashion-and-luxury/

Coombs, W. T., & Holladay, S. J. (2007). The negative communication dynamic: Exploring the impact of stakeholder affect on behavioral intention. *Journal of Communication Management (London)*, *11*(4), 300–312. doi:10.1108/13632540710843913

Cornelissen, J. (2020). *Corporate communications: A guide to theory & practice*. Sage Publications.

Cusumano, M., Gawer, A., & Yoffie, D. (2019). *The business of platforms: Strategy in the age of digital competition, innovation, and power*. HarperBus.

Daimler Mobility Activities. (n.d.). Retrieved from https://group.mercedes-benz.com/innovation/digitalisation/mobility-services/?r=dai

Daimler. (n.d.). *A.I. guidelines*. Retrieved from https://www.daimler.com/sustainability/data/ki-guidelines.html

Daimler. (n.d.). *Future battery cells.* Retrieved from https://www.daimler.com/sustainability/human-rights/certified-raw-materials-and-less-cobalt-in-future-battery-cells.html

Daniel, B., McCalla, G., & Schwier, R. (2002). A process model for building social capital in virtual learning communities. *International Conference on Computers in Education, 1*, 575. Retrieved from https://ieeexplore.ieee.org/document/1186008

Davis, A. (2005). Placing promotional culture. In J. Curran & D. Morley (Eds.), *Media and cultural theory* (pp. 149–163). Routledge.

Diehl, S. (n.d.). *Web3 is bullshit.* Retrieved from https://www.stephendiehl.com/blog/web3-bullshit.html#:~:text=At%20its%20core%20web3%20is,train%20of%20evading%20securities%20regulation

Dimov, C. (2021). Should marketing be on corporate boards? *LinkedIn*. Retrieved from https://www.linkedin.com/pulse/should-marketing-corporate-boards-charles-dimov/

Donaldson, T., & Preston, L. E. (1995). The stakeholder theory of the corporation: Concepts, evidence and implications. *Academy of Management Review, 20*(1), 65–91. doi:10.2307/258887

Dupont, Q. (2017). *Experiments in algorithmic governance: A history and ethnography of 'the DAO', 'A failed decentralized autonomous organization'*. Academic Press.

Elliott, L. (2015). *Margaret Thatcher's deregulation of the city a myth, says thinktank.* Retrieved from https://www.theguardian.com/business/2015/may/25/margaret-thatcher-deregulated-city-london

Falconi, T. (2009). *Global stakeholder relationship governance.* Retrieved from https://instituteforpr.org/wpcontent/uploads/Global_Stakeholder_Relationship_Governance1.pdf

Ferrell, O. C., & Ferrell, L. (2021). Applying the Hunt Vitell ethics model to artificial intelligence ethics. *Journal of Global Scholars of Marketing Science, 31*(2), 178–188. doi:10.1080/21639159.2020.1785918

Fletcher, R. (2011). *Top performing companies incorporating the public sector* (11th ed.). Topco Media.

Franceschi, M., Morelli, D., Plans, D., Brown, A., Collomosse, J., & Coutts, L. (2018). *ComeHere: Exploiting Ethereum for secure sharing of healthcare data*. European conference on parallel processing [Euro-Par 2018]: parallel processing workshops. *Lect. Notes Comput. Sci.* Cham: Springer 11338, 585–596. doi:10.1007/978-3-030-10549-5_46.

Frenkel, A. K. (2017). *Confusion over security responsibility in cloud.* https://www.cioinsight.com/cloud-virtualization/confusion-over-security-responsibility-in-cloud/

Friedman, L. A., & Miles, S. (2006). *Stakeholders: theory and practice.* Oxford University Press.

Friedman, M. (1970). A Friedman doctrine - The social responsibility of business is to increase its profits. *New York Times.* Retrieved from https://www.nytimes.com/1970/09/13/archives/a-friedman-doctrine-the-social-responsibility-of-business-is-to.html

Fuchs, C., Hofkirchner, W., Schafranek, M., Raffl, C., Sandoval, M., & Bichler, R. (2010). Theoretical foundations of the web: Cognition, communication, and co-operation. Towards an understanding of Web 1.0, 2.0, 3.0. *Future Internet*, *2*(1), 41–59. doi:10.3390/fi2010041

Gabarro, J. J. (1978). The development of trust influence and expectations. In A. G. Athos & J. J. Gabarro (Eds.), *Interpersonal behavior: Communication and understanding in relationships* (pp. 290–303). Prentice Hall.

Gabarro, J. J., & Athos, J. (1976). *Interpersonal relations and communications.* Prentice-Hall.

Genesis. (2018). What are dApps (decentralized applications), and how do they work? *Developers Convention.* Retrieved from https://medium.com/@genesishack/know-your-track-dapp-decentralized-applications-1e1e0d29cc88

Governancetoday. (n.d.). *What does governance mean?* Retrieved from https://www.governancetoday.com/GT/Material/Governance__what_is_it_and_why_is_it_important_.aspx

Greyser, S. (2012). *The strategic role of the corporate communication officer at IE University.* Retrieved from https://www.youtube.com/watch?v=rf6ud_H8oKc

Griffith, J. (2021). *What you need to know about centralized vs decentralized identity management.* Retrieved from https://www.pingidentity.com/en/resources/blog/posts/2021/centralized-decentralized-identity-management.html

Griffith, J. (2022). *What is knowledge-based authentication (KBA)?* Retrieved from https://www.pingidentity.com/en/resources/blog/posts/2022/what-is-knowledge-based-authentication-kba.html

Grogan, M., & Peebles, H. (2021). *OpenChat: A truly decentralized alternative to WhatsApp.* Retrieved from https://medium.com/dfinity/openchat-a-truly-decentralized-alternative-to-whatsapp-d0d051479b9a

Grunig, J. E., & Hunt, T. (1980). *Managing public relations.* Cengage Learning.

Hackl, C. (2021). *What are DAOs and why you should pay attention.* Retrieved from https://www.forbes.com/sites/cathyhackl/2021/06/01/what-are-daos-and-why-you-should-pay-attention/

Hassan, S., & De Filippi, P. (2017). The expansion of algorithmic governance: From code is law. *Code Field Actions Science Reports.* Retrieved from https://journals.openedition.org/factsreports/4518

Hawlitschek, F., Notheisen, B., & Teubner, T. (2018). The limits of trust-free systems: A literature review on blockchain technology and trust in the sharing economy. *Electronic Commerce Research and Applications*, *29*, 50–63. doi:10.1016/j.elerap.2018.03.005

Hay, L. (2019). *Hacker lexicon: What are zero-knowledge proofs?* Retrieved from https://www.wired.com/story/zero-knowledge-proofs/

Hayes, A. (2021). *Disintermediation.* Retrieved from https://www.investopedia.com/terms/d/disintermediation.asp

Helebrandt, P., Belluš, M., Ries, M., Kotuliak, I., & Khilenko, V. (2018). Blockchain adoption for monitoring and management of enterprise networks. *2018 IEEE 9th Annual Information Technology, Electronics and Mobile Communication Conference (IEMCON).* Retrieved from https://www.researchgate.net/publication/330478223_Blockchain_Adoption_for_Monitoring_and_Management_of_Enterprise_Networks

Hendler, J. (2009). Web 3.0 emerging. *Computer*, *42*(1), 111–113. doi:10.1109/MC.2009.30

Huang, M., & Rust, R. (2018). Artificial intelligence in service. *Journal of Service Research*, *21*(2), 155–172. doi:10.1177/1094670517752459

Icertis Blockchain. (n.d.). *Framework.* Retrieved from https://www.icertis.com/contract-management/blockchain/

Jenkins, H., Ford, S., & Green, J. (2013). *Spreadable media creating value and meaning in a networked culture*. New York University. doi:10.18574/9780814743515

Kai-fu-lee. (n.d.). On the power of A.I. to transform humanity. Interview by Andrew Zuckerman. *Time Sensitive.* Retrieved from https://timesensitive.fm/episode/kai-fu-lee-power-artificial-intelligence-transform-humanity/

Kampakis, S. (2018). Why do we need tokenomics? *The Journal of The British Blockchain Association*, *1*(1), 1–4. doi:10.31585/jbba-1-1-(8)2018

Kaplan, A., & Haenlein, M. (2019). Siri, siri, in my hand: Who's the fairest in the land? On the interpretations, illustrations, and implications of artificial intelligence. *Business Horizons*, *62*(1), 15–25. doi:10.1016/j.bushor.2018.08.004

Karl, J. (2022). The Web3 you've heard of does not exist. *Bloomberg.* Retrieved from https://www.bloomberg.com/opinion/articles/2022-01-11/the-web3-you-ve-heard-of-does-not-exist

Kavanagh, R. (2022). *Hash rate: A measure of the computing power on a cryptocurrency network that is a key security indicator.* Retrieved from https://www.businessinsider.com/personal-finance/hash-rate?r=US&IR=T#:~:text=Hash20rate%20is%20a%20measure,miner's%20machines%20complete%20these%20computations

Ketokivi, M. & Mahoney, T. J. (2017). *Transaction cost economics as a theory of the firm, management, and governance free.* Retrieved from doi:10.1093/acrefore/9780190224851.013.6

Kotler, P., & Mindak, W. (1978). *Marketing and public relations: Should they be partners or rivals?* Sage Publication.

Lee, F. K. (2019). *Ai superpowers: China, Silicon Valley, and the New World Order.* Harper Bus.

Lee, K. (2018). *The four waves of A.I.* Retrieved from https://kaifulee.medium.com/the-four-waves-of-a-i-46e7e627c054

Lehdonvirta, V., & Ali, R. (2016). Governance and regulation: Digital currencies. Bank of England Oxford Internet Institute, University of Oxford.

Liberto, D. (2021). *What is reintermediation?* Retrieved from https://www.investopedia.com/terms/r/reintermediation.asp

Lustgarten, A. (2012). BP agrees to plead guilty to crimes in Gulf oil spill - Environmental sustainability, regulation & legislation. *The Magazine of Corporate Responsibility.*

Lustig, C., & Nardi, B. (2015). Algorithmic authority: The case of Bitcoin. *48th Hawaii international Conference on System Sciences*, 743–752.

Mack, O. (2018). *How smart contracts will change the world.* Retrieved from https://www.ted.com/talks/olga_mack_how_smart_contracts_will_change_the_world

Madhavaram, S., Badrinarayanan, V., & McDonald, E. R. (2005). Integrated marketing communication (IMC) and brand identity as critical components of brand equity strategy: A conceptual framework and research propositions. *Journal of Advertising*, *34*(4), 69–80. doi:10.1080/00913367.2005.10639213

MOBI. (n.d.). *The Mobility Open Blockchain Initiative.* Retrieved from https://dlt.mobi/standards/

Moore, K. (2017). *Content marketing in the 90s: What was it like?* Retrieved from https://www.business2community.com/content-marketing/content-marketing-90s-like-01903791

Myers, J., & Ulloa, J. (2018). California lawmakers agree to new consumer privacy rules that would avert showdown on the November ballot. *Los Angeles Times*. Retrieved from https://www.latimes.com/politics/la-pol-ca-privacy-initiative-legislature-agreement-20180621-story.html

Nagy, N. (2017). *Trends in social media marketing within the small and medium-sized business industry and how small and medium-sized businesses are using social media to grow their business.* doi:10.13140/RG.2.2.19426.58560

Nahapiet, J., & Ghoshal, S. (1998). Social capital, intellectual capital, and the organizational advantage. *Academy of Management Review, 23*(2), 242–266. doi:10.5465/amr.1998.533225

Netimperative. (2021). *Global social media ad spend grows 60% year-over-year.* Retrieved from https://www.netimperative.com/2021/04/27/global-social-media-ad-spend-grows-60-year-over-year/

Nield, D. (2021). *What is Web3 and why should you care? The next internet revolution is upon us—here's why it matters.* Retrieved from https://gizmodo.com/what-is-web-3-and-why-should-you-care-1848204799

Nohria, N., & Eccles, R. C. (1992). *Networks and organizations: Structure, form, and action*. Harvard Business School Press.

OpenChat: A truly decentralized alternative to WhatsApp. (n.d.). Retrieved from https://medium.com/dfinity/openchat-a-truly-decentralized-alternative-to-whatsapp-d0d051479b9a

Ostrom, A., Fotheringham, D., & Bitner, M. J. (2018). Customer acceptance of AI in service encounters: Understanding antecedents and consequences. In P. P. Maglio, C. A. Kieliszewski, J. C. Spohrer, K. Lyons, L. Patricio, & Y. Swatani (Eds.), Handbook of Service Science (Vol. 2, pp. 77–103). Academic Press.

Parry, G., & Collomosse, J. (2021). *Perspectives on 'good' in blockchain for good.* Frontiers Blockchain. doi:10.3389/fbloc.2020.609136

Peake, J. (1981). *Public relations in business: Review article*. Harper and Row. doi:10.1177/002194368101800211

Pelt, R. V., Jansen, S., Baars, D., & Overbeek, S. (2020). *Defining blockchain governance: A framework for analysis and comparison*. Taylor & Francis Publication. doi:10.1080/10580530.2020.1720046

Pratley, N. (2005). *Tesco faces questions over true value of its computer vouchers.* Retrieved from https://www.theguardian.com/technology/2005/mar/07/schools.supermarkets#:~:text=Computers%20for%20Schools%20works%20by,of%20computer%20equipment%20to%20schools

Puldford, A., Smith, P. R., & Berry, C. (1999). *Strategic marketing communications: New ways to build and integrate communications.* Kogan Page.

Ratnasingam, P. (2003). *Inter-organizational trust for business to business e-commerce.* IGI Global. doi:10.4018/978-1-931777-75-9

Rawlins, B. L., & Bowen, S. A. (2005). Publics. In L. R. Heath (Ed.), *Encyclopedia of Public Relations* (Vol. 2). SAGE.

Ray, S. (2021). *NFTs & virtual reality, emerging technology blog.* Retrieved from https://medium.com/lansaar/nfts-virtual-reality-cba66cacc7e1

Ripple. (n.d.). Retrieved from https://www.investopedia.com/terms/r/ripple-cryptocurrency.asp

RLYL. (2020). *Blockchain public relations: The building blocks to success.* Retrieved from https://bit.ly/3nw4Y7q

RSK. (n.d.). *The difference between a cryptocurrency and a token.* Retrieved from https://developers.rsk.co/kb/get-crypto-on-rsk/cryptocurrency-vs-token/

Sarraf, S. (2021). UNESCO launches global standard for AI ethics. *InfoWorld.*

Sedita, R. S. (2017). *Cause related marketing.* Retrieved from https://advancedmarketingunipd.wordpress.com/2017/10/27/cause-related-marketing/

Sekhon, H., Roy, S., Shergill, G., & Pritchard, A. (2013). Modelling trust in service relationships: A transnational perspective. *Journal of Services Marketing*, *27*(1), 76–86. doi:10.1108/08876041311296392

Serto. (2021). *The DAO plutocracy problem: Off-chain reputation is the key to meritocracy.* Retrieved from https://serto.medium.com/the-dao-plutocracy-problem-a8841546a0f2

Shane, S., & Wakabayashi, D. (2018). *'The business of war': Google employees protest work for the Pentagon.* Retrieved from https://www.nytimes.com/2018/04/04/technology/google-letter-ceo-pentagon-project.html

Shuttleworth, D. (2021). *What is a DAO and how do they work?* Retrieved from https://consensys.net/blog/blockchain-explained/what-is-a-dao-and-how-do-they-work/

Simonite, T. (2021). *3 years after the Project Maven uproar, Google cozies to the Pentagon.* Retrieved from https://www.wired.com/story/3-years-maven-uproar-google-warms-pentagon/

Smith, H. (2003). The shareholders vs. stakeholders debate. *MIT Sloan Management Review*, *44*(4), 85–90.

Smith, P., & Taylor, J. (2004). *Marketing communications: An integrated approach* (4th ed.). Kogan Page.

Smith, P. R., & Zook, Z. (2019). Marketing communications - Integrating online and offline. In *Customer engagement and digital technologies* (7th ed.). Kogan Page.

Spitzeck, H., & Hansen, E. G. (2010). Stakeholder governance: How stakeholders influence corporate decision making. *Corporate Governance*, *10*(4), 378–391. doi:10.1108/14720701011069623

Sriramesh, K., & Verci, C. D. (2012). *Culture and public relations: Links and implications*. Routledge. doi:10.4324/9780203149232

Startup-autobahn. (n.d.). *Mercedes-benz – Innovation.* Retrieved from https://group.mercedes-benz.com/innovation/venture/startup-autobahn/en/?r=dai

Syam, N., & Sharma, A. (2018). Waiting for a sales renaissance in the fourth industrial revolution: Machine learning and artificial intelligence in sales research and practice. *Industrial Marketing Management*, *69*, 69. doi:10.1016/j.indmarman.2017.12.019

Tapscott, D. & Tapscott, A. (2016). *Blockchain revolution: How the technology behind Bitcoin is changing money, business, and the world.* Academic Press.

Target. (n.d.). *Asymmetric communications.* Retrieved from https://www.techtarget.com/searchnetworking/definition/asymmetric-communications

Terbu, O. (2020). *Trusted P2P messaging with DIDs, DIDComm and VCs.* Retrieved from https://medium.com/uport/trusted-p2p-messaging-with-dids-didcomm-and-vcs-398f4c3f3cda

The Institute of Directors in Southern Africa (IoDSA). (n.d.). Retrieved from https://www.iodsa.co.za/page/KingIII

The Internet Corporation for Assigned Names and Numbers (ICANN). (2022). Retrieved from https://www.icann.org/

Thompson, G. (2020). *Post-truth public relations: Communication in an era of digital disinformation*. Routledge. doi:10.4324/9780429429125

Tsoukas, H. (2009). A dialogical approach to the creation of new knowledge in organizations. *Organization Science*, *20*(6), 941–957. doi:10.1287/orsc.1090.0435

Tuten, T. L., & Solomon, M. R. (2014). *Social media marketing*. Sage Publications.

UNESCO. (2021). *Ethics of artificial intelligence.* Retrieved from https://en.unesco.org/news/unesco-member-states-adopt-first-ever-global-agreement-ethics-artificial-intelligence

United Nations. (2018). *Let's talk about artificial intelligence.* Retrieved from https://www.undp.org/blog/lets-talk-about-artificial-intelligence

Wall Street Journal. (2022). *Why some see Web 3.0 as the future of the Internet.* Retrieved from https://newsfeedplus.com/why-some-see-web-3-0-as-the-future-of-the-internet-wsj/

Waller, B. N. (2005). *Consider ethics: Theory, readings, and contemporary issues.* Pearson Longman.

What Is Reaganomics. (n.d.). Retrieved from https://corporatefinanceinstitute.com/resources/knowledge/economics/reaganomics/

What Was the Share a Coke Campaign. (2022). Retrieved from https://www.coca-colacompany.com/au/faqs/what-was-the-share-a-coke-campaign

Williams, D. (2019). *How DFINITY is reinventing the internet.* Retrieved from https://www.youtube.com/watch?v=QUhceX6I81U

Williams, M. (2019). *Mercedes-Benz to boost visibility via blockchain.* Retrieved from https://www.automotivelogistics.media/digital-technology/mercedes-benz-to-boost-visibility-via-blockchain/37673.article

Williams, M. (2019). *Mercedes-Benz to boost visibility via blockchain.* Retrieved from https://www.automotivelogistics.media/digital-technology/mercedes-benz-to-boost-visibility-via-blockchain/37673.article#:~:text=Mercedes%2DBenz%20Cars%20has%20announced,the%20use%20of%20blockchain%20technology

Wood, T. (2020). *Visualizing the evolution of global advertising spend (1980–2020).* Retrieved from https://www.visualcapitalist.com/evolution-global-advertising-spend-1980-2020/

Xiong, H., Keogh, J. G., Gipp, B., Schubotz, M., & Schlager, S. (2018). How blockchain technology can benefit marketing: Six pending research areas. In *Frontiers in blockchain*. Frontiers Media SA. Retrieved from https://www.researchgate.net/publication/339354050_How_Blockchain_Technology_Can_Benefit_Marketing_Six_Pending_Research_Areas

XRPL I XRP Ledger Overview. (n.d.). *XRPL today and the vision for tomorrow*. Retrieved from https://xrpl.org/xrp-ledger-overview.html

Yanık, S., & Kiliç, S. A. (2018). *Energy management—Collective and computational intelligence with theory and applications*. Springer Publication.

Yanik & Kiliç. (2018). *A framework for the performance evaluation of an energy blockchain*. Springer. Retrieved from https://link.springer.com/chapter/10.1007/978-3-319-75690-5_23

Zwitter, A., & Hazenberg, J. (2020). Decentralized network governance: Blockchain technology and the future of regulation. *Frontiers*, *3*, 12. Advance online publication. doi:10.3389/fbloc.2020.00012

Chapter 11
The Impact of IT Technologies on Management Accounting

Alharbi Habbab Husam
Mansoura University, Egypt

ABSTRACT

Because changes are quick in the digital age, the decision maker will actively seek the optimal solution for managerial accounting that he considers satisfactory and will put it into practice as soon as possible, given the conditions for materialising the decision. The use of digital programs and technologies to simulate the company's managerial accounting decisions can avoid these shortcomings, at least for a short period of time. This chapter illustrates that, in an increasingly digitalis environment, it is generally recognised that the use of IT technology in management accounting is critical for every company. Properly managing stakeholders' increasing expectations also contributes to the confidence required for a firm to survive and develop.

INTRODUCTION

The struggle between corporations grows beyond the global level and, indirectly, transfers into the virtual environment as a result of the digital era (Andon, Baxter & Chua, 2007). Companies that have the power provided by digital technology are the ones that can manage the exponential changes that define today's business environment. As a minimum requirement, the availability and implementation of numerous alternatives in the organization and operation of establishments' accounting information systems must satisfy the following essential functions: making decisions and documenting operating procedures (Ahrens, 2008).

DOI: 10.4018/978-1-6684-4595-2.ch011

In other words, the digital solutions provided by the digital age create new opportunities for businesses, encourage the development of dependable technologies, promote an open and democratic society, create a dynamic and viable economy, and contribute to the fight against climate change and the transition to a green economy (Bettner & Kate, 2013). Furthermore, a considerable number of CEOs believe that the world has a positive impact on regulatory harmonization, personal data protection, and geopolitical risk management. What is clear is that chances for company development are dependent on the speed and quality of the internet connection, as well as investments in cutting-edge technology Barth, Landsman, Young & Zhuang, 2014). As a result, we will become increasingly linked.

On the other hand, conditioned by the method in which the total economic potential is structured, turned to profit, and made to operate toward the fulfillment of budgetary commitments with maximum efficiency, economic management is a process that administers the assets that constitute an economic entity's patrimony and manages the activity that is carried out based on that patrimony (Dennis, 2014; Fan et al., 2016). Economic management is defined as the administration of the assets that form an economic entity's patrimony and the management of the activity that is carried out based on that patrimony (Ball, 2013; Brown, 2010).

Managers are often concerned with continual issues: understanding the future, and managing others' activities. Managerial accounting refers to an accounting system designed for managers, but it does not preclude the use of financial accounting information (Schleicher, Tahoun & Walker, 2010; Doukakis, 2014; Allen & Ramanna, 2013).

Also, the foundation of economic management - as a management vehicle - is the achievement of required to collect at the lowest possible cost, so that when the activity is completed, the revenue exceeds the costs, i.e. there is a profit that ensures a level of profitability as high as possible both at the overall level and by product, department, or service performed (Richardson, 2011; Lukka, 2010; He, Pan & Tian, 2017; Cahan & Sun, 2015).

It can be noted that business organizations with significant economic and social performance are those that strive to satisfy all stakeholders (shareholders, employees, surrounding communities, suppliers, customers, state, unions); have a higher purpose (job creators and suppliers of goods and services), and have high standards (Arsenault & Faerman, 2014; Barth, 2013; Caylor, 2010; Hou et al., 2015; Parker, 2012).

Businesses in the digital economy have new frontiers, endless shapes, and opportunities for development (Byard, Li & Yu, 2011; Damayant, 2013; Florou & Pope, 2012). The rise of digital technology is fundamentally altering how businesses operate. To attain the expected aim (profit), the organization must employ digital technology. First and foremost, corporate organizations should digital their business processes. (Baker & Bettner, 1997; Barth, M., Landsman, W., & Lang, 2008).

In this context, an ERP solution can be defined as one that maps a company's processes and integrates all important functions of the company, such as accounting, logistics, production, and human resources, into a common database. companies. As a result, planning and control should be much easier throughout the company. ERP systems thus promise high-efficiency increases for companies (Jackson, & Liu, 2010; Vladu et al., 2016).

BACKGROUND

It is worth stressing that each component of this circuit may be bearing risks impacting the configuration and quality of accounting information (Chen, Tang, Jiang & Lin, 2010). Thus, (Holthausen & Watts, 2001). Management accounting systems that operate in parallel can also be replaced with a new ERP implementation; the database can be upgraded and operating, and maintenance expenses can be reduced. In general, installing ERP should increase a company's competitiveness and help it obtain critical information faster so that it can make better strategic decisions (Ozkan et al., 2012).

In this way, consolidated data about customers, suppliers, product information, and financial information may be accessed much more readily in electronic format by individuals interested in streamlining business (Ramanna, 2008) Once a company's operations have been digitized, they are easily accessible on a variety of platforms, devices, and interfaces. This enables business people to build their companies using a variety of different programs, platforms, or technical solutions (Alstete & Beutell, 2018).

Over the course of time, managers' information requirements about expenses have developed into significantly more complex forms. In light of the increased level of competition, which has the impact of transferring economic power from the producer to the consumer, the rise of new management styles, and the accelerated evolution of technical advancement, techniques of cost calculation, information provision, control, and analysis have had to develop.

As is only natural, the procedure of arranging budgeting, management accounting, and costing is affected by a number of elements. The following are some of the most significant of these aspects: the size of the firm, the organizational structure of the enterprise, the kind of production and the organization of its production technology, the degree to which the enterprise is concentrated, profiled, and specialized; the degree to which the enterprise is integrated; the nature of the production process; and the character of the production.

The primary goal of an effective budgeting system is to gather accurate data on the company's most critical operations at a cheap cost and in a timely manner so that the required corrective actions can be done based on budgetary control and managers' performance can be evaluated at various stages.

Managers need to have all of the necessary tools at their disposal to discern between relevant and irrelevant expenses and exclude the latter from the decision-making process in order to be successful in their decision-making activity (Chen, Qu & Sun, 2017). The manager can review the facts at his disposal for each choice and separate the relevant expenses. Otherwise, the management runs the danger of employing useless data.

Such an information system is inefficient unless the manner in which it was designed adheres to specific standards, both in terms of function and content. The manner in which the information is presented may vary, but it must adhere to certain constraints of concision and pertinence. In this regard, company dashboards, for example, encourage communication and inspire people in charge. (Englund & Gerdin, 2018).

Accounting data derived from electronic business operations is more trustworthy if the accounting system adheres to both security and processing criteria for accounting information. On top of that, essential for a successful implementation of an ERP system is the effective integration of technical and psychological knowledge.

THE SPECIFIC ASPECTS OF THE IMPACT OF IT TECHNOLOGIES ON THE ACCOUNTING INFORMATION

In a world that is becoming increasingly digitized, it is becoming increasingly common knowledge that a robust organizational objective is vital for every firm, and it is also becoming increasingly common knowledge that trust is becoming increasingly harder to obtain. Comparable phases or a selection of them can also be assumed for IT tools smaller than ERP. There are also comparable effects on the organization and end users (Stoian, 2001).

New IT technologies are usually considered to be the responsibility of the IT department. As a result, they are often incorrectly referred to as "IT projects." The more work or process steps that include a new IT technology, the more appropriate it is to introduce technology as a project of change because it standardizes business processes and harmonizes them.

From this perspective, the introduction of a new ERP system often affects everything at three levels, albeit to varying degrees. Processes are being redefined, which has a clear impact on a company's organizational chart and culture.

Large IT providers offer introductions to ERP systems, which also include change management offerings. In such cases, it may be a mixture of professional, technical, and interdisciplinary aspects. This is a good way to do things, but the technical side of these kinds of offers is still too one-sided.

Change and resilience are closely linked. This is reflected in the fact that decisions and measures associated with the introduction of IT technology for managerial accounting are often greeted with rejection by individuals or groups in the workforce (IFRS, 2013). Resistance is a very important part of change projects, so a constructive way to deal with it is key to the project's success.

An ERP project is considered successful if the introduction of the new system can be implemented within the specified time and within the calculated financial framework. Finding a motivating vision for introducing a new IT system in the project preparation phase is a demanding undertaking, as it means connecting a technical tool with feelings. The aim is to present short and objective images of the future that fit those who will be affected in the future. What is certain is that the new technology is often bought out of an emergency and that the main concern is to avoid a dreaded final state, namely a deadlock in the old system.

If the new technology is introduced by an external supplier, the ordering organization becomes subject to technical dependency, which makes it difficult for it to verify the quality of the service provided and to conclude an appropriate contract. Also, there are no standards that the client can use to make sure that the outside consultants who are then called are good enough.

Anyone challenged with the introduction of a new IT technology for the first time finds it difficult to comprehend all of the project's linkages. This is made more difficult by the additional words and abbreviations used by external experts. Suddenly, an accounting manager cannot depend on his tried-and-true expertise anymore.

The more familiar the top management, the steering committee and the project organization are with a change project, the more uniform the terms used become. Those involved develop a project language that is increasingly difficult for outsiders to understand.

However, the more customized an ERP solution is, the more expensive it becomes. There is rarely room for individual desires. If new processes are defined and subsequently implemented, the employees of an organization have few real opportunities for co-determination. Opportunities to help shape new system processes and solutions, however, promote acceptance and reduce resilience during subsequent implementation. At the same time, those affected by the change have many fears, desires, and goals to avoid. They know what they want more often than they can clearly articulate their desires.

For some ERP systems, there are clear specifications as to where printers printing central forms should be located. The proximity of this device is an expression of status. Important employees have it right next to their offices; the least important ones have to walk many meters to get their prints. And not everyone takes it athletically. It makes perfect sense to talk in-depth about where the printer is and come up with a solution together.

As part of an introduction to IT, changing groups of people need to be able to work together temporarily, forming a temporary team. External specialists often mingle with internal employees in the business and IT departments. Qualification refers to increasing the knowledge, learning, and practical skills that enable employees and future end-users to take on a new role after the change or to keep it despite the change. This includes knowing how to use new templates and how to work with new processes, as well as knowing how to do new jobs.

With larger projects, there is a risk that project management will give more weight to the technical aspect, especially if time and financial frameworks are tight. The people involved, on the other hand, will ensure that there is sufficient communication and negotiation with those affected, which repeatedly costs money, time, and extra work. The people involved and the project management have a common interest in a change that is as smooth as possible but sometimes combines opposite measures with it. The people involved and the project manager should not see each other as opponents, but rather work closely and constructively together.

The people involved should not report directly to the project manager. Instead, it should report directly to the project management or steering committee and be endowed with the appropriate decision-making powers. In terms of technical skills, it does not necessarily need an IT background, but a great willingness to understand the core elements of an ERP implementation. Being unfamiliar with the ERP system, he will ask many useful clarification questions. In addition, he should have extensive knowledge of management conflicts, communication, and support for the psychological work process.

As a philosophy of business administration, the three stages of budget accounting management — estimating, budgeting, and control — go beyond accounting. These three processes give the managers the information they need for the dashboard, which is the primary method for optimizing the fundamental economic information subsystem at the firm level.

This process may be carried out by a business economist, or it can be the result of the reflections of a company responsible factor who may issue three hypotheses (maximal, average, minimal) and then establish the probable budgets for future periods on the basis of these hypotheses, Forecasts, as opposed to estimates, include predicting a probable future outcome that is not supported by any source or logic.

A strong link between the budget and the overall organization of the firm is required for accountability. The latter method necessitates the creation of an organizational chart as well as a paycheck that details all of the responsibilities that are expected of the person holding the role. The budget is only a numerical representation of the documents, as each action has a monetary identifier and value. However, this does not imply that the budget must always conform to the company's current structure.

Because of the persistent impact that the expansion of the economy as a whole has on the operations of the firm, it is necessary to make a number of modifications over the course of the relevant time period. At the corporate level, adjustment is accomplished through two methods: a flexible budget and budget revision. The flexibility of the budget may be understood as the fact that every spending budget can be established in accordance with the activity that is carried out by the appropriate department.

A budget may be thought of as an economic model that is a simplified description of the way in which a unit works. Economically, it is a mathematical and accounting model, or a schematic depiction of a monetarily appraised reality. It is made up of a set of equations, some of which are accounting equations and others of which are behavioral equations. Accounting equations allow specific locations to be linked.

Because it is not enough for a company to acquire new and more capable pieces of equipment, the balanced scorecard draws attention to the significance of keeping a long-run view of the activity. This is because it is necessary for a company to invest in human capital in addition to purchasing new and more capable pieces of equipment.

Employees who are well-informed about the aims and decisions of their bosses will be able to actively contribute to those goals and implicitly fulfill the selected strategy if they are well educated. The "top-down" route is another name for the path that is taken by the information as it travels from the executive sectors, specifically the managers, to the people in the productive and operational sectors.

Considering the benefits, accessibility, and global reach that the Internet offers has helped many businesses of all sizes learn how to use it effectively in their operations. As a consequence of this, a great number of firms have either transitioned into the world of virtual reality or improved their existing infrastructure for doing business online. This has led to modifications in work processes that are associated with online e-business solutions or the new opportunities that these solutions make available.

The interaction of the information and planning systems is what distinguishes the controlling process from other similar procedures. Using the company's strategic goals as a guide, the various divisions design their own specific plans. Individual department plans are then collated and standardized at a higher level (the consolidated plan). The managing activity is carried out in a coordinated fashion based on the three-year strategy that is described yearly. Indicators of management that are measurable can be used to indicate plans and measures.

As a result, standard measurement units must be utilized to calculate the indicators, and publishing intervals should be defined so that accounting data may be reorganized and updated at the same time. The accounting management dashboard provides control over assigned duties as well as a synthesis of the outcomes acquired by subordinates.

Companies used to focus on building standard goods and service lines and then incentivizing their sales team to push and sell them to current customers and prospects. However, many goods or service lines are one-size-fits-all and have devolved into commodities. Most banks, for example, provide identical checking and deposit services. Furthermore, rivals can simply copy a company's conventional products and services. As a consequence of this, the significance of services grows, which leads to a transition away from differentiation based on products and toward differentiation based on services, in addition to distinct customer microsegments, in order to obtain a competitive edge. To put it another way, as the competitive edge gained from product advantages is diminished or eliminated altogether, the value of the connection with the customer increases.

There are many different approaches to running a business in the online age. There is a fundamentally new organizational structure emerging today, based on Internet capabilities and the development of new information and communication technologies. In place of a specified location and an actual organizational structure, the virtual model uses a configuration of a network instead of the traditional model's location.

This new digital business model is rather unpredictable, which results in the emergence of new challenges. Organizational decision-making offers new opportunities for success, and communication takes on new meanings and forms when physical labor dematerializes and becomes digital.

A structure with a linearly functional function and predictable occurrences substitutes a well-defined, sometimes rigid, organizational structure with departments, compartments, and responsibilities. Probabilistic thinking patterns are used to anticipate the outcomes of random events. Because one interconnection leads to another, the complexity of the digital business model refers to a high number of interconnections and the ongoing dynamic of their existence.

In spite of the fact that the Internet has spread to all areas of human endeavor, many developing and emerging economies are falling farther and further behind in terms of their level of digitization. Furthermore, a large number of people still do not have access to information and communication technologies (ICT), and there are significant disparities between urban and rural regions within nations. Evidently, a government's digital economy performance is determined by its capacity to promote technical innovation, entrepreneurship, education, specialized skills, and the transition of all public and commercial organizations from bureaucratic hierarchy to learning networks.

However, we must remember that human resources are the most important resource, and that digital technology continues to be a significant tool. During the pandemic crises, when they were used to relay vital information, telecommunications and information technology technologies demonstrated their significance.

In the digital era, new ways of business development and information transmission have evolved. The system facilitates the interface through which a company engages with its customers. Internet have also grown into powerful advertising and commercial tools, having uses in a range of businesses.

Accounting and e-accounting have become more popular in organizations and businesses because of increased confidence in the technology and the simplicity with which accountants and accounting staff can do their jobs more efficiently. In contrast to the conventional corporate environment, all the developments in the communication sector, as well as the economic and social repercussions of globalization, have necessitated the involvement of organizations in a dynamic environment through the analysis of archives and stored documents. These elements compel firms to conduct internal restructuring studies and to employ worldwide standards and applications.

Accounting data is processed using high-performance technologies that ensure the reliability and security of the data saved and utilized to provide the most trustworthy accounting information. IT infrastructure is critical in guaranteeing data protection and processing it to gather the information required to generate accounting documents or tax returns. When it comes to ensuring that the requirements for the security of accounting information are met, the management of a company bears direct responsibility. Additionally, management is accountable for adopting, developing, and maintaining the organization's information security that they are in charge of managing.

The development of corporate financial reports that are as relevant as possible for management and external users in order to make suitable decisions has resulted in advancement in information technology, particularly with the advent of e-accounting. This has allowed for proper decisions to be made. E-accounting is software that was developed to automate and integrate all of a company or organization's different business operations. As a result, it makes the management of a company's or organization's business processes significantly simpler and more cost-efficient. A few of the advantages of e-accounting include the capacity to swiftly and efficiently manage large amounts of information, as well as the potential to boost daily visibility or the speed of access to essential information.

Due to technology advancements, the tax authorities' reliance on this will grow and audit costs will drop, since quick processing is desirable. Governments will be able to better and more frequently audit compliance with tax and accounting rules and regulations thanks to the internet environment's interaction, which will make things more challenging and alert for both accountants and the authorities. The speed with which online consulting services, online accounting, online financial statement preparation, and online auditing are spreading leads to the quick accumulation of benefits in the form of profits for businesses whose primary focus is the supply of these kinds of services to customers.

SOLUTIONS AND RECOMMENDATIONS

Given these considerations, it is clear that the specialists in the business environment offer strategies for changing organizations into successful business models. It is critical that business development begins on the inside. The value may be produced from the inside, which can then manifest in the corporate environment as an improvement in competitiveness and performance. And this internal development may be done by concentrating on digital and circular methods for business expansion, customer happiness, and business excellence.

The definition of enterprise performance management is the integration of several techniques (such as strategy maps, balanced scorecards, performance metrics, driver-based budgeting, lean management, and customer relationship management) to meet the goals of the executive team, enhance control, and boost financial profitability through better decision-making. Each strategy incorporates business analytics, such as segmentation and correlation analysis, and notably predictive analytics, and this accounts for a significant portion of this phenomenon. The output of a management accounting system is always the input used to obtain insights and manage activities and operations.

Regulators of the financial markets are impacted by the public policy perspectives of their governments, and this influence takes different forms in different regions. It is becoming more and more common for businesses to fail to accurately disclose the effects of climate change that are caused by their actions.

The ultimate expense are represented by the unit of goods, work, or service for which the unit cost is computed. When one-off items are manufactured, this factor is present throughout the entirety of the production process and at each level of cost generation. In other circumstances, the final expenditure bearers only function at the conclusion of the production process, at the final cost-formation step.

There are several methods to do business in the digital age. Organic growth is a successful company development technique for an increasing number of business owners. They seek to form new strategic alliances or joint ventures, while others intend to enter into fresh mergers and acquisitions.

Dashboards that are automated can only be created if there is already an information system in place that can collect, process, and display the relevant data. In terms of the information sources, dashboards need to be able to analyse a constant volume of data while adhering to limits in terms of confidentiality, offering differentiated user access, and providing opportunities for growth and development.

In order to design a panel for an accounting dashboard, we need to choose the indicators that will be displayed on the panel and describe the information that will be provided by the hierarchical levels below the top level. Indicators regarding the present condition as well as past indicators are shown on the panels of the dashboard.

This illustrates the evolution of accounting indicators, informing relevant parties prior to the emergence of crucial results and predicting future actions.

Analytical and Big Data are prominent issues in business nowadays. Because complexity, uncertainty, and volatility are on the rise, they are here to stay. When some managers hear these phrases, it causes them to respond with some dread and cause them to consider. Due to the fact that old generic methods such as having the lowest cost supplier, differentiation of products and customers are vulnerable to swift rivals who can match a supplier's price or invade your client base, this is the situation.

FUTURE RESEARCH DIRECTIONS

As a result, the divisions' financial goals would be sacrificed to the corporation's plan. Finally, all of the other three main axis' aims and targets should be linked to the realization of one or more of the financial objectives.

Because the development of new technologies may satisfy the clients' new wants while assuring a certain profit for the firm, the present needs of the clients, as well as their post-sale needs, must be given additional attention. The learning and development axis is concerned with the company's ability to adapt and innovate in order to accomplish its strategic goals.

Furthermore, process monitoring, and control are critical stages if the intended objectives are to be met by adopting the particular innovation. It is necessary for the size and characteristics of the business organization to serve as the primary determinants of the various activities that comprise the innovation process. In addition, the innovation process must be consistent with the organization's policy, strategy, vision, and objectives, especially those related to innovation.

The firm has to place its primary emphasis on preserving and enhancing its position in those markets in which it is already operating by boosting the degree of customer satisfaction, the number of customers, and its market share. In addition to doing all in their power to fulfill the requirements of their customers, division managers are responsible for translating the purpose and the strategy into customer-market-specific goals.

CONCLUSION

To summarize, the future is neither foreseeable nor predictable, and innovation has emerged as a critical component that may contribute value in any environment, whether individual, corporate, or societal. The development of information-technology-based systems for generating information for management purposes based on an integrated accounting information system has become a requirement in all businesses. There are several accounting software options for unifying accounting, however firms are increasingly turning to and utilizing e-accounting systems.

An organization's growth is always accompanied by a deliberate process of change that affects all or parts of daily operations. Generally, every progress implies and necessitates a shift in corporate culture. Digital technologies are parts of a corporate organization's material culture.

It's important to remember that the ultimate goal of any company development is to improve the organization's performance and competitiveness in the marketplace. Business development is a planned, coordinated activity that targets the entire firm and tries to boost efficiency through process intervention.

It is imperative that every organization regularly analyze its present and potential innovation capabilities, taking into account the following factors: existing practices in the field of innovation management, skills and knowledge in innovation and organizational culture, equipment performance and investment opportunities from sources internal and / or external connected to innovation, external partnerships, business models and product enhancements for ecological, economic a / or societal reasons The process of innovation must be validated, planned, and implemented.

On the basis of these considerations, we consider that a crucial factor in the performance management, respectively entity's objectives overall information system must address three principal issues: ensuring comprehensive documentation and detailed, offering information needed to operate the current systems, and ensuring all information essential for decision-making structures.

REFERENCES

Ahrens, T. (2008). Overcoming the subjective–objective divide in interpretive management accounting research. *Accounting, Organizations and Society*, *33*(2), 292–297. doi:10.1016/j.aos.2007.03.002

Allen, A., & Ramanna, K. (2013). Towards an understanding of the role of standard setters in standard setting. *Journal of Accounting and Economics*, *55*(1), 1–66. doi:10.1016/j.jacceco.2012.05.003

Andon, P., Baxter, J., & Chua, W. F. (2007). Accounting change as relational drifting: A field study of experiments with performance measurement. *Management Accounting Research*, *18*(2), 273–308. doi:10.1016/j.mar.2006.06.007

Arsenault, P., & Faerman, S. R. (2014). Embracing paradox in management: The value of the competing values framework. *Organizational Management Journal, 11*(3), 147–158. doi:10.1080/15416518.2014.949614

Baker, C., & Bettner, M. (1997). Interpretive and Critical Research in Accounting: A Commentary on its Absence from Mainstream Research||. *Critical Perspectives on Accounting, 8*(4), 293–310. doi:10.1006/cpac.1996.0116

Ball, R. (2013). Accounting informs investors and earnings management is rife: Two questionable beliefs. *Accounting Horizons, 27*(4), 847–853. doi:10.2308/acch-10366

Barth, M., Landsman, W., & Lang, M. (2008). International accounting standards and accounting quality. *Journal of Accounting Research, 46*(3), 467–498. doi:10.1111/j.1475-679X.2008.00287.x

Barth, M. E. (2013). Global comparability in financial reporting: What, why, how, and when? *China Journal of Accounting Studies, 1*(1), 2–12. doi:10.1080/21697221.2013.781765

Barth, M. E., Landsman, W. R., Young, D., & Zhuang, Z. (2014). Relevance of Differences between Net Income based on IFRS and Domestic Standards for European Firms. *Journal of Business Finance & Accounting, 41*(3-4), 297–506. doi:10.1111/jbfa.12067

Bettner, M., & Kate, K. (2013). Changes in annual reporting rituals of financial services firms in periods of market crisis. *International Journal of Critical Accounting, 5*(6), 577–593. doi:10.1504/IJCA.2013.059027

Brown, J. (2010). Accounting and visual cultural studies: Potentialities, challenges and prospects. *Accounting, Auditing & Accountability Journal, 23*(4), 482–505. doi:10.1108/09513571011041598

Byard, D., Li, Y., & Yu, Y. (2011). The effect of mandatory IFRS adoption on financial analysts' information environment. *Journal of Accounting Research, 49*(1), 69–96. doi:10.1111/j.1475-679X.2010.00390.x

Cahan, S. F., & Sun, J. (2015). The effect of audit experience on audit fees and audit quality. *Journal of Accounting, Auditing & Finance, 30*(1), 78–100. doi:10.1177/0148558X14544503

Caylor, M. L. (2010). Strategic revenue recognition to achieve earnings benchmarks. *Journal of Accounting and Public Policy, 29*(1), 82–95. doi:10.1016/j.jaccpubpol.2009.10.008

Chen, H., Tang, Q., Jiang, Y., & Lin, Z. (2010). The role of international financial reporting standards in accounting quality: Evidence from the European Union. *Journal of International Financial Management & Accounting*, *21*(3), 220–278. doi:10.1111/j.1467-646X.2010.01041.x

Damayant, T. (2013). Who is afraid of Qualitative Research? A Compromise Accounting Research Failure in Improving Accounting Practices. *International Journal of Advances in Management and Economics*, *2*(2), 89-94.

Dennis, I. (2014). *The Nature of Accounting Regulation*. Routledge.

Doukakis, L. C. (2014). The effect of mandatory IFRS adoption on real and accrual-based earnings management activities. *Journal of Accounting and Public Policy*, *33*(6), 551–572. doi:10.1016/j.jaccpubpol.2014.08.006

Fan, J. P. H., Li, J., & Zheng, G. (2016). Revisiting the bright and dark sides of capital flows in business groups. *Journal of Business Ethics*, *134*(4), 509–528. doi:10.100710551-014-2382-6

Florou, A., & Pope, P. (2012). Mandatory IFRS adoption and institutional investment decisions. *The Accounting Review*, *87*(6), 1993–2025. doi:10.2308/accr-50225

He, K., Pan, X., & Tian, G. (2017). Legal liability, government intervention, and auditor behavior: Evidence from structural reform of audit firms in China. *European Accounting Review*, *26*(1), 61–95. doi:10.1080/09638180.2015.1100547

Holthausen, R. W., & Watts, R. L. (2001). The relevance of the value-relevance literature for financial accounting standard setting. *Journal of Accounting and Economics*, *31*(1-3), 3–75. doi:10.1016/S0165-4101(01)00029-5

Hou, Q., Jin, Q., Yang, R., Yuan, H., & Zhang, G. (2015). Performance commitments of controlling shareholders and earnings management. *Contemporary Accounting Research*, *32*(3), 1099–1127. doi:10.1111/1911-3846.12111

Jackson, S. B., & Liu, X. K. (2010). The allowance for uncollectible accounts, conservatism, and earnings management. *Journal of Accounting Research*, *48*(3), 565–601. doi:10.1111/j.1475-679X.2009.00364.x

Li, S. (2010). Does mandatory adoption of international accounting standards in the European Union reduce the cost of equity capital? *The Accounting Review*, *85*(2), 607–636. doi:10.2308/accr.2010.85.2.607

Lukka, K. (2010). The roles and effects of paradigms in accounting research. *Management Accounting Research*, *21*(2), 110–115. doi:10.1016/j.mar.2010.02.002

Ozkan, N., Singer, Z., & You, H. (2012). Mandatory IFRS adoption and the contractual usefulness of accounting information in executive compensation. *Journal of Accounting Research*, *50*(4), 1077–1107. doi:10.1111/j.1475-679X.2012.00453.x

Parker, L. (2012). Qualitative management accounting research: Assessing deliverables and relevance. *Critical Perspectives on Accounting*, *23*(1), 54–70. doi:10.1016/j.cpa.2011.06.002

Ramanna, K. (2008). The implications of unverifiable fair-value accounting: Evidence from the political economy of goodwill accounting. *Journal of Accounting and Economics*, *45*(2-3), 253–281. doi:10.1016/j.jacceco.2007.11.006

Richardson, A. (2011). Myth, Paradigms and Academic Accounting Research: A Comment on Reading and Understanding Academic Research in Accounting. *Global Perspectives on Accounting Education*, *8*, 67–77.

Schleicher, T., Tahoun, A., & Walker, M. (2010). IFRS adoption in Europe and investment-cash flow sensitivity: Outsider versus insider economies. *The International Journal of Accounting*, *45*(2), 143–168. doi:10.1016/j.intacc.2010.04.007

Vladu, A. B., Amat, O., & Cuzdriorean, D. D. (2016). Truthfulness in accounting: How to discriminate accounting manipulators from non-manipulators. *Journal of Business Ethics*, *140*(4), 633–648. doi:10.100710551-016-3048-3

ADDITIONAL READING

Ahmed, A., Neel, M., & Wang, D. (2013). Does mandatory adoption of IFRS improve accounting quality? Preliminary evidence. *Contemporary Accounting Research*, *30*(4), 388–423. doi:10.1111/j.1911-3846.2012.01193.x

Alstete, J. W., & Beutell, N. J. (2018). Designing learning spaces for management education: A mixed methods research approach. *Journal of Management Development*, *37*(2), 201–211. doi:10.1108/JMD-08-2017-0247

Ball, R., Li, X., & Shivakumar, L. (2015). Contractibility and transparency of financial statement information prepared under IFRS: Evidence from debt contracts around IFRS adoption. *Journal of Accounting Research*, *53*(5), 915–963. doi:10.1111/1475-679X.12095

Chen, M., Qu, X., & Sun, X. (2017). Whose cost of equity capital reduces after IFRS convergence and why? Heterogeneity evidence from Chinese stock market. *China Journal of Accounting Studies*, *5*(1), 1–27. doi:10.1080/21697213.2017.1304539

Englund, H., & Gerdin, J. (2018). Management accounting and the paradox of embedded agency: A framework for analyzing sources of structural change. *Management Accounting Research*, *38*(1), 1–11. doi:10.1016/j.mar.2017.12.001

Li, L., Qi, B., Tian, G., & Zhang, G. (2017). The contagion effect of low-quality audits at the level of individual auditors. *The Accounting Review*, *92*(1), 137–163. doi:10.2308/accr-51407

Compilation of References

Accenture. (2021). *Artificial intelligence.* Retrieved from https://www.accenture.com/gb-en/insights/artificial-intelligence-summary-index

AccountAbility. (2003). *Impacts of Reporting: The Role of Social and Sustainability Reporting in Organisational Transformation.* Retrieved February 10, 2022 from http://accountability.com

Adams, C. A., & Abhayawansa, S. (2021). Connecting the COVID-19 pandemic, environmental, social and governance (ESG) investing and calls for 'harmonization' of sustainability reporting. *Critical Perspectives on Accounting.*

Agha, S., Alrubaiee, L., & Jamhour, M. (2012). Effect of core competence on competitive advantage and organizational performance. *International Journal of Business and Management, 7*(1), 192–204.

Ahearne, M., Lam, S. K., Mathieu, J. E., & Bolander, W. (2010). Why are some sales people better at adapting to organizational change? *Journal of Marketing, 74*(3), 65–79. doi:10.1509/jmkg.74.3.065

Ahmed, A., Neel, M., & Wang, D. (2013). Does mandatory adoption of IFRS improve accounting quality? Preliminary evidence. *Contemporary Accounting Research, 30*(4), 388–423. doi:10.1111/j.1911-3846.2012.01193.x

Ahrens, T. (2008). Overcoming the subjective–objective divide in interpretive management accounting research. *Accounting, Organizations and Society, 33*(2), 292–297. doi:10.1016/j.aos.2007.03.002

Aidemark, G. (2010). Cooperation and competition: Balanced scorecard and hospital privatization. *International Journal of Health Care Quality Assurance, 23*(8), 730–748. doi:10.1108/09526861011081868 PMID:21125968

Aidemark, L. G. (2001). The meaning of Balanced Scorecards in the health care organization. *Financial Accountability & Management, 17*(1), 23–40. doi:10.1111/1468-0408.00119

Aidemark, L. G., & Funck, E. K. (2009). Measurement and health care management. *Financial Accountability & Management, 25*(2), 253–276. doi:10.1111/j.1468-0408.2009.00476.x

Akgün, A. E., Keskin, H., & Byrne, J. (2009). Organizational emotional capability, product and process innovation, and firm performance: An empirical analysis. *Journal of Engineering and Technology Management*, *26*(3), 103–130. doi:10.1016/j.jengtecman.2009.06.008

Al Lawati, H., & Hussainey, K. (2022). Does Sustainable Development Goals Disclosure Affect Corporate Financial Performance? *Sustainability*, *14*(13), 7815. doi:10.3390u14137815

Alcaraz, A. S., & Rodenas, S. P. (2013). The Spanish Banks in face of the Corporate Social Responsibility Standards: Previous analysis of the financial crisis. *Review of Business Management*, *15*(49), 562–581.

Alhyari, S., Alazab, M., Venkatraman, S., Alazab, M., & Alazab, A. (2013). Performance evaluation of e-government services using balanced scorecard. *Benchmarking*, *20*(4), 512–536. doi:10.1108/BIJ-08-2011-0063

Allen, A., & Ramanna, K. (2013). Towards an understanding of the role of standard setters in standard setting. *Journal of Accounting and Economics*, *55*(1), 1–66. doi:10.1016/j.jacceco.2012.05.003

Alsop, T. (2021). *PC market in Europe - Statistics & facts*. https://www.statista.com/topics/3889/pc-market-in-europe/

Alstete, J. W., & Beutell, N. J. (2018). Designing learning spaces for management education: A mixed methods research approach. *Journal of Management Development*, *37*(2), 201–211. doi:10.1108/JMD-08-2017-0247

Alsultanny, Y. A., & Alotaibi, M. F. (2015). Evaluating the Factors Affecting on Intension to Use of E-Recruitment. *American Journal of Information Science and Computer Engineering*, *1*(5), 324–331.

Alzola, M. A. (2017). Beware of the watchdog: Rethinking the normative justification of gatekeeper liability. *Journal of Business Ethics*, *140*(4), 705–721. doi:10.100710551-017-3460-3

Amado, C. A., Santos, S. P., & Marques, P. M. (2012). Integrating the Data Envelopment Analysis and the Balanced Scorecard approaches for enhanced performance assessment. *Omega*, *40*(3), 390–403. doi:10.1016/j.omega.2011.06.006

Amagoh, F. (2008). Perspectives on organizational change: Systems and complexity theories. *The Innovation Journal*, *13*(3), 1–14.

Anand, G., & Kodali, R. (2010). A mathematical model for the evaluation of roles and responsibilities of human resources in a lean manufacturing environment. *International Journal of Human Resources Development and Management*, *10*(1), 63–100. doi:10.1504/IJHRDM.2010.029447

Anand, J., & Devi, C. S. (2016). The Impact of e-recruitment and challenges faced by HR professionals. *International Journal of Applied Research*, *2*(3), 410–413. https:// www.allresearchjournal.com/archives/2016/vol2issue3/PartG/2-2-84.pdf

Anand, M., Sahay, B. S., & Saha, S. (2005). Balanced Scorecard in Indian Companies. *Vikalpa*, *30*(2), 11–25. doi:10.1177/0256090920050202

Andersson, P. M., Persson, J. E., & Ramberg, U. (2000). Balanced Scorecard i landsting: erfarenheter från tolv projekt i region Skäne. Institutet fo¨r ekonomisk forskning vid Lunds universitet, Lund.

Andon, P., Baxter, J., & Chua, W. F. (2007). Accounting change as relational drifting: A field study of experiments with performance measurement. *Management Accounting Research*, *18*(2), 273–308. doi:10.1016/j.mar.2006.06.007

Andriole, S. J. (2010). Business impact of Web 2.0 Technologies. *Communications of the ACM*, *53*(12), 67–79. doi:10.1145/1859204.1859225

Ansari, J. A. N., & Khan, N. A. (2020). Exploring the role of social media in collaborative learning the new domain of learning. *Smart Learning Environments*, *7*(1), 9. Advance online publication. doi:10.118640561-020-00118-7

Anthroplous, A. (2018). *Mastering Ethereum: Building smart contracts and dApps*. O'Reilly Publication.

Antipova, T., & Bourmistrov, A. (2013). Is Russian Public Sector Accounting in the Process of Modernization? An Analysis of Accounting Reforms in Russia. *Financial Accountability & Management*, *29*(4), 442–478. Advance online publication. doi:10.1111/faam.12021

Aqeel, S., & Siddiqui, D. (2019). The effect of social media following on recruitment in service industries of Pakistan. *Business Management and Strategy*, *10*(1), 41–77. doi:10.5296/bms.v10i1.14633

Aras, G., & Crowther, D. (2009). Corporate Sustainability Reporting: A Study in Disingenuity? *Journal of Business Ethics*, *87*(S1), 279–288. doi:10.100710551-008-9806-0

Armbester, K., Clay, T., & Roberts, L. (2011). Integrated Reporting: An Irreversible Tipping Point. Accountancy SA, 29-31.

Armstrong, M. (2006). *A handbook of human resources management practice*. Kogan Page.

Arsenault, P., & Faerman, S. R. (2014). Embracing paradox in management: The value of the competing values framework. *Organizational Management Journal*, *11*(3), 147–158. doi:10.1080/15416518.2014.949614

Asher, C. C., Mahoney, J. M., & Mahoney, J. T. (2005). Towards a property rights foundation for a stakeholder theory of the firm. *The Journal of Management and Governance*, *9*(1), 5–32. doi:10.100710997-005-1570-2

Ashkanasy, N. (2011). International happiness; a multilevel perspective. *The Academy of Management Perspectives*, (February), 23–29.

Assiri, A., Zairi, M., & Eid, R. (2006). How to profit from the balanced scorecard: An implementation roadmap. *Industrial Management & Data Systems*, *106*(7), 937–952. doi:10.1108/02635570610688869

Atkinson, H. (2006). Strategy Implementation: A Role for the Balanced Scorecard? *Management Decision*, *44*(10), 1441–1460. doi:10.1108/00251740610715740

Atkinson, M. (2012). Developing and using a performance management framework – a case study. *Measuring Business Excellence*, *16*(3), 102–132. doi:10.1108/13683041211257402

Attestation. (n.d.). Retrieved from https://alphawallet.com/for-user/attestation/

Bach, S. (2005). *Managing human resources: personnel management in transition*. Blackwell Pub.

Badr, G., & Aboul-Ela, E. (2014). Development of a scale to measure the perceived benefits of e-recruitment from the viewpoint of the recruiter. *The Journal of Business and Retail Management Research*, *9*(1), 40–51.

Bailey, A. (2021). *Roadblocks and concerns on the way to a decentralized ecosystem*. Retrieved from https://www.kuppingercole.com/insights/decentralized-identity#Chapter4

Bakar, C., Akgün, H. S., & Assaf, A. F. (2008). The role of expectations in patients' hospital assessments: A Turkish university hospital example. *International Journal of Health Care Quality Assurance*, *21*(5), 503–516. doi:10.1108/09526860810890477 PMID:18785349

Baker, C., & Bettner, M. (1997). Interpretive and Critical Research in Accounting: A Commentary on its Absence from Mainstream Research||. *Critical Perspectives on Accounting*, *8*(4), 293–310. doi:10.1006/cpac.1996.0116

Baker, G. R., & Pink, G. H. (1995). A balanced scorecard for Canadian hospitals. *Healthcare Management Forum*, *8*(2), 7–21. doi:10.1016/S0840-4704(10)60926-X PMID:10156487

Balachandran, B., & Faff, R. (2015). Corporate governance, firm value and risk: Past, present, and future. *Pacific-Basin Finance Journal, 35*(A), 1-12.

Ball, R. (2013). Accounting informs investors and earnings management is rife: Two questionable beliefs. *Accounting Horizons*, *27*(4), 847–853. doi:10.2308/acch-10366

Ball, R., Li, X., & Shivakumar, L. (2015). Contractibility and transparency of financial statement information prepared under IFRS: Evidence from debt contracts around IFRS adoption. *Journal of Accounting Research*, *53*(5), 915–963. doi:10.1111/1475-679X.12095

Balva, C. (2017). *The blockchain: Reinventing relationships of trust* [La Blockchain: réinventer les rapports de confiance]. Retrieved from https://www.youtube.com/watch?v=JID9c-MABis

Bamford, D., & Chaziaislan, E. (2009). Healthcare capacity measurement. *International Journal of Productivity and Performance Management*, *58*(8), 748–766. doi:10.1108/17410400911000390

Banyai, T. (2019). *Sustainable Human Resource Management*. MDPI.

Baret, P., & Helfrich, V. (2016). Cas 10. Rémy Cointreau. 10 cas de RSE, 219-232. doi:10.3917/dunod.baret.2016.01.0219

Barraud, J., Guillemin, M., & Kittel, F. (2008). The Human Resources function-3rd ed.: Trades, skills and training [La fonction Ressources Humaines-3e éd.: Métiers, compétences et formation]. Hachette.

Barth, M. E. (2013). Global comparability in financial reporting: What, why, how, and when? *China Journal of Accounting Studies*, *1*(1), 2–12. doi:10.1080/21697221.2013.781765

Barth, M. E., Konchitchki, Y. L., & Landsman, W. R. (2013). Cost of capital and earnings transparency. *Journal of Accounting and Economics*, *55*(2–3), 206–224. doi:10.1016/j.jacceco.2013.01.004

Barth, M. E., Landsman, W. R., Young, D., & Zhuang, Z. (2014). Relevance of Differences between Net Income based on IFRS and Domestic Standards for European Firms. *Journal of Business Finance & Accounting*, *41*(3-4), 297–506. doi:10.1111/jbfa.12067

Barth, M., Landsman, W., & Lang, M. (2008). International accounting standards and accounting quality. *Journal of Accounting Research*, *46*(3), 467–498. doi:10.1111/j.1475-679X.2008.00287.x

BDO. (2018). *Driving value creation through integrated thinking and reporting*. Retrieved February 10, 2022 from https://www.bdo.global/ getattachment/Insights/Audit-Assurance/BDO-integrated-thinking-and-reporting-journey-guid/IRSTF-IR-journey-guide-FINAL.pdf.aspx?lang=en-GB&ext=.pdf

Beasley, M. S., Buckless, F. A., Glover, S. M., & Prawitt, D. F. (2009). *Auditing Cases. An Interactive Learning Approach* (4th ed.). Prentice Hall.

Becker, B. E., & Huselid, M. A. (2006). Strategic human resources management: Where do we go from here? *Journal of Management*, *32*(6), 898–925. doi:10.1177/0149206306293668

Bedenik, N., & Barišić, P. (2019). Nonfinancial Reporting: Theoretical and Empirical Evidence. In M. Sarfraz, M. I. Adbullah, A. Rauf, & M. S. G. Shah (Eds.), *Business. Sustainable Management Practices*. IntechOpen. doi:10.5772/intechopen.87159

Beer, M., & Eisenstat, R. A. (2004). How to have an honest conversation about your business strategy. *Harvard Business Review*, *82*(2), 82–89. PMID:14971272

Behery, M., Jabeen, F., & Parakandi, M. (2014). Adopting a contemporary performance management system. *International Journal of Productivity and Performance Management*, *63*(1), 22–43. doi:10.1108/IJPPM-07-2012-0076

Bellini, E., Iraqi, Y., & Damiani, E. (2020). Blockchain-based distributed trust and reputation management systems. *IEEE Access: Practical Innovations, Open Solutions*, *8*, 8. doi:10.1109/ACCESS.2020.2969820

Bellucci, M., & Manetti, G. (2018). *Stakeholder Engagement and Sustainability Reporting*. Routledge. doi:10.4324/9781351243957

Benchemam, F., & Galindo, G. (2009). Human Resources Management [Gestion des resources humaines] (2nd ed.). Gualino ed..

Berg, R. J., & McCoy, H. (2012). *Let's Talk Business!: Introduction to economic and commercial French* [Parlons affaires!: Initiation au français economique et commercial]. Cengage Learning.

Bernays, E. (1928). *Propaganda*. Horace Liveright.

Berry, M. (2005). *Top companies lead online recruitment revolution*. www.personneltoday.com

Bettner, M., & Kate, K. (2013). Changes in annual reporting rituals of financial services firms in periods of market crisis. *International Journal of Critical Accounting*, *5*(6), 577–593. doi:10.1504/IJCA.2013.059027

Beyer, R. (1963). *Profitability accounting for planning and control*. Ronald Press Company.

Bhagyashree, P., Margaret, R., & Victor, P. (2006). Performance measurement systems: Successes, failures and future? A review. *Measuring Business Excellence*, *10*(3), 4–14. doi:10.1108/13683040610685748

Bhalla, A. (n.d.). *What is decentralization in blockchain?* Retrieved from https://www.blockchain-council.org/blockchain/what-is-decentralization-in-blockchain/

Bickerton, P., Bickerton, M., & Pardesi, U. (2000). *Cybermarketing*. Routledge.

Billsberry, J. (2008). *Experiencing recruitment and selection*. John Wiley & Sons.

Bini, L., Dainelli, F., Giunta, F., & Simoni, L. (2019). Are non-financial KPIs in annual reports really "key"? An investigation of company disclosure and analyst reports in the UK. In *Business Integrated Sustainability Reporting*. ICAS.

Bini, L., & Bellucci, M. (2020). *Integrated Sustainability Reporting: Linking Environmental and Social Information to Value Creation Processes*. Springer. doi:10.1007/978-3-030-24954-0

Bitcoin Magazine. (2020). *What is a Bitcoin Improvement Proposal (BIP)*. Retrieved from https://bitcoinmagazine.com/guides/what-is-a-bitcoin-improvement-proposal-bip

Blau, P. (1964). *Blau, exchange and power in social life*. John Wiley and Sons.

Blockchain Framework. (n.d.). Retrieved from https://www.icertis.com/contract-management/blockchain

Blockchain-governance. (n.d.). Retrieved from https://101blockchains.com/blockchain-governance/

Bock, E. D., Wolter, S. J., & Ferrell, C. O. (2020). Artificial intelligence: Disrupting what we know about services. *Journal of Services Marketing*, *34*(3), 317–334. doi:10.1108/JSM-01-2019-0047

Bondarouk, T., Ruël, H., & Looise, J. K. (2011). *Electronic HRM in theory and practice*. Emerald Group Publishing. doi:10.1108/S1877-6361(2011)8

Boşcai, B. G. (2017). The evolution of e-recruitment: The introduction of online recruiter. In *Management and Organization: Concepts, Tools and Applications* (pp. 161-170). Pearson. http://real.mtak.hu/54549/1/162_Management_and_Organization-Pearson-2017j%C3%BAn08-DOI_CrossRef-2017j%C3% BAn 13f.pdf

Bosch. (n.d.). *AI code of ethics*. Retrieved from https://www.bosch.com/stories/ethical-guidelines-for-artificial-intelligence/#:~:text=Bosch's%20AI%20code%20of%20ethics,based%20products%20that%20are%20trustworthy

Boukis, A. (2020). Exploring the implications of blockchain technology for brand–consumer relationships: A future research agenda. *Journal of Product and Brand Management, 29*(3), 307–320. doi:10.1108/JPBM-03-2018-1780

Bourgoin, A., Marchessaux, F., & Bencherki, N. (2018). We need to talk about strategy: How to conduct effective strategic. *Business Horizons, 61*(4), 587–597. doi:10.1016/j.bushor.2018.03.008

Bourne, M., Mills, J., Wilcox, M., Neely, A., & Platts, K. (2000). Designing, implementing and updating performance measurement systems. *International Journal of Operations & Production Management, 20*(7), 754–771. doi:10.1108/01443570010330739

Bournois, F., Point, S., Rojot, J., & Scaringella, J. L. (2007). *RH: Les meilleures pratiques du CAC 40/SBF 120*. Editions Eyrolles.

Bovenberg, L., & Zaidi, A. (2010). *Ageing, Health and Pensions in Europe*. Springer. doi:10.1057/9780230307346

Bozec, Y. (2008). Ownership Concentration, Separation of Voting Rights from Cash Flow Rights, and Earnings Management: An Empirical Study in Canada. *Canadian Journal of Administrative Sciences, 25*(1), 1–15. doi:10.1002/cjas.52

Bradutanu, D. (2015). *Resistance to change: a new perspective*. Lulu Press.

Brahambhatt, R. (2021). *What is Web 3.0? A new horizon for your online life*. Retrieved from https://interestingengineering.com/web-3-the-new-internet-is-about-to-arrive#:~:text=Web%203.0%3A%20The%20internet%20of%20tomorrow&text=Web%203.0%20is%20in%20many,is%20no%20central%20controlling%20node

Brown, S. (2021). *Machine learning, explained*. Retrieved from https://mitsloan.mit.edu/ideas-made-to-matter/machine-learning-explained

Brown, H. S., De Jong, M., & Lessidrenska, T. (2009a). The rise of the Global Reporting Initiative: A case of institutional entrepreneurship. *Environmental Politics, 18*(2), 182–200. doi:10.1080/09644010802682551

Brown, H. S., De Jong, M., & Levy, D. L. (2009b). Building institutions based on information disclosure: Lessons from GRI's sustainability reporting. *Journal of Cleaner Production, 17*(6), 571–580. doi:10.1016/j.jclepro.2008.12.009

Brown, J. (2010). Accounting and visual cultural studies: Potentialities, challenges and prospects. *Accounting, Auditing & Accountability Journal, 23*(4), 482–505. doi:10.1108/09513571011041598

Brüggemann, U., Hitz, J.-M., & Sellhorn, T. (2013). Intended and unintended consequences of mandatory IFRS adoption: A review of extant evidence and suggestions for future research. *European Accounting Review, 22*(1), 1–37. doi:10.1080/09638180.2012.718487

Brusca, I., & Martınez, J. C. (2015). Adopting international public sector accounting standards: A challenge for modernizing and harmonizing public sector accounting. *International Review of Administrative Sciences International, 0*(0), 1–21.

Bryant, L., Jones, D. A., & Widener, S. K. (2004). Managing Value Creation within the Firm: An Examination of Multiple Performance Measures. *Journal of Management Accounting Research, 16*(1), 107–131. doi:10.2308/jmar.2004.16.1.107

Buhalis, D., & Licata, M. C. (2002). The future etourism intermediaries. *Tourism Management, 23*(3), 207–220. Advance online publication. doi:10.1016/S0261-5177(01)00085-1

Burgess, M. (2021). How France tamed Google. *Wired Magazine.* Retrieved from https://www.wired.co.uk/article/google-france-fines

Busco, C., Frigo, M., Quattrone, P., & Riccaboni, A. (2014). Leading practices in Integrated Reporting. *Strategic Finance, 9*, 23–32.

Byard, D., Li, Y., & Yu, Y. (2011). The effect of mandatory IFRS adoption on financial analysts' information environment. *Journal of Accounting Research, 49*(1), 69–96. doi:10.1111/j.1475-679X.2010.00390.x

Cadin, L., Guerin, F., & Pigeyre, F. (2009). *Human resources management* [Gestion des ressources humaines]. Dunod.

Cahan, S. F., & Sun, J. (2015). The effect of audit experience on audit fees and audit quality. *Journal of Accounting, Auditing & Finance, 30*(1), 78–100. doi:10.1177/0148558X14544503

Cairns, D., Massoudi, D., Taplin, R., & Tarca, A. (2011). IFRS fair value measurement and accounting policy choice in the United Kingdom and Australia. *The British Accounting Review, 43*(1), 1–21. doi:10.1016/j.bar.2010.10.003

Callegaro, M., Manfreda, K. L., & Vehovar, V. (2015). Web survey methodology. *Sage.*

Cameron, K. S., & Quinn, R. E. (2011). *Diagnosing and Changing Organizational Culture: Based on the Competing Values Framework.* Jossey-Bass.

Campbell-Verduyn, M. (Ed.). (2019). *Bitcoin and beyond cryptocurrencies, blockchains, and global governance.* Routledge.

Carnini Pulino, S., Ciaburri, M., Magnanelli, B. S., & Nasta, L. (2022). Does ESG Disclosure Influence Firm Performance? *Sustainability, 14*(13), 7595. doi:10.3390u14137595

Caylor, M. L. (2010). Strategic revenue recognition to achieve earnings benchmarks. *Journal of Accounting and Public Policy*, *29*(1), 82–95. doi:10.1016/j.jaccpubpol.2009.10.008

Celma, D., Buil, M., & Patau, J. (2017). Management control in startups with high growth success in the Technology sector: The case of Netrivals. *European Accounting and Management Review*, *3*(2), 17–44. doi:10.26595/eamr.2014.3.2.2

Chaffey, D. (2022). *What is digital marketing?* Retrieved from https://www.smartinsights.com/digital-marketing-strategy/what-is-digital-marketing/

Champniss, G., & Vila, R. (2011). *Brand valued: How socially valued brands hold the key to a sustainable future and business success*. Wiley and Sons.

Chan, L. L., Shaffer, M. A., & Snape, E. (2004). In search of sustained competitive advantage: The impact of organizational culture, competitive strategy and human resource management practices on firm performance. *International Journal of Human Resource Management*, *15*(1), 17–35. doi:10.1080/0958519032000157320

Chan, Y. L. (2009). How strategy map works for Ontario's health system. *International Journal of Public Sector Management*, *22*(4), 349–363. doi:10.1108/09513550910961628

Chavan, M. (2009). The Balanced Scorecard: A new challenge. *Journal of Management Development*, *28*(5), 393–406. doi:10.1108/02621710910955930

Chavez-Dreyfuss, G. (2019). Harvard, Levi Strauss, U.S. think tank in blockchain tie-up on worker welfare. *Reuters*. Retrieved from https://reut.rs/3alm7g

Chebaane, S., & Othman, H. B. (2014). The Impact of IFRS Adoption on Value Relevance of Earnings and Book Value of Equity: The Case of Emerging Markets in African and Asian Regions. *Procedia: Social and Behavioral Sciences*, *145*, 70–80. doi:10.1016/j.sbspro.2014.06.012

Cheffi, W., Rao, A., & Beldi, A. (2010). Designing a Performance Measurement System: Accountants and Managers Diverge. *Management Accounting Quarterly*, *11*(3), 8–21.

Chen, H. M., & Fu, P. C. (2008). A systematic framework for performance appraisal and compensation strategy. *Human Systems Management*, *27*(2), 161–175. doi:10.3233/HSM-2008-0674

Chen, H., Tang, Q., Jiang, Y., & Lin, Z. (2010). The role of international financial reporting standards in accounting quality: Evidence from the European Union. *Journal of International Financial Management & Accounting*, *21*(3), 220–278. doi:10.1111/j.1467-646X.2010.01041.x

Chen, M., Qu, X., & Sun, X. (2017). Whose cost of equity capital reduces after IFRS convergence and why? Heterogeneity evidence from Chinese stock market. *China Journal of Accounting Studies*, *5*(1), 1–27. doi:10.1080/21697213.2017.1304539

Chen, X. Y., Yamauchi, K., Kato, K., Nishimura, A., & Ito, K. (2006). Using the balanced scorecard to measure Chinese and Japanese hospital performance. *International Journal of Health Care Quality Assurance*, *19*(5), 339–350. doi:10.1108/09526860610671391 PMID:16961099

Chitkara, H. (2019). *Daimler will use a blockchain platform to track the value of used cars in real time.* Retrieved from https://www.businessinsider.com/daimler-to-use-blockchain-platform-for-valuing-used-cars-2019-9?r=US&IR=T

Choi, Y.-S., Peasnell, K., & Toniato, J. (2013). Has the IASB been successful in making accounting earnings more useful for prediction and valuation? UK evidence. *Journal of Business Finance & Accounting*, *40*(7–8), 741–768. doi:10.1111/jbfa.12025

Christiaens, J., Vanhee, C., Manes-Rossi, F., Aversano, N., & van Cauwenberge, P. (2015). The effect of IPSAS on reforming governmental financial reporting: an international comparison. *International Review of Administrative Sciences (IRAS), 81*(1), 158-177. doi:10.1177/0020852314546580

Churet, C., & Eccles, R. (2014). Integrated Reporting, Quality of Management, and Financial Performance. *Journal of Applied Corporate Finance*, *26*(1), 56–64.

Cialdini, R. (2007). *Influence: The psychology of persuasion.* HarperBus.

Cifalino, A., & Baraldi, S. (2009). Training programs and performance measurement: Evidence from healthcare organizations. *Journal of Human Resource Costing and Accounting*, *13*(4), 294–315. doi:10.1108/14013381011010141

Cîrstea, A., Nistor, C.S., & Tiron-Tudor, A. (2017). Consolidated financial statements – a new challenge for the public sector administration. *Journal of Economic and Administrative Sciences, 33*(1), 46-65. doi:10.1108/JEAS-04-2016-0012

Cisco. (n.d.). *The Cisco Responsible AI Framework.* Retrieved from https://www.cisco.com/c/dam/en_us/about/doing_business/trust-center/docs/cisco-responsible-artificial-intelligence-framework.pdf?CCID=cc000742&DTID=odicdc000016

Ciurea, M. (2018). Considerations on the Need to Implement International Accounting Standards for the Public Sector in Romania. *Annals of the University of Petrosani. Economics*, *18*(1), 35–44.

Čizmić, E., & Crnkić, K. (2010). Enhancing Organizational Effectiveness and Efficiency through Balanced Scorecard Application. *Problems and Perspectives in Management*, *8*(4), 14–26.

Coca-Cola. (2022). *Coca-Cola's Coke's Share A Coke Campaign*. Retrieved from https://www.coca-colacompany.com/au/faqs/what-was-the-share-a-coke-campaign

Cocca, P., & Alberti, M. (2010). A framework to assess performance measurement in SMEs. *International Journal of Productivity and Performance Management*, *59*(2), 186–200. doi:10.1108/17410401011014258

Cohen, J., Holder-Webb, L., Kanellakou, L., & Wood, D. (2012). Corporate Reporting of Non-Financial Leading Indicators of Economic Performance and Sustainability. *Accounting Horizons*, *26*(1), 65–90. doi:10.2308/acch-50073

Cohen, S., & Karatzimas, S. (2017). Accounting information quality and decision usefulness of governmental financial reporting. Moving from cash to modified cash. *Meditary Accounting Research*, *25*(1), 95–113. doi:10.1108/MEDAR-10-2015-0070

Coin Insider. (2018). Daimler AG launches MobiCoin; a cryptocurrency that rewards eco-friendly driving. *Coin Insider.* Retrieved from https://www.coininsider.com/daimler-ag-mercedes-benz-mobicoin/

Columbus, L. (2017). How artificial intelligence is revolutionizing business in 2017. *Forbes Magazine.* Retrieved from https://www.forbes.com/sites/louiscolumbus/2017/09/10/how-artificial-intelligence-is-revolutionizing-business-in-2017/

Compeau, R. D., & Higgins, A. C. (1995). Application of social cognitive theory to training for computer skills. *Information Systems Research*, *6*(2), 118–143. Advance online publication. doi:10.1287/isre.6.2.118

Consensys. (n.d.). *Blockchain in retail fashion & luxury*. Retrieved from https://consensys.net/blockchain-use-cases/retail-fashion-and-luxury/

Coombs, W. T., & Holladay, S. J. (2007). The negative communication dynamic: Exploring the impact of stakeholder affect on behavioral intention. *Journal of Communication Management (London)*, *11*(4), 300–312. doi:10.1108/13632540710843913

Cornelissen, J. (2020). *Corporate communications: A guide to theory & practice*. Sage Publications.

Cornet, A., & Warlaud, Ph. (2008). *Human resources management and diversity management* [Gestion de ressources humaines et gestion de la diversité]. Dunod.

Cross, O. D. (2018). E-Recruitment and its Effects on Organizational Creativity and Innovation in Nigerian Manufacturing Firms. *Nile Journal of Business and Economics*, *8*, 3–12.

Crowther, D. (2013). *A Social Critique of Corporate Reporting; Semiotics and web-based integrated reporting*. Routledge.

Cusumano, M., Gawer, A., & Yoffie, D. (2019). *The business of platforms: Strategy in the age of digital competition, innovation, and power*. HarperBus.

D'Silva, C. (2020). A study on increase in e-recruitment and selection process. *International Journal of Research in Engineering, Science and Management, 3*(8), 205-213. https:// www.journals.resaim.com/ijresm/article/view/162

Dabbicco, G., & Mattei, M. (2020). The reconciliation of budgeting with financial reporting: A comparative study of Italy and the UK. *Public Money & Management*, 1–11.

Daft, R. L. (2010). *Organization Theory and Design* (10th ed.). South-Western Cengage Learning.

Daimler Mobility Activities. (n.d.). Retrieved from https://group.mercedes-benz.com/innovation/digitalisation/mobility-services/?r=dai

Daimler. (n.d.). *A.I. guidelines*. Retrieved from https://www.daimler.com/sustainability/data/ki-guidelines.html

Daimler. (n.d.). *Future battery cells.* Retrieved from https://www.daimler.com/sustainability/human-rights/certified-raw-materials-and-less-cobalt-in-future-battery-cells.html

Damayant, T. (2013). Who is afraid of Qualitative Research? A Compromise Accounting Research Failure in Improving Accounting Practices. *International Journal of Advances in Management and Economics, 2*(2), 89-94.

Daniel, B., McCalla, G., & Schwier, R. (2002). A process model for building social capital in virtual learning communities. *International Conference on Computers in Education, 1*, 575. Retrieved from https://ieeexplore.ieee.org/document/1186008

Daske, H., & Gebhardt, G. (2006). International financial reporting standards and experts' perceptions of disclosure quality. *Abacus, 42*(3/4), 461–498. doi:10.1111/j.1467-6281.2006.00211.x

Davila, A. (2012). New trends in performance measurement and management control. *In Performance Measurement and Management Control. Global Issues (Washington, D.C.), 25*, 65–87.

Davis, A. (2005). Placing promotional culture. In J. Curran & D. Morley (Eds.), *Media and cultural theory* (pp. 149–163). Routledge.

De Geuser, F., Mooraj, S., & Oyon, D. (2009). Does the Balanced Scorecard Add Value? Empirical Evidence on its Effect on Performance. *European Accounting Review, 18*(1), 93–122. doi:10.1080/09638180802481698

de Villiers, C., Rinaldi, L., & Unerman, J. (2014). Integrated Reporting: Insights, gaps and an agenda for future research. *Accounting, Auditing & Accountability Journal, 27*(7), 1042–1067. doi:10.1108/AAAJ-06-2014-1736

Deaconu, A., Nistor, S. C., & Filip, C. (2011). The Impact of Accrual Accounting on Public Sector Management: An Exploratory Study for Romania. *Transylvanian Review of Administrative Sciences, 32E*, 74–97.

Dechow, P., Sloan, R., & Sweeney, A. (1996). Causes and consequences of earnings manipulation: An analysis of firms subject to enforcement actions by the SEC. *Contemporary Accounting Research, 13*(1), 1–36. doi:10.1111/j.1911-3846.1996.tb00489.x

Decoene, V., & Bruggeman, W. (2006). Strategic alignment and middle-level managers' motivation in a balanced scorecard setting. *International Journal of Operations & Production Management, 26*(4), 429–448. doi:10.1108/01443570610650576

DeFond, M. L. (2010). Earnings quality research: Advances, challenges and future research. *Journal of Accounting and Economics, 50*(2-3), 402–409. doi:10.1016/j.jacceco.2010.10.004

Deloitte. (2015). *Integrated Reporting as a driver for Integrated Thinking?* Retrieved February 8, 2022 from https://www2.deloitte.com/content/dam/Deloitte/nl/Documents/risk/deloitte-nl-risk-integrated-reporting-a-driver-for-integratedthinking.pdf

Dennis, I. (2014). *The Nature of Accounting Regulation*. Routledge.

Deutsch, P., & Silcox, B. (2003). Learning from other libraries: Benchmarking to assess library performance. *Information Outlook, 7*(7), 18–25.

Diehl, S. (n.d.). *Web3 is bullshit.* Retrieved from https://www.stephendiehl.com/blog/web3-bullshit.html#:~:text=At%20its%20core%20web3%20is,train%20of%20evading%20securities%20 regulation

Dimov, C. (2021). Should marketing be on corporate boards? *LinkedIn.* Retrieved from https://www.linkedin.com/pulse/should-marketing-corporate-boards-charles-dimov/

Donaldson, T., & Preston, L. E. (1995). The stakeholder theory of the corporation: Concepts, evidences, and implications. *Academy of Management Review, 20*(1), 65–91. doi:10.2307/258887

Dong, L. (2017). Understanding investors' reliance on disclosures of nonfinancial information and mitigating mechanisms for underreliance. *Accounting and Business Research, 47*(4), 431–454. doi:10.1080/00014788.2016.1277969

Doran, A. (2001). *E-work arhitect-how HR leads the way using the Internet.* IHRIM Press Book.

Doukakis, L. C. (2010). The persistence of earnings and earnings components after the adoption of IFRS. *Managerial Finance, 36*(11), 969–980. doi:10.1108/03074351011081286

Doukakis, L. C. (2014). The effect of mandatory IFRS adoption on real and accrual-based earnings management activities. *Journal of Accounting and Public Policy, 33*(6), 551–572. doi:10.1016/j.jaccpubpol.2014.08.006

Downes, S. (2015). *Special GAAP Report 'Integrated Reporting.* GAAP Consulting.

Drăcea, M., Mitu, E. N., & Drăcea, R. (2016). *Elaboration and execution of the public budget* [Elaborarea şi execuţia bugetului public]. Editura Universitaria.

Dupont, Q. (2017). *Experiments in algorithmic governance: A history and ethnography of 'the DAO', 'A failed decentralized autonomous organization'.* Academic Press.

Eccles, R. G., & Armbrester, K. (2011). Two Disruptive Ideas Combined: Integrated Reporting in the Cloud. *IESE Insight, 8*, 13–20. doi:10.15581/002.ART-1890

Eccles, R. G., & Krzus, M. P. (2010). *One Report: Integrated Reporting for a Sustainable Strategy.* John Wiley & Sons.

Elliott, L. (2015). *Margaret Thatcher's deregulation of the city a myth, says thinktank.* Retrieved from https://www.theguardian.com/business/2015/may/25/margaret-thatcher-deregulated-city-london

EU Commission. (2014). *Directive 2014/95/EU of the European Parliament and the Council of 22 October 2014 Amending Directive 2013/34/EU as Regards Disclosure of Non-Financial and Diversity Information by Certain Large Undertakings and Groups.* Brussels: EU Commission.

Eurostat. (2020). *Labour productivity per person employed and hour worked (EU27_2020=100).* https://ec.europa.eu/eurostat/databrowser/view/tesem160/default/table?lang=en

Eurostat. (2021a). *Individuals using the internet for looking for a job or sending a job application.* https://ec.europa.eu/eurostat/databrowser/view/tin00102/default/table?lang=en

Eurostat. (2021b). *Internet use by individuals.* https://ec.europa.eu/eurostat/databrowser/view/tin00028/default/table?lang=en

Eurostat. (2021c). *Households - Availability of computers.* https://appsso.eurostat.ec.europa.eu/nui/show.do?dataset=isoc_ci_cm_h&lang=en

Falconi, T. (2009). *Global stakeholder relationship governance.* Retrieved from https://instituteforpr.org/wpcontent/uploads/Global_Stakeholder_Relationship_Governance1.pdf

Fan, J. P. H., Li, J., & Zheng, G. (2016). Revisiting the bright and dark sides of capital flows in business groups. *Journal of Business Ethics, 134*(4), 509–528. doi:10.100710551-014-2382-6

FEE. (2015). *The Future of Corporate Reporting – creating the dynamics for change.* FEE.

FEE. (2016). *EU Directive on disclosure of nonfinancial and diversity information: Achieving good quality and consistent reporting.* FEE.

Ferrara, W. L. (1963). Relevant costing—Two points of view. *The Accounting Review, 38*(4), 719–722. https://www.jstor.org/stable/242395

Ferrell, O. C., & Ferrell, L. (2021). Applying the Hunt Vitell ethics model to artificial intelligence ethics. *Journal of Global Scholars of Marketing Science, 31*(2), 178–188. doi:10.1080/21639159.2020.1785918

Fielding, M. (2005). Effective communication in organizations (3rd ed.). Juta & Co. Ltd.

Fisher, C. D. (2010). Happiness at Work. *International Journal of Management Reviews, 12*(4), 384–412. doi:10.1111/j.1468-2370.2009.00270.x

Fletcher, R. (2011). *Top performing companies incorporating the public sector* (11th ed.). Topco Media.

Florea, N. V. (2013). Human resources audit [Auditul resurselor umane]. C.H. Beck.

Florea, N. V. (2017). *Simulation and modeling in business* [Simulare si modelare in afaceri]. Mustang.

Florea, N. V., & Duica, A. (2019). *Customer relationship management* [Managementul relatiei cu clientii]. Mustang.

Florou, A., & Pope, P. (2012). Mandatory IFRS adoption and institutional investment decisions. *The Accounting Review, 87*(6), 1993–2025. doi:10.2308/accr-50225

Franceschi, M., Morelli, D., Plans, D., Brown, A., Collomosse, J., & Coutts, L. (2018). *ComeHere: Exploiting Ethereum for secure sharing of healthcare data.* Academic Press.

Fred, M. O., & Kinange, U. M. (2018). Effectiveness of E-Recruitment in Organization Development. *Management and Economic Journal, 2*(4), 294–301.

Freeman, R. E. (1984). *Strategic management: A stakeholder approach.* Pitman.

Frenkel, A. K. (2017). *Confusion over security responsibility in cloud.* https://www.cioinsight.com/cloud-virtualization/confusion-over-security-responsibility-in-cloud/

Friedman, M. (1970). A Friedman doctrine - The social responsibility of business is to increase its profits. *New York Times.* Retrieved from https://www.nytimes.com/1970/09/13/archives/a-friedman-doctrine-the-social-responsibility-of-business-is-to.html

Friedman, M. (1970). The Social Responsibility of Business Is to Increase Its Profits. *New York Times Magazine*, 122-126.

Friedman, L. A., & Miles, S. (2006). *Stakeholders: theory and practice.* Oxford University Press.

Frolova, I., & Lapiņa, I. (2015). Integration of CSR principles in quality management. *International Journal of Quality and Service Sciences*, *7*(2/3), 260–273. doi:10.1108/IJQSS-03-2015-0033

Fuchs, C., Hofkirchner, W., Schafranek, M., Raffl, C., Sandoval, M., & Bichler, R. (2010). Theoretical foundations of the web: Cognition, communication, and co-operation. Towards an understanding of Web 1.0, 2.0, 3.0. *Future Internet*, *2*(1), 41–59. doi:10.3390/fi2010041

Funck, E. K. (2009). Ordination Balanced Scorecard – översättning av ett styrinstrument inom hälso- och sjukvården [Prescription Balanced Scorecard – Translation of a Management Control Instrument in Health Care]. Ekonomihögskolan, Växjö universitet.

Funck, E. (2007). The Balanced Scorecard Equates Interests in Healthcare Organizations. *Journal of Accounting & Organizational Change*, *3*(2), 88–103. doi:10.1108/18325910710756122

Fu, R., Kraft, A., & Zhang, H. (2012). Financial reporting frequency, information asymmetry, and the cost of equity. *Journal of Accounting and Economics*, *54*(2–3), 132–149. doi:10.1016/j.jacceco.2012.07.003

Gabarro, J. J. (1978). The development of trust influence and expectations. In A. G. Athos & J. J. Gabarro (Eds.), *Interpersonal behavior: Communication and understanding in relationships* (pp. 290–303). Prentice Hall.

Gabarro, J. J., & Athos, J. (1976). *Interpersonal relations and communications.* Prentice-Hall.

Galanaki, E. (2002). The Decision to recruit Online: A Descriptive Study. *Career International Development*, *7*(4), 243–251. doi:10.1108/13620430210431325

Galas, E. S., & Forte, S. H. A. C. (2005). Fatores que interferem na implantação de um modelo de gestão estratégica baseado no balanced scorecard: estudo de caso em uma instituição pública. *Revista de Administração do Mackenzie*, *6*(2), 88-111.

Genesis. (2018). What are dApps (decentralized applications), and how do they work? *Developers Convention.* Retrieved from https://medium.com/@genesishack/know-your-track-dapp-decentralized-applications-1e1e0d29cc88

Ghazzawi, K., & Accoumeh, A. (2014). Critical Success Factors of the E-Recruitment System. *Journal of Human Resources Management and Labor Studies*, *2*(2), 159–170.

Ghosh, A., & Olsen, L. (2008). Environmental uncertainty and managers' use of discretionary accruals. *Accounting, Organizations and Society, 34*(2), 188–205. doi:10.1016/j.aos.2008.07.001

Gilmore, C., & Willmott, H. (1992). Company Law and Financial Reporting: A Sociological History of the UK Experience. In M. Bromwich & A. G. Hopwood (Eds.), *Accounting and the Law* (pp. 159–190). Prentice-Hall/ICAEW.

Global Reporting Initiative (GRI) (2016). *Consolidated set of GRI sustainability reporting standards 2016: Global Reporting Initiative*. Academic Press.

Gokten, S. (Ed.). (2017). Accounting and Corporate Reporting - Today and Tomorrow. IntechOpen. doi:10.5772/66609

Gopalia, A. (2011). *Effectiveness of Online Recruitment and Selection Process: A Case of Tesco.* http://www.pbr.co.in/2011/2011_month/Jan_March/0002.pdf

Governancetoday. (n.d.). *What does governance mean?* Retrieved from https://www.governancetoday.com/GT/Material/Governance__what_is_it_and_why_is_it_important_.aspx

Greyser, S. (2012). *The strategic role of the corporate communication officer at IE University.* Retrieved from https://www.youtube.com/watch?v=rf6ud_H8oKc

GRI. (2021). Retrieved February 6, 2022 from https://www.globalreporting.org/standards/download-the-standards/

Griffith, J. (2021). *What you need to know about centralized vs decentralized identity management.* Retrieved from https://www.pingidentity.com/en/resources/blog/posts/2021/centralized-decentralized-identity-management.html

Griffith, J. (2022). *What is knowledge-based authentication (KBA)?* Retrieved from https://www.pingidentity.com/en/resources/blog/posts/2022/what-is-knowledge-based-authentication-kba.html

Grogan, M., & Peebles, H. (2021). *OpenChat: A truly decentralized alternative to WhatsApp.* Retrieved from https://medium.com/dfinity/openchat-a-truly-decentralized-alternative-to-whatsapp-d0d051479b9a

Grunig, J. E., & Hunt, T. (1980). *Managing public relations*. Cengage Learning.

Gueutal, H., & Stone, D. L. (2015). *The Brave New World of eHR: Human Resources in the Digital Age*. John Wiley & Sons.

Gurd, B., & Gao, T. (2007). Lives in the balance: An analysis of the balanced scorecard (BSC) in healthcare organizations. *International Journal of Productivity and Performance Management, 57*(1), 6–21. doi:10.1108/17410400810841209

Hackl, C. (2021). *What are DAOs and why you should pay attention.* Retrieved from https://www.forbes.com/sites/cathyhackl/2021/06/01/what-are-daos-and-why-you-should-pay-attention/

Hada, B. S., & Gairola, S. (2015). Opportunities & Challenges of E- Recruitment. *Journal of Management Engineering and Information Technology, 2*(2), 1–4.

Hallin, B., & Kastberg, G. (2002). Balanced Scorecard i teori och praktik. En flerdimensionell styrmodell i hälso- och sjukvå rden. Göteborgs universitet.

Harris, J. N. (1936). What did we earn last month? NACA Bulletin, 501–527.

Hartnell, C. A., Ou, A. Y., & Kinicki, A. (2011). Organizational culture and organizational effectiveness: A meta-analytic investigation of the competing values framework's theoretical suppositions. *The Journal of Applied Psychology*, *96*(4), 677–694. doi:10.1037/a0021987 PMID:21244127

Hassan, S., & De Filippi, P. (2017). The expansion of algorithmic governance: From code is law. *Code Field Actions Science Reports*. Retrieved from https://journals.openedition.org/factsreports/4518

Hassan, A., Elamer, A. A., Lodh, S., Roberts, L., & Nandy, M. (2021). The future of non-financial businesses reporting: Learning from the Covid-19 pandemic. *Corporate Social Responsibility and Environmental Management*, *28*(4), 1231–1240. doi:10.1002/csr.2145 PMID:34220362

Hassanein, A., & Hussainey, K. (2015). Is Forward-Looking Financial Disclosure Really Informative? Evidence from UK Narrative Statements. *International Review of Financial Analysis*, *41*, 52–61. doi:10.1016/j.irfa.2015.05.025

Havlová, K. (2015). What Integrated Reporting Changed: The Case Study of Early Adopters. *Procedia Economics and Finance*, *34*, 231–237. doi:10.1016/S2212-5671(15)01624-X

Hawlitschek, F., Notheisen, B., & Teubner, T. (2018). The limits of trust-free systems: A literature review on blockchain technology and trust in the sharing economy. *Electronic Commerce Research and Applications*, *29*, 50–63. doi:10.1016/j.elerap.2018.03.005

Hay, L. (2019). *Hacker lexicon: What are zero-knowledge proofs?* Retrieved from https://www.wired.com/story/zero-knowledge-proofs/

Hayes, A. (2021). *Disintermediation.* Retrieved from https://www.investopedia.com/terms/d/disintermediation.asp

Headworth, A. (2015). *Social media recruitment.* Kogan Page Publishers.

He, K., Pan, X., & Tian, G. (2017). Legal liability, government intervention, and auditor behavior: Evidence from structural reform of audit firms in China. *European Accounting Review*, *26*(1), 61–95. doi:10.1080/09638180.2015.1100547

Helebrandt, P., Belluš, M., Ries, M., Kotuliak, I., & Khilenko, V. (2018). Blockchain adoption for monitoring and management of enterprise networks. *2018 IEEE 9th Annual Information Technology, Electronics and Mobile Communication Conference (IEMCON).* Retrieved from https://www.researchgate.net/publication/330478223_Blockchain_Adoption_for_Monitoring_and_Management_of_Enterprise_Networks

Henczel, S. (2002). Benchmarking – measuring and comparing for continuous improvement. *Information Outlook*, *6*(7), 12–20.

Hendler, J. (2009). Web 3.0 emerging. *Computer*, *42*(1), 111–113. doi:10.1109/MC.2009.30

Hillman, A. J., & Keim, G. D. (2001). Shareholder Value, Stakeholder Management, and Social Issues: What's the Bottom Line? *Strategic Management Journal*, *22*(2), 125–139. doi:10.1002/1097-0266(200101)22:2<125::AID-SMJ150>3.0.CO;2-H

Holm, A. B. (2012). E-recruitment: Towards an Ubiquitous Recruitment Process and Candidate Relationship Management. *German Journal of Human Resource Management*, 241-259.

Holthausen, R. W., & Watts, R. L. (2001). The relevance of the value-relevance literature for financial accounting standard setting. *Journal of Accounting and Economics*, *31*(1-3), 3–75. doi:10.1016/S0165-4101(01)00029-5

Homburg, C., & Pflesser, C. (2000). A Multiple Layer Model of Market-Oriented Organizational Culture: Measurement Issues and Performance Outcomes. *JMR, Journal of Marketing Research*, *37*(4), 449–462. doi:10.1509/jmkr.37.4.449.18786

Hooghiemstra, R. (2000). Corporate Communication and Impression Management – New Perspectives Why Companies Engage in Corporate Social Reporting. *Journal of Business Ethics*, *27*(1), 55–68. doi:10.1023/A:1006400707757

Hopkins, B., & Markham, J. (2003). *E-HR: using intranets to improve the effectiveness of your people*. Gower Pub.Ltd.

Hoque, Z. (2014). 20 years of studies on the balanced scorecard: Trends, accomplishments, gaps and opportunities for future research. *The British Accounting Review*, *46*(1), 33–59. doi:10.1016/j.bar.2013.10.003

Horngren, C. T., & Sorter, G. H. (1961). Direct costing for external reporting. *The Accounting Review*, *36*(January), 84–93. https://www.jstor.org/stable/243122

Horton, J., Serafeim, G., & Serafeim, I. (2013). Does mandatory IFRS adoption improve the information environment? *Contemporary Accounting Research*, *30*(1), 388–423. doi:10.1111/j.1911-3846.2012.01159.x

Hosain, M., & Liu, P. (2020). LinkedIn for searching better job opportunity: Passive jobseekers' perceived experience. *Qualitative Report*, *25*(10), 3719–3732. doi:10.46743/2160-3715/2020.4449

Hou, Q., Jin, Q., Yang, R., Yuan, H., & Zhang, G. (2015). Performance commitments of controlling shareholders and earnings management. *Contemporary Accounting Research*, *32*(3), 1099–1127. doi:10.1111/1911-3846.12111

Houque, M. N. (2012). The effect of IFRS adoption and investor protection on earnings quality around the world. *The International Journal of Accounting*, *47*(3), 333–355. doi:10.1016/j.intacc.2012.07.003

Huang, H.-C., Chu, W., Lai, M.-C., & Lin, L.-H. (2009). Strategic Linkage Process and Value-Driven System: A Dynamic Analysis of High-Tech Firms in a Newly-Industrialized Country. *Expert Systems with Applications*, *36*(2), 3965–3974. doi:10.1016/j.eswa.2008.02.038

Huang, M., & Rust, R. (2018). Artificial intelligence in service. *Journal of Service Research, 21*(2), 155–172. doi:10.1177/1094670517752459

Hurley, R. F. (2002). Putting people back into organizational learning. *Journal of Business and Industrial Marketing, 17*(4), 270–281. doi:10.1108/08858620210431679

Iatridis, G. (2010). International Financial Reporting Standards and the quality of financial statement information. *International Review of Financial Analysis, 19*(3), 193–204. doi:10.1016/j.irfa.2010.02.004

Iatridis, G. (2012). Hedging and earnings management in the light of IFRS implementation: Evidence from the UK stock market. *The British Accounting Review, 44*(1), 21–35. doi:10.1016/j.bar.2011.12.002

Icertis Blockchain. (n.d.). *Framework.* Retrieved from https://www.icertis.com/contract-management/blockchain/

International Integrated Reporting Council (IIRC). (2011). *The International <IR> Framework.* Retrieved February 7, 2022 from http//:www.iirc.org

International Integrated Reporting Council (IIRC). (2013a). *Consultation draft of the international <IR> framework.* IIRC.

International Integrated Reporting Council (IIRC). (2013b). *Integrated reporting.* The IIRC.

International Integrated Reporting Council (IIRC). (2021). *The International <IR> Framework.* Available at: https://www.integratedreporting.org/resource/international-ir-framework/

Internet Live Stats. (2016). *Romania Internet Users.* https://www.internetlivestats.com/internet-users/romania/

Internet World Stats. (2021). *Internet users in the world.* https://www.internetworldstats.com/stats.htm

IPSASB. (2010). *Conceptual Framework for General Purpose Financial Reporting by Public Sector Entities: Elements and Recognition in Financial Statements.* IPSASB.

Ittner, C. D., Larcker, D. F., & Randall, T. (2003). Performance Implications of Strategic Performance Measurement in Financial Services Firms. *Accounting, Organizations and Society, 28*(7-8), 715–741. doi:10.1016/S0361-3682(03)00033-3

Jackson, S. B., & Liu, X. K. (2010). The allowance for uncollectible accounts, conservatism, and earnings management. *Journal of Accounting Research, 48*(3), 565–601. doi:10.1111/j.1475-679X.2009.00364.x

Janeš, A. (2014). Empirical Verification of the Balanced Scorecard. *Industrial Management & Data Systems, 114*(2), 203–219. doi:10.1108/IMDS-04-2013-0195

Jeanjean, T., & Stolowy, H. (2008). Do accounting standards matter? An exploratory analysis of earnings management before and after IFRS adoption. *Journal of Accounting and Public Policy*, *27*(6), 480–490. doi:10.1016/j.jaccpubpol.2008.09.008

Jenkins, H., Ford, S., & Green, J. (2013). *Spreadable media creating value and meaning in a networked culture*. New York University. doi:10.18574/9780814743515

Johnson, J. (2021). *Internet usage in Europe - Statistics & Facts*. https://www.statista.com/topics/3853/internet-usage-in-europe/#dossierKeyfigures

Jones, D. A., & Smith, K. J. (2012). Comparing the value relevance, predictive value, and persistence of other comprehensive income and special items. *The Accounting Review*, *86*(6), 2047–2073. doi:10.2308/accr-10133

Jones, T. M. (1995). Instrumental Stakeholder Theory: A Synthesis of Ethics and Economics. *Academy of Management Review*, *20*(2), 404–437. doi:10.5465/amr.1995.9507312924

Juhmani, O. I. H. (2007). Usage, motives and usefulness of the Balanced Scorecard (BSC): Evidence from Bahrain. *International Journal of Business Research*, *7*(5), 106–117.

Kai-fu-lee. (n.d.). On the power of A.I. to transform humanity. Interview by Andrew Zuckerman. *Time Sensitive*. Retrieved from https://timesensitive.fm/episode/kai-fu-lee-power-artificial-intelligence-transform-humanity/

Kampakis, S. (2018). Why do we need tokenomics? *The Journal of The British Blockchain Association*, *1*(1), 1–4. doi:10.31585/jbba-1-1-(8)2018

Kaplan, A., & Haenlein, M. (2019). Siri, siri, in my hand: Who's the fairest in the land? On the interpretations, illustrations, and implications of artificial intelligence. *Business Horizons*, *62*(1), 15–25. doi:10.1016/j.bushor.2018.08.004

Kaplan, R. S., & Norton, D. P. (1996). *The Balanced Scorecard: Translating Strategy into Action*. Harvard Business School Press.

Kaplan, R. S., & Norton, D. P. (2006). How to implement a new strategy without disrupting your organization. *Harvard Business Review*, *84*(3), 100. doi:10.1108d.2006.05622had.002 PMID:16515159

Kapse, A. S., Patil, V. S., & Patil, N. V. (2012). E-recruitment. *International Journal of Engineering and Advanced Technology*, *1*(4), 82–86.

Karim, M. R., Miah, S., & Asma, K. (2015). E-Recruitment in Practice: A Study on Jobseekers' Perception in Bangladesh. *Munich Personal RePEc Archive*, 33-42.

Karl, J. (2022). The Web3 you've heard of does not exist. *Bloomberg*. Retrieved from https://www.bloomberg.com/opinion/articles/2022-01-11/the-web3-you-ve-heard-of-does-not-exist

Kaufmann, L., & Becker, A. (2005). Overcoming the barriers during Implementation and use of the balanced scorecard by multinational companies in Brazil. *Latin American Business Review*, *6*(3), 39–62. doi:10.1300/J140v06n03_02

Kaur, J., Arianayagam, S., & Singh, P. (2020). The usage of social media networks as a tool by employers to screen job candidates. *The European Journal of Social & Behavioural Sciences*, *3*(3), 191–207. doi:10.15405/ejsbs.282

Kavanagh, R. (2022). *Hash rate: A measure of the computing power on a cryptocurrency network that is a key security indicator.* Retrieved from https://www.businessinsider.com/personal-finance/hash-rate?r=US&IR=T#:~:text=Hash20rate%20is%20a%20measure,miner's%20machines%20complete%20these%20computations

Kershaw, R., & Kershaw, S. (2001). Developing a balanced scorecard to implement strategy at St. Elsewhere hospital. *Management Accounting Quarterly*, *2*(2), 28–35.

Ketokivi, M. & Mahoney, T. J. (2017). *Transaction cost economics as a theory of the firm, management, and governance free.* Retrieved from doi:10.1093/acrefore/9780190224851.013.6

Klein, A. (2002). Audit committee, board of director characteristics and earnings management. *Journal of Accounting and Economics*, *33*(3), 375–400. doi:10.1016/S0165-4101(02)00059-9

Kocakülâh, M., & Austill, A. D. (2007). Balanced scorecard application in the Health Care Industry: a case study. *Journal of Health Care Finance, 34*(1), 72-99.

Kochalski, C. (2016). *Green Controlling and Finance. Theoretical Framework.* Helion SA Publishing Group.

Kollberg, B. (2007). *Performance Measurement Systems in Swedish Health Care Services, Division of Quality Technology and Management*. Linköping University.

Kollberg, B., & Elg, M. (2011). The practice of the Balanced Scorecard in health care services. *International Journal of Productivity and Performance Management*, *60*(5), 427–445. doi:10.1108/17410401111140374

Korschun, D., Bhattacharya, C. B., & Swain, S. (2016). CSR and the Frontline Context: How Social Programs Improve Customer Service. *NIM Marketing Intelligence Review*, *8*(1), 24–29. doi:10.1515/gfkmir-2016-0004

Kothari, S. P., Leone, A. J., & Wasley, C. E. (2005). Performance matched discretionary accrual measures. *Journal of Accounting and Economics*, *39*(1), 163–197. doi:10.1016/j.jacceco.2004.11.002

Kotler, P., & Mindak, W. (1978). *Marketing and public relations: Should they be partners or rivals?* Sage Publication.

Kramer, M. (2020). *Larry Fink Isn't Going to Read Your Sustainability Report.* Harvard Business Practices. Retrieved February 5, 2022 from https://hbr.org/2020/01/larry-fink-isnt-going-to-read-your-sustainability-report

Kumbakara, N. (2008). Managed IT Services: The Role of IT Standards. *Information Management & Computer Security*, *16*(4), 336–359. doi:10.1108/09685220810908778

La Torre, M., Sabelfeld, S., Blomkvist, M., Tarquinio, L., & Dumay, J. (2018). Harmonising non-ðnancial reporting regulation in Europe: Practical forces and projections for future research. *Meditari Accountancy Research*, *26*(4), 598–621. doi:10.1108/MEDAR-02-2018-0290

Lai, A., Melloni, G., & Stacchezzini, R. (2018). Integrated reporting and narrative accountability: The role of preparers. *Accounting, Auditing & Accountability Journal*, *31*(5), 1381–1405. doi:10.1108/AAAJ-08-2016-2674

Lakhdar, S. (2001). *Human Resources Management* [Gestion de ressources humaines]. Universite de Boeck.

Landsman, W. R., Maydew, E. L., & Thornock, J. R. (2012). The information content of annual earnings announcements and mandatory adoption of IFRS. *Journal of Accounting and Economics*, *53*(1-2), 34–54. doi:10.1016/j.jacceco.2011.04.002

Lang, M., Raedy, J. S., & Wilson, W. (2006). Earnings management and cross listing: Are reconciled earnings comparable to US earnings? *Journal of Accounting and Economics*, *42*(1-2), 255–283. doi:10.1016/j.jacceco.2006.04.005

Lee, F. K. (2019). *Ai superpowers: China, Silicon Valley, and the New World Order.* Harper Bus.

Lee, K. (2018). *The four waves of A.I.* Retrieved from https://kaifulee.medium.com/the-four-waves-of-a-i-46e7e627c054

Legenkova, M. (2016). International Public Sector Accounting Standards Implementation in the Russian Federation. *International Journal of Economics and Financial Issues*, *6*(4), 1304–1309.

Lehdonvirta, V., & Ali, R. (2016). Governance and regulation: Digital currencies. Bank of England Oxford Internet Institute, University of Oxford.

Leuz, C., Nanda, D., & Wysocki, P. D. (2003). Earnings management and investor protection: An international comparison. *Journal of Financial Economics*, *69*(3), 505–527. doi:10.1016/S0304-405X(03)00121-1

Lewis, D. K. (1969). *Convention a philosophical study*. Harvard University Press.

Liberto, D. (2021). *What is reintermediation?* Retrieved from https://www.investopedia.com/terms/r/reintermediation.asp

Li, L., Qi, B., Tian, G., & Zhang, G. (2017). The contagion effect of low-quality audits at the level of individual auditors. *The Accounting Review*, *92*(1), 137–163. doi:10.2308/accr-51407

Lim, S., Matolcsy, Z., & Chow, D. (2007). The association between board composition and different types of voluntary disclosure. *European Accounting Review*, *16*(3), 555–583. doi:10.1080/09638180701507155

Lin, C. H., Peng, C. H., & Kao, D. T. (2008). The innovativeness effect of market orientation and learning orientation on business performance. *International Journal of Manpower, 29*(8), 752–772. doi:10.1108/01437720810919332

Lin, S., Riccardi, W., & Wang, C. (2012). Does accounting quality change following a switch from U.S.GAAP to IFRS? Evidence from Germany. *Journal of Accounting and Public Policy, 31*(6), 641–657. doi:10.1016/j.jaccpubpol.2012.10.006

Li, S. (2010). Does mandatory adoption of international accounting standards in the European Union reduce the cost of equity capital? *The Accounting Review, 85*(2), 607–636. doi:10.2308/accr.2010.85.2.607

Lisi, I. E. (2018). Determinants and Performance Effects of Social Performance Measurement Systems. *Journal of Business Ethics, 152*(1), 225–251. doi:10.100710551-016-3287-3

Lobo, G. L., & Zhou, J. (2001). Disclosure quality and earning management. *Asia-Pacific Journal of Accounting & Economics, 8*(1), 1–20. doi:10.1080/16081625.2001.10510584

Louwers, T. J., Ramsay, R. J., Sinason, D. H., & Strawser, J. R. (2007). *Auditing and Assurance Services* (2nd ed.). McGraw-Hill Irwin.

Lueg, R., & Carvalho e Silva, A. L. (2013). When One Size does not Fit All: A Literature Review on the Modifications of the Balanced Scorecard. *Problems and Perspectives in Management, 11*(3), 86–94.

Lukka, K. (2010). The roles and effects of paradigms in accounting research. *Management Accounting Research, 21*(2), 110–115. doi:10.1016/j.mar.2010.02.002

Lustgarten, A. (2012). BP agrees to plead guilty to crimes in Gulf oil spill - Environmental sustainability, regulation & legislation. *The Magazine of Corporate Responsibility.*

Lustig, C., & Nardi, B. (2015). Algorithmic authority: The case of Bitcoin. *48th Hawaii international Conference on System Sciences*, 743–752.

Mabuza, M. P. (2019). *Evaluating international public health issues*. Springer Nature.

Machado, C. F., & Davim, J. P. (2019). *Higher Education and the Evolution of Management. Applied Sciences, and Engineering Curricula*. IGI Global. doi:10.4018/978-1-5225-7259-6

Mack, O. (2018). *How smart contracts will change the world.* Retrieved from https://www.ted.com/talks/olga_mack_how_smart_contracts_will_change_the_world

Madhavaram, S., Badrinarayanan, V., & McDonald, E. R. (2005). Integrated marketing communication (IMC) and brand identity as critical components of brand equity strategy: A conceptual framework and research propositions. *Journal of Advertising, 34*(4), 69–80. doi:10.1080/00913367.2005.10639213

Malik, Z., & Ullah, R. (2013). The Role of E-recruitment Towards Attraction of Workforce: A Case of Telecom Sector Organization. *Abasyn Journal of Social Sciences, 6*(1), 104–115.

Malina, M. A., & Selto, F. H. (2001). Communicating and controlling strategy: An empirical study of the effectiveness of the balanced scorecard. *Journal of Management Accounting Research*, *13*(1), 47–90. doi:10.2308/jmar.2001.13.1.47

Man, M., & Ciurea, M. (2017). The current economic context to measuring performance in the Romanian public system. *Proceedings of the 29th IBIMA on Education Excellence and Innovation Management through Vision 2020: from Regional Development Sustainability to Global Economic Growth*, 370-379.

Man, M., & Ciurea, M. (2016). Elements of Corporate Governance Implementation in Romania, in the European Context. *Annals of the University of Petrosani. Economics*, *16*(1), 151–166.

Maroun, W. (2017). Assuring the integrated report: Insights and recommendations from auditors and preparers. *The British Accounting Review*, *49*(3), 329–346. doi:10.1016/j.bar.2017.03.003

Marra, A., Mazzola, P., & Prencipe, A. (2011). Board Monitoring and Earnings Management Pre- and Post-IFRS. *The International Journal of Accounting*, *46*(2), 205–230. doi:10.1016/j.intacc.2011.04.007

Maruf, M., Ku Nor Izah Ku, I., & Halimah Nasibah, A. (2017). Contingency for Financial Reporting Quality in the Public Sector under Cash-Basis IPSAS: a Conceptual Approach. *Proceedings of the Global Conference on Business and Economics Research.*

Maurer, D. S., & Liu, Y. (2007). Developing effective e-recruiting websites: Insights for managers from marketers. *Business Horizons*, *50*(4), 305–314. doi:10.1016/j.bushor.2007.01.002

McAdam, R., & Walker, T. (2003). An Inquiry into Balanced Scorecards within Best Value Implementation in UK Local Government. *Public Administration*, *81*(4), 873–892. doi:10.1111/j.0033-3298.2003.00375.x

Meah, M. M., & Sarwar, A. (2021). Social Networking Sites for e-Recruitment: A Perspective of Malaysian Employers. *Journal of Asian Finance, Economics and Business*, *8*(8), 613–624. doi:10.13106/jafeb.2021

Mechelli, A., & Cimini, R. (2014). Is comprehensive income value relevant and does location matter? A European study. *Accounting in Europe*, *16*(25), 1–35. doi:10.1080/17449480.2014.890777

Messier, W. F., Glover, S. M., & Prawitt, D. F. (2008). *Auditing and Assurance Services. A Systematic Approach* (5th ed.). McGraw-Hill Irwin.

Mindia, P. M., & Hoque, K. (2018). Effects of E-recruitment and internet on recruitment process: An Empirical study on Multinational companies of Bangladesh. *International Journal of Scientific Research and Management*, *6*(1), 2321–3418. doi:10.18535/ijsrm/v6i1.em01

Miska, C., Stahl, G., & Mendenhall, M. (2013). Intercultural competencies as antecedents of responsible global leadership. *European Journal of International Management*, *7*(5), 550–569. doi:10.1504/EJIM.2013.056477

Mnif, Y., & Gafsi, Y. (2020). A contingency theory perspective on the analysis of central government accounting disclosure under International Public Sector Accounting Standards (IPSAS). *Meditari Accountancy Research, 28*(6), 1089-1117. doi/ doi:10.1108/MEDAR-04-2019-0480

MOBI. (n.d.). *The Mobility Open Blockchain Initiative*. Retrieved from https://dlt.mobi/standards/

Mohammad, J., Quoquab, F., Sulaiman, A., & Salam, Z. (2020). I voice out because I care: The effect of online social networking on employees' likelihood to voice and retention. *Asia-Pacific Journal of Business Administration, 13*(1), 117–137. doi:10.1108/APJBA-05-2020-0142

Moore, K. (2017). *Content marketing in the 90s: What was it like?* Retrieved from https://www.business2community.com/content-marketing/content-marketing-90s-like-01903791

Moratis, L., & Cochius, T. (2011). *ISO26000: the business guide to the new standard on social responsibility*. Greenleaf.

Morrós Ribera, J. (2016). The integrated reporting: A presentation of the current state of art and aspects of integrated reporting that need further development. *Intangible Capital, 12*(1), 336–356.

Muduli, A., & Trivedi, J. (2020). Social media recruitment: The role of credibility and satisfaction. Evidence-based HRM: A global forum for empirical scholarship. *Evidence-based HRM, 8*(2), 237–251. doi:10.1108/EBHRM-08-2019-0069

Myers, J., & Ulloa, J. (2018). California lawmakers agree to new consumer privacy rules that would avert showdown on the November ballot. *Los Angeles Times*. Retrieved from https://www.latimes.com/politics/la-pol-ca-privacy-initiative-legislature-agreement-20180621-story.html

Nagy, N. (2017). *Trends in social media marketing within the small and medium-sized business industry and how small and medium-sized businesses are using social media to grow their business*. doi:10.13140/RG.2.2.19426.58560

Nahapiet, J., & Ghoshal, S. (1998). Social capital, intellectual capital, and the organizational advantage. *Academy of Management Review, 23*(2), 242–266. doi:10.5465/amr.1998.533225

Netimperative. (2021). *Global social media ad spend grows 60% year-over-year*. Retrieved from https://www.netimperative.com/2021/04/27/global-social-media-ad-spend-grows-60-year-over-year/

Newsome, D. A. (2007). *Bridging the gaps in global communication*. Blackwell Pub.

Nguti, V. N., & Mose, T. (2021). The Role Of E-Recruitment And Selection Functions on the Organizational Outcomes in Helb, Kenya. International Academic Journal of Human Resource and Business Administration, 3(9), 554-565.

Nicula, V. C., & Bragadireanu, C. (2017). International Accounting Standards for the Public Sector (IPSAS) in Romania [Standardele Internaţionale de Contabilitate pentru Sectorul Public (IPSAS) în Romania]. *Romanian Court of Accounts Journal, 9*, 11–18.

Nield, D. (2021). *What is Web3 and why should you care? The next internet revolution is upon us—here's why it matters.* Retrieved from https://gizmodo.com/what-is-web-3-and-why-should-you-care-1848204799

Nistor, C. S. (2011). A New Aproach of conceptual Framework for General Purpose Financial Reporting by Public Sector Entities. *Annals of Faculty of Economics*, *1*(2), 603–609.

Nistor, S. C. (2017). European Union under the pressure of creating a competitive public accounting system. *International Journal of Competitiveness*, *1*(2), 136–154. doi:10.1504/IJC.2017.084726

Nohria, N., & Eccles, R. C. (1992). *Networks and organizations: Structure, form, and action.* Harvard Business School Press.

Nørreklit, H. (2000). The Balance on the Balanced Scorecard a Critical Analysis of Some of Its Assumptions. *Management Accounting Research*, *11*(1), 65–88. doi:10.1006/mare.1999.0121

Nørreklit, H. (2003). The balanced scorecard: What is the score? a rhetorical analysis of the balanced scorecard. *Accounting, Organizations and Society*, *28*(6), 591–619. doi:10.1016/S0361-3682(02)00097-1

Olson, E. M., Slater, S. F., Tomas, G., & Hult, M. (2005). The performance implications of fit among business strategy, marketing organization structure, and strategic behavior. *Journal of Marketing*, *69*(3), 49–65. doi:10.1509/jmkg.69.3.49.66362

Olsson, B., Karlsson, M., & Sharma, E. (2000). Towards a Theory of Implementing the Balance Scorecard: A Study in Association with the Swedish Telecommunication Firm Ericsson. *Journal of Human Resource Costing & Accounting*, *5*(1), 59–84. doi:10.1108/eb029064

OpenChat: A truly decentralized alternative to WhatsApp. (n.d.). Retrieved from https://medium.com/dfinity/openchat-a-truly-decentralized-alternative-to-whatsapp-d0d051479b9a

Orlitzky, M., & Benjamin, J. (2001). Corporate Social Performance and Firm Risk: A Meta-Analytic Review. *Business & Society*, *40*(4), 369–396. doi:10.1177/000765030104000402

Osama, A. (2006). *Multi-Attribute Strategy and Performance Architectures in R&D: The Case of The Balanced Scorecard.* PhD Thesis.

Ostrom, A., Fotheringham, D., & Bitner, M. J. (2018). Customer acceptance of AI in service encounters: Understanding antecedents and consequences. In P. P. Maglio, C. A. Kieliszewski, J. C. Spohrer, K. Lyons, L. Patricio, & Y. Swatani (Eds.), Handbook of Service Science (Vol. 2, pp. 77–103). Academic Press.

Othman, R. (2006). Balanced Scorecard and causal model development: Preliminary findings. *Management Decision*, *44*(5), 690–702. doi:10.1108/00251740610668923

Ozkan, N., Singer, Z., & You, H. (2012). Mandatory IFRS adoption and the contractual usefulness of accounting information in executive compensation. *Journal of Accounting Research*, *50*(4), 1077–1107. doi:10.1111/j.1475-679X.2012.00453.x

Pande, S., & Basak, S. (2015). *Human resource management: text and cases.* Vikas Publishing House.

Parker, L. (2012). Qualitative management accounting research: Assessing deliverables and relevance. *Critical Perspectives on Accounting, 23*(1), 54–70. doi:10.1016/j.cpa.2011.06.002

Parmenter, D. (2010). *Key Performance Indicators: Developing, Implementing, and Using Winning KPIs* (2nd ed.). John Wiley & Sons.

Parry, E., & Tyson, S. (2008a). Can technology transform HR processes? The case of UK recruitment. *The Second European Academic Workshop on Electronic Human Resource Management.*

Parry, E., & Tyson, S. (2008b). An analysis of the use and success of online recruitment methods in the UK. *Human Resource Management Journal, 18*(3), 257–174. doi:10.1111/j.1748-8583.2008.00070.x

Parry, G., & Collomosse, J. (2021). *Perspectives on 'good' in blockchain for good.* Frontiers Blockchain. doi:10.3389/fbloc.2020.609136

Paton, W. A., & Littleton, A. C. (1940). *An introduction to corporate accounting standards.* American Accounting Association.

Peake, J. (1981). *Public relations in business: Review article.* Harper and Row. doi:10.1177/002194368101800211

Pelt, R. V., Jansen, S., Baars, D., & Overbeek, S. (2020). *Defining blockchain governance: A framework for analysis and comparison.* Taylor & Francis Publication. doi:10.1080/10580530.2020.1720046

Peng, T. A., Pike, S., & Roos, G. (2007). Intellectual capital and performance indicators: Taiwansese healthcare sector. *Journal of Intellectual Capital, 8*(3), 535–556. doi:10.1108/14691930710774902

Perrini, F., Pogutz, S., & Tencati, A. (2006). *Developing Corporate Social Responsibility: A European Perspective.* Edward Elgar.

Phillips, P. A. (2007). The balanced scorecard and strategic control: a hotel case study analysis. *Service Industries Journal, 27*(6), 731-746.

Pope, P., & McLeay, S. (2011). The European IFRS experiment: Objectives, research challenges and some early evidence. *Accounting and Business Research, 41*(3), 233–266. doi:10.1080/00014788.2011.575002

Posthumus, J. (2015). *Use of Market Data in the Recruitment of High Potentials.* Springer. doi:10.1007/978-3-658-10376-7

Pratley, N. (2005). *Tesco faces questions over true value of its computer vouchers.* Retrieved from https://www.theguardian.com/technology/2005/mar/07/schools.supermarkets#:~:text=Computers%20for%20Schools%20works%20by,of%20computer%20equipment%20to%20schools

Prieto, V. C., & de Carvalho, M. M. (2009). *Literature review on Balanced Scorecard – Types of research, difficulties and benefits.*, Annual Conference on Production and Operations Management Society, Orlando, FL.

Prieto, V. C., Pereira, F. L. A., de Carvalho, M. M., & Laurindo, F. J. B. (2006). Critical Factors in Balanced Scorecard Implementation. *Gestão & Produção, 13*(1), 81–92. doi:10.1590/S0104-530X2006000100008

Priyadarshini, C., Kumar, Y., & Jha, R. R. (2017a). Employer Attractiveness Through Social Media: A Phenomenological Study. *Qualitative Report, 22*(4), 969–983. doi:10.46743/2160-3715/2017.2663

Priyadarshini, C., Sreejesh, S., & Anusree, M. R. (2017b). Effect of information quality of employment website on attitude toward the website A moderated mediation study. *International Journal of Manpower, 38*(5), 729–745. doi:10.1108/IJM-12-2015-0235

Priyadarshini, C., Sreejesh, S., & Jha, R. R. (2019). Impact of Informational Characteristics of the Recruitment Website on Graduating Students' Job Pursuit Intention: A Moderated Mediation Study. *International Journal of Human Capital and Information Technology Professionals, 10*(2), 1–19. doi:10.4018/IJHCITP.2019040101

Puldford, A., Smith, P. R., & Berry, C. (1999). *Strategic marketing communications: New ways to build and integrate communications*. Kogan Page.

Purbey, S., Mukherjee, K., & Bhar, C. (2007). Performance measurement system for healthcare processes. *International Journal of Productivity and Performance Management, 56*(3), 241–251. doi:10.1108/17410400710731446

Radnor, Z., & Lovell, B. (2003). Success factors for implementation of the balanced scorecard in a NHS multi-agency setting. *International Journal of Health Care Quality Assurance, 16*(2), 99–108. doi:10.1108/09526860310465618 PMID:12870249

Rahm, C., Henriks, G., & Skreding, M. (2002). *Insiktsboken – en skrift om ett nätverk som arbetar med Balanced Scorecard*. Landstingsförbundet.

Ramanna, K. (2008). The implications of unverifiable fair-value accounting: Evidence from the political economy of goodwill accounting. *Journal of Accounting and Economics, 45*(2-3), 253–281. doi:10.1016/j.jacceco.2007.11.006

Randev, K., & Jha, J. (2019). Sustainable Human Resource Management: A Literature-based Introduction. *NHRD Network Journal, 12*(3), 1–13. doi:10.1177/2631454119873495

Ratnasingam, P. (2003). *Inter-organizational trust for business to business e-commerce*. IGI Global. doi:10.4018/978-1-931777-75-9

Rawlins, B. L., & Bowen, S. A. (2005). Publics. In L. R. Heath (Ed.), *Encyclopedia of Public Relations* (Vol. 2). SAGE.

Ray, S. (2021). *NFTs & virtual reality, emerging technology blog*. Retrieved from https://medium.com/lansaar/nfts-virtual-reality-cba66cacc7e1

Retolaza, J., Ruíz-Roqueñi, M., & San-Jose, L. (2015). An Innovative Approach to Stakeholder Theory: Application in spanish transnational corporations. *Review of Business Management*, *17*(55), 1007–1020. doi:10.7819/rbgn.v17i55.2056

Richardson, A. (2011). Myth, Paradigms and Academic Accounting Research: A Comment on Reading and Understanding Academic Research in Accounting. *Global Perspectives on Accounting Education*, *8*, 67–77.

Ripple. (n.d.). Retrieved from https://www.investopedia.com/terms/r/ripple-cryptocurrency.asp

Rittenberg, L. E., & Schwieger, B. J. (2005). *Auditing. Concepts for a Changing Environment* (5th ed.). Thomson South-Western.

RLYL. (2020). *Blockchain public relations: The building blocks to success.* Retrieved from https://bit.ly/3nw4Y7q

Roca, L. C., & Searcy, C. (2012). An analysis of indicators disclosed in corporate sustainability reports. *Journal of Cleaner Production*, *20*(1), 103–118. doi:10.1016/j.jclepro.2011.08.002

Rodrigues Quesado, P., Frenandes Branco, J. C., & Rodrigues, F. J. (2017). Proposal to Implement the Balanced Scorecard in a Non-profit Organization. *European Accounting and Management Review*, *4*(1), 49–74. doi:10.26595/eamr.2014.4.1.3

Roje, G., Vašiček, D., & Vašiček, V. (2010). Accounting regulation and IPSAS implementation: Efforts of transition countries toward IPSAS compliance. *Journal of Modern Accounting and Auditing*, *6*(12), 1–16.

Rosoiu, O., & Popescu, C. (2016). E-recruiting Platforms: Features that Influence the Efficiency of Online Recruitment Systems. *Informações Econômicas*, *20*(2), 46–55. doi:10.12948/issn14531305/20.2.2016.05

Rowland, C., & Hall, R. (2014). Management learning, performance and reward: Theory and practice revisited. *Journal of Management Development*, *33*(4), 342–356. doi:10.1108/JMD-08-2012-0110

RSK. (n.d.). *The difference between a cryptocurrency and a token.* Retrieved from https://developers.rsk.co/kb/get-crypto-on-rsk/cryptocurrency-vs-token/

Salehi, M. (2009). *Investigating Website Success in the Context of e-Recruitment: An Analytic Network Process (ANP) Approach* [Master's thesis]. Lulea University of Technology.

Salmen, S. (2012). What's Next -Die nächsten Trends. In *Recruiting im Social Web*. BusinessVillage GmbH.

Sarioglu, M., Dalkilic, A. F., & Durak, M. G. (2019). The Future of Corporate Reporting: Integrated Reporting. *International Journal of Contemporary Economics and Administrative Sciences*, *9*(2), 327–347.

Sarraf, S. (2021). UNESCO launches global standard for AI ethics. *InfoWorld.*

Sawe, B. E. (2017). *Countries With The Most Personal Computers Per Capita.* https://www.worldatlas.com/articles/countries-with-the-most-personal-computers-per-capita

Scarpello, V. G. (2008). *The Handbook of Human Resource Management Education.* SAGE.

Schleicher, T., Tahoun, A., & Walker, M. (2010). IFRS adoption in Europe and investment-cash flow sensitivity: Outsider versus insider economies. *The International Journal of Accounting*, *45*(2), 143–168. doi:10.1016/j.intacc.2010.04.007

Schneider, M., & Somers, M. (2006). Organizations as complex adaptive systems: Implications of complexity theory for leadership research. *The Leadership Quarterly*, *17*(4), 351–365. doi:10.1016/j.leaqua.2006.04.006

Sedita, R. S. (2017). *Cause related marketing.* Retrieved from https://advancedmarketingunipd.wordpress.com/2017/10/27/cause-related-marketing/

Sekhon, H., Roy, S., Shergill, G., & Pritchard, A. (2013). Modelling trust in service relationships: A transnational perspective. *Journal of Services Marketing*, *27*(1), 76–86. doi:10.1108/08876041311296392

Serto. (2021). *The DAO plutocracy problem: Off-chain reputation is the key to meritocracy.* Retrieved from https://serto.medium.com/the-dao-plutocracy-problem-a8841546a0f2

Shane, S., & Wakabayashi, D. (2018). *'The business of war': Google employees protest work for the Pentagon.* Retrieved from https://www.nytimes.com/2018/04/04/technology/google-letter-ceo-pentagon-project.html

Sharma, N. (2014). Recruitment Strategies: A power of E-Recruiting and Social Media. *International Journal of Core Engineering & Management*, *1*(5), 15–35.

Sherkar, A. (2011). A Study on Use of E- Resources in Recruitment and Selection Process in 5 Star Hotels. *Atythia: A Journal of Hospitality*, 14-19. http://www.publishingindia.com

Shin, J., Choi, J., & Kim, I. (2015). Development of BIM Performance Measurement System for Architectural Design Firms. In G. Celani, D. M. Sperling, & J. M. S. Franco (Eds.), *Computer-Aided Architectural Design Futures. The Next City - New Technologies and the Future of the Built Environment* (pp. 348–365). Springer Berlin Heidelberg. doi:10.1007/978-3-662-47386-3_19

Shuttleworth, D. (2021). *What is a DAO and how do they work?* Retrieved from https://consensys.net/blog/blockchain-explained/what-is-a-dao-and-how-do-they-work/

Sierra-Garcia, L., Garcia-Benau, M. A., & Bollas-Araya, H. M. (2018). Empirical Analysis of Non-Financial Reporting by Spanish Companies. *Administrative Sciences*, *8*(3), 29. doi:10.3390/admsci8030029

Sills, M. (2014). *E-recruitment: A comparison with traditional recruitment and the influences of social media. A qualitative and quantitative review.* https://www.theseus.fi/bitstream/handle/10024/80428/Sills_Maureen.pdf

Silva, S., Silva, C., & Martins, D. (2017). Online Recruitment for Organizational Knowledge Management: A Quantitative Study. *Proceedings of the 18th European Conference on Knowledge Management*, *1*(2), 890-896.

Simonite, T. (2021). *3 years after the Project Maven uproar, Google cozies to the Pentagon.* Retrieved from https://www.wired.com/story/3-years-maven-uproar-google-warms-pentagon/

Sims, R. R. (2002). *Organizational success through effective human resources management.* Greenwood Pub. Inc.Group.

Singh, S. (2017). Recruitment: A New Dimension of Human Resource Management in India. *International Journal of Advance Research in Computer Science and Management Studies*, *5*(3), 99–105.

Sinha, V., & Thaly, P. (2013). A Review on Changing Trend of Recruitment Practice to Enhance the Quality of Hiring in Global Organizations. *Management*, *18*(2), 141–156.

Smith, H. (2003). The shareholders vs. stakeholders debate. *MIT Sloan Management Review*, *44*(4), 85–90.

Smith, P. R., & Zook, Z. (2019). Marketing communications - Integrating online and offline. In *Customer engagement and digital technologies* (7th ed.). Kogan Page.

Smith, P., & Taylor, J. (2004). *Marketing communications: An integrated approach* (4th ed.). Kogan Page.

Soltani, B. (2014). The anatomy of corporate fraud: A comparative analysis of high profile American and European corporate scandals. *Journal of Business Ethics*, *120*(2), 251–274. doi:10.100710551-013-1660-z

Spitzeck, H., & Hansen, E. G. (2010). Stakeholder governance: How stakeholders influence corporate decision making. *Corporate Governance*, *10*(4), 378–391. doi:10.1108/14720701011069623

Sriramesh, K., & Verci, C. D. (2012). *Culture and public relations: Links and implications.* Routledge. doi:10.4324/9780203149232

Startup-autobahn. (n.d.). *Mercedes-benz – Innovation.* Retrieved from https://group.mercedes-benz.com/innovation/venture/startup-autobahn/en/?r=dai

Statista. (2020). *Share of households with internet access in the European Union (EU) from 2007 to 2020.* https://www.statista.com/statistics/377585/household-internet-access-in-eu28/

Stefanovska, L., & Soklevski, T. (2014). Benefits of Using Balanced Scorecard in Strategic and Operational Planning, *Universal. Journal of Management, 2*(4), 165–171.

Stettina, C. J., & Hörz, J. (2015). Agile portfolio management: An empirical perspective on the practice in use. *International Journal of Project Management, 33*(1), 140–152. doi:10.1016/j.ijproman.2014.03.008

Steyn, M. (2014). Organisational benefits and implementation challenges of mandatory integrated reporting. *Sustainability Accounting. Management and Policy Journal, 5*(4), 476–503.

Stredwick, J. (2000). *An introduction to HRM, Butter-Heinemann.* Reed Edu & Prof. Pub. Ltd.

Svendsen, A., Boutilier, R., Abbott, R. M., & Wheeler, D. (2001). *Measuring the business value of stakeholder relationships (part one).* The Center for Innovation in Management (CIN).

Syam, N., & Sharma, A. (2018). Waiting for a sales renaissance in the fourth industrial revolution: Machine learning and artificial intelligence in sales research and practice. *Industrial Marketing Management, 69*, 69. doi:10.1016/j.indmarman.2017.12.019

Sylva, H., & Mol, S. T. (2009). E-Recruitment: A study into applicant perceptions of an online application system. *International Journal of Selection and Assessment, 17*(3), 311–323. doi:10.1111/j.1468-2389.2009.00473.x

Taipaleenmäki, J., & Ikäheimo, S. (2013). On the convergence of management accounting and financial accounting—The role of information technology in accounting change. *International Journal of Accounting Information Systems, 14*(4), 321–348. doi:10.1016/j.accinf.2013.09.003

Tallon, P. P., & Pinsonneault, A. (2011). Competing Perspectives on the Link Between Strategic Information Technology Alignment and Organizational Agility: Insights from a Mediation Model. *Management Information Systems Quarterly, 35*(2), 463–486. doi:10.2307/23044052

Tapanainen, T. (2012). Information Technology (IT) managers' contribution to IT agility in organizations–views from the field. Publications of Turku School of Economics, serie A.

Tapanainen, T., Hallanoro, M., Päivärinta, J., & Salmela, H. (2008). Towards an Agile IT Organization: A Review of Prior Literature. In *Proceedings of the 2nd European Conference on Information Management and Evaluation* (pp. 425-432). London, UK: Academic Conferences Limited.

Tapscott, D. & Tapscott, A. (2016). *Blockchain revolution: How the technology behind Bitcoin is changing money, business, and the world.* Academic Press.

Target. (n.d.). *Asymmetric communications.* Retrieved from https://www.techtarget.com/searchnetworking/definition/asymmetric-communications

Taticchi, P., Tonelli, F., & Cagnazzo, L. (2010). Performance measurement and management: A literature review and a research agenda. *Measuring Business Excellence, 14*(1), 4–18. doi:10.1108/13683041011027418

Tendeloo, B., & Vanstrelen, A. (2005). Earnings management under German GAAP versus IFRS. *European Accounting Review, 14*(1), 155–180. doi:10.1080/0963818042000338988

Terbu, O. (2020). *Trusted P2P messaging with DIDs, DIDComm and VCs.* Retrieved from https://medium.com/uport/trusted-p2p-messaging-with-dids-didcomm-and-vcs-398f4c3f3cda

The Institute of Directors in Southern Africa (IoDSA). (n.d.). Retrieved from https://www.iodsa.co.za/page/KingIII

The Internet Corporation for Assigned Names and Numbers (ICANN). (2022). Retrieved from https://www.icann.org/

Thompson, G. (2020). *Post-truth public relations: Communication in an era of digital disinformation.* Routledge. doi:10.4324/9780429429125

Thong, T. Y., Ding, D. K., & Lim, C. Y. (2008). Firm diversification and earning management: Evidence from seasoned equity offerings. *Review of Quantitative Finance and Accounting, 30*(1), 69–92. doi:10.100711156-007-0043-x

Tiron-Tudor, A. (2010). Romanian Public Institutions Financial Statements on the way of Harmonization with IPSAS. *Accounting and Management Information Systems, 9*(3), 422–447.

Tong, Y. K., & Arvey, R. D. (2015). Managing complexity via the Competing Values Framework. *Journal of Management Development, 34*(6), 653–673. doi:10.1108/JMD-04-2014-0029

Tsiakis, T. (2015). *Trends and Innovations in Marketing Information Systems.* IGI Global. doi:10.4018/978-1-4666-8459-1

Tsoukas, H. (2009). A dialogical approach to the creation of new knowledge in organizations. *Organization Science, 20*(6), 941–957. doi:10.1287/orsc.1090.0435

Tuten, T. L., & Solomon, M. R. (2014). *Social media marketing.* Sage Publications.

Tyagi, A. (2012). Effective Talent Acquisition Through E-Recruitment:A Study. *International Journal of Multidisciplinary Research, 2*(3), 302–312.

Tyagi, A. (2016). *Impact of e-recruitment on human resource.* Horizon Books.

UNESCO. (2021). *Ethics of artificial intelligence.* Retrieved from https://en.unesco.org/news/unesco-member-states-adopt-first-ever-global-agreement-ethics-artificial-intelligence

United Nations. (2018). *Let's talk about artificial intelligence.* Retrieved from https://www.undp.org/blog/lets-talk-about-artificial-intelligence

Urrutia, I., & Eriksen, S. D. (2005). Application of the balanced scorecard in Spanish private health-care management. *Measuring Business Excellence, 9*(4), 16–26. doi:10.1108/13683040510634808

Vaassen, E. H. J., & Hunton, J. E. (2009). An eclectic approach to accounting information systems. *International Journal of Accounting Information Systems, 10*(4), 173–176. doi:10.1016/j.accinf.2009.10.004

van Esch, P., Black, J. S., & Arli, D. (2021). Job candidates' reactions to AI-enabled job application processes. *AI Ethics*, *1*(2), 119–130. doi:10.100743681-020-00025-0

Vatansever, K. (2017). Using multi criteria decision making approaches for evaluating and selecting website: A literature review. *International Journal of Current Advanced Research*, *6*(4), 3388–3399. doi:10.24327/ijcar.2017.3399.0281

Verheyden, T., Eccles, R., & Feiner, A. (2016). ESG for All? The Impact of ESG Screening on Return, Risk, and Diversification. *Journal of Applied Corporate Finance*, *28*(2), 47–55.

Vladu, A. B., Amat, O., & Cuzdriorean, D. D. (2016). Truthfulness in accounting: How to discriminate accounting manipulators from non-manipulators. *Journal of Business Ethics*, *140*(4), 633–648. doi:10.100710551-016-3048-3

Wade, D., & Recardo, R. (2001). *Corporate Performance Management: How to Build a Better Organization Through Measurement-Driven Strategic Alignment*. Butterworth-Heinemann. doi:10.1016/B978-0-87719-386-9.50005-7

Wadee, N. (2011). Integrated reporting: An opportunity to reshape business. *Accountancy SA*, (December), 6–8.

Wall Street Journal. (2022). *Why some see Web 3.0 as the future of the Internet*. Retrieved from https://newsfeedplus.com/why-some-see-web-3-0-as-the-future-of-the-internet-wsj/

Waller, B. N. (2005). *Consider ethics: Theory, readings, and contemporary issues*. Pearson Longman.

Watson, G., & Reissner, S. (2014). *Developing skills for business leadership*. Kogan Page Pub.

Watts, R., & Zimmerman, J. (1978). Towards a Positive Theory of the Determination of Accounting Standards. *The Accounting Review*, *53*(1), 112–134.

Webber, L., & Wallace, M. (2011). *Quality control for dummies*. JohnWiley&Sons.

What Is Reaganomics. (n.d.). Retrieved from https://corporatefinanceinstitute.com/resources/knowledge/economics/reaganomics/

What Was the Share a Coke Campaign. (2022). Retrieved from https://www.coca-colacompany.com/au/faqs/what-was-the-share-a-coke-campaign

Whittington, O. R., & Pany, K. (2008). *Principles of Auditing & Other Assurance Services* (16th ed.). McGraw-Hill Irwin.

Wilkinson, A., & Dundon, T. (2021). Contemporary HRM. *Sage (Atlanta, Ga.)*.

Williams, D. (2019). *How DFINITY is reinventing the internet*. Retrieved from https://www.youtube.com/watch?v=QUhceX6I81U

Williams, M. (2019). *Mercedes-Benz to boost visibility via blockchain.* Retrieved from https://www.automotivelogistics.media/digital-technology/mercedes-benz-to-boost-visibility-via-blockchain/37673.article

Williams, M. (2019). *Mercedes-Benz to boost visibility via blockchain.* Retrieved from https://www.automotivelogistics.media/digital-technology/mercedes-benz-to-boost-visibility-via-blockchain/37673.article#:~:text=Mercedes%2DBenz%20Cars%20has%20announced,the%20use%20of%20blockchain%20technology

Wilson, E. (2017). School-based researcg: A guide for education students. *Sage (Atlanta, Ga.).*

Wood, T. (2020). *Visualizing the evolution of global advertising spend (1980–2020).* Retrieved from https://www.visualcapitalist.com/evolution-global-advertising-spend-1980-2020/

Xiong, H., Keogh, J. G., Gipp, B., Schubotz, M., & Schlager, S. (2018). How blockchain technology can benefit marketing: Six pending research areas. In *Frontiers in blockchain.* Frontiers Media SA. Retrieved from https://www.researchgate.net/publication/339354050_How_Blockchain_Technology_Can_Benefit_Marketing_Six_Pending_Research_Areas

Xiong, Y. (2006). Earning management and its measurement; a theoretical perspective. *The Journal of American Academy of Business, Cambridge, 9*(1), 214–219.

XRPL | XRP Ledger Overview. (n.d.). *XRPL today and the vision for tomorrow.* Retrieved from https://xrpl.org/xrp-ledger-overview.html

Yadav, N., & Sagar, M. (2013). Performance measurement and management frameworks. *Business Process Management Journal, 19*(6), 947–971. doi:10.1108/BPMJ-01-2013-0003

Yanik & Kiliç. (2018). *A framework for the performance evaluation of an energy blockchain.* Springer. Retrieved from https://link.springer.com/chapter/10.1007/978-3-319-75690-5_23

Yanık, S., & Kiliç, S. A. (2018). *Energy management—Collective and computational intelligence with theory and applications.* Springer Publication.

Yuen, P. P., & Ng, A. W. (2012). Towards a balanced performance measurement system in public health care organization. *International Journal of Health Care Quality Assurance, 25*(5), 421–430. doi:10.1108/09526861211235919 PMID:22946241

Zakrizevska, M., & Litvina, A. (2016). First Impresion And Belief Importance In Candidate Recruitment Decisions. *SGEM, Psychology And Psychiatry, Sociology And Healthcare, Education Conference Proceedings*, 1, 177-184.

Zarzycka, E., & Krasodomska, J. (2021). Non-financial key performance indicators: What determines the differences in the quality and quantity of the disclosures? *Journal of Applied Accounting Research, 23*(1), 139–162. doi:10.1108/JAAR-02-2021-0036

Zeghal, D., Chtourou, S., & Fourati, M. Y. (2012). The effect of mandatory adoption of IFRS on earning quality: Evidence from the European Union. *Journal of International Accounting Research, 11*(2), 1–25. doi:10.2308/jiar-10221

Zéghal, D., Chtourou, S., & Mnif, S. Y. (2011). An analysis of the effect of mandatory adoption of IAS/IFRS on earnings Management. *Journal of International Accounting, Auditing & Taxation*, *20*(2), 61–72. doi:10.1016/j.intaccaudtax.2011.06.001

Zelman, W. N., Pink, G. H., & Matthias, C. B. (2003). Use of the balanced scorecard in health care. *Journal of Health Care Finance*, *29*(4), 1–16. PMID:12908650

Zhou, S., Simnett, R., & Green, W. (2017). Does Integrated Reporting Matter to the Capital Market? *Abacus*, *53*(1), 94–132. doi:10.1111/abac.12104

Zin, S. M., & Jaafar, N. N. (2016). *E-Recruitment Technology: The Effective Source of Recruitment*. https://www.semanticscholar.org/paper/E-Recruitment-Technology%3A-The-Effective-Source-of-Zin-Jaafar/490e8d7069007b8ee4105d714c0ad725dddbed4b

Zumente, I., & Bistrova, J. (2021). ESG Importance for Long-Term Shareholder Value Creation: Literature vs. Practice. *Journal of Open Innovation*, *7*(2), 127. doi:10.3390/joitmc7020127

Zwitter, A., & Hazenberg, J. (2020). Decentralized network governance: Blockchain technology and the future of regulation. *Frontiers*, *3*, 12. Advance online publication. doi:10.3389/fbloc.2020.00012

About the Contributors

Ionica Oncioiu holds a Ph.D. in economy and accounting. Her research interests include the development of SMEs innovation, Project Management, Accounting Information Systems, Asset Management and E-Commerce Marketing. She has had more than 10 years of experience in this area and has published 10 textbooks and more than 70 papers in scholarly peer reviewed international journals.

* * *

Ijaz Ali is Assistant Professor of Accounting and Finance in Fahad Bin Sultan-Tabuk. Before joining FBSU, he previously served as an Assistant Professor of Accounting at Ghulam Ishaq Khan University of Science & Technology. Ali received his Masters (Accounting) and Ph.D. (Management Sciences) from the University of Grenoble-France. Ali's research investigates the impact of dividend payment and earnings announcements on the stock prices of firms. Specifically, he examines whether dividends and earnings convey information about firms' future prospects. He earned MS/Ph.D. scholarship for a duration of 4 years starting from July 2007. The scholarship has been awarded on merit in reference to an agreement signed between Higher Education Commission of Pakistan and the Ambassador of France in Pakistan. Ali was awarded the best research paper award in the 14th Annual Doctoral Conference on Accounting and Finance, May 2013, Prague, Czech Republic.

Asif Baig received M.com and Ph.D. from the Department of Commerce Aligarh Muslim University, India, in 2003 and 2011 respectively. Currently working as Assistant Professor, Department of Business, Jubail University College, Saudi Arabia. He has published various papers in journals of international repute. His research interests include financial analysis, strategic cost management, fintech, etc.

Teodora Raluca Odett Tâmpănariu Breaz is a PhD. student at the Lucian Blaga University of Sibiu and PhD. associate professor at Faculty of Economic Sciences, 1 Decembrie 1918 University of Alba-Iulia. His research focus is the area of Economics, Management Accounting, Performance Management, Strategic Management. She has participated in many international conferences and published articles and coauthored books.

Sorinel Căpuşneanu is a PhD. Professor at Titu Maiorescu University of Bucharest. His research focus is the area of Management Accounting, Management Performance, Management Information Systems, Audit and Controlling, and Business Ethics. He is the author of the following books: Elements of Cost Management, Economica Publishing House (2008) and Management Accounting. Performance Assessment Tool, University Publishing House (2013) and co-author of Deontology and Accounting Expertise. Judicial Accounting and Tax Expertise (2019) published by Lambert Academic Publishing and Management Accounting Standards for Sustainable Business Practices (2019) published by IGI-Global. He has participated in numerous national and international conferences and has made a remarkable contribution to managerial accounting by publishing several articles.

Mihaela Denisa Coman, PhD, is scientific researcher at Valahia University of Targoviste, Institute of Multidisciplinary Research for Science and Technology. Her scientific activity includes 18 scientific papers in international journals Indexed ISI and proceeding ISI, more than 25 scientific papers in national and international journals and conferences, 2 books and 2 book-chapters as co-author.

Teodora Cucerzan is a PhD student at the 1 Decembrie 1918 University of Alba-Iulia, Faculty of Economic Sciences. Her research focus is the area of non-financial reporting,company performance and integrated reporting. The working title of her thesis is “The Impact of Integrated Reporting on the Performance of Companies Listed on the Capital Market.” The thesis will cover concepts such as: non-financial information and stakeholders, integrated reporting and globalization, implementation of integrated reporting and capital market.

Cristina Didea (Castrase) is a PhD student at the Doctoral School of Accounting, under the coordination of Prof. PhD. Topor Ioan Dan, graduate of Faculty of Economic Scienses with a master`s degree in Accounting Information System in Management Decision Making, within 1 Decembrie 1918 University of Alba Iulia. Currently, management economist with responsibility in plant controlling, budget controlling and cost calculation area with over six years of experience.

Alharbi Habbab Husam has a M.Sc. degree in Software Engineering from Mansoura University, Egypt. Her research interest is in digital transformation, internet of things, and digital business.

Constantin Aurelian Ionescu, Ph.D., is Lecturer at the Faculty of Economic Sciences, Hyperion University of Bucharest, and Researcher III at Valahia University of Targoviste, Institute of Multidisciplinary Research for Science and Technology. His research interests include financial accounting, managerial accounting, environmental accounting, and audit. He has published his works in various journals, has participated at numerous conferences, and is a member of the editorial board of Annals of Romanian Scientists, New Series on economy, law, and sociology.

Imran Khan has done a Ph.D. in commerce with a concentration in accounting and has vast teaching experience in different subjects in accounting and finance. The author has published around 35 papers on various topics in accounting and finance.

Asma Khatoon, Assistant Professor, Imam Abdulrahman Bin Faisal University of Dammam, Saudi Arabia, holds a B.Com. from MJP Rohilkhand University, India, and both M.Com. and Ph.D. Degrees from Aligarh Muslim University, India. She is working at the College of Business Administration, the Imam Abdulrahman Bin Faisal University of Dammam since 2015 to date. She taught courses in the Department of Accounting as well as a good number of research papers in the area of finance and accounting. She has been awarded Junior Research Fellowship (JRF) by University Grant Commission, India in 2010 and qualified National Eligibility Test for Lectureship. She has also attended various national and international conferences, workshops, symposiums held in India & Saudi Arabia and acted as an Invigilator several times in various National Level Entrance Tests conducted by Aligarh Muslim University. She has held administrative positions from 2015 to 2018 as Quality Coordinator at College of Business Administration, Imam Abdulrahman Bin Faisal University, Saudi Arabia, and held positions of course leader and co-op supervisor several times at IAU, Dammam. Over her 6-year teaching career, she taught different accounting courses.

Nabil Ahmed Mareai Senan is currently working as executive manager of entrepreneurship center and an associate Professor, College of Business Administration, Prince Sattam Bin Abdulaziz University, Kingdom of Saudi Arabia. He obtained his Ph.D in Auditing in 2010, and MSc in Advance Accounting and Taxation, from University of Pune India, in 2015 and also Bachelor`s Degree in Accounting, in 2000 from Faculty of Commerce and economic, Sana`a University, Yemen. Moreover, he is a Certified Public Accountant (CPA) from Yemen in 2012. Additionally, he has participated in various conferences and has published in the fields of Accounting, Auditing, and Finance, in several SCOPUS, ISI journals, and international journals.

Manea Marinela Daniela is Associate Professor at Accounting Finance Department, Faculty of Economic Sciences, Valahia University of Targoviste. She is doctor of accounting at Bucharest Academy of Economic Studies and have an postdoctoral studies at Alexandru Ioan Cuza University of Iasi. She published 10 books and 65 articles in accounting and related fields.

Florea Nicoleta Valentina, PhD, is a Lecturer at Management-Marketing Department, Faculty of Economic Sciences, Valahia University of Targoviste. She is a member in research and editorial board at EUMMAS. She had a PhD stage at UPEC, France and a teaching Erasmus + scholarship at CUT, Poland. She published 10 books and 5 chapters and 75 articles in customer relationship management, marketing simulation and modelling, human resources management, and business communication.

Ileana-Sorina Rakos is a PhD. lecturer at the University of Petrosani, Department of Economic Sciences. Her research focus is the area of Finance and Accounting. She is the author of the book: Management of public institutions. Theoretical and Applied Fundamentals (2018). She has published numerous articles on Finance and Accounting, and she has participated in numerous national and international conferences.

Raj Bahadur Sharma is an intellectual academician of high caliber with an extensive experience of over seventeen years in the higher education industry in India and Abroad. He has been acknowledged for Accounting & Finance courses along with the specialized area of Accounting. Presently, Dr. Raj is providing his services as an 'Assistant Professor' at the Department of Accounting, College Business Administration, University of Bahrain, Kingdom of Bahrain. Before this, He has worked in the Department of Accounting, College of Business Administration, Prince Sattam Bin Abdulaziz University (PSAU), Kingdom of Saudi Arabia from year 2010, to 2021. Along with his Master and doctorial academic degrees in accounting, he has patents of two books in the area of Accounting. He has a nearly forty research papers published in the Scopus, Web of Sciences, peer-reviewed, UGC care listed journals. He has completed three funded research projects. Besides, he has presented several research papers in the national and international conferences in India and abroad. He has also attended workshops, reference courses, Faculty Development Program (FDP) in India and abroad. Apart from his teaching and research, Dr. Raj rendered services to many academic and administrative committees. He is a Life Member of Indian Accounting Association (IAA), Indian Accounting Association Research Foundation (IAARF), Member of Bar Council of Rajasthan. He is also a research supervisor at Jai Narain Vyas University, Jodhpur, India.

Sorina-Geanina Stanescu, PhD, is scientific researcher at Valahia University of Targoviste, Institute of Multidisciplinary Research for Science and Technology. She has the following results: 15 ISI articles, more than 20 articles BDI, member in research projects with national/international funding, numerous scientific works presented in conferences. Expertise and interest topics: environmental accounting, management, economic statistics.

Adela-Ioana Staraş is a PhD. senior researcher 3rd degree at National Institute for Chemical Pharmaceutical Research and Development, Bucharest, Pharmacology Department. She has theoretical and practical knowledge in cellular and molecular biology, biochemistry, tissue engineering, microbiology. She is responsible for microbiological control of pharmaceuticals. She works in research projects and in services contracts with companies and institutes (e.g., potential antibiotics and antimicrobials). She also has a management of health services and quality systems graduation accredited by the ANMCS (National Authority of Health Quality Management) and ANC (National Authority for Qualification). She published papers in ISI (WoS) indexed journals and several patent applications in Romania and participated in many international and national conferences.

Melinda Timea Fülöp is a Lecturer at the Faculty of Economics and Business Administration in the Babeş-Bolyai University, Cluj-Napoca, Romania. She holds a PhD in Audit and her teaching and research fields are audit profession and ethics, the tripartite function of audit in the context of corporate governance and financial accounting and auditing.

Dan Ioan Topor is a PhD. Professor at the 1 Decembrie 1918 University of Alba-Iulia, Faculty of Economic Sciences. His research focus is the area of Management Accounting, Management Performance and Management Information Systems, Audit and Controlling, and Business Ethics. He is the author of the following books: New dimensions of cost-related cost information for winemaking (2014), Basics of Accounting (2016) and and coauthor of Management Accounting Standards for Sustainable Business Practices published by IGI-Global (USA, 2019) and Deontology and Accounting Expertise. Judicial Accounting and Tax Expertise, published by Lambert Academic Publishing (Germany, 2019). He has published numerous articles on Managerial Accounting and Management Control and has participated in numerous national and international conferences.

Moin Uddin is working with the College of Administrative & Financial Sciences, Saudi Electronic University, Jeddah, Kingdom of Saudi Arabia since 2013. He has completed his Master's in International Business Management from Aligarh Muslim University, Aligarh U.P. (India). He has completed his Ph.D. from Chhatrapati Shahu Ji Maharaj University, Kanpur U.P. (India).The title of his research was "An Analytical Study of Entrepreneurial Opportunities in Emerging Global Scenario". He has fifteen years of teaching experience that include teaching in STEP-HBTI, Kanpur from 2005 to September 2013. He has been working in finance and accounting, in which he has been studying Innovation, project management techniques, fintech, etc. He has been involved in teaching and developing Master's and Undergraduates' courses like Principles of Finance, Global Economics, Operations Management & Microeconomics. He has developed his aptitude in public sharing and the deliverance of knowledge through classroom teachings. He believes in conscious teaching and practices effective management techniques such as interpersonal skills, motivation, and constructive feedback and strives to enhance students' competence. He has participated in and organized various national and international workshops and seminars. He is aspiring in the field of developing financial innovations through innovative practices. He believes in continuous improvement and teamwork.

Lavinia Yildirim is a PhD student in Ankara University where her major is management in the Faculty of Political Science.

Mariana Zamfir, PhD, is Associate Professor at Department of Accounting and Finance, Valahia University of Targoviste. Also, she was the member of POSDRU projects. She is a member of the Center for Research and Scientific Studies in Accounting and Finance, ICSTM-Valahia University of Targoviste. His research interests include financial accounting, managerial accounting, controlling. She has published his works in various books, journals, and has participated at numerous conferences.

Ze Zook is a Digital Content Strategist and Developer with more than fifteen years' experience gained delivering innovative business and educational solutions, making the apparently illogical logical. Demonstrating strong capabilities for successfully repositioning brands, working across digital channels and optimising services with exceptional analytical insight as well as introducing a unique perspective on EU markets.

Index

G

H

I

M

N

O

P

R

S

T

V

W

www.ingramcontent.com/pod-product-compliance
Lightning Source LLC
LaVergne TN
LVHW061539290926
849162LV00004B/846